T0192805

Software Languages

Ralf Lämmel

Software Languages

Syntax, Semantics, and Metaprogramming

 Springer

Ralf Lämmel
Computer Science Department
Universität Koblenz-Landau
Koblenz, Germany

ISBN 978-3-030-08104-1   ISBN 978-3-319-90800-7   (eBook)
https://doi.org/10.1007/978-3-319-90800-7

© Springer International Publishing AG, part of Springer Nature 2018
Softcover re-print of the Hardcover 1st edition 2018
This work is subject to copyright. All rights are reserved by the Publisher, whether the whole or part of the material is concerned, specifically the rights of translation, reprinting, reuse of illustrations, recitation, broadcasting, reproduction on microfilms or in any other physical way, and transmission or information storage and retrieval, electronic adaptation, computer software, or by similar or dissimilar methodology now known or hereafter developed.
The use of general descriptive names, registered names, trademarks, service marks, etc. in this publication does not imply, even in the absence of a specific statement, that such names are exempt from the relevant protective laws and regulations and therefore free for general use.
The publisher, the authors and the editors are safe to assume that the advice and information in this book are believed to be true and accurate at the date of publication. Neither the publisher nor the authors or the editors give a warranty, express or implied, with respect to the material contained herein or for any errors or omissions that may have been made. The publisher remains neutral with regard to jurisdictional claims in published maps and institutional affiliations.

Printed on acid-free paper

This Springer imprint is published by the registered company Springer International Publishing AG part of Springer Nature.
The registered company address is: Gewerbestrasse 11, 6330 Cham, Switzerland

Copyright and Attribution

Copyright for Code

The code in this book is part of the open-source YAS project:
http://www.softlang.org/yas.

YAS is licensed under the MIT license.

Copyright 2016–2018 Ralf Lämmel

Permission is hereby granted, free of charge, to any person obtaining a copy of the YAS code including software and associated documentation files (the "Software"), to deal in the Software without restriction, including without limitation the rights to use, copy, modify, merge, publish, distribute, sublicense, and/or sell copies of the Software, and to permit persons to whom the Software is furnished to do so, subject to the following conditions:

The above copyright notice and this permission notice shall be included in all copies or substantial portions of the Software.

THE SOFTWARE IS PROVIDED "AS IS", WITHOUT WARRANTY OF ANY KIND, EXPRESS OR IMPLIED, INCLUDING BUT NOT LIMITED TO THE WARRANTIES OF MERCHANTABILITY, FITNESS FOR A PARTICULAR PURPOSE AND NONINFRINGEMENT. IN NO EVENT SHALL THE AUTHORS OR COPYRIGHT HOLDERS BE LIABLE FOR ANY CLAIM, DAMAGES OR OTHER LIABILITY, WHETHER IN AN ACTION OF CONTRACT, TORT OR OTHERWISE, ARISING FROM, OUT OF OR IN CONNECTION WITH THE SOFTWARE OR THE USE OR OTHER DEALINGS IN THE SOFTWARE.

Artwork Credits

Cover artwork:
Wojciech Kwasnik, *The Tower of Software Languages*, 2017.
With the assistance of Archina Void and Daniel Dünker.
Licensed under CC BY-SA 4.0.
Artwork *DMT*, acrylic, 2006 by Matt Sheehy is quoted with the artist's permission.

Credits for per-chapter artwork:
Wojciech Kwasnik.
See the individual chapters for details.

Preface

You must not fall into the trap of rejecting a surgical technique because it is beyond the capabilities of the barber in his shop around the corner.
– Edsger W. Dijkstra, EWD 512[1]

Welcome to the *Software Languages Book*!

The Notion of a Software Language

A software language is an "artificial language," the syntax and semantics of which may be realized in software. Software languages are particularly omnipresent in software and systems engineering. While a proper attempt at classification will follow later, here are some illustrative categories of software languages:

- programming languages (e.g., Python, Java, and Haskell);
- modeling languages (e.g., UML, Simulink, and Modelica);
- exchange formats (e.g., JSON and XML);
- markup languages (e.g., HTML);
- domain-specific languages (DSLs) for domains such as the following:

  - parsing;
  - build management;
  - machine control;
  - documentation;
  - configuration.

---

[1]   https://www.cs.utexas.edu/users/EWD/transcriptions/EWD05xx/
EWD512.html

Software Language Engineering (SLE)

We shall honor fundamental concepts and engineering techniques across different use cases and forms of software languages, with different software technologies used for realization. That is, we endorse and advertise *software language engineering* (SLE). To quote from the website of (an edition of) the SLE conference,[2]: "Software language engineering is the application of systematic, disciplined, and quantifiable approaches to the development (design, implementation, testing, deployment), use, and maintenance (evolution, recovery, and retirement) of these languages."

A Particular SLE Book

SLE is a relatively young field. (The term "SLE" may be dated back to 2007.) The knowledge of fundamental concepts and engineering techniques is scattered over multiple research communities and technological spaces. Thus, there exist "knowledge silos" with limited understanding of commonalities and specifics in different contexts. The present book is aimed at collecting and organizing scattered knowledge in the form of an accessible textbook. Given the breadth of the SLE field, this book cannot claim full coverage and a balanced presentation of the SLE field. This book is biased as follows:

- Coverage of language processors for source code analysis and manipulation informed by programming language theory and implementation. There is no coverage of runtime forms of metaprogramming such as reflection.
- A focus on application areas such as software analysis (software reverse engineering), software transformation (software re-engineering), software composition (modularity), and domain-specific languages.
- Usage of several programming languages (Java, Python, and Haskell) for illustration with Haskell taking a leading role. There are no illustrations for particular metaprogramming systems, language workbenches, or model-driven engineering technologies, but some of the underlying principles are discussed and pointers to further reading are provided.
- Code blocks (programs and executable specifications) form an integral part of the sequential text flow in this book. Code blocks are placed in non-floating "Illustration" blocks, as opposed to being moved into floating figures. The code is typically explained in subsequent text paragraphs (less so in code comments).

---

[2] http://www.sleconf.org/2012/

Complementary Online Material

There is a website for the book.[3] All software artifacts in the book are part of YAS[4] (*Yet Another SLR* (*Software Language Repository*)); The code of YAS is hosted on GitHub. The book's website provides complementary material, for example, lecture slides and videos.

Structure of the Preface

The rest of this preface provides descriptions as follows: the *audience* targeted by the book, the *background* assumed by the book, the *characteristics* of the book, an *outline* of the book, *trails* offered for using the book selectively, and the style of the *exercises* included throughout the book.

Audience Targeted by this Book

This book is designed as a textbook for self-organized learning and university courses for Bachelor (advanced level) or Master of Computer Science, in the broader context of software engineering.

This book serves those who have an intention of understanding the fundamental concepts and important engineering principles underlying software languages. Readers will acquire much of the operational intelligence needed for dealing with software languages in software development practice. Of course, readers may also need to consult more technology-specific resources when addressing specific problems with the help of specific technologies.

This book is primarily targeted at people in higher education. However, because of the book's pragmatic (applied) approach, practitioners on a self-learning path may also appreciate the book.

The typical developer may have encountered language design and implementation in practice and may have used technologies, as dictated by the moment. This book raises the developer's view to a higher level of abstraction and delivers more advanced techniques, for example, small-step semantics, formal type systems, quasi-quotation, term rewriting, and program analysis. The objective is that the book will enable readers to design, implement, assess, integrate, and evolve language-based software. This is an important skill set for software engineers, as languages are permeating software development in an increasing manner.

---

[3] http://www.softlang.org/book
[4] http://www.softlang.org/yas

This book admits several different 'trails' (see below), thereby making it useful for different learning objectives and different course designs on the basis of adjusting the level of sophistication and selective inclusion of chapters. Depending on individual background or the local curriculum, some chapters or sections may be skipped or processed by cursory reading or the short videos available may be consulted instead.

Background Assumed by this Book

Required Knowledge

Moderate programming skills   One needs to be fluent in an object-oriented and a functional programming language. The illustrative examples in the book are written in many different notations and programming languages. Chapter 2 ("A Story of a Domain-Specific Language") uses Java and Python in going through many aspects of language implementation in an introductory manner. Beyond Chapter 2, the functional programming language Haskell dominates as the language used for illustration. The book's Haskell code is straightforward; advanced language features and idioms are avoided.

Basic software engineering knowledge   A basic understanding of the software lifecycle (analysis, design, implementation, testing, deployment, maintenance) is required. In particular, the reader needs to have mastered basic aspects of software design and testing. That is, the reader should have previously leveraged and designed domain models (e.g., object models) for different domains. Also, the reader should have some experience with unit testing and in testing the input/output behavior of software components.

Optional Knowledge

Basic knowledge of theoretical computer science   The book rehashes the relevant background in a pragmatic manner and hence, such knowledge is optional. This includes notions such as formal languages and computability.

Basic knowledge of metaprogramming   Such knowledge is optional because the book develops a particular (limited) view of metaprogramming from the ground up. We focus on source code analysis and manipulation. A few metaprogramming *recipes* are highlighted in the text. Runtime forms of metaprogramming such as reflection are not discussed.

Characteristics of this Book

SLE concepts and techniques   This book aims to identify, define, and illustrate
the fundamental concepts and engineering techniques as relevant to applications
of software languages in software development. Examples of these concepts include abstract syntax, compositionality, and type system. Examples of these techniques include parser generation and template processing. Some concepts and
techniques will be explained by referring to a lifecycle for software languages or
to the architecture of a typical language implementation such as a compiler.

Software engineering perspective   This book presents software languages primarily from a software engineering perspective. That is, the book basically addresses the following question: how to parse, analyze, transform, generate, format, and otherwise process software artifacts in different software languages, as
they turn up in software development? This question is of interest in many areas
of software engineering, most notably software reverse engineering, software re-
engineering, model-driven engineering, program comprehension, software analysis, program generation, and mining software repositories.

Diverse languages   This book covers a wide range of software languages–most
notably programming languages, domain-specific languages, modeling languages,
exchange formats, and specifically also language definition languages (notably
grammar and metamodeling notations). Several different technological spaces
are exercised, with some emphasis on grammarware and with excursions to modelware, XMLware, and JSONware. Several different programming paradigms are
exercised, most notably, functional and object-oriented programming.

Polyglot illustration   Different languages are leveraged to illustrate SLE concepts
and techniques. The functional programming language Haskell dominates the
book. Additionally, the mainstream programming languages Python and Java are
used for illustration. Further, XML, XML Schema, JSON, and JSON Schema are
leveraged as mainstream options for exchange formats. ANTLR is used for mainstream parser development. A number of syntax definition formalisms (inspired
by Backus-Naur form, Ecore, and algebraic signatures) are developed and systematically used in the book. The standard notion of inference rules for deductive
systems is used for representing operational semantics and type systems.

Bits of theory   A deeper understanding of software languages must take into account some fundamental concepts typically studied in the field of programming
language theory. In particular, this concerns semantics and type systems. This
book presents these topics in a pragmatic manner so that the practical value of
semantics definitions and type systems may become clear more easily and the
knowledge gained can be applied to software languages other than programming
languages; see Chapter 8–11.

Bits of language implementation   The development of interpreters or compilers
for programming languages as well as runtime systems, is well understood and
covered by existing textbooks. We take a more general view of language implementation, which covers languages other than programming languages and
language-based software components other than compilers and interpreters. The

book covers the topic of interpreters relatively well. Compiler construction is
covered only in a superficial manner. Runtime systems are not covered.

Bits of programming paradigms   Just as this book is not a book on compiler
construction, it is not a book on programming paradigms either. Nevertheless,
the book exercises several paradigms to some extent. That is, languages of different paradigms are defined and implemented with a cursory discussion of the
underlying language concepts. Further, languages of different paradigms are used
in implementing the examples in the book. A systematic discussion of programming paradigms is beyond the scope of this book.

Outline of this Book

Preface
This is the current chapter.
Chapter 1: *The Notion of a Software Language*
The notion of a software language is introduced broadly by means of introducing
example languages, classifying languages, discussing the language lifecycle, and
identifying the roles of languages in software engineering.
Chapter 2: *A Story of a Domain-Specific Language*
A domain-specific modeling language, FSML, for finite state machines (FSMs) is
discussed in terms of language concepts, lifecycle, syntax, operational semantics,
and provision of a code generator. Mainstream implementation languages and
technologies are leveraged.
Chapter 3: *Foundations of Tree- and Graph-Based Abstract Syntax*
The signature- and metamodel-based definitions of tree- and graph-based syn-
tax and the accompanying notion of conformance are described in a pragmatic
manner. The abstract syntaxes of several example languages are defined.
Chapter 4: *Representation of Object Programs in Metaprograms*
The implementation of abstract syntax is discussed, where object models in
object-oriented programming or algebraic data types in functional programming
serve the purpose of object-program representation in metaprogramming.
Chapter 5: *A Suite of Metaprogramming Scenarios*
Typical scenarios of metaprogramming are discussed and illustrated: interpre-
tation, semantic analysis, transformation, translation. Only the basic idioms of
metaprogramming are exercised. Concrete syntax is not considered yet.
Chapter 6: *Foundations of Textual Concrete Syntax*
The grammar-based definition of textual concrete syntax and the accompanying
notions of acceptance and parsing are described in a pragmatic manner. The con-
crete syntaxes of several example languages are defined.
Chapter 7: *Implementation of Textual Concrete Syntax*
Several aspects of the implementation of concrete syntax are discussed: parsing
(e.g., by using a parser generator or parser combinators), abstraction (i.e., the

mapping of concrete to abstract syntax), formatting (e.g., by means of template processing), and concrete object syntax.

Chapter 8: *A Primer on Operational Semantics*

The operational approach to semantics definition is described in a pragmatic manner. This approach leverages inference rules (deductive systems) to model the stepwise computation of programs in either big-step or small-step style. The operational semantics of several example languages are defined. The formal definitions can be used, for example, in the implementation of interpreters.

Chapter 9: *A Primer on Type Systems*

The notion of type systems is described in a pragmatic manner. The approach, again, leverages inference rules to assign properties to programs as sound, static predictions of runtime behavior. The type systems of several example languages are defined. The formal definitions can be used, for example, in the implementation of type checkers.

Chapter 10: *An Excursion into the Lambda Calculus*

The lambda calculus is described as a well-known vehicle for studying semantics and type systems of programming language constructs. In fact, a number of specific lambda calculi are discussed, and thereby we encounter polymorphism, structural and nominal typing, and subtyping.

Chapter 11: *An Ode to Compositionality*

The denotational approach to semantics definition is described in a pragmatic manner. This approach leverages functional equations to map program phrases to elements of suitable domains in a compositional (i.e., inductive) style. The denotational semantics of several example languages are defined.

Chapter 12: *A Suite of Metaprogramming Techniques*

Several metaprogramming techniques are described in a pragmatic manner: term rewriting, attribute grammars, multi-stage programming, partial evaluation, and abstract interpretation. The techniques are applied to different metaprogramming scenarios and example languages.

Postface

This final chapter summarizes the key concepts covered by the book, identifies omissions in this particular book on software languages, lists complementary textbooks, and mentions relevant academic conferences.

Trails Offered by this Book

This book may be walked through several different trails for selective self-learning experiences or course designs. Each trail listed below itemizes chapters to be include at different levels of detail:

low   cursory/highly selective coverage;
medium   incomplete coverage;
high   comprehensive coverage.

All these trails, when understood as course designs, correspond to advanced Bachelor's or regular Master's courses. Based on the author's experience, these trails can be upgraded to research-oriented course designs for Master's courses. To this end, the literature references provided and specifically, also those from the *Postface* of the book, and relevant technologies, for example, for metaprogramming, may be studied by students as part of their literature research and project work.

Trail "An Introduction to Metaprogramming"

- Chapter 1: *The Notion of a Software Language*   [none–low]
- Chapter 2: *A Story of a Domain-Specific Language*   [high]
- Chapter 3: *Foundations of Tree- and Graph-Based Abstract Syntax* [medium]
- Chapter 4: *Representation of Object Programs in Metaprograms*   [medium]
- Chapter 5: *A Suite of Metaprogramming Scenarios*   [medium]
- Chapter 6: *Foundations of Textual Concrete Syntax*   [medium]
- Chapter 7: *Implementation of Textual Concrete Syntax*   [medium]

This is an introductory trail with Chapters 2 and 5 at its heart, complemented by modest coverage of the foundations and implementation of abstract and concrete syntax and, possibly, the notion of a software language in general. The assumption is here that this trail should touch upon different metalanguages (including mainstream options) and a broad variety of relatively simple metaprogramming scenarios and techniques. The complexity of the trail could be tuned by including more or less detail from Chapter 5.

Trail "A Primer on Programming Language Theory"

- Chapter 3: *Foundations of Tree- and Graph-Based Abstract Syntax*   [low]
- Chapter 4: *Representation of Object Programs in Metaprograms*   [low]
- Chapter 5: *A Suite of Metaprogramming Scenarios*   [low]
- Chapter 8: *A Primer on Operational Semantics*   [high]
- Chapter 9: *A Primer on Type Systems*   [high]
- Chapter 10: *An Excursion into the Lambda Calculus*   [medium–high]
- Chapter 11: *An Ode to Compositionality*   [medium–high]

This trail excludes the two introductory chapters, as a broad view of software languages is not required. The trail starts off with a short discussion of abstract syntax. The trail skips over the topic of concrete syntax. The excursion to scenarios of metaprogramming is recommended to introduce the notions of interpretation and type checking without reliance on formal notation. The remaining chapters in the trail deal with formal semantics and type systems in a pragmatic manner. Haskell serves as the implementation language. The complexity of the trail can be tuned by including more or less detail of the lambda calculus and denotational semantics. For instance, abstract interpretation and structural and nominal typing and subtyping may be considered optional.

Trail "Metaprogramming in Haskell"

- Chapter 1: *The Notion of a Software Language*   [none–low]
- Chapter 3: *Foundations of Tree- and Graph-Based Abstract Syntax*   [low]
- Chapter 4: *Representation of Object Programs in Metaprograms*   [low]
- Chapter 5: *A Suite of Metaprogramming Scenarios*   [high]
- Chapter 6: *Foundations of Textual Concrete Syntax*   [low]
- Chapter 7: *Implementation of Textual Concrete Syntax*   [low]
- Chapter 12: *A Suite of Metaprogramming Techniques*   [high]

Chapters 5 and 12 provide the technical meat for this trail, prepared by modest coverage of the foundations and implementation of abstract and concrete syntax and, possibly, the notion of a software language in general.

Trail "Software Language Engineering"

This is a long trail through all chapters. This trail may be too long for an actual course.

Exercises in the Book

Each exercise is marked with a level of difficulty:

Basic   These exercises are concerned with using the relevant techniques in a basic manner; the book's coverage should suffice for solving these exercises.

Intermediate   These exercises are concerned with aspects of techniques or scenarios of their usage that may go beyond the book's coverage. Some research ("googling"), teamwork, and advice from an instructor may be needed for solving the exercises.

Advanced   These exercises are at the level of project assignments that may require weeks of work depending on background and supervision. These exercises could also be used for giving focus to research efforts in a course, for example.

Except for the exercises at the basic level, the formulations given intentionally leave room for creativity. In general, solutions to the exercises will not be explicitly published by the book's author, although the resources for the book may provide some relevant pieces of information.

Acknowledgments

I am grateful to my academic peers, who have helped me to learn many of the things that I now want to pass on with this book. I list these peers in somewhat chronological order, Günter Riedewald (my diploma and PhD supervisor to whom I owe so much), Uwe Lämmel (an early mentor who put me on the Prolog and grammar quest), Mark van den Brand (a mentor who helped me during my PhD period in diverse ways), Paul Klint (my key mentor during my PostDoc and senior researcher times at CWI, Amsterdam), Chris Verhoef (my boss at VU, Amsterdam, who introduced me to the art of writing), Simon L. Peyton Jones (with whom I wrote a few great papers and from whom I learned other aspects of the art of writing), Erik Meijer (a very exciting mentor at Microsoft and, more recently, at Facebook), and Jean-Marie Favre (an inspiring colleague and friend of whom you have one of the kind in a lifetime).

There are yet other peers with whom I may have collaborated only more briefly, but they also have helped me to learn things I want to pass on with this book; they are stated here in no well-defined order: Eelco Visser, Dragan Gasevic, Simon Thompson, Krzysztof Czarnecki, Jean Bézivin, James R. Cordy, Oleg Kiselyov, Peter Thiemann, Wolfram Schulte, Walid Taha, Tijs van der Storm, Frédéric Jouault, Robert Hirschfeld, William R. Cook, Alfonso Pierantonio, Marjan Mernik, Dietrich Paulus, Steffen Staab, and Jan Maluszynski.

I kindly acknowledge collaboration with Anya Helene Bagge on initial attempts at a textbook design and continued efforts regarding education in software language engineering. I envy people who can write a textbook in a team effort; I cannot.

Further, I am very grateful to those who provided input for or feedback on (parts of) the book. I want to mention specifically Mahdi Derakhshanmanesh, Torsten Grust, Bradford Larsen, Nicolas Laurent, Eliot Miranda, Friedrich Steimann, and Vadim Zaytsev.

I kindly acknowledge collaboration on relevant subjects with current or former graduate or undergraduate students at the University of Rostock; Universiteit van Amsterdam; the Dutch Centre of Mathematics and Computer Science, Amsterdam (CWI); Vrije Universiteit, Amsterdam; Universität Koblenz-Landau; and other places. I want to mention specifically Jan Kort, Joost Visser, Wolfgang Lohmann,

Thiago T. Bartolomei, Markus Kaiser, Ekaterina Pek, Andrei Varanovich, Vadim Zaytsev, Marcel Heinz, Lukas Härtel, Johannes Härtel, Kevin Klein, and Simon Schauss.

Several editions of my courses on software language engineering and programming language theory have helped in collecting and maturing the content; thanks to all the students on these courses for bearing with me.

I kindly acknowledge the artistic work of Wojciech Kwasnik and his collaborators on the book's cover and the per-chapter artwork. I very much enjoyed the endeavor–a "deep art" approach. The artwork on the book's cover shows a tower (inspired by the Tower of Babel), suggesting a notion of a "Tower of Software Languages". The tower is the output of a neural algorithm applied to a simpler (computed) tower and used a style image by Matt Sheehy for "morphing". "Tron design" was applied at the border of the tower's shape. The images for the per-chapter artwork were derived based on the following pattern: the image of a computer scientist to be honored was composed with artwork by Vincent van Gogh for the person's background; artwork by Matt Sheehy (the same as for the book's cover) was used to morph the person's clothes and "Tron design" was applied at the border of the person's shape. Thus, there is a constructive similarity between the "Tower of Software Languages" and the morphed images of the persons. See http://www.softlang.org/book-art for information on the art and the way in which computer scientists are honored in this book.

Much of the book was written in Koblenz in proximity to the Mosel and Rhine river, perhaps, in the morning, while eating scrambled eggs and drinking coffee at Baeckerei Hoefer (Ferdinand-Sauerbruch-Straße); in the Sunday afternoons, while drinking Darjeeling or, possibly, Riesling at Kaffeewirtschaft (Münzplatz); or on Saturday or Sunday evenings on Holger's rocking chair.

Dear Olya, thank you for being there and sharing your life with me.

Ralf Lämmel (Software Language Engineer)
March 1st, 2018

Contents

List of Recipes

Acronyms

Fabricated Languages

In this book, several software languages have been "fabricated" to capture core design aspects of diverse real-world software languages. See Section 1.1.2 for a detailed discussion. Here is a summary:

BAL   Basic Assembly Language
BFPL   Basic Functional Programming Language
BGL   Basic Grammar Language
BIPL   Basic Imperative Programming Language
BL   Buddy Language
BML   Basic Machine Language
BNL   Binary Number Language
BSL   Basic Signature Language
BTL   Basic TAPL Language
EFPL   Extended Functional Programming Language
EGL   Extended Grammar Language
EIPL   Extended Imperative Programming Language
EL   Expression Language
ESL   Extended Signature Language
FSML   Finite State Machine Language
MML   MetaModeling Language
TLL   Typed Lambda Language
ULL   Untyped Lambda Language

Other Acronyms

ADT	abstract data type
AG	attribute grammar
AOP	aspect-oriented programming
ASG	abstract syntax graph
AST	abstract syntax tree
BNF	Backus Naur form
ccpo	chain complete partial order
CFG	context-free grammar
COP	context-oriented programming
CPS	continuation-passing style
CST	concrete syntax tree
DSL	domain-specific language
DSML	domain-specific modeling language
EBNF	extended Backus Naur form
FSM	finite state machine
IDE	integrated development environment
IR	intermediate representation
JIT	just in time
LMS	lightweight modular staging
MDE	model-driven engineering
OO	object oriented/orientation
OOP	object-oriented programming
PEG	parsing expression grammar
RDF	resource description framework
SLR	software language repository
UML	unified modeling language

Chapter 1
The Notion of a Software Language

JEAN-MARIE FAVRE.[1]

Abstract In this chapter, we characterize the notion of "software language" in a broad sense. We begin by setting out diverse examples of programming, modeling, and specification languages to cover a wide range of use cases of software languages in software engineering. Then, we classify software languages along multiple dimensions and describe the lifecycle of software languages, with phases such as language definition and implementation. Finally, we identify areas in software engineering that involve software languages in different ways, for example, software reverse engineering and software re-engineering.

---

[1] When the "Software Languages" community was formed around 2005–2007, Jean-Marie Favre was perhaps the key pillar and visionary and community engineer. His views and interests are captured very well in publications like these: [105, 104, 106, 100, 103].

Artwork Credits for Chapter Opening: This work by Wojciech Kwasnik is licensed under CC BY-SA 4.0. This artwork quotes the artwork *DMT*, acrylic, 2006 by Matt Sheehy with the artist's permission. This work also quotes `https://commons.wikimedia.org/wiki/File:Vincent_van_Gogh_-_Zeegezicht_bij_Les_Saintes-Maries-de-la-Mer_-_Google_Art_Project.jpg`, subject to the attribution "Vincent van Gogh: Seascape near Les Saintes-Maries-de-la-Mer (1888) [Public domain], via Wikimedia Commons." This work artistically morphes an image, `https://www.flickr.com/photos/eelcovisser/4772847104`, showing the person honored, subject to the attribution "Permission granted by Eelco Visser for use in this book."

© Springer International Publishing AG, part of Springer Nature 2018
R. Lämmel, *Software Languages*,
https://doi.org/10.1007/978-3-319-90800-7_1

1.1 Examples of Software Languages

In this book, we discuss diverse software languages; we may use them for illustrative purposes, and we may even define or implement them or some subsets thereof. For clarity, we would like to enumerate all these languages here in one place so that the reader will get an impression of the "language-related profile" of this book.

1.1.1 Real-World Software Languages

By "real-world language", we mean a language that exists independently of this book and is more or less well known. We begin with *programming languages* that will be used for illustrative code in this book. We order these languages loosely in terms of their significance in this book.

- *Haskell*[2]: The functional programming language Haskell
- *Java*[3]: The Java programming language
- *Python*[4]: The dynamic programming language Python

We will use some additional software languages in this book; these languages serve the purpose of specification, modeling, or data exchange rather than programming; we order these languages alphabetically.

- *ANTLR*[5]: The grammar notation of the ANTLR technology
- *JSON*[6]: The JavaScript Object Notation
- *JSON Schema*[7]: The JSON Schema language
- *XML*[8]: Extensible Markup Language
- *XSD*[9]: XML Schema Definition

Furthermore, we will refer to diverse software languages in different contexts, for example, for the purpose of language classification in Section 1.2; we order these languages alphabetically.

- *Alloy*[10]: The Alloy specification language
- *CIL*[11]: Bytecode of .NET's CLR

---

[2] Haskell language: https://www.haskell.org/

[3] Java language: https://en.wikipedia.org/wiki/Java_(programming_language)

[4] Python language: https://www.python.org/

[5] ANTLR language: http://www.antlr.org/

[6] JSON language: https://en.wikipedia.org/wiki/JSON

[7] JSON Schema language: http://json-schema.org/

[8] XML language: https://en.wikipedia.org/wiki/XML

[9] XSD language: https://en.wikipedia.org/wiki/XML_Schema_(W3C)

[10] Alloy language: http://alloy.mit.edu/alloy/

[11] CIL language: https://en.wikipedia.org/wiki/Common_Intermediate_Language

- *Common Log Format*[12]: The NCSA Common log format
  DocBook[13]: The DocBook semantic markup language for documentation
- *FOAF*[14]: The friend of a friend ontology
- *INI file*[15]: The INI file format
- *Java bytecode*[16]: Bytecode of the JVM
- *make*[17]: The make tool and its language
- *OWL*[18]: Web Ontology Language
- *Prolog*[19]: The logic programming language Prolog
- *QTFF*[20]: QuickTime File Format
- *RDF*[21]: Resource Description Framework
- *RDFS*[22]: RDF Schema
- *Scala*[23]: The functional OO programming language Scala
- *Smalltalk*[24]: The OO reflective programming language Smalltalk
- *SPARQL*[25]: SPARQL Protocol and RDF Query Language
- *UML*[26]: Unified Modeling Language
- *XPath*[27]: The XML path language for querying
- *XSLT*[28]: Extensible Stylesheet Language Transformations

1.1.2 Fabricated Software Languages

In this book, we "fabricated" a few software languages: these are small, idealized languages that have been specifically designed and implemented for the purposes of the book, although in fact these languages are actual or de facto subsets of real-world software languages. The language names are typically acronyms with expansions hinting at the nature of the languages. Language definitions of language-based

---

[12] Common Log Format language: https://en.wikipedia.org/wiki/Common_Log_Format

[13] DocBook language: https://en.wikipedia.org/wiki/DocBook

[14] FOAF language: http://semanticweb.org/wiki/FOAF.html

[15] INI file language: https://en.wikipedia.org/wiki/INI_file

[16] Java bytecode language: https://en.wikipedia.org/wiki/Java_bytecode

[17] make language: https://en.wikipedia.org/wiki/Make_(software)

[18] OWL language: https://en.wikipedia.org/wiki/Web_Ontology_Language

[19] Prolog language: https://en.wikipedia.org/wiki/Prolog

[20] QTFF language: https://en.wikipedia.org/wiki/QuickTime_File_Format

[21] RDF language: https://www.w3.org/RDF/

[22] RDFS language: https://www.w3.org/TR/rdf-schema/

[23] Scala language: https://en.wikipedia.org/wiki/Scala_(programming_language)

[24] Smalltalk language: https://en.wikipedia.org/wiki/Smalltalk

[25] SPARQL language: https://en.wikipedia.org/wiki/SPARQL

[26] UML language: https://en.wikipedia.org/wiki/Unified_Modeling_Language

[27] XPath language: https://en.wikipedia.org/wiki/XPath

[28] XSLT language: https://en.wikipedia.org/wiki/XSLT

software components are available for these languages from the book's repository.[29]
The footnotes in the following list link to the repository locations for the languages.

- *BAL*: Basic Assembly Language
- *BFPL*: Basic Functional Programming Language
- *BGL*: Basic Grammar Language
- *BIPL*: Basic Imperative Programming Language
- *BML*: Binary Machine Language
- *BNL*: Binary Number Language
- *BSL*: Basic Signature Language
- *BTL*: Basic TAPL Language
- *BL*: Buddy Language
- *EFPL*: Extended Functional Programming Language
- *EGL*: Extended Grammar Language
- *EIPL*: Extended Imperative Programming Language
- *EL*: Expression Language
- *ESL*: Extended Signature Language
- *FSML*: Finite State Machine Language
- *MML*: Meta Modeling Language
- *TLL*: Typed Lambda Language
- *Text*: The "language" of text (such as Unicode 8.0 strings)
- *ULL*: Untyped Lambda Language

In the rest of this section, we quickly introduce some of these languages, thereby
providing a first indication of the diversity of language aspects covered by the book.

Binary Number Language (BNL)   A trivial language of binary numbers with an
intended semantics that maps binary to decimal values.

Basic TAPL Language (BTL)   A trivial expression language in reference to the
TAPL textbook (Types and programming languages [210]).

Buddy Language (BL)   A trivial language for modeling persons in terms of their
names and buddy relationships.

Basic Functional Programming Language (BFPL)   A really simple functional
programming language which is an actual syntactic subset of the established programming language *Haskell*.

Basic Imperative Programming Language (BIPL)   A really simple imperative
programming language which is a de-facto subset of the established programming language C.

Finite State Machine Language (FSML)   A really simple language for behavioral modeling which is variation on statecharts of the established modeling language UML.

Basic Grammar Language (BGL)   A specification language for concrete syntax,
which can also be executed for the purpose of parsing; it is a variation on the
established Backus-Naur form (BNF).

---

[29] http://github.com/softlang/yas

1.1.2.1 BNL: A Language of Binary Numbers

We introduce *BNL* (*B*inary *N*umber *L*anguage). This is a trivial language whose elements are essentially the binary numbers. Here are some binary numbers and their associated "interpretations" as decimal numbers:

- **0**: 0 as a decimal number;
- **1**: 1 as a decimal number;
- **10**: 2 as a decimal number;
- **11**: 3 as a decimal number;
- **100**: 4 as a decimal number;
- **101**: 5 as a decimal number;
- **101.01**: 5.25 as a decimal number.

Thus, the language contains integer and rational numbers – only positive ones, as it happens. BNL is a trivial language that is nevertheless sufficient to discuss the most basic aspects of software languages such as *syntax* and *semantics*. A syntax definition of BNL should define valid sequences of digits, possibly containing a period. A semantics definition of BNL could map binary to decimal numbers. We will discuss BNL's abstract syntax in Chapter 3 and the concrete syntax in Chapter 6.

1.1.2.2 BTL: An Expression Language

We introduce *BTL* (*B*asic *T*APL *L*anguage). This is a trivial language whose elements are essentially expressions over natural numbers and Boolean values. Here is a simple expression:

```
pred if iszero zero then succ succ zero else zero
```

The meaning of such expressions should be defined by expression evaluation. For instance, the expression form iszero e corresponds to a test of whether e evaluates to the natural number zero; evaluation of the form is thus assumed to return a Boolean value. The expression shown above evaluates to zero because iszero zero should compute to true, making the if-expression select the then-branch succ succ zero, the predecessor of which is succ zero.

An interpreter of BTL expressions should recursively evaluate BTL expression forms. BTL is a trivial language that is nevertheless sufficient to discuss basic aspects of interpretation (Chapter 5), semantics (Chapter 8), and type systems (Chapter 9).

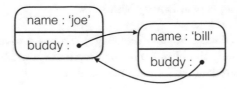

Fig. 1.1 Illustrative graph of buddy relationships.

1.1.2.3 BL: A Language for Buddy Relationships

We introduce *BL* (*Buddy Language*). This is a trivial language whose elements are essentially graphs of persons with their names and buddy relationships. Figure 1.1 shows an illustrative graph of buddy relationships between two persons; we leverage an ad hoc visual, concrete syntax.

BL is a trivial ontology-like language. It can be considered a trivial variation on FOAF, the "friend of a friend" ontology. Importantly, BL involves references in an essential manner. Thus, BL calls for a graph-based abstract syntax, whereas the other language examples given above (arguably) need only a tree-based abstract syntax. BL also involves an interesting constraint: a person must not be his or her own buddy. We will discuss BL as an example of graph-based abstract syntax in Chapter 3.

1.1.2.4 BFPL: A Functional Programming Language

We introduce *BFPL* (*Basic Functional Programming Language*). Here is an illustration of BFPL – a sample program which defines the factorial function recursively and applies to an actual argument:

```
−− The factorial function
factorial :: Int −> Int
factorial x =
  if ((==) x 0)
    then 1
    else ((*) x (factorial ((−) x 1)))

−− Apply the function to 5
main = print $ factorial 5 −− Prints 120
```

(The execution of the program would print "120".) BFPL is a trivial language exercising basic *functional programming* concepts such as function application and recursive function definition. A semantics definition of BFPL should define expression evaluation, including parameter passing for function application. We will develop such a semantics in Chapter 8.

For what it matters, BFPL is a "small" syntactic subset of the established functional programming language *Haskell*. In fact, the sample shown is a valid Haskell program as is, and the Haskell semantics would agree on the output – 120 for the factorial of 5. BFPL was fabricated to be very simple. Thus, BFPL lacks many language constructs of Haskell and other real-world functional programming languages. For instance, BFPL does not feature higher-order functions and algebraic data types.

1.1.2.5 BIPL: An Imperative Programming Language

We introduce *BIPL* (*B*asic *I*mperative *P*rogramming *L*anguage). Here is an illustration of BIPL – a sample program which performs Euclidean division:

```
{
    // Sample operands for Euclidean division
    x = 14;
    y = 4;

    // Compute quotient q=3 and remainder r=2
    q = 0;
    r = x;
    while (r >= y) {
        r = r – y;
        q = q + 1;
    }
}
```

Division is applied to specific arguments x and y. The result is returned as the quotient q and the remainder r. The execution of the sample program would terminate with the variable assignment x=14, y=4, q=3, r=2.

BIPL is a trivial language exercising basic *imperative programming* concepts such as mutable variable, assignment, and control-flow constructs for sequence, selection, and iteration. For what it matters, BIPL is roughly a "small" syntactic subset of the established but much more complicated imperative programming language C. BIPL lacks many language constructs that are provided by C and other real-world imperative programming languages. For instance, BIPL does not feature procedures (functions) and means of type definition such as structs. Further, C requires declaration of variables, whereas BIPL does not. A semantics of BIPL should define statement execution. We will develop such a semantics in Chapter 8.

1.1.2.6 FSML: A Language for Finite State Machines

We introduce *FSML* (*FSM L*anguage, i.e., *F*inite *S*tate *M*achine *L*anguage). Figure 1.2 shows an illustrative FSM (finite state machine) which models the behavior of a turnstile or some sort of revolving door, as possibly used in a metro system. The FSM identifies possible states of the turnstile; see the nodes in the visual notation.

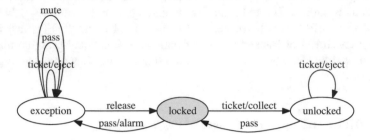

Fig. 1.2 A finite state machine for a turnstile.

The FSM also identifies possible transitions between states triggered by "events," possibly causing "actions"; see the edges in the visual notation.

These are these states in the turnstile FSM:

- *locked*: The turnstile is locked. No passenger is allowed to pass.
- *unlocked*: The turnstile is unlocked. A passenger may pass.
- *exception*: A problem has occurred and metro personnel need to intervene.

There are input symbols which correspond to the events that a user or the environment may trigger. There are output symbols which correspond to the actions that the state machine should perform upon a transition. These are some of the events and actions of the turnstile FSM:

- Event *ticket*: A passenger enters a ticket into the card reader.
- Event *pass*: A passenger passes through the turnstile, as noticed by a sensor.
- Action *collect*: The ticket is collected by the card reader.
- Action *alarm*: An alarm is turned on, thereby requesting metro personnel.

The meanings of the various transitions should be clear. Consider, for example, the transition from the source state "locked" to the target state "unlocked", which is annotated by "ticket/collect" to mean that the transition is triggered by entering a ticket and the transition causes ticket collection to happen.

FSML is a domain-specific modeling language (DSML). FSML supports *state-based modeling* of systems. The specification can be executed to simulate possible behaviors of a turnstile. The specification could also be used to generate a code skeleton for controlling an actual turnstile, as part of an actual metro system. FSML is a trivial language that can be used to discuss basic aspects of domain-specific language definition and implementation. For what it matters, languages for state-based behavior are widely established in software and systems engineering. For instance, the established modeling language UML consists, in fact, of several modeling languages; UML's state machine diagrams are more general than FSML. We will discuss FSML in detail in Chapter 2.

1.1.2.7 BGL: A Language for Context-Free Grammars

We introduce *BGL* (*B*asic *G*rammar *L*anguage). This language can be used to define the *concrete textual syntax* of other software languages. Thus, BGL gets us to the metalevel. Here is an illustration of BGL – a definition of the syntax of BNL – the language of binary numbers, as introduced earlier:

```
[number] number : bits rest ; // A binary number
[single] bits : bit ; // A single bit
[many] bits : bit bits ; // More than one bit
[zero] bit : '0' ; // The zero bit
[one] bit : '1' ; // The nonzero bit
[integer] rest : ; // An integer number
[rational] rest : '.' bits ; // A rational number
```

Each line is a grammar production (a rule) with the syntactic category (or the so-called nonterminal) to the left of ":" and its definition to the right of ":". For instance, the first production defines that a binary number consists of a bit sequence bits for the integer part followed by rest for the optional rational part. The right-hand phrases compose so-called terminals ("0", "1", and ".") and nonterminals (bit, bits, rest, and number) by juxtaposition. The rules are labeled, thereby giving a name to each construct.

BGL is a domain-specific modeling language in that it supports modeling (or specifying or defining) concrete textual syntax. One may "execute" BGL in different ways. Most obviously, one may execute a BGL grammar for the purpose of accepting or *parsing* input according to the syntax defined. BGL, like many other notations for syntax definition, is grounded in the fundamental formalism of *context-free grammars* (CFGs). BGL is a variation on BNF [21]. There exist many real-world notations for syntax definition [277]; they are usually more complex than BGL and may be tied to specific technology, for example, for parsing. We will develop BGL in detail in Chapter 6.

1.2 Classification of Software Languages

There are hundreds or even thousands of established software languages, depending on how we count them. It may be useful to group languages in an ontological manner. In particular, a *classification* of software languages (i.e., a language taxonomy) is a useful (if not necessary) pillar of a definition of "software language".

Wikipedia, which actually uses the term "computer language" at the root of the classification, identifies the following top-level classifiers:[30]

- data-modeling languages;
- markup languages;
- programming languages;
- specification languages;
- stylesheet languages;
- transformation languages.

Any such branch can be classified further in terms of constructs and concepts. For instance, in the case of programming languages, there exist textbooks on programming languages, programming paradigms, and programming language theory such as [199, 232], which identify constructs and concepts. There is also scholarly work on the classification of programming languages [20, 90] and the identification of language concepts and corresponding paradigms [258].

Several classes of software languages (other than programming languages) have been identified, for example, *model transformation languages* [75], *business rule modeling languages* [239], *visual languages* [46, 49, 190], and *architecture description languages* [192]. There is more recent work aimed at the classification of software languages (or computer languages) more broadly [13, 237, 3, 171]. The *101companies* project[31] [102, 101, 173, 166] is also aimed at a taxonomy of software languages, but the results are of limited use, at the time of writing.

In the remainder of this section, we classify software languages along different dimensions. A key insight here is that a single classification tree is insufficient. Multiple inheritance may be needed, or orthogonal dimensions may need to be considered separately.

1.2.1 Classification by Paradigm

When focusing on programming languages as a category of software languages, classification may be based on the *programming paradigm*. A paradigm is characterized by a central notion of programming or computing. Here is an incomplete, classical list of paradigms:

Imperative programming   Assignable (updatable) variables and updatable (in-place) data structures and sequential execution of statements of operations on variables. Typically, procedural abstractions capture statements that describe control flow with basic statements for updates. We exercise imperative programming with the fabricated language BIPL (Section 1.1.2.5) in this book.

---

[30] We show Wikipedia categories based on a particular data-cleaning effort [171]. This is just a snapshot, as Wikipedia is obviously evolving continuously.

[31] http://101companies.org

Functional programming   The application of functions models computation with compound expressions to be reduced to values. Functions are first-class citizens in that functions may receive and return functions; these are higher-order functions. We exercise functional programming with the fabricated language BFPL (Section 1.1.2.4) in this book – however, though higher-order functions are not supported.

Object-oriented (OO) programming   An object is a capsule of state and behavior. Objects can communicate with each other by sending messages, the same message being implementable differently by different kinds of objects. Objects also engage in structural relationships, i.e., they can participate in whole–part and reference relationships. Objects may be constructed by instantiation of a given template (e.g., a class). *Java* and C# are well-known OO programming languages.

Logic programming   A program is represented as a collection of logic formulae. Program execution corresponds to some kind of proof derivation. For instance, *Prolog* is a well-known logic programming language; computation is based on depth-first, left-to-right proof search through the application of definite clauses.

There exist yet other programming or computing notions that may characterize a paradigm, for example, message passing and concurrency. Many programming languages are, in fact, *multi-paradigm* languages in that they support several paradigms. For instance, *JavaScript* is typically said to be both a functional and an imperative OO programming language and a scripting language. Programming languages may be able to support programming according to a paradigm on the basis of some encoding scheme without being considered a member of that paradigm. For instance, in Java prior to version 8, it was possible to encode functional programs in Java, while proper support was added only in version 8.

Van Roy offers a rich discussion of programming paradigms [258]. Programming concepts are the basic primitive elements used to construct programming paradigms. Often, two paradigms that seem quite different (for example, functional programming and object-oriented programming) differ by just one concept. The following are the concepts discussed by Van Roy: record, procedure, closure, continuation, thread, single assignment, (different forms of) cell (state), name (unforgeable constant), unification, search, solver, log, nondeterministic choice, (different forms of) synchronization, port (channel), clocked computation. Van Roy identifies 27 paradigms, which are characterized as sets of programming concepts. These paradigms can be clearly related in terms of the concepts that have to be added to go from one paradigm to another.

1.2.2 Classification by Type System

Furthermore, languages may also be classified in terms of their typing discipline or type system [210] (or the lack thereof). Here are some important options for programming languages in particular:

Static typing   The types of variables and other abstractions (e.g., the argument and result types of methods or functions) are statically known, i.e., without executing the program – this is at compile time for compiled languages. For instance, Haskell and Java are statically typed languages.

Dynamic typing   The types of variables and other abstractions are determined at runtime. A variable's type is the type of the value that is stored in that variable. A method or function's type is the one that is implied by a particular method invocation or function application. For instance, Python is a dynamically typed language.

Duck typing   The suitability of a variable (e.g., an object variable in object-oriented programming) is determined at runtime on the basis of checking for the presence of certain methods or properties. Python uses duck typing.

Structural typing   The equivalence or subtyping relationship between types in a static typing setting is determined on the basis of type structure, such as the components of record types. Scala supports some form of structural typing.

Nominal typing   The equivalence or subtyping relationship between types in a static typing setting is determined on the basis of explicit type names and declared relationships between them. Java's reference types (classes and interfaces including "extends" and "implements" relationships) commit to nominal typing.

1.2.3 Classification by Purpose

Languages may be classified on the basis of the *purpose* of the language (its usage) or its elements. Admittedly, the term "purpose" may be somewhat vague, but the illustrative classifiers in Table 1.1 may convey our intuition. We offer two views: the purpose of the language versus that of its elements; these two views are very similar.

Table 1.1 Classification by the purpose of language elements

Purpose (language)	Purpose (element)	Classifier	Example
Programming	Program	Programming language	Java
Querying	Query	Query language	XPath
Transformation	Transformation	Transformation language	XSLT
Modeling	Model	Modeling language	UML
Specification	Specification	Specification language	Alloy
Data representation	Data	Data format	QTFF (QuickTime file format)
Documentation	Documentation	Documentation language	DocBook
Configuration	Configuration	Configuration language	INI file
Logging	Log	Log format	Common Log Format
...	...	...	...

In some cases, owing to the ambiguity of natural language, we may even end up with (about) the same purpose for both views, language elements versus language. These classifiers are not necessarily disjoint. For instance, it may be hard to decide in all cases whether some artifact should be considered a model, a specification, or a program. The classifiers can also be further broken down. For instance, "data" may be classified further as "audio", "image", or "video" data; "models" may be classified further as "structural", "behavioral", or "architectural" models.

Let us apply this classification to the illustrative languages of Section 1.1. The basic functional and imperative languages (BFPL and BIPL) are programming languages. The languages for buddy relationships (BL) and finite state machines (FSML) are (domain-specific) modeling languages. The BNF-like grammar language BGL is a specification language. We may also characterize BGL as a syntax-modeling language. We may also characterize the languages for binary numbers (BNL) and buddy relationships (BL) as data formats or data representation languages.

In many cases, when speaking of purposes, we may also speak of domains and, more specifically, of problem or programming domains. For instance, (a) transformation may be considered as a purpose, as an artifact, and a domain. We discuss the domain notion in more detail below.

Exercise 1.1 (Another purpose for classification)   [Intermediate level]
Study the classification of languages based on the references given earlier. For instance, you may study the classification of languages according to Wikipedia. Find another classifier to serve for classification based on purpose.

1.2.4 Classification by Generality or Specificity

There is a long-standing distinction between general-purpose (programming) languages (GPLs) versus domain-specific languages (DSLs). The term "domain" may be meant here in the sense of "problem" or "application" domain such as image manipulation, hardware design, or financial products; see [81, 157] for many examples. The term "domain" may also be meant in the sense of "programming" or "solution" domain such as XML, GUI, or database programming [219]. This distinction is not clear-cut; it also depends on the point of view. We do not make much use of this distinction in the sequel.

We quote from [81] to offer a definition of a DSL: "A domain-specific language (DSL) is a programming language or executable specification language that offers, through appropriate notations and abstractions, expressive power focused on, and usually restricted to, a particular problem domain." We also extract some distinguishing characteristics of GPLs and DSLs from [265]:

Domain   Only DSLs have a relatively small and well-defined domain.

Language size   GPLs are large. DSLs are typically small.

Turing completeness   DSLs may not be Turing complete.

Lifespan   GPLs live for years to decades. DSLs may live for months only.

Designed by   GPLs are designed by gurus or committees. DSLs are designed by a few software engineers and domain experts.

Evolution   GPLs evolve slowly. The evolution of DSLs is fast-paced.

Deprecation/incompatible changes   This is almost impossible for GPLs; it is feasible and relatively common for DSLs.

DSLs, in turn, may be subdivided into domain-specific programming versus modeling languages; see [147] for an introduction to domain-specific modeling. However, we argue that the distinction between programming and modeling is somewhat vague, because many modeling languages end up being executable eventually and it is also not uncommon to use programming languages for modeling. DSLs may also be subdivided based on the style of implementation: *internal* versus *external DSLs* [265, 214, 94, 78]. An internal DSL is basically a DSL implementation inside another language (the so-called *host language*) – typically as a library inside a GPL, for example, *Parsec* [182] is implemented as a Haskell-based combinator library for parsing. The DSL user accesses the DSL by means of an API. Internal style may leverage metaprogramming-related facilities of the host language.

An external DSL is a language that is implemented in its own right, for example, *make* as a DSL (and a tool) for build management. There is also the notion of an *embedded DSL* [214], where the DSL's syntax and semantics are integrated into a host language. This may be achieved by the host language's ability to define the DSL syntax and to model the semantics by means of a mapping from DSL syntax to host language syntax.

There is also the related notion of *language composition*. That is, when multiple languages are integrated to be used together, then their semantics may need to be coordinated [141, 48, 95, 78]. Language composition is particularly relevant in the context of (domain-specific) modeling languages.

1.2.5 Classification by Representation

One may distinguish three fundamental representation options: strings versus trees versus graphs. That is, the terms "string", "tree", and "graph" hint at the fundamental structure of language elements. The terms are drawn from formal language theory. Accordingly, there are these language classifiers:

String language   (See also "textual language" below.) Language elements are represented, viewed, and edited as strings, i.e., sequences of characters. A string language would be typically defined in terms of a string grammar in the sense of formal language theory, as supported, for example, by the BGL grammar notation of Section 1.1.2.7. Several of the illustrative languages of Section 1.1 were introduced as string languages.

Tree language   (See also "markup language" below.) Language elements are represented, viewed, and edited as trees, for example, as XML trees or JSON dictionaries. A tree language is defined in terms of a suitable grammar or data modeling notation, for example, XSD in the case of XML. As it happens, we did not present any tree languages in Section 1.1.2.7, but we will discuss tree-based abstract syntax definitions later for some of the string languages that we have already seen. Tree languages play an important role in language implementation.

Graph language   Language elements are represented, viewed, and edited as graphs, i.e., more or less constrained collections of nodes and edges. Appropriate grammar and data modeling notations exist for this case as well. The language BL for buddy relationships (Section 1.1.2.3) was introduced as a graph language and we hinted at a visual concrete syntax. A graph language may be coupled with a string or tree language in the sense of alternative representations of the same "conceptual" language. For instance, BL may be represented in a string-, tree-, or graph-based manner.

1.2.6 Classification by Notation

One may also distinguish languages in terms of notation; this classification is very similar to the classification by representation:

Textual (text) language   This is essentially a synonym for "string language".

Markup language   Markup, as in XML, is used as the main principle for expressing language elements. The use of markup is one popular notation for tree languages. With an appropriate semantics of identities, markup can also be used as a notation for graphs. Not every tree language relies on markup for the notation. For instance, JSON provides another, more dictionary-oriented notation for tree languages.

Visual (graphical) language   A visual notation is used. The languages BL for buddy relationships (Section 1.1.2.3) and FSML for state-based modeling (Section 1.1.2.6) were introduced in terms of a visual notation.

1.2.7 Classification by Degree of Declarativeness

An (executable) language may be said to be (more or less) *declarative*. It turns out to be hard to identify a consensual definition of declarativeness, but this style of classification is nevertheless common. For instance, one may say that programs (or models) of a declarative language describe more the "what" than the "how". That is, a declarative program's semantics is not strongly tied to execution order.

Let us review the languages of Section 1.1:

Binary Number Language (BNL)   A trivial language.

Buddy Language (BL)   A trivial language.

Basic Functional Programming Language (BFPL)   This language is "pure", i.e., free of side effects. Regardless of the evaluation order of subexpressions, complete evaluation of a main expression should lead to the same result – modulo some constraints to preserve termination. For instance, argument expressions of a function application could be evaluated in different orders without affecting the result. Thus, BFPL is a declarative programming language.

Basic Imperative Programming Language (BIPL)   This language features imperative variables such that the execution order of statements affects the result of computation. Thus, BIPL is not a declarative programming language.

Finite State Machine Language (FSML)   This language models finite states and event- and action-labeled transitions between states. Its actual semantics or execution order is driven by an event sequence. FSML would usually be regarded as a declarative (modeling) language.

Basic Grammar Language (BGL)   This grammar notation defines sets of strings in a rule-based manner. Thus, BGL's most fundamental semantics is "declarative" in the sense that it is purely mathematical, without reference to any operational details. Eventually, we may attach a more or less constrained operational interpretation to BGL so that we can use it for efficient, deterministic parsing. Until that point, BGL would be usually regarded as a declarative (specification) language.

We may also consider subcategories of declarative languages such that it is emphasized how declarativeness is achieved. Two examples may suffice:

Rule-based language   Programs are composed from rules, where a rule typically combines a condition and an action part. The condition part states when the rule is applicable; the action part states the implications of rule application. Some logic programming languages, for example, Prolog, can be very well considered to be rule-based languages. Some schemes for using functional programming, for example, in interpretation or program transformation, also adopt the rule-based approach. Event-driven approaches may also use rules with an additional "event" component, for example, the "event condition action" (ECA) paradigm, as used in active databases [88].

Constraint-based language   Programs involve constraints as means of selecting or combining computations. These constraints are aggregated during program execution and constraint resolution is leveraged to establish whether and how given constraints can be solved. For instance, there exist various constraint-logic programming languages which enrich basic logic programming with constraints on sets of algebras for numbers [117].

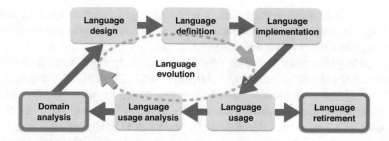

Fig. 1.3 The lifecycle of a software language. The nodes denote phases of the lifecycle. The edges denote transitions between these phases. The lifecycle starts with *domain analysis*. The lifecycle ends (theoretically) with *language retirement*. We may enter cycles owing to language evolution.

Exercise 1.2 (Classification of *make*)   [Basic level]
Study the language used by the well-known make *utility and argue that the language is declarative and identify what subcategory of declarativeness applies.*

1.3 The Lifecycle of Software Languages

The notion of a software lifecycle can be usefully adopted for languages. That is, a language goes through a lifecycle, possibly iterating or skipping some phases; see Fig. 1.3. These phases are described in some detail as follows:

Domain analysis   A domain analysis is required to discover the domain that is to be addressed by a new language. A domain analysis answers these questions: What are the central concepts in the domain? For instance, the central concepts are states and transitions between states for FSML, differential equations and their solution in a language for weather forecasts, or layouts and their rendering in a language for HTML/XML stylesheets. These concepts form the foundation of language design and for everything onwards. Arguably, no domain analysis is performed for general-purpose programming languages.

Language design   The domain concepts are mapped, at the design level of abstraction, to language constructs and language concepts. The emerging language should be classified in terms of paradigm, degree of declarativeness, and other characteristics. A language may be presented as a composition of very specific language constructs as well as reusable language constructs, for example, for basic expressions or modules. The first samples are written so that a syntax emerges, and the transition to the phase of language definition has then begun.

Language definition   The language design is refined into a language definition. Most notably, the syntax and semantics of the language are defined. Assuming an executable language definition, a first language implementation (a proof of concept) is made available for experiments, so that the transition to the phases of language implementation and usage has begun.

Language implementation   The language is properly implemented. Initially, a usable and efficient compiler or interpreter needs to provided. Eventually, additional *language processors* and tool support may be provided, for example, documentation tools, formatters, style checkers, and refactorings. Furthermore, support for an integrated development environment (IDE) may be implemented.

Language usage   The language is used in actual software development. That is, language artifacts are "routinely" authored and a body of software artifacts acquire dependencies on the language. This is not explicitly modeled in Fig. 1.3, but the assumption is, of course, that the language implementation is continuously improved and new language processors are made available.

Language evolution   Language definitions may revised to incorporate new language features or respond to experience with language usage. Obviously, changes to language definitions imply work on language implementations. Language changes may even break backward compatibility, in which cases these changes will necessitate migration of existing code in those languages.

Language usage analysis   Language evolution and the systematic improvement of domain analysis as well as language design, definition, and implementation, may benefit from language usage analysis [155, 100, 172], as an empirical element of the lifecycle. By going through the lifecycle in cycles, the language may evolve in different ways. For instance, the language may be extended so that a new version becomes available, which again needs to be implemented and put to use.

Language retirement   In practice, languages, once adopted, are rarely retired completely, because the costs and risks of retirement are severe impediments. Retirement may still happen in the narrow scope of projects or organizations. In theory, a language may become obsolete, i.e., there are no software artifacts left that depend on that language. Otherwise, *language migration* may be considered. That is, software artifacts that depend on a language are migrated (i.e., transformed manually or automatically) to another language.

Many aspects of these phases, with some particular emphasis on the lifecycle of DSLs are discussed in [133, 272, 273, 197, 214, 56, 98, 94, 78, 265, 229]. In the present book, the focus is on language definition and implementation; we are concerned only superficially with domain analysis, language design, evolution, and retirement.

1.3.1 Language Definition

Let us have a deeper look at the lifecycle phase of language definition. A language is defined to facilitate implementation and use of the language. There are these aspects of language definition:

Syntax The definition of the syntax consists of rules that describe the valid language elements which may be drawn from different "universes": the set of all strings (say, text), the set of all trees (of some form, e.g., XML-like trees), or the set of all graphs (of some form). Different kinds of formalisms may be used to specify the rules defining the syntax. We may distinguish *concrete* and *abstract syntax* – the former is tailored towards users who need to read and write language elements, and the latter is tailored towards language implementation. Abstract syntax is discussed in Chapters 3and 4. Concrete syntax is discussed in Chapters 6and 7.

Semantics The definition of semantics provides a mapping from the syntactic categories of a language (such as statements and expressions) to suitable domains of meanings. The actual mapping can be defined in different ways. For instance, the mapping can be defined as a set of syntax-driven inference rules which model the stepwise execution or reduction of a program; this is known as small-step operational semantics (Chapter 8). The mapping can also be applied by a translation, for example, by a model-to-model transformation in model-driven engineering (MDE).

Pragmatics The definition of the pragmatics explains the purpose of language concepts and provides recommendations for their usage. Language pragmatics is often defined only informally through text and samples. For instance, the pragmatics definition for a C-like language with arrays may state that arrays should be used for efficient (constant-time) access to indices in ordered collections of values of the same type. Also, arrays should be favored over (random-access) files or databases for as long as in-memory representation of the entire data structure is reasonable. In modeling languages for finite state machine (e.g., FSML), events proxy for sensors and actions proxy for actors in an embedded system.

Types Some languages also feature a *type system* as a part of the language definition. A type system provides a set of rules for assigning or verifying *types*, i.e., properties of language phrases, for example, different expression types such as "int" or "string" in a program with expressions. We speak of *type checking* if the type system is used to check explicitly declared types. We speak of *type inference* if the type system is used additionally to infer missing type declarations. A type system needs to be able to bind names in the sense that any use of an abstraction such as a variable, a method, or a function is linked to the corresponding declaration. Such *name binding* may defined as part of the type system or they may be defined somewhat separately. We discuss types in detail in Chapter 9. Even when a language does not have an interesting type system, i.e., different types and rules about their use in abstractions, the language may still feature other constraints regarding, for example, the correct use of names. Thus, we may also speak of *well-formedness* more generally, as opposed to *well-typedness* more specifically. For instance, in FSML, the events handled by a given source state must be distinct for the sake of determinism.

When definitions of syntax, types, and semantics are considered formal artifacts such that these artifacts are treated in a formal (mathematical) manner, then we operate within the context of *programming language theory*. A formal approach is helpful, for example, when approaching the question of *soundness*. That is: *Are the type system and semantics in alignment in that properties described by the type system agree with the actual runtime behavior described by the semantics?*

In the present book, we use semiformal language definitions and we assume them to be useful as concise executable specifications that will help software engineers in implementing software languages, as discussed below. For reasons of limiting the scope and size of the book, we are not much concerned with the formal analysis ("metatheory") of language definitions, in the sense of soundness or otherwise.

1.3.2 Language Implementation

Let us also have a deeper look at the lifecycle phase of language implementation. The discussion gravitates slightly towards programming languages, but most elements apply similarly to MDE and DSLs.

1.3.2.1 Compilation versus Interpretation

One may distinguish two approaches to language implementation:

Interpretation   An interpreter executes elements of a software language to produce, for example, the I/O behavior of a function, the result of a database query, or the object graph corresponding to method invocations in an OO program. We will develop some interpreters in Chapter 5. We will relate semantics and interpretation in Chapters 8 and 11.

Compilation   A compiler translates (transforms) elements of an executable software language into elements of another executable software language. This translation may or may not lower the level of abstraction. For instance, a compiler may translate a high-level programming language into low-level assembly or virtual machine code. Likewise, a compiler for a DSL may target a GPL, thereby also lowering the level of abstraction. Alternatively, a compiler may be more of a translator between similar languages without much lowering the level of abstraction. In particular, a compiler may piggyback on yet another compiler for its target language. We will develop a simple compiler in Chapter 5.

In a formalist's view, an interpreter would be derived more or less directly from a suitable form of semantics definition for a language. However, this does not cover all forms of interpretation, because a given semantics may not directly enable a practically motivated form of interpretation. For instance, consider the semantics of a formal grammar as a language (a set) generated by that grammar. This semantics is not immediately usable for "interpretation" in the sense of parsing.

Executing a program by interpretation is usually assumed to be slower than executing the target of compilation. Interpretation allows a code base to be extended as the program runs, whereas compilation prevents this.

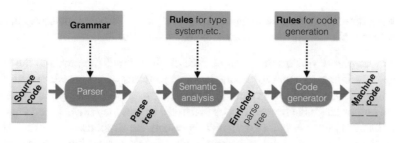

Fig. 1.4 Simplified data flow in a compiler. The rectangles with rounded edges represent logical phases of compilation. The remaining nodes (rectangles and triangles) correspond to input and output, as expressed by the direction of the arrows.

Interpretation versus compilation is not a clear-cut dichotomy; neither do we usually deal with a single layer of program execution. Consider the usual scheme of compiling languages to virtual machines. For instance, Java is compiled to Java bytecode and C# is compiled to.NET's CIL. These target languages are implemented in turn by virtual machines which may be regarded as interpreters of the bytecode languages at hand or, in fact, compilers, as they may translate bytecode into native machine code on a target platform. There is also the notion of just-in-time (JIT) compilation which can be seen as a compilation/interpretation hybrid in that compilation happens as part of interpretation such that compilation can be adjusted to the runtime context. Virtual machines, as mentioned before, usually leverage JIT compilation. In other words, a JIT compiler is therefore an optimization of an interpreter which tries to achieve the performance of a compiler while preserving the dynamicity of an interpreter.

In addition to the basic dichotomy of compilation versus interpretation, there is also the specific classification of implementation strategies for domain-specific languages – internal versus external versus embedded DSL, as discussed in Section 1.2.4.

In MDE, one does not necessarily speak of compilation, but instead of model-to-model transformation, code generation, or model-to-text transformation. However, the underlying principles are very much alike.

1.3.2.2 Architecture of a Compiler

Compilers and interpreters consist of several components. The decomposition of a compiler into standard components with the associated data flow is summarized in Fig. 1.4; see textbooks on compiler construction [2, 186, 14] for an in-depth discussion. Thus, the source code ("text") is mapped to a syntax tree (i.e., a parse tree, a concrete syntax tree (CST), or an abstract syntax tree (AST)), which is then further enriched with attributes and links. Eventually, code for a virtual or actual machine is generated. These conceptual phases may be properly separated ("multi-pass compilation") or may be integrated into one phase ("single-pass compilation"). The components are explained more in detail as follows:

Parser   A parser verifies the conformance of given input (i.e., text) to the syntax rules of a language and represents the input in terms of the structure defined by the rules. A parser performs parsing. Compilers and interpreters begin by parsing. Many other language processors, as discussed below, also involve parsing.

Semantic analysis   A syntax tree only represents the structure of the source code. For any sort of nontrivial treatment such as code generation, the syntax tree needs to be enriched with attributes and links related to typing and name binding. Names with their bindings and other attributes may be aggregated in a data structure which is referred to as a symbol table or environment.

Code generator   The enriched syntax tree is translated, more or less directly, into machine code, i.e., code of some actual or virtual machine. In particular, code generation involves resource and storage decisions such as register allocation, i.e., assigning program variables to processor registers of the target machine. In this book, few technicalities of code generation are discussed; this topic is covered perfectly by the literature on compiler construction.

Ideally, the components are described by specifications such as grammars, type systems, name-binding rules, and rewrite systems, as indicated in Fig. 1.4. In practice, the components are often implemented in a more ad hoc fashion.

This is a simplified data flow, because actual compilers may involve additional phases. That is, parsing may consist of several phases in itself: preprocessing; lexical analysis (scanning, lexing, or tokenization); syntax analysis including parse-tree construction and syntax desugaring. Also, there may be extra steps preceding code generation: translation to a (simpler) *intermediate representation* (IR) and IR-level optimization. Further, code generation may also involve *optimization* at the level of the target language and a separation between translation to assembly code, mapping to machine code, and some elements of linking. Finally, code generation may actually rely on translation such that the given input language is translated into a well-defined subset of an existing (programming) language so that an available compiler can be used afterwards.

Exercise 1.3 (An exercise on language implementation)   [Basic level]
Research the current version of the JDK (Java Development Kit) and identify and characterize at least two language implementations that are part of it.

1.3.2.3 Classification of Language Processors

Languages are implemented in many ways other than just regular compilers and interpreters. We use the term "language processor" to refer to any sort of functionality for automated processing of software artifacts in a language-aware manner, i.e., with more or less awareness of the syntax, types, and semantics of the artifacts. Examples of language processors include documentation generators, refactoring tools, bug checkers, and metrics calculation tools. Language processors often consist of several components and perform processing in phases, as we discussed above for compilers. Rather than classifying language processors directly, let us classify language-based software components. We do not make any claim of completeness for this classification. Several of the classifiers below will reappear in the discussion of the role of software languages across different software engineering areas (Section 1.4):

Parser or text-to-model transformation   The term "parser" has already been introduced in the context of compilation and interpretation. The term "text-to-model transformation" is specifically used in the MDE community when one wants to emphasize that the result of parsing is not a parse *tree*, but rather a model in the sense of metamodeling, thus potentially involving, for example, references after completing name binding.

Unparser, formatter, pretty printer, or model-to-text transformation   An artifact is formatted as text, possibly also subject to formatting conventions for the use of spaces and line breaks. Formatting may start from source code (i.e., text), concrete syntax trees (i.e., parse trees), or abstract syntax trees. Formatting is typically provided as a service in an IDE.

Preprocessor   As part of parsing, code may be subject to macro expansion and conditional compilation. Such preprocessing may serve the purpose of, for example, configuration management in the sense of software variability and desugaring in the sense of language extension by macros. Interestingly, preprocessing gives rise to a language of its own for the preprocessing syntax such that the preprocessor can be seen as an interpreter of that language; the result type of this sort of interpretation is, of course, text [99]. One may also assume that a base language is extended by preprocessing constructs so that preprocessing can be modeled as a translation from the extended to the base language. In fact, some macro system work in that manner. In practice, preprocessing is often used in an undisciplined (i.e., not completely syntax-aware) manner [29, 18, 184].

Software transformation or model-to-model transformation   A software transformation is a mapping between software languages. The term "model-to-model transformation" is used in the model transformation and MDE community. We may classify transformations in terms of whether the source and target languages are the same and whether the source and target reside at the same level of abstraction [195]. Thus:

> **Exogenous transformation**   The source and target languages are different, as in the case of code generation (translation) or language migration.
> **Endogenous transformation**   The source and target languages are the same, as in the case of program refactoring or compiler optimization [116, 196]. We can further distinguish in-place and out-place transformations [195, 35] in terms of whether the source model is "reused" to produce the target model. (Exogenous transformations are necessarily out-place transformations.)

Horizontal transformation   The source and target languages reside at the same level of abstraction, as in the case of refactoring or language migration.

Vertical transformation   The source and target languages reside at different levels of abstraction. In fact, both directions, i.e., lowering and raising the level of abstraction, make sense. An example of lowering is code generation or formal refinement (such as refining a specification into an implementation). An example of raising is architectural recovery [158].

Software analysis or software analyzer   A software analysis verifies or computes some property of a given language element. Here are a few well-known objectives of software analysis:

Termination analysis   The termination of a program is verified or potential or actual termination problems are detected; see, e.g., [235].

Performance analysis   The performance of a program (or a model or a system) is predicted or performance problems are detected (see, e.g., [138]).

Alias analysis   It is determined whether or not a given storage cell can be addressed in multiple ways (see, e.g., [243]).

Bug analysis   Bad smells and potential or actual bugs in a program (or a model or a system) are detected (see, e.g., [19]).

Usage analysis   Data about the usage of a language is collected, for example, the frequency or presence of constructs or idioms in a corpus (see, e.g., [172, 167, 120]).

As mentioned before, compilers and interpreters perform a semantic analysis that verifies conformance to rules for typing, naming, scoping, etc. Compilers also perform data-flow analysis and control-flow analysis to facilitate optimizations. Overall, software transformations often rely on software analyses to accomplish their work. One may argue that software analysis is a form of software transformation; we avoid this discussion here.

There are many analyses in software engineering that leverage methods from different areas of computer science, for example, search-based algorithms, text analysis, natural language processing, model checking, and SAT solving. In this book, we focus on the software language- and software engineering-specific aspects of software analysis. We will discuss simple instances of software analysis in Chapter 5.

Software translator   The notion of translation generalizes the more basic notion of compilation. A translator implements a mapping between different software languages. A migration tool, for example, to accommodate breaking changes due to language evolution, is an example of a translator that is not also a compiler. Typically, we assume that translation is semantics-preserving. A translation is an exogenous transformation. We will develop a simple compiler (translator) in Chapter 5.

Software generator   Generation, as in the case of program generation or generative programming [74], is very similar to translation. The key focus is here on how the generator lowers the level of abstraction and optimizes a program by eliminating inefficiency due to the use of abstraction mechanisms or domain-specific concepts, subject to specialized analyses and optimizations. Software generation is used, for example, to derive language-processing components (e.g., parsers, rewrite engines, pretty printers, and visitor frameworks) from grammars or rule-based specifications. The implementation of software generators may rely on dedicated language concepts, for example, multi-staged programming [248, 217] (Chapter 12) and templates [236, 76, 256, 211].

Test-data generator   Given a grammar or a metamodel, valid language elements are generated in a systematic manner. Such generation may also be controlled by additional parameters and specifications and may be tailored towards a particular use case, for example, for testing a compiler frontend, a virtual machine implementation, or a serialization framework [174].

Program specializer   As a special case of program optimization, program specializers or partial evaluators aim at simplifying a given program (or software system) on the basis of statically available partial input [139, 129, 68]. We will discuss partial evaluation in Chapter 12.

Additional details regarding the classification of transformations (software transformations, software analyses, model transformations, source-to-source transformations) can be found elsewhere [59, 195, 75, 249, 121, 8].

Exercise 1.4 (Classification of conference papers)   [Intermediate level]
Study the most recent edition of the International Conference on Model Transformation (ICMT) and extract the forms of transformations that are discussed in the papers. Classify these forms according to the classifiers given above. (You may want to follow some of the guidelines for a systematic mapping study [206, 207].)

With reference to "language usage" (as in Fig. 1.3), we should mention another category of language implementation: IDEs integrate a basic language implementation (e.g., a compiler) with other language services for editing, code completion, refactoring, formatting, exploration, etc. Thus, an IDE is an integrated system of components supporting language users.

1.3.2.4 Metaprogramming Systems

Language implementations, including all kinds of language processors, are implemented by means of metaprogramming. A metaprogram is a program that consumes or produces (object) programs. To this end, "normal" programming environments may be used. However, there also exist dedicated *metaprogramming systems* that incorporate expressiveness or tool support for transformation, analysis, and possibly concrete object syntax, for example, Rascal [151, 150], TXL [69, 70], Stratego XT [262, 47], Converge [255], and Helvetia [215, 214].

In the neighborhood of metaprogramming systems, there are also *language definition* or *executable semantic frameworks* (e.g., the K semantic framework [221]

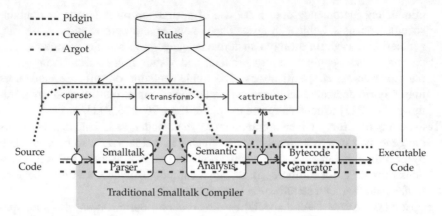

Fig. 1.5 The code compilation pipeline of Helvetia, showing multiple interception paths; there are hooks to intercept parsing <parse>, AST transformation <transform>, and semantic analysis <attribute>. Source: [215]. Additional capabilities of Helvetia support editing (coloring), debugging, etc. © 2010 Springer.

and PLT Redex [107]), *compiler frameworks* (e.g., LLVM [180]), and *modeling frameworks* (e.g., AM3 [24]).

Metaprogramming and software language engineering efforts may be "advertised" through *software language repositories* (SLRs) [165], i.e., repositories with components for language processing (interpreters, translators, analyzers, transformers, pretty printers, etc.). Further examples of SLRs include the repositories for Krishnamurthi's textbook on programming languages [160], Batory's Prolog-based work on teaching MDE [28], Zaytsev et al.'s software language processing suite (SLPS) [278], and Basciani et al.'s extensible web-based modeling platform MDE-Forge [26].

1.3.2.5 Language Workbenches

Metaprogrammers may also be supported in an interactive and integrated fashion. Accordingly, the notion of *language workbenches* [96, 97, 144, 143, 267, 266, 269, 263] encompasses enhanced metaprogramming systems that are, in fact, IDEs for language implementation. A language workbench assumes specialized language definitions that cater for IDE services such as syntax-directed, structural, or projectional editing, coloring, synthesis of warnings and errors, package exploration, quick fixes, and refactorings.

Figure 1.5 illustrates the compilation pipeline of the metaprogramming system Helvetia [214, 215]. In fact, Helvetia is an extensible development environment for embedding DSLs into a host language (Smalltalk) and its tools such as the editor and debugger. Thus, Helvetia is a language workbench.

1.3.3 Language Evolution

Let us briefly discuss more concrete scenarios of language evolution; see also [48] for more background:

Language extension   A language construct or concept is added to the language design. The language definition (syntax, semantics, pragmatics) and implementation, as well as the documentation are to be extended accordingly.

Language restriction   Some language construct or concept has been found to be problematic in terms of, for example, its semantics or implementation. The language definition (syntax, semantics, pragmatics) and implementation, as well as the documentation need to be restricted accordingly. A migration path may need to be offered to users.

Language revision   A language extension can be formally seen as moving to a superset, when looking at languages in a set-theoretic manner. A language restriction is then seen as moving to a subset. We speak of language revision when neither of these clear-cut cases applies. A migration path may need to be offered to users.

Language integration   The scenarios named above are concerned with a single language on the time line. We use the term "language integration" here for situations when more than one language needs to be somehow combined. For instance, one language may need be embedded into another language (e.g., SQL is embedded into Java) or multiple variants of a given language need to be unified or handled in an interoperable manner.

In the context of language revision and integration, we face challenges in terms of coupling between language definitions and existing artifacts. For instance, the evolution of a concrete syntax needs to be complemented by the evolution of the corresponding abstract syntax and vice versa; also, the existing language elements may need to be co-evolved [260, 176].

Exercise 1.5 (Extension of the Java language)   [Intermediate level]
Research the available documents on the evolution of the Java language and identify a language extension added in a specific language version. Demonstrate the extension with a sample and argue what syntactic categories of the Java language are affected.

Exercise 1.6 (Restriction of the Haskell language)   [Intermediate level]
Research the available documents on the evolution of the Haskell language and identify a language restriction in a specific language version. Demonstrate the restriction with a sample and summarize the reasoning behind the restriction. Why was the restriction considered reasonable? What is the migration path, if any?

1.4 Software Languages in Software Engineering

Various software engineering areas, and, in fact, more broadly, many areas in computer science, involve software languages in an essential manner, i.e., these areas necessitate parsing, analysis, transformation, generation, and other forms of processing software language-based artifacts. Several software engineering areas are discussed in the sequel. For each area, we identify a few typical application domains for software languages. This will give us a good sense of the omnipresence of software languages in software engineering, software development, and IT.

1.4.1 Software Re-Engineering

We quote: "re-engineering ... is the examination and alteration of a subject system to reconstitute in a new form" [59]. These are some application domains for software languages in the re-engineering area:

Refactoring   The improvement (in fact, the possibly automated transformation) of the design of code or models without changing its "behavior" [116, 196]. In particular, the "functional" behavior has to to preserved; some nonfunctional aspects such as execution time may be modified. Refactorings are often meant to be performed interactively, for example, by means of an IDE integration. Refactorings may also be recorded and "replayed" to propagate changes, for example, from a refactored library to client code [130, 227]. Ultimately, refactorings may be as complex as system restructuring to serve a different architecture [6].
Migration   A migration can be viewed as a more or less automated transformation of a program or a software system to conform to a different API, language, or architectural requirement. For instance, a language migration is concerned with rewriting a system written in one high-level language to use another high-level language instead [250, 44, 241]. Language migrations may be challenging because of an array of aspects, for example, different platforms for source and target, or different type systems or primitive types.
Wrapping   A wrapper is a form of adaptor that provides a different interface for existing functionality. The interfaces involved may be essentially object-oriented APIs [227, 25]. We may also wrap a legacy system in terms of its user interface or procedural abstractions as a service [242, 63, 240, 55]. In many cases, wrappers may be semiautomatically generated or vital information may be gathered by an automated analysis.

Figure 1.6 illustrates a very simple refactoring scenario in an OO programming context: the boxed statements at the top are to be extracted into a new method, as shown in completed form at the bottom of the figure. In terms of the structural rules for transforming source code, refactorings may be relatively simple, but they often involve nontrivial preconditions and constraints to be met for correctness' sake [253,

```
void printOwing(double amount) {
    printBanner();
    System.out.println("name: " + name);
    System.out.println("amount: " + amount);
}
```

```
void printOwing(double amount) {
    printBanner();
    printDetails(amount);
}
void printDetails(double amount) {
    System.out.println ("name: " + name);
    System.out.println ("amount: " + amount);
}
```

Fig. 1.6 Illustration of the "extract method" refactoring.

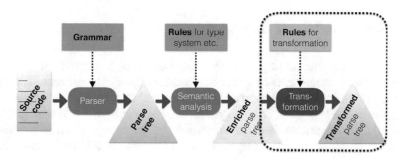

Fig. 1.7 Overall data flow for a re-engineering transformation. We have marked the phase which replaces code generation in the standard data flow for compilation.

228]. Even in the simple example at hand, some constraints have to be met; for example, the extracted statements must not return.

Figure 1.7 shows the overall data flow for a re-engineering transformation as needed, for example, for refactoring or restructuring. This data flow should be compared with the data flow for compilation; see Fig. 1.4. The two data flows share the phases of parsing and semantic analysis. The actual transformation is described (ideally) by declarative rules of a transformation language. Not every re-engineering use case requires a full-blown semantic analysis, which is why we have grayed out slightly the corresponding phase in Fig. 1.7. In fact, not even a proper syntax-aware transformation is needed in all cases, but instead a lexical approach may be applicable [152].

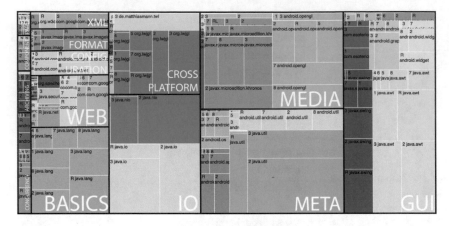

Fig. 1.8 An API-usage map for an open-source Java project. The complete rectangle (in terms of its size) models the references to all APIs made by all developers. The nested rectangles partition references by domain (e.g., GUI rather than Swing or AWT). The rectangles nested further partition references by API; one color is used per API. Within each such rectangle, the contributions of distinct developers (1, ..., 8 for the top-eight committers and "R" for the rest) are shown. Source: [4].

1.4.2 Software Reverse Engineering

We quote: "reverse engineering is the process of analyzing a subject system to identify the system's components and their interrelationships and create representations of the system in another form or at a higher level of abstraction" [59]. For instance, we may extract a call graph from a system, thereby identifying call sites (such as packages, files, classes, methods, or functions) and actual calls (such as method or function calls). Reverse engineering may also be concerned with *architecture recovery* [126, 128, 158, 33], for example, the identification of components in a legacy system. Overall, reverse engineering is usually meant to help with program comprehension and to prepare for software re-engineering or to otherwise facilitate software development.

Figure 1.8 shows the visual result of a concrete reverse engineering effort aimed at understanding API usage in Java projects [4]. The tree map groups API references (i.e., source code-level references to API methods) so that we can assess the contributions of different APIs and of individual developers for each API to the project.

Figure 1.9 shows the overall data flow for a reverse engineering component that is based on the paradigm of fact extraction [109, 201, 185, 27]. Just as in the cases of compilation or transformation for re-engineering, we begin with parsing and (possibly customized) semantic analysis. The data flow differs in terms of last phase for fact extraction. The extracted facts can be thought of as sets of tuples, for example, pairs of caller/callee sites to be visualized eventually as a call graph.

Reverse engineering often starts from some sort of fact extraction. Reverse engineering may also involve data analysis based, for example, on relational alge-

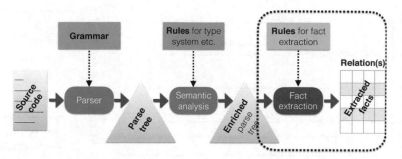

Fig. 1.9 Overall data flow for fact extraction in reverse engineering. We have marked the phase which replaces code generation in the standard data flow for compilation. The resulting tables represent "projections" of the source code, for example, call relationships between functions.

bra [134, 38, 37, 135]. Reverse engineering is by no means limited to source code artifacts, but may also involve, for example, documentation, models, and commits. The results are often communicated to software engineers or other stakeholders by means of software visualization [148, 187, 177, 1, 178]. In the earlier example concerned with API-usage analysis, fact extraction from Java source code was used to extract API references, commits were analyzed to associate API references with developers, and visualization as a tree map was used to communicate the result.

1.4.3 Software Analysis

There exist diverse forms of software analysis that support software reverse engineering, software maintenance, software evolution, and program comprehension. Here are some forms:

Program slicing   This is the computation of a simplified program, for example, the statements which affects the state or the result at some point of interest [271, 136, 252, 43, 10].

Feature location   This is the semiautomated process of locating features or specific program functionality in software systems or product lines, based on different forms of source-code analysis, helping ultimately with code refactoring, software maintenance, clone detection, and product-line engineering [224, 86, 270, 111, 34, 191, 12, 166].

Clone detection   This is the largely automated process of determined duplicated source code, using various means of attesting the presence of equal or similar code at a textual, lexical, syntactic, or semantic level [22, 30, 222, 223].

Traceability recovery   This is the largely automated process of recovering trace links between different kinds of artifacts, for example, documentation and source code, to attest that the linked artifacts or fragments thereof are related [64, 145, 118, 188, 233].

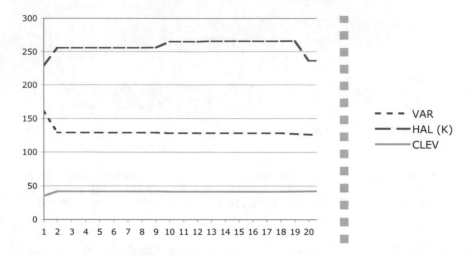

Fig. 1.10 Three different grammar metrics over time for the versions of an industrial-strength parser for a specification language. Source: [7]. © 2008 Springer.

Design-pattern detection   This is the automated process of detecting instances of design patterns in actual code, subject to checking structural and behavioral constraints [218, 114, 112, 154, 153, 276]. This area also relates to the detection and analysis of micro-patterns, for example, in bytecode [120], decompilation [110], and disassembly, for example, for the purpose of detecting security issues [9].

Change-impact analysis   This is the semiautomated process of "identifying the potential consequences of a change, or estimating what needs to be modified to accomplish a change" [15]; see also [246, 183, 119, 87, 212, 213].

Code smell   This is an automatically checkable symptom in source code that possibly indicates a deeper problem such as abnormal complexity or insufficient modularity [92, 257, 275, 205, 113, 115]. The corresponding checking or detection activity is accordingly referred to as code smell detection.

Software metric   This is a computable standard measure of the degree to which given source code or a complete software system possesses some property, for example, complexity in terms of lines-of-code (LOC) or McCabe (i.e., Cyclomatic complexity) [108, 179, 209, 79, 50, 198, 259, 57].

Coding convention   This is a mechanized (executable and checkable) convention for authoring code in a language, possibly also specific to a project; such conventions are checked by corresponding tools that are typically integrated into an IDE so that developers receive continuous feedback on the code's compliance with the conventions [123].

Software analysis is often combined with software visualization; for example, the values of computed software metrics are typically visualized [177, 23] to better access the distribution of metrics over a system or changes in the metrics over time.

Figure 1.10 gives an example of how metrics and simple visualization can be combined to analyze a software process – in this case, a process for the improvement of a grammar [7]. The changes of the values of the metrics can be explained as consequences of the specific grammar revisions applied at the corresponding commit points.

1.4.4 Technological Spaces

We quote: "A technological space is a working context with a set of associated concepts, body of knowledge, tools, required skills, and possibilities. It is often associated to a given user community with shared know-how, educational support, common literature and even workshop and conference regular meetings" [161].

For instance, there are the following technological spaces, which we characterize in a keyword style by pointing out associated languages, technologies, and concepts:

Grammarware string, grammar, parsing, CST, AST, term, rewriting, . . .
XMLware XML, XML infoset, DOM, DTD, XML Schema, XPath, XQuery, XSLT, . . .
JSONware JSON, JSON Schema, . . .
Modelware UML, MOF, EMF, class diagram, modeling, metamodeling, model transformation, MDE, . . .
SQLware table, SQL, relational model, relational algebra, . . .
RDFware resource, triple, Linked Data, WWW, RDF, RDFS, OWL, SPARQL, . . .
Objectware objects, object graphs, object models, state, behavior, . . .
Javaware Java, Java bytecode, JVM, Eclipse, JUnit, . . .

We refer to [40] for a rather detailed discussion of one technological space – modelware (MDE). We refer to [89] for a discussion of multiple technological spaces with focus on Modelware and RDFware centric and cursory coverage of grammarware, Javaware, and XMLware and the interconnections between these spaces.

Technological spaces are deeply concerned with software languages:

Data models The data in a space conforms to some data model, which can be viewed as a "semantic domain" in the sense of semantics in the context of language definition. For instance, the data model of XML is defined by a certain set of trees, according to the XML infoset [274]; the data model JSON is a dictionary format that is a simple subset of Javascript objects; and the data model of SQLware is the relational model [67].
Schema languages Domain- or application-specific data can be defined by appropriate schema-like languages. Schemas are to tree- or graph-based data what (context-free) grammars are to string languages [149]. For instance, the schema language of JSON is JSON Schema [208]; the schema language of grammarware is EBNF [137] in many notational variations [277]; and the schema languages of

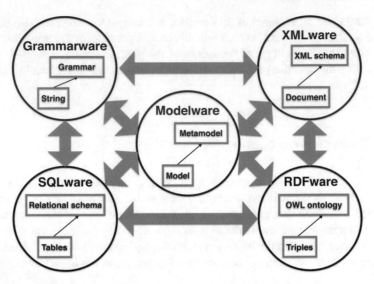

Fig. 1.11 A few technological spaces with their instance (data) level and the schema level. The thin arrows model "conformance" such as an XML document conforming to an XML schema. The thick arrows hint at expected "bridges" between the spaces as needed for technological space travel. Inspired by [161].

RDF are RDFS and OWL. Schemas and their instances give rise to a conformance relationships; see Fig. 1.11 for a few examples.

Query languages   A technological space tends to offer one or more languages for querying data in that space. For instance, the query languages of XMLware are XPath and XQuery; the query language of RDFware is SPARQL; and the query language of SQLware is SQL (specifically, the SELECT part of it).

Transformation languages   A technological space tends to offer one or more languages for transforming data in that space. For instance, the transformation language of XMLware is XSLT; the transformation language of RDFware is SPARQL with updates; and the transformation language of SQLware is SQL (specifically, the DELETE, UPDATE, and CREATE parts of it).

Programming language integration   Technological spaces may be integrated into programming languages by either appropriate APIs for the underlying query and transformation languages, or some form of mapping (see below), or proper language integration. The JDBC approach in the Java platform is a basic example of the API option for integrating SQLware (SQL) into Java.

Mapping   There is a recurrent need to map across technological spaces such as objectware, XMLware, and SQLware [169], leading to what we refer to as technological space travel; this is also referred to as operational bridges in [161]; see Fig. 1.11 for a few examples. For instance, object/relational mapping allows one to make objects persistent in a database and to access a database in an object-

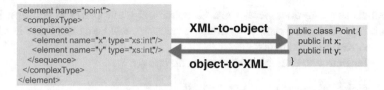

Fig. 1.12 Mapping object models to XML schemas and vice versa

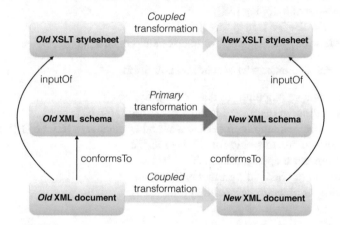

Fig. 1.13 Mapping in an XML context at the instance (XML), the type (XSD), and the stylesheet (XSLT) level.

oriented program. Mapping, as such, is a translation problem – thus the link to software languages.

Coupling Mapping, as just explained, may need to be accomplished at multiple levels: the data level, the schema level, and the processing level (i.e., queries and transformations). Depending on the space, each level may be challenging in itself. For instance, mapping schema languages is complicated in the presence of space-specific constraint forms. However, mapping is specifically challenging because all the levels need to be mapped in a coupled ("synchronized") manner [162, 149, 73, 164].

Figure 1.12 illustrates the XMLware instance of mapping at the schema level; we assume that the XML type on the left may be mapped to the Java/C# class on the right and vice versa. Of course, such a mapping is not straightforward, because of the many differences in the underlying data models and schema languages, giving rise to an impedance mismatch [170].

Figure 1.13 illustrates three levels of mapping for the XMLware space. Consider the following scenario. There is an XML document meant to conform to an XML schema; there is also a document processor (an XSLT stylesheet) that is used to process the XML document. Now assume that the schema is changed to refactor the format. Existing documents must be converted ("mapped") to conform to the new schema. Also, the existing document processor must be converted to be able to process converted documents.

We refer below to examples of work on mappings:

- XML/object mapping [170, 163, 251, 5];
- XML/grammar mapping [202];
- object/relational mapping [52, 51, 53, 200, 36, 254, 238];
- XML/relational mapping [58];
- relational/RDF+OWL mapping [234];
- XML/relational with support for queries and constraints [32, 264].

We also refer to examples of work on coupling:

- schema/instance mapping for databases [124, 261];
- metamodel/model mapping for modelware [268, 60, 62];
- program/schema mapping for databases and applications [65, 66, 125];
- document/schema mapping for XML [168, 72];
- string/grammar mapping [260, 176];
- co-evolution of GMF editor models [225];
- refactoring of object/relational mapping [230].

1.4.5 Model-Driven Engineering

MDE [39, 40, 231] (see also some related model-based approaches [247, 181]) combines the broad notions of modeling, metamodeling [203], modeling languages, and model transformation. This area constitutes an important space for language definition, implementation, usage, processing, and evolution. We identify the key notions of the MDE (modelware) space as follows:

Modeling languages   Models (artifacts, programs, etc.) are elements of suitable modeling languages, of which there are many. For instance, the mainstream UML approach offers a family of modeling notations for behavioral and structural modeling.

Domain-specific modeling languages (DSMLs)   On the basis of metamodeling and other modeling concepts, DSMLs are modeled and enable the application of modeling to specific domains. The semantics of these DSMLs are also developed in the modelware space, for example, by means of model transformation [16].

Model transformation   Foremost, there are model-to-model transformations. Additionally, there are special kinds of transformations to import and export text-based artifacts, i.e., text-to-model and model-to-text transformations. There are dedicated model-transformation languages [194, 75, 140, 8, 142].

Model evolution   Models are subject to evolution. Specifically, metamodels and model transformations are also subject to evolution [204]. There are a number of concepts (see below) which help in understanding or automating evolution, for example, model comparison and model co-evolution.

Model management With the increase in the numbers of models, metamodels, model transformations, versions of models, and relationships, some sort of management needs to be applied to systematically maintain repositories of models. Such model management gives rise to yet another form of model – megamodels [41, 42, 103, 84, 175, 165, 127].

Model comparison In the context of model evolution, models also need to be compared [244, 122, 146] to extract differences also on the basis of suitable diff models [61, 60].

Model merging We quote: "merging is the action of combining two models, such that their common elements are included only once and the other ones are preserved" [189]; see also [156, 93, 45, 189, 220, 77]. Model merging can be viewed as a form of model synchronization; see below.

Model weaving We quote: "weaving involves two actors: an aspect and a base model. The aspect is made of two parts, a pointcut, which is the pattern to match in the base model, and an advice, which represents the modification made to the base model during the weaving" [189]; see also [226, 193, 159]. Model weaving helps with, for example, crosscutting concerns to be addressed by models.

Model synchronization Software systems may involve multiple models to be related by some consistency relation. Model synchronization is the process of establishing consistency in response to changes in individual models, for example, by means of propagating changes in the form of a difference (a "delta") from one model to another; see [11, 82, 85, 83].

Models@run.time This notion applies when any sort of model is used during the operation of a system. We quote: "the key property of models@run.time systems is their use and provision of manageable reflection, which is characterized to be tractable and predictable and by this overcomes the limitation of reflective systems working on code" ([17] which was part of the seminar [31]). In different terms, the program and model become essentially united or integrated [71, 80]. Arguably, reflective language infrastructures (e.g., Smalltalk-based ones) may also provide manageable reflection and other aspects of models@run.time [91, 54, 245].

Model co-evolution When multiple modeling languages are used simultaneously, the models may involve common entities and, thus, coupled with respect to evolution; see, for example, the coupled evolution of the models of GMF-based editors [225]. Language evolution, as mentioned earlier, is a special case of model co-evolution. That is, language evolution is model/metamodel co-evolution. Language evolution is a particularly important problem in the context of domain-specific (modeling) languages because these languages may evolve rapidly and significantly without being limited by backward compatibility [268, 131, 132, 216].

Summary and Outline

We have argued that software languages permeate software engineering, software development, and IT. We have classified software languages in different ways. We have presented a lifecycle for software languages; the lifecycle covers, for example, language implementation in a compiler or language processor for re- and reverse engineering. Software languages deserve to be treated in an engineering manner, thereby giving rise to the discipline of software language engineering (SLE). All of the example languages and most of the SLE scenarios introduced in this chapter will play a role in the rest of the book.

References

1. Abdeen, H., Ducasse, S., Pollet, D., Alloui, I., Falleri, J.: The Package Blueprint: Visually analyzing and quantifying packages dependencies. Sci. Comput. Program. **89**, 298–319 (2014)
2. Aho, A., Monica S., Sethi, R., Ullman, J.: Compilers: Principles, Techniques, and Tools. Addison Wesley (2006). 2nd edition
3. Akinin, A., Zubkov, A., Shilov, N.: New developments of the computer language classification knowledge portal. In: Proc. Spring/Summer Young Researchers' Colloquium on Software Engineering (2012)
4. Aksu, H., Lämmel, R., Kwasnik, W.: Visualization of API experience. Softwaretechnik-Trends **36**(2) (2016)
5. Alagic, S., Bernstein, P.A., Jairath, R.: Object-oriented constraints for XML schema. In: Proc. ICOODB, *LNCS*, vol. 6348, pp. 100–117. Springer (2010)
6. Almonaies, A.A., Alalfi, M.H., Cordy, J.R., Dean, T.R.: A framework for migrating web applications to web services. In: Proc. ICWE, *LNCS*, vol. 7977, pp. 384–399. Springer (2013)
7. Alves, T.L., Visser, J.: A case study in grammar engineering. In: Proc. SLE 2008, *LNCS*, vol. 5452, pp. 285–304. Springer (2009)
8. Amrani, M., Combemale, B., Lucio, L., Selim, G.M.K., Dingel, J., Traon, Y.L., Vangheluwe, H., Cordy, J.R.: Formal verification techniques for model transformations: A tridimensional classification. J. Object Technol. **14**(3), 1–43 (2015)
9. Andriesse, D.: Analyzing and Securing Binaries Through Static Disassembly. Ph.D. thesis, Vrije Universiteit Amsterdam (2017)
10. Androutsopoulos, K., Clark, D., Harman, M., Krinke, J., Tratt, L.: State-based model slicing: A survey. ACM Comput. Surv. **45**(4), 53 (2013)
11. Antkiewicz, M., Czarnecki, K.: Design space of heterogeneous synchronization. In: GTTSE 2007, Revised Papers, *LNCS*, vol. 5235, pp. 3–46. Springer (2008)
12. Antkiewicz, M., Ji, W., Berger, T., Czarnecki, K., Schmorleiz, T., Lämmel, R., Stanciulescu, S., Wasowski, A., Schaefer, I.: Flexible product line engineering with a virtual platform. In: Proc. ICSE, pp. 532–535. ACM (2014)
13. Anureev, I.S., Bodin, E., Gorodnyaya, L., Marchuk, A.G., Murzin, A.G., Shilov, N.V.: On the problem of computer language classification. Joint NCC&IIS Bulletin, Series Computer Science **27**, 1–20 (2008)
14. Appel, A., Palsberg, J.: Modern Compiler Implementation in Java. Cambridge University Press (2002). 2nd edition
15. Arnold, R., Bohner, S.: Software Change Impact Analysis. Wiley-IEEE Computer Society (1996)

16. Aßmann, U., Bartho, A., Bürger, C., Cech, S., Demuth, B., Heidenreich, F., Johannes, J., Karol, S., Polowinski, J., Reimann, J., Schroeter, J., Seifert, M., Thiele, M., Wende, C., Wilke, C.: DropsBox: the Dresden Open Software Toolbox – Domain-specific modelling tools beyond metamodels and transformations. SoSyM **13**(1), 133–169 (2014)
17. Aßmann, U., Götz, S., Jézéquel, J., Morin, B., Trapp, M.: A reference architecture and roadmap for models@run.time systems. In: Bencomo et al. [31], pp. 1–18
18. Aversano, L., Penta, M.D., Baxter, I.D.: Handling preprocessor-conditioned declarations. In: Proc. SCAM, pp. 83–92. IEEE (2002)
19. Ayewah, N., Hovemeyer, D., Morgenthaler, J.D., Penix, J., Pugh, W.: Using static analysis to find bugs. IEEE Software **25**(5), 22–29 (2008)
20. Babenko, L.P., Rogach, V.D., Yushchenko, E.L.: Comparison and classification of programming languages. Cybern. Syst. Anal. **11**, 271–278 (1975)
21. Backus, J.W., Bauer, F.L., Green, J., Katz, C., McCarthy, J., Perlis, A.J., Rutishauser, H., Samelson, K., Vauquois, B., Wegstein, J.H., van Wijngaarden, A., Woodger, M.: Revised report on the Algorithm Language ALGOL 60. Commun. ACM **6**(1), 1–17 (1963)
22. Baker, B.S.: On finding duplication and near-duplication in large software systems. In: Proc. WCRE, pp. 86–95. IEEE (1995)
23. Balogh, G.: Validation of the city metaphor in software visualization. In: Proc. ICCSA, *LNCS*, vol. 9159, pp. 73–85. Springer (2015)
24. Barbero, M., Jouault, F., Bézivin, J.: Model driven management of complex systems: Implementing the macroscope's vision. In: Proc. ECBS 2008, pp. 277–286. IEEE (2008)
25. Bartolomei, T.T., Czarnecki, K., Lämmel, R.: Swing to SWT and back: Patterns for API migration by wrapping. In: Proc. ICSM, pp. 1–10. IEEE (2010)
26. Basciani, F., Rocco, J.D., Ruscio, D.D., Salle, A.D., Iovino, L., Pierantonio, A.: MDEForge: An extensible web-based modeling platform. In: Proc. CloudMDE@MoDELS, *CEUR Workshop Proceedings*, vol. 1242, pp. 66–75. CEUR-WS.org (2014)
27. Basten, H.J.S., Klint, P.: DeFacto: Language-parametric fact extraction from source code. In: Proc. SLE 2008, *LNCS*, vol. 5452, pp. 265–284. Springer (2009)
28. Batory, D.S., Latimer, E., Azanza, M.: Teaching model driven engineering from a relational database perspective. In: Proc. MODELS, *LNCS*, vol. 8107, pp. 121–137. Springer (2013)
29. Baxter, I.D., Mehlich, M.: Preprocessor conditional removal by simple partial evaluation. In: Proc. WCRE, pp. 281–290. IEEE (2001)
30. Baxter, I.D., Yahin, A., de Moura, L.M., Sant'Anna, M., Bier, L.: Clone detection using abstract syntax trees. In: Proc. ICSM, pp. 368–377. IEEE (1998)
31. Bencomo, N., France, R.B., Cheng, B.H.C., Aßmann, U. (eds.): Models@run.time – Foundations, Applications, and Roadmaps, Dagstuhl Seminar 11481, November 27 – December 2, 2011, *LNCS*, vol. 8378. Springer (2014)
32. Berdaguer, P., Cunha, A., Pacheco, H., Visser, J.: Coupled schema transformation and data conversion for XML and SQL. In: Proc. PADL, *LNCS*, vol. 4354, pp. 290–304. Springer (2007)
33. Berger, B.J., Sohr, K., Koschke, R.: Extracting and analyzing the implemented security architecture of business applications. In: Proc. CSMR, pp. 285–294. IEEE (2013)
34. Berger, T., Lettner, D., Rubin, J., Grünbacher, P., Silva, A., Becker, M., Chechik, M., Czarnecki, K.: What is a feature?: A qualitative study of features in industrial software product lines. In: Proc. SPLC, pp. 16–25. ACM (2015)
35. Bergmayr, A., Troya, J., Wimmer, M.: From out-place transformation evolution to in-place model patching. In: Proc. ASE, pp. 647–652. ACM (2014)
36. Bernstein, P.A., Jacob, M., Pérez, J., Rull, G., Terwilliger, J.F.: Incremental mapping compilation in an object-to-relational mapping system. In: Proc. SIGMOD, pp. 1269–1280. ACM (2013)
37. Beyer, D.: Relational programming with CrocoPat. In: Proc. ICSE, pp. 807–810. ACM (2006)
38. Beyer, D., Noack, A., Lewerentz, C.: Efficient relational calculation for software analysis. IEEE Trans. Softw. Eng. **31**(2), 137–149 (2005)

39. Bézivin, J.: On the unification power of models. SoSyM **4**(2), 171–188 (2005)
40. Bézivin, J.: Model driven engineering: An emerging technical space. In: GTTSE 2005, Revised Papers, *LNCS*, vol. 4143, pp. 36–64. Springer (2006)
41. Bézivin, J., Jouault, F., Rosenthal, P., Valduriez, P.: Modeling in the large and modeling in the small. In: European MDA Workshops MDAFA 2003 and MDAFA 2004, Revised Selected Papers, *LNCS*, vol. 3599, pp. 33–46. Springer (2005)
42. Bézivin, J., Jouault, F., Valduriez, P.: On the need for megamodels. In: Proc. OOPSLA/G-PCE: Best Practices for Model-Driven Software Development Workshop (2004)
43. Binkley, D., Harman, M., Krinke, J. (eds.): Beyond Program Slicing, *Dagstuhl Seminar Proceedings*, vol. 05451. Internationales Begegnungs- und Forschungszentrum fuer Informatik (IBFI), Schloss Dagstuhl, Germany (2006)
44. Blasband, D.: Compilation of legacy languages in the 21st century. In: GTTSE 2011, Revised Papers, *LNCS*, vol. 7680, pp. 1–54. Springer (2013)
45. Boronat, A., Carsí, J.A., Ramos, I., Letelier, P.: Formal model merging applied to class diagram integration. ENTCS **166**, 5–26 (2007)
46. Bottoni, P., Grau, A.: A suite of metamodels as a basis for a classification of visual languages. In: Proc. VL/HCC, pp. 83–90. IEEE (2004)
47. Bravenboer, M., Kalleberg, K.T., Vermaas, R., Visser, E.: Stratego/XT 0.17. A language and toolset for program transformation. Sci. Comput. Program. **72**(1-2), 52–70 (2008)
48. Bryant, B.R., Jézéquel, J., Lämmel, R., Mernik, M., Schindler, M., Steinmann, F., Tolvanen, J., Vallecillo, A., Völter, M.: Globalized domain specific language engineering. In: Globalizing Domain-Specific Languages – International Dagstuhl Seminar, Dagstuhl Castle, Germany, October 5–10, 2014 Revised Papers, *LNCS*, vol. 9400, pp. 43–69. Springer (2015)
49. Burnett, M.M., Baker, M.J.: A classification system for visual programming languages. J. Vis. Lang. Comput. **5**(3), 287–300 (1994)
50. Byelas, H., Telea, A.: The metric lens: Visualizing metrics and structure on software diagrams. In: Proc. WCRE, pp. 339–340. IEEE (2008)
51. Cabibbo, L.: A mapping system for relational schemas with constraints. In: Proc. SEBD, pp. 237–244. Edizioni Seneca (2009)
52. Cabibbo, L.: On keys, foreign keys and nullable attributes in relational mapping systems. In: Proc. EDBT, *ACM International Conference Proceeding Series*, vol. 360, pp. 263–274. ACM (2009)
53. Cabibbo, L., Carosi, A.: Managing inheritance hierarchies in object/relational mapping tools. In: Proc. CAiSE, *LNCS*, vol. 3520, pp. 135–150. Springer (2005)
54. Callaú, O., Robbes, R., Tanter, É., Röthlisberger, D.: How (and why) developers use the dynamic features of programming languages: The case of Smalltalk. Empir. Softw. Eng. **18**(6), 1156–1194 (2013)
55. Canfora, G., Fasolino, A.R., Frattolillo, G., Tramontana, P.: A wrapping approach for migrating legacy system interactive functionalities to service oriented architectures. J. Syst. Softw. **81**(4), 463–480 (2008)
56. Ceh, I., Crepinsek, M., Kosar, T., Mernik, M.: Ontology driven development of domain-specific languages. Comput. Sci. Inf. Syst. **8**(2), 317–342 (2011)
57. Chaparro, O., Bavota, G., Marcus, A., Penta, M.D.: On the impact of refactoring operations on code quality metrics. In: Proc. ICSME, pp. 456–460. IEEE (2014)
58. Chen, L.J., Bernstein, P.A., Carlin, P., Filipovic, D., Rys, M., Shamgunov, N., Terwilliger, J.F., Todic, M., Tomasevic, S., Tomic, D.: Mapping XML to a wide sparse table. IEEE Trans. Knowl. Data Eng. **26**(6), 1400–1414 (2014)
59. Chikofsky, E.J., II, J.H.C.: Reverse engineering and design recovery: A taxonomy. IEEE Softw. **7**(1), 13–17 (1990)
60. Cicchetti, A., Ruscio, D.D., Eramo, R., Pierantonio, A.: Automating co-evolution in model-driven engineering. In: Proc. ECOC, pp. 222–231. IEEE (2008)
61. Cicchetti, A., Ruscio, D.D., Pierantonio, A.: A metamodel independent approach to difference representation. J. Object Technol. **6**(9), 165–185 (2007)
62. Cicchetti, A., Ruscio, D.D., Pierantonio, A.: Managing dependent changes in coupled evolution. In: Proc. ICMT, *LNCS*, vol. 5563, pp. 35–51. Springer (2009)

63. Cimitile, A., de Carlini, U., Lucia, A.D.: Incremental migration strategies: Data flow analysis for wrapping. In: Proc. WCRE, pp. 59–68. IEEE (1998)
64. Cleland-Huang, J., Gotel, O., Zisman, A. (eds.): Software and Systems Traceability. Springer (2012)
65. Cleve, A.: Automating program conversion in database reengineering: A wrapper-based approach. In: Proc. CSMR, pp. 323–326. IEEE (2006)
66. Cleve, A., Hainaut, J.: Co-transformations in database applications evolution. In: GTTSE 2005, Revised Papers, *LNCS*, vol. 4143, pp. 409–421. Springer (2006)
67. Codd, E.F.: A relational model of data for large shared data banks. Commun. ACM **13**(6), 377–387 (1970)
68. Cook, W.R., Lämmel, R.: Tutorial on online partial evaluation. In: Proc. DSL, *EPTCS*, vol. 66, pp. 168–180 (2011)
69. Cordy, J.R.: The TXL source transformation language. Sci. Comput. Program. **61**(3), 190–210 (2006)
70. Cordy, J.R.: Excerpts from the TXL cookbook. In: GTTSE 2009, Revised Papers, *LNCS*, vol. 6491, pp. 27–91. Springer (2011)
71. Cuadrado, J.S., Guerra, E., de Lara, J.: *The Program Is the Model*: Enabling transformations@run.time. In: Proc. SLE 2012, *LNCS*, vol. 7745, pp. 104–123. Springer (2013)
72. Cunha, A., Oliveira, J.N., Visser, J.: Type-safe two-level data transformation. In: Proc. FM, *LNCS*, vol. 4085, pp. 284–299. Springer (2006)
73. Cunha, A., Visser, J.: Strongly typed rewriting for coupled software transformation. ENTCS **174**(1), 17–34 (2007)
74. Czarnecki, K., Eisenecker, U.: Generative Programming: Methods, Tools, and Applications. Addison-Wesley Professional (2000)
75. Czarnecki, K., Helsen, S.: Feature-based survey of model transformation approaches. IBM Syst. J. **45**(3), 621–646 (2006)
76. Czarnecki, K., O'Donnell, J.T., Striegnitz, J., Taha, W.: DSL implementation in MetaOCaml, Template Haskell, and C++. In: Domain-Specific Program Generation, International Seminar, Dagstuhl Castle, Germany, March 23-28, 2003, Revised Papers, *LNCS*, vol. 3016, pp. 51–72. Springer (2004)
77. Dam, H.K., Egyed, A., Winikoff, M., Reder, A., Lopez-Herrejon, R.E.: Consistent merging of model versions. J. Syst. Softw. **112**, 137–155 (2016)
78. Degueule, T.: Composition and interoperability for external domain-specific language engineering. Ph.D. thesis, Université de Rennes 1 (2016)
79. Demeyer, S., Ducasse, S., Lanza, M.: A hybrid reverse engineering approach combining metrics and program visualization. In: Proc. WCRE, pp. 175–186. IEEE (1999)
80. Derakhshanmanesh, M., Ebert, J., Iguchi, T., Engels, G.: Model-integrating software components. In: Proc. MODELS, *LNCS*, vol. 8767, pp. 386–402. Springer (2014)
81. van Deursen, A., Klint, P., Visser, J.: Domain-specific languages: An annotated bibliography. SIGPLAN Not. **35**(6), 26–36 (2000)
82. Diskin, Z.: Model synchronization: Mappings, tiles, and categories. In: GTTSE 2009, Revised Papers, *LNCS*, vol. 6491, pp. 92–165. Springer (2011)
83. Diskin, Z., Gholizadeh, H., Wider, A., Czarnecki, K.: A three-dimensional taxonomy for bidirectional model synchronization. J. Syst. Softw. **111**, 298–322 (2016)
84. Diskin, Z., Kokaly, S., Maibaum, T.: Mapping-aware megamodeling: Design patterns and laws. In: Proc. SLE 2013, *LNCS*, vol. 8225, pp. 322–343. Springer (2013)
85. Diskin, Z., Wider, A., Gholizadeh, H., Czarnecki, K.: Towards a rational taxonomy for increasingly symmetric model synchronization. In: Proc. ICMT, *LNCS*, vol. 8568, pp. 57–73. Springer (2014)
86. Dit, B., Revelle, M., Gethers, M., Poshyvanyk, D.: Feature location in source code: A taxonomy and survey. J. Softw.: Evol. Process **25**(1), 53–95 (2013)
87. Dit, B., Wagner, M., Wen, S., Wang, W., Vásquez, M.L., Poshyvanyk, D., Kagdi, H.H.: ImpactMiner: A tool for change impact analysis. In: Proc. ICSE, pp. 540–543. ACM (2014)
88. Dittrich, K.R., Gatziu, S., Geppert, A.: The active database management system manifesto: A rulebase of ADBMS features. In: Proc. RIDS, *LNCS*, vol. 985, pp. 3–20. Springer (1995)

89. Djuric, D., Gasevic, D., Devedzic, V.: The tao of modeling spaces. J. Object Technol. **5**(8), 125–147 (2006)
90. Doyle, J.R., Stretch, D.D.: The classification of programming languages by usage. Int. J. Man–Machine Stud. **26**(3), 343–360 (1987)
91. Ducasse, S., Gîrba, T., Kuhn, A., Renggli, L.: Meta-environment and executable metalanguage using Smalltalk: An experience report. SoSyM **8**(1), 5–19 (2009)
92. Emden, E.V., Moonen, L.: Java quality assurance by detecting code smells. In: Proc. WCRE, p. 97. IEEE (2002)
93. Engel, K., Paige, R.F., Kolovos, D.S.: Using a model merging language for reconciling model versions. In: Proc. ECMDA-FA, *LNCS*, vol. 4066, pp. 143–157. Springer (2006)
94. Erdweg, S.: Extensible languages for flexible and principled domain abstraction. Ph.D. thesis, Philipps-Universität Marburg (2013)
95. Erdweg, S., Giarrusso, P.G., Rendel, T.: Language composition untangled. In: Proc. LDTA, p. 7. ACM (2012)
96. Erdweg, S., van der Storm, T., Völter, M., Boersma, M., Bosman, R., Cook, W.R., Gerritsen, A., Hulshout, A., Kelly, S., Loh, A., Konat, G.D.P., Molina, P.J., Palatnik, M., Pohjonen, R., Schindler, E., Schindler, K., Solmi, R., Vergu, V.A., Visser, E., van der Vlist, K., Wachsmuth, G., van der Woning, J.: The state of the art in language workbenches – conclusions from the language workbench challenge. In: Proc. SLE, *LNCS*, vol. 8225, pp. 197–217. Springer (2013)
97. Erdweg, S., van der Storm, T., Völter, M., Tratt, L., Bosman, R., Cook, W.R., Gerritsen, A., Hulshout, A., Kelly, S., Loh, A., Konat, G.D.P., Molina, P.J., Palatnik, M., Pohjonen, R., Schindler, E., Schindler, K., Solmi, R., Vergu, V.A., Visser, E., van der Vlist, K., Wachsmuth, G., van der Woning, J.: Evaluating and comparing language workbenches: Existing results and benchmarks for the future. Comput. Lang. Syst. Struct. **44**, 24–47 (2015)
98. Erwig, M., Walkingshaw, E.: Semantics first! – rethinking the language design process. In: Proc. SLE 2011, *LNCS*, vol. 6940, pp. 243–262. Springer (2012)
99. Favre, J.: Preprocessors from an abstract point of view. In: Proc. WCRE, pp. 287–296. IEEE (1996)
100. Favre, J., Gasevic, D., Lämmel, R., Pek, E.: Empirical language analysis in software linguistics. In: Proc. SLE 2010, *LNCS*, vol. 6563, pp. 316–326. Springer (2011)
101. Favre, J., Lämmel, R., Leinberger, M., Schmorleiz, T., Varanovich, A.: Linking documentation and source code in a software chrestomathy. In: Proc. WCRE, pp. 335–344. IEEE (2012)
102. Favre, J., Lämmel, R., Schmorleiz, T., Varanovich, A.: 101companies: A community project on software technologies and software languages. In: Proc. TOOLS, *LNCS*, vol. 7304, pp. 58–74. Springer (2012)
103. Favre, J., Lämmel, R., Varanovich, A.: Modeling the linguistic architecture of software products. In: Proc. MODELS, *LNCS*, vol. 7590, pp. 151–167. Springer (2012)
104. Favre, J.M.: Foundations of meta-pyramids: Languages vs. metamodels – Episode II: Story of Thotus the baboon. In: Language Engineering for Model-Driven Software Development, no. 04101 in Dagstuhl Seminar Proceedings (2005)
105. Favre, J.M.: Foundations of model (driven) (reverse) engineering: Models – Episode I: Stories of the Fidus Papyrus and of the Solarus. In: Language Engineering for Model-Driven Software Development, no. 04101 in Dagstuhl Seminar Proceedings (2005)
106. Favre, J.M., Gasevic, D., Lämmel, R., Winter, A.: Guest editors' introduction to the special section on software language engineering. IEEE Trans. Softw. Eng. **35**(6), 737–741 (2009)
107. Felleisen, M., Findler, R., Flatt, M.: Semantics Engineering with PLT Redex. MIT Press (2009)
108. Fenton, N.E., Pfleeger, S.L.: Software metrics – A practical and rigorous approach. International Thomson (1996). 2nd edition
109. Ferenc, R., Siket, I., Gyimóthy, T.: Extracting facts from open source software. In: Proc. ICSM, pp. 60–69. IEEE (2004)
110. Fokin, A., Derevenetc, E., Chernov, A., Troshina, K.: SmartDec: Approaching C++ decompilation. In: Proc. WCRE, pp. 347–356. IEEE (2011)

111. Font, J., Arcega, L., Haugen, Ø., Cetina, C.: Leveraging variability modeling to address meta-model revisions in model-based software product lines. Comput. Lang. Syst. Struct. **48**, 20–38 (2017)
112. Fontana, F.A., Caracciolo, A., Zanoni, M.: DPB: A benchmark for design pattern detection tools. In: CSMR 2012, pp. 235–244. IEEE (2012)
113. Fontana, F.A., Ferme, V., Marino, A., Walter, B., Martenka, P.: Investigating the impact of code smells on system's quality: An empirical study on systems of different application domains. In: Proc. ICSM, pp. 260–269. IEEE (2013)
114. Fontana, F.A., Zanoni, M.: A tool for design pattern detection and software architecture reconstruction. Inf. Sci. **181**(7), 1306–1324 (2011)
115. Fontana, F.A., Zanoni, M., Marino, A., Mäntylä, M.: Code smell detection: Towards a machine learning-based approach. In: Proc. ICSM, pp. 396–399. IEEE (2013)
116. Fowler, M.: Refactoring: Improving the Design of Existing Code. Addison Wesley (1999)
117. Frühwirth, T., Abdennadher, S.: Essentials of constraint programming. Springer (2003)
118. Galvao, I., Goknil, A.: Survey of traceability approaches in model-driven engineering. In: Proc. EDOC, pp. 313–326. IEEE (2007)
119. Gethers, M., Dit, B., Kagdi, H.H., Poshyvanyk, D.: Integrated impact analysis for managing software changes. In: Proc. ICSE, pp. 430–440. IEEE (2012)
120. Gil, J., Maman, I.: Micro patterns in Java code. In: Proc. OOPSLA, pp. 97–116. ACM (2005)
121. Gomes, C., Barroca, B., Amaral, V.: Classification of model transformation tools: Pattern matching techniques. In: Proc. MODELS, *LNCS*, vol. 8767, pp. 619–635. Springer (2014)
122. Gonçales, L., Farias, K., Scholl, M., Veronez, M., de Oliveira, T.C.: Comparison of design models: A systematic mapping study. Int. J. Softw. Eng. Knowl. Eng. **25**(9-10), 1765–1770 (2015)
123. Goncharenko, B., Zaytsev, V.: Language design and implementation for the domain of coding conventions. In: Proc. SLE, pp. 90–104. ACM (2016)
124. Hainaut, J.: The transformational approach to database engineering. In: GTTSE 2005, Revised Papers, *LNCS*, vol. 4143, pp. 95–143. Springer (2006)
125. Hainaut, J., Cleve, A., Henrard, J., Hick, J.: Migration of legacy information systems. In: Software Evolution, pp. 105–138. Springer (2008)
126. Han, M., Hofmeister, C., Nord, R.L.: Reconstructing software architecture for J2EE web applications. In: Proc. WCRE, pp. 67–79. IEEE (2003)
127. Härtel, J., Härtel, L., Heinz, M., Lämmel, R., Varanovich, A.: Interconnected linguistic architecture. The Art, Science, and Engineering of Programming Journal **1** (2017). 27 pages. Available at http://programming-journal.org/2017/1/3/
128. Hassan, A.E., Jiang, Z.M., Holt, R.C.: Source versus object code extraction for recovering software architecture. In: Proc. WCRE, pp. 67–76. IEEE (2005)
129. Hatcliff, J.: Foundations of partial evaluation and program specialization (1999). Available at http://people.cis.ksu.edu/~hatcliff/FPEPS/
130. Henkel, J., Diwan, A.: CatchUp!: capturing and replaying refactorings to support API evolution. In: Proc. ICSE, pp. 274–283. ACM (2005)
131. Herrmannsdoerfer, M., Benz, S., Jürgens, E.: Automatability of coupled evolution of metamodels and models in practice. In: Proc. MoDELS, *LNCS*, vol. 5301, pp. 645–659. Springer (2008)
132. Herrmannsdoerfer, M., Benz, S., Jürgens, E.: COPE – Automating coupled evolution of metamodels and models. In: Proc. ECOOP, *LNCS*, vol. 5653, pp. 52–76. Springer (2009)
133. Hoare, C.A.R.: Hints on programming language design. Tech. rep., Stanford University (1973)
134. Holt, R.C.: Structural manipulations of software architecture using Tarski relational algebra. In: Proc. WCRE, pp. 210–219. IEEE (1998)
135. Holt, R.C.: WCRE 1998 most influential paper: Grokking software architecture. In: Proc. WCRE, pp. 5–14. IEEE (2008)
136. Horwitz, S., Reps, T.W., Binkley, D.: Interprocedural slicing using dependence graphs. ACM Trans. Program. Lang. Syst. **12**(1), 26–60 (1990)

137. ISO/IEC: ISO/IEC 14977:1996(E). Information Technology. Syntactic Metalanguage. Extended BNF. (1996). Available at `http://www.cl.cam.ac.uk/~mgk25/iso-14977.pdf`
138. Jin, G., Song, L., Shi, X., Scherpelz, J., Lu, S.: Understanding and detecting real-world performance bugs. In: Proc. PLDI, pp. 77–88. ACM (2012)
139. Jones, N.D., Gomard, C.K., Sestoft, P.: Partial evaluation and automatic program generation. Prentice-Hall, Inc. (1993)
140. Jouault, F., Allilaire, F., Bézivin, J., Kurtev, I.: ATL: A model transformation tool. Sci. Comput. Program. **72**(1-2), 31–39 (2008)
141. Jouault, F., Vanhooff, B., Brunelière, H., Doux, G., Berbers, Y., Bézivin, J.: Inter-DSL coordination support by combining megamodeling and model weaving. In: Proc. SAC, pp. 2011–2018. ACM (2010)
142. Kappel, G., Langer, P., Retschitzegger, W., Schwinger, W., Wimmer, M.: Model transformation by-example: A survey of the first wave. In: Conceptual Modelling and Its Theoretical Foundations – Essays Dedicated to Bernhard Thalheim on the Occasion of His 60th Birthday, *LNCS*, vol. 7260, pp. 197–215. Springer (2012)
143. Kats, L.C.L., Visser, E.: The Spoofax language workbench. In: Companion SPLASH/OOPSLA, pp. 237–238. ACM (2010)
144. Kats, L.C.L., Visser, E.: The Spoofax language workbench: rules for declarative specification of languages and IDEs. In: Proc. OOPSLA, pp. 444–463. ACM (2010)
145. Keenan, E., Czauderna, A., Leach, G., Cleland-Huang, J., Shin, Y., Moritz, E., Gethers, M., Poshyvanyk, D., Maletic, J.I., Hayes, J.H., Dekhtyar, A., Manukian, D., Hossein, S., Hearn, D.: TraceLab: An experimental workbench for equipping researchers to innovate, synthesize, and comparatively evaluate traceability solutions. In: Proc. ICSE, pp. 1375–1378. IEEE (2012)
146. Kehrer, T., Kelter, U., Pietsch, P., Schmidt, M.: Operation-based model differencing meets state-based model comparison. Softwaretechnik-Trends **32**(4) (2012)
147. Kelly, S., Tolvanen, J.: Domain-Specific Modeling. IEEE & Wiley (2008)
148. Kienle, H.M., Müller, H.A.: Rigi – An environment for software reverse engineering, exploration, visualization, and redocumentation. Sci. Comput. Program. **75**(4), 247–263 (2010)
149. Klint, P., Lämmel, R., Verhoef, C.: Toward an engineering discipline for grammarware. ACM Trans. Softw. Eng. Methodol. **14**(3), 331–380 (2005)
150. Klint, P., van der Storm, T., Vinju, J.J.: RASCAL: A domain specific language for source code analysis and manipulation. In: Proc. SCAM, pp. 168–177. IEEE (2009)
151. Klint, P., van der Storm, T., Vinju, J.J.: EASY meta-programming with Rascal. In: GTTSE 2009, Revised Papers, *LNCS*, vol. 6491, pp. 222–289. Springer (2011)
152. Klusener, A.S., Lämmel, R., Verhoef, C.: Architectural modifications to deployed software. Sci. Comput. Program. **54**(2-3), 143–211 (2005)
153. Kniesel, G., Binun, A.: Standing on the shoulders of giants – A data fusion approach to design pattern detection. In: Proc. ICPC, pp. 208–217. IEEE (2009)
154. Kniesel, G., Binun, A., Hegedüs, P., Fülöp, L.J., Chatzigeorgiou, A., Guéhéneuc, Y., Tsantalis, N.: DPDX–towards a common result exchange format for design pattern detection tools. In: Proc. CSMR, pp. 232–235. IEEE (2010)
155. Knuth, D.E.: An empirical study of FORTRAN programs. Softw., Pract. Exper. **1**(2), 105–133 (1971)
156. Kolovos, D.S., Paige, R.F., Polack, F.: Merging models with the Epsilon Merging Language (EML). In: Proc. MoDELS, *LNCS*, vol. 4199, pp. 215–229. Springer (2006)
157. Kosar, T., Bohra, S., Mernik, M.: Domain-specific languages: A systematic mapping study. Inf. Softw. Technol. **71**, 77–91 (2016)
158. Koschke, R.: Architecture reconstruction. In: Software Engineering, International Summer Schools, ISSSE 2006-2008, Salerno, Italy, Revised Tutorial Lectures, *LNCS*, vol. 5413, pp. 140–173. Springer (2009)
159. Kramer, M.E., Klein, J., Steel, J.R.H., Morin, B., Kienzle, J., Barais, O., Jézéquel, J.: Achieving practical genericity in model weaving through extensibility. In: Proc. ICMT, *LNCS*, vol. 7909, pp. 108–124. Springer (2013)

160. Krishnamurthi, S.: Programming Languages: Application and Interpretation. Brown University (2007). https://cs.brown.edu/~sk/Publications/Books/ProgLangs/
161. Kurtev, I., Bézivin, J., Akşit, M.: Technological spaces: An initial appraisal. In: Proc. CoopIS, DOA 2002, Industrial track (2002)
162. Lämmel, R.: Coupled software transformations. In: Proc. SET, pp. 31–35 (2004). Extended Abstract. Available at http://post.queensu.ca/~zouy/files/set-2004.pdf#page=38
163. Lämmel, R.: LINQ to XSD. In: Proc. PLAN-X, pp. 95–96 (2007)
164. Lämmel, R.: Coupled software transformations revisited. In: Proc. SLE, pp. 239–252. ACM (2016)
165. Lämmel, R.: Relationship maintenance in software language repositories. The Art, Science, and Engineering of Programming Journal **1** (2017). 27 pages. Available at http://programming-journal.org/2017/1/4/
166. Lämmel, R., Leinberger, M., Schmorleiz, T., Varanovich, A.: Comparison of feature implementations across languages, technologies, and styles. In: Proc. CSMR-WCRE, pp. 333–337. IEEE (2014)
167. Lämmel, R., Linke, R., Pek, E., Varanovich, A.: A framework profile of .NET. In: Proc. WCRE, pp. 141–150. IEEE (2011)
168. Lämmel, R., Lohmann, W.: Format evolution. In: Proc. RETIS, vol. 155, pp. 113—134. OCG, books@ocg.at (2001)
169. Lämmel, R., Meijer, E.: Mappings make data processing go 'round. In: GTTSE 2005, Revised Papers, *LNCS*, vol. 4143, pp. 169–218. Springer (2006)
170. Lämmel, R., Meijer, E.: Revealing the X/O impedance mismatch – (changing lead into gold). In: Datatype-Generic Programming – International Spring School, SSDGP 2006, Revised Lectures, *LNCS*, vol. 4719, pp. 285–367. Springer (2007)
171. Lämmel, R., Mosen, D., Varanovich, A.: Method and tool support for classifying software languages with Wikipedia. In: Proc. SLE, *LNCS*, vol. 8225, pp. 249–259. Springer (2013)
172. Lämmel, R., Pek, E.: Understanding privacy policies – A study in empirical analysis of language usage. Empir. Softw. Eng. **18**(2), 310–374 (2013)
173. Lämmel, R., Schmorleiz, T., Varanovich, A.: The 101haskell chrestomathy: A whole bunch of learnable lambdas. In: Proc. IFL, p. 25. ACM (2013)
174. Lämmel, R., Schulte, W.: Controllable combinatorial coverage in grammar-based testing. In: Proc. TestCom, *LNCS*, vol. 3964, pp. 19–38. Springer (2006)
175. Lämmel, R., Varanovich, A.: Interpretation of linguistic architecture. In: Proc. ECMFA, *LNCS*, vol. 8569, pp. 67–82. Springer (2014)
176. Lämmel, R., Zaytsev, V.: Recovering grammar relationships for the Java language specification. Softw. Qual. J. **19**(2), 333–378 (2011)
177. Lanza, M., Ducasse, S.: Polymetric views – A lightweight visual approach to reverse engineering. IEEE Trans. Softw. Eng. **29**(9), 782–795 (2003)
178. Lanza, M., Ducasse, S., Demeyer, S.: Reverse engineering based on metrics and program visualization. In: ECOOP 1999 Workshop Reader, *LNCS*, vol. 1743, pp. 168–169. Springer (1999)
179. Lanza, M., Marinescu, R.: Object-Oriented Metrics in Practice – Using Software Metrics to Characterize, Evaluate, and Improve the Design of Object-Oriented Systems. Springer (2006)
180. Lattner, C., Adve, V.S.: LLVM: A compilation framework for lifelong program analysis & transformation. In: Proc. CGO, pp. 75–88. IEEE (2004)
181. Lédeczi, Á., Bakay, A., Maroti, M., Völgyesi, P., Nordstrom, G., Sprinkle, J., Karsai, G.: Composing domain-specific design environments. IEEE Computer **34**(11), 44–51 (2001)
182. Leijen, D., Meijer, E.: Parsec: Direct style monadic parser combinators for the real world. Tech. Rep. UU-CS-2001-27, Department of Computer Science, Universiteit Utrecht (2001)
183. Li, B., Sun, X., Leung, H., Zhang, S.: A survey of code-based change impact analysis techniques. Softw. Test., Verif. Reliab. **23**(8), 613–646 (2013)

184. Liebig, J., Kästner, C., Apel, S.: Analyzing the discipline of preprocessor annotations in 30 million lines of C code. In: Proc. AOSD, pp. 191–202. ACM (2011)
185. Lin, Y., Holt, R.C.: Formalizing fact extraction. ENTCS **94**, 93–102 (2004)
186. Louden, K.: Compiler Construction: Principles and Practice. Cengage Learning (1997)
187. Lungu, M., Lanza, M., Gîrba, T., Robbes, R.: The small project observatory: Visualizing software ecosystems. Sci. Comput. Program. **75**(4), 264–275 (2010)
188. Mäder, P., Egyed, A.: Do developers benefit from requirements traceability when evolving and maintaining a software system? Empir. Softw. Eng. **20**(2), 413–441 (2015)
189. Marchand, J.Y., Combemale, B., Baudry, B.: A categorical model of model merging and weaving. In: Proc. MiSE, pp. 70–76. IEEE (2012)
190. Marriott, K., Meyer, B.: On the classification of visual languages by grammar hierarchies. J. Vis. Lang. Comput. **8**(4), 375–402 (1997)
191. Martinez, J., Ziadi, T., Bissyandé, T.F., Klein, J., Traon, Y.L.: Automating the extraction of model-based software product lines from model variants (T). In: Proc. ASE, pp. 396–406. IEEE (2015)
192. Medvidovic, N., Taylor, R.N.: A classification and comparison framework for software architecture description languages. IEEE Trans. Softw. Eng. **26**(1), 70–93 (2000)
193. Mehner, K., Monga, M., Taentzer, G.: Analysis of aspect-oriented model weaving. In: Trans. Aspect-Oriented Software Development, vol. 5, pp. 235–263 (2009)
194. Mens, T.: Model Transformation: A Survey of the State of the Art, pp. 1–19. John Wiley & Sons, Inc. (2013)
195. Mens, T., Gorp, P.V.: A taxonomy of model transformation. ENTCS **152**, 125–142 (2006)
196. Mens, T., Tourwé, T.: A survey of software refactoring. IEEE Trans. Softw. Eng. **30**(2), 126–139 (2004)
197. Mernik, M., Heering, J., Sloane, A.M.: When and how to develop domain-specific languages. ACM Comput. Surv. **37**(4), 316–344 (2005)
198. Mordal-Manet, K., Anquetil, N., Laval, J., Serebrenik, A., Vasilescu, B., Ducasse, S.: Software quality metrics aggregation in industry. J. Softw.: Evol. Process **25**(10), 1117–1135 (2013)
199. Mosses, P.D.: Action Semantics. Cambridge University Press (1992)
200. Murakami, T., Amagasa, T., Kitagawa, H.: DBPowder: A flexible object-relational mapping framework based on a conceptual model. In: Proc. COMPSAC, pp. 589–598. IEEE (2013)
201. Murphy, G.C., Notkin, D.: Lightweight lexical source model extraction. ACM Trans. Softw. Eng. Methodol. **5**(3), 262–292 (1996)
202. Neubauer, P., Bergmayr, A., Mayerhofer, T., Troya, J., Wimmer, M.: XMLText: from XML schema to Xtext. In: Proc. SLE, pp. 71–76. ACM (2015)
203. Paige, R.F., Kolovos, D.S., Polack, F.A.C.: A tutorial on metamodelling for grammar researchers. Sci. Comput. Program. **96**, 396–416 (2014)
204. Paige, R.F., Matragkas, N.D., Rose, L.M.: Evolving models in model-driven engineering: State-of-the-art and future challenges. J. Syst. Softw. **111**, 272–280 (2016)
205. Palomba, F., Bavota, G., Penta, M.D., Oliveto, R., Poshyvanyk, D., Lucia, A.D.: Mining version histories for detecting code smells. IEEE Trans. Softw. Eng. **41**(5), 462–489 (2015)
206. Petersen, K., Feldt, R., Mujtaba, S., Mattsson, M.: Systematic mapping studies in software engineering. In: Proc. EASE, Workshops in Computing. BCS (2008)
207. Petersen, K., Vakkalanka, S., Kuzniarz, L.: Guidelines for conducting systematic mapping studies in software engineering: An update. Inf. Softw. Technol. **64**, 1–18 (2015)
208. Pezoa, F., Reutter, J.L., Suarez, F., Ugarte, M., Vrgoc, D.: Foundations of JSON schema. In: Proc. WWW, pp. 263–273. ACM (2016)
209. Pfleeger, S.L.: Software metrics: Progress after 25 years? IEEE Softw. **25**(6), 32–34 (2008)
210. Pierce, B.: Types and Programming Languages. MIT Press (2002)
211. Porkoláb, Z., Sinkovics, Á., Siroki, I.: DSL in C++ template metaprogram. In: CEFP 2013, Revised Selected Papers, *LNCS*, vol. 8606, pp. 76–114. Springer (2015)
212. Rajlich, V.: A model and a tool for change propagation in software. ACM SIGSOFT Software Engineering Notes **25**(1), 72 (2000)

213. Ren, X., Shah, F., Tip, F., Ryder, B.G., Chesley, O.C.: Chianti: A tool for change impact analysis of Java programs. In: Proc. OOPSLA, pp. 432–448. ACM (2004)
214. Renggli, L.: Dynamic language embedding with homogeneous tool support. Ph.D. thesis, Universität Bern (2010)
215. Renggli, L., Gîrba, T., Nierstrasz, O.: Embedding languages without breaking tools. In: Proc. ECOOP, *LNCS*, vol. 6183, pp. 380–404. Springer (2010)
216. Rocco, J.D., Ruscio, D.D., Iovino, L., Pierantonio, A.: Dealing with the coupled evolution of metamodels and model-to-text transformations. In: Proc. Workshop on Models and Evolution, *CEUR Workshop Proceedings*, vol. 1331, pp. 22–31. CEUR-WS.org (2015)
217. Rompf, T.: The essence of multi-stage evaluation in LMS. In: A List of Successes That Can Change the World – Essays Dedicated to Philip Wadler on the Occasion of His 60th Birthday, *LNCS*, vol. 9600, pp. 318–335. Springer (2016)
218. Roover, C.D.: A logic meta-programming foundation for example-driven pattern detection in object-oriented programs. In: Proc. ICSM, pp. 556–561. IEEE (2011)
219. Roover, C.D., Lämmel, R., Pek, E.: Multi dimensional exploration of API usage. In: Proc. ICPC 2013, pp. 152–161. IEEE (2013)
220. Rosa, M.L., Dumas, M., Uba, R., Dijkman, R.M.: Business process model merging: An approach to business process consolidation. ACM Trans. Softw. Eng. Methodol. **22**(2), 11 (2013)
221. Rosu, G., Serbanuta, T.: An overview of the K semantic framework. J. Log. Algebr. Program. **79**(6), 397–434 (2010)
222. Roy, C.K., Cordy, J.R., Koschke, R.: Comparison and evaluation of code clone detection techniques and tools: A qualitative approach. Sci. Comput. Program. **74**(7), 470–495 (2009)
223. Roy, C.K., Zibran, M.F., Koschke, R.: The vision of software clone management: Past, present, and future (keynote paper). In: Proc. CSMR-WCRE, pp. 18–33. IEEE (2014)
224. Rubin, J., Chechik, M.: A survey of feature location techniques. In: Domain Engineering, Product Lines, Languages, and Conceptual Models, pp. 29–58. Springer (2013)
225. Ruscio, D.D., Lämmel, R., Pierantonio, A.: Automated co-evolution of GMF editor models. In: Proc. SLE 2010, *LNCS*, vol. 6563, pp. 143–162. Springer (2011)
226. Sánchez, P., Fuentes, L., Stein, D., Hanenberg, S., Unland, R.: Aspect-oriented model weaving beyond model composition and model transformation. In: Proc. MoDELS, *LNCS*, vol. 5301, pp. 766–781. Springer (2008)
227. Savga, I., Rudolf, M., Goetz, S., Aßmann, U.: Practical refactoring-based framework upgrade. In: Proc. GPCE, pp. 171–180. ACM (2008)
228. Schäfer, M., Thies, A., Steimann, F., Tip, F.: A comprehensive approach to naming and accessibility in refactoring Java programs. IEEE Trans. Softw. Eng. **38**(6), 1233–1257 (2012)
229. Schauss, S., Lämmel, R., Härtel, J., Heinz, M., Klein, K., Härtel, L., Berger, T.: A chrestomathy of DSL implementations. In: Proc. SLE. ACM (2017). 12 pages
230. Schink, H., Kuhlemann, M., Saake, G., Lämmel, R.: Hurdles in multi-language refactoring of Hibernate applications. In: Proc. ICSOFT, pp. 129–134. SciTePress (2011)
231. Schmidt, D.C.: Guest editor's introduction: Model-driven engineering. IEEE Computer **39**(2), 25–31 (2006)
232. Sebesta, R.W.: Concepts of Programming Languages. Addison-Wesley (2012). 10th edition
233. Seibel, A., Hebig, R., Giese, H.: Traceability in model-driven engineering: Efficient and scalable traceability maintenance. In: Software and Systems Traceability., pp. 215–240. Springer (2012)
234. Sequeda, J., Arenas, M., Miranker, D.P.: On directly mapping relational databases to RDF and OWL. In: Proc WWW 2012, pp. 649–658. ACM (2012)
235. Sereni, D., Jones, N.D.: Termination analysis of higher-order functional programs. In: Proc. APLAS, *LNCS*, vol. 3780, pp. 281–297. Springer (2005)
236. Sheard, T., Peyton Jones, S.L.: Template meta-programming for Haskell. SIGPLAN Not. **37**(12), 60–75 (2002)
237. Shilov, N.V., Akinin, A.A., Zubkov, A.V., Idrisov, R.I.: Development of the computer language classification knowledge portal. In: Perspectives of Systems Informatics – 8th International Andrei Ershov Memorial Conference, PSI 2011, Novosibirsk, Russia, June 27–July 1, 2011, Revised Selected Papers, *LNCS*, vol. 7162, pp. 340–348. Springer (2012)

238. Singh, R., Bezemer, C., Shang, W., Hassan, A.E.: Optimizing the performance-related configurations of object-relational mapping frameworks using a multi-objective genetic algorithm. In: Proc. ICPE, pp. 309–320. ACM (2016)
239. Skalna, I., Gawel, B.: Model driven architecture and classification of business rules modelling languages. In: Proc. FedCSIS, pp. 949–952 (2012)
240. Sneed, H.M.: Wrapping legacy COBOL programs behind an XML-interface. In: Proc. WCRE, p. 189. IEEE (2001)
241. Sneed, H.M.: Migrating PL/I code to Java. In: Proc. CSMR, pp. 287–296. IEEE (2011)
242. Sneed, H.M., Majnar, R.: A case study in software wrapping. In: Proc. ICSM, pp. 86–93. IEEE (1998)
243. Sridharan, M., Chandra, S., Dolby, J., Fink, S.J., Yahav, E.: Alias analysis for object-oriented programs. In: Aliasing in Object-Oriented Programming. Types, Analysis and Verification, *LNCS*, vol. 7850, pp. 196–232. Springer (2013)
244. Stephan, M., Cordy, J.R.: A survey of model comparison approaches and applications. In: Proc. MODELSWARD, pp. 265–277. SciTePress (2013)
245. Stinckwich, S., Ducasse, S.: Introduction to the Smalltalk special issue. Comput. Lang. Syst. Struct. **32**(2-3), 85–86 (2006)
246. Sun, X., Li, B., Leung, H., Li, B., Zhu, J.: Static change impact analysis techniques: A comparative study. J. Syst. Softw. **109**, 137–149 (2015)
247. Sztipanovits, J., Karsai, G.: Model-integrated computing. IEEE Computer **30**(4), 110–111 (1997)
248. Taha, W.: A gentle introduction to multi-stage programming, part II. In: GTTSE 2007, Revised Papers, *LNCS*, vol. 5235, pp. 260–290. Springer (2008)
249. Tamura, G., Cleve, A.: A comparison of taxonomies for model transformation languages. Paradigma **4**(1), 1–14 (2010)
250. Terekhov, A.A., Verhoef, C.: The realities of language conversions. IEEE Softw. **17**(6), 111–124 (2000)
251. Terwilliger, J.F., Bernstein, P.A., Melnik, S.: Full-fidelity flexible object-oriented XML access. PVLDB **2**(1), 1030–1041 (2009)
252. Tip, F.: A survey of program slicing techniques. J. Program. Lang. **3**(3) (1995)
253. Tip, F., Fuhrer, R.M., Kiezun, A., Ernst, M.D., Balaban, I., Sutter, B.D.: Refactoring using type constraints. ACM Trans. Program. Lang. Syst. **33**(3), 9 (2011)
254. Torres, A., de Matos Galante, R., Pimenta, M.S.: ENORM: An essential notation for object-relational mapping. SIGMOD Record **43**(2), 23–28 (2014)
255. Tratt, L.: Domain specific language implementation via compile-time meta-programming. ACM Trans. Program. Lang. Syst. **30**(6) (2008)
256. Trujillo, S., Azanza, M., Díaz, O.: Generative metaprogramming. In: Proc. GPCE, pp. 105–114. ACM (2007)
257. Tufano, M., Palomba, F., Bavota, G., Oliveto, R., Penta, M.D., Lucia, A.D., Poshyvanyk, D.: When and why your code starts to smell bad. In: Proc. ICSE, pp. 403–414. IEEE (2015)
258. van Roy, P.: Programming paradigms for dummies: What every programmer should know. In: New Computational Paradigms for Computer Music, IRCAM/Delatour, France, pp. 9–38 (2009)
259. Vasilescu, B., Serebrenik, A., van den Brand, M.: You can't control the unfamiliar: A study on the relations between aggregation techniques for software metrics. In: ICSM 2011, pp. 313–322. IEEE (2011)
260. Vermolen, S., Visser, E.: Heterogeneous coupled evolution of software languages. In: Proc. MoDELS, *LNCS*, vol. 5301, pp. 630–644. Springer (2008)
261. Vermolen, S.D., Wachsmuth, G., Visser, E.: Generating database migrations for evolving web applications. In: Proc. GPCE, pp. 83–92. ACM (2011)
262. Visser, E.: Stratego: A language for program transformation based on rewriting strategies. In: Proc. RTA, *LNCS*, vol. 2051, pp. 357–362. Springer (2001)
263. Visser, E., Wachsmuth, G., Tolmach, A.P., Neron, P., Vergu, V.A., Passalaqua, A., Konat, G.: A language designer's workbench: A one-stop-shop for implementation and verification of language designs. In: Proc. SPLASH, Onward!, pp. 95–111. ACM (2014)

264. Visser, J.: Coupled transformation of schemas, documents, queries, and constraints. ENTCS **200**(3), 3–23 (2008)
265. Voelter, M., Benz, S., Dietrich, C., Engelmann, B., Helander, M., Kats, L.C.L., Visser, E., Wachsmuth, G.: DSL Engineering – Designing, Implementing and Using Domain-Specific Languages. dslbook.org (2013)
266. Voelter, M., Ratiu, D., Kolb, B., Schätz, B.: mbeddr: instantiating a language workbench in the embedded software domain. Autom. Softw. Eng. **20**(3), 339–390 (2013)
267. Völter, M., Visser, E.: Language extension and composition with language workbenches. In: Companion SPLASH/OOPSLA, pp. 301–304. ACM (2010)
268. Wachsmuth, G.: Metamodel adaptation and model co-adaptation. In: Proc. ECOOP, *LNCS*, vol. 4609, pp. 600–624. Springer (2007)
269. Wachsmuth, G., Konat, G.D.P., Visser, E.: Language design with the Spoofax language workbench. IEEE Softw. **31**(5), 35–43 (2014)
270. Wang, J., Peng, X., Xing, Z., Zhao, W.: How developers perform feature location tasks: A human-centric and process-oriented exploratory study. J. Softw.: Evol. Process **25**(11), 1193–1224 (2013)
271. Weiser, M.: Program slicing. IEEE Trans. Softw. Eng. **10**(4), 352–357 (1984)
272. Wile, D.S.: Lessons learned from real DSL experiments. In: Proc. HICSS-36, p. 325. IEEE (2003)
273. Wile, D.S.: Lessons learned from real DSL experiments. Sci. Comput. Program. **51**(3), 265–290 (2004)
274. WWW: XML Information Set (2004). https://www.w3.org/TR/xml-infoset/
275. Yamashita, A.F., Moonen, L.: Do code smells reflect important maintainability aspects? In: Proc. ICSM, pp. 306–315. IEEE (2012)
276. Zanoni, M., Fontana, F.A., Stella, F.: On applying machine learning techniques for design pattern detection. J. Syst. Softw. **103**, 102–117 (2015)
277. Zaytsev, V.: BNF WAS HERE: What have we done about the unnecessary diversity of notation for syntactic definitions. In: Proc. SAC, pp. 1910–1915. ACM (2012)
278. Zaytsev, V., et al.: Software language processing suite (2008). http://slps.github.io/

Chapter 2
A Story of a Domain-Specific Language

MARTIN FOWLER.[1]

Abstract In this chapter, several fundamental concepts and engineering techniques for software languages are explained by means of an illustrative domain-specific language. In particular, we exercise the internal and external styles of DSL implementation, textual and visual syntax, parsing, interpretation, and code generation. As a running example, we deal with a DSL for finite state machines FSML (*FSM Language*). In addition to implementing FSML with mainstream languages and technologies, we discuss design and implementation options and concerns overall and we describe a number of "recipes" for DSL development.

---

[1] There is no "Greek" in Martin Fowler's textbooks on refactoring [4] and DSLs [5], both addressing important topics in software language engineering. These accessible textbooks triggered research on these topics and connected research better with "mainstream" software development. Martin Fowler was again visionary when he asked in 2005 "Language Workbenches: The Killer-App for Domain Specific Languages?" (https://www.martinfowler.com/articles/languageWorkbench.html), thereby fueling the development of and research on language workbenches [2, 3, 9, 8, 16, 15, 17, 13].

Artwork Credits for Chapter Opening: This work by Wojciech Kwasnik is licensed under CC BY-SA 4.0. This artwork quotes the artwork *DMT*, acrylic, 2006 by Matt Sheehy with the artist's permission. This work also quotes https://en.wikipedia.org/wiki/Wheat_Field_with_Cypresses#/media/File:Wheat-Field-with-Cypresses-(1889)-Vincent-van-Gogh-Met.jpg, subject to the attribution "Vincent van Gogh: Wheat Field with Cypresses (1889) [Public domain], via Wikipedia." This work artistically morphes an image, https://en.wikipedia.org/wiki/Martin_Fowler, showing the person honored, subject to the attribution "By Webysther Nunes - Own work, CC BY-SA 4.0, https://commons.wikimedia.org/w/index.php?curid=39594469."

© Springer International Publishing AG, part of Springer Nature 2018
R. Lämmel, *Software Languages*,
https://doi.org/10.1007/978-3-319-90800-7_2

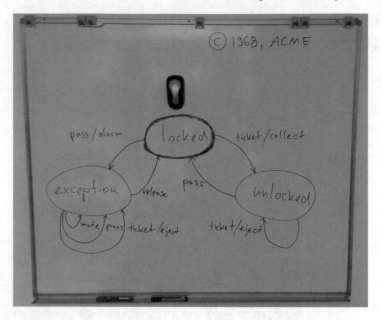

Fig. 2.1 A turnstile FSM in visual notation on the whiteboard.

2.1 Language Concepts

We assume an imaginary business context: a company *Acme*[2], which develops *embedded systems*.[3] *Acme* is an international leader in embedded systems development. Over the last 50 years, *Acme* has matured a number of development techniques that are specifically tailored to the area of embedded systems development. For instance, *Acme* uses FSMs[4] in the development of embedded systems. In this chapter, we discuss a corresponding language for FSMs, FSML (*FSM L*anguage). FSML is a domain-specific language that was grown at *Acme* over many years; the language and its implementation have emerged and evolved in various ways, as described below.

FSML is introduced here by means of an example. In an ongoing project, *Acme* is developing a turnstile component, as part of a bigger contract to modernize the metro system in an undisclosed city. Metro passengers need to pass through the turnstile (a hub or spider) and insert a valid ticket into the turnstile's card reader when they want to reach the platform in a legal manner. The *Acme* architects and the customer agree on the basic functionality for turnstiles in a meeting, where they draw an FSM on the whiteboard as shown in Fig. 2.1.

---

[2] http://en.wikipedia.org/wiki/Acme_Corporation

[3] http://en.wikipedia.org/wiki/Embedded_system

[4] http://en.wikipedia.org/wiki/Finite-state_machine

FSML is quickly explained in terms of its visual notation with the example at hand. FSMs comprise states (nodes) and transitions (directed edges). The initial state of the machine is indicated by a bolder border. These are these states in the turnstile FSM:

- *locked*: The turnstile is locked. No passenger is allowed to pass.
- *unlocked*: The turnstile is unlocked. A passenger may pass.
- *exception*: A problem has occurred and metro personnel need to intervene.

Each transition connects two states and is annotated by two parts, e/a, an event e and an action a, where the latter is optional. The event may be triggered by the user; this may involve sensors in an embedded system. An event causes a transition. An action corresponds to functionality to be performed upon a transition; this may involve actors in an embedded system. The source of a transition is the source state; the target of a transition is the target state. The turnstile FSM involves these *events*:

- *ticket*: A passenger inserts a ticket into the card reader.
- *pass*: A passenger passes through the turnstile as noticed by a sensor.
- *mute*: Metro personnel turn off the alarm after an exception.
- *release*: Metro personnel turn on normal operation again.

The turnstile FSM involves these *actions*:

- *collect*: The ticket is collected by the card reader.
- *eject*: The ticket is ejected by the card reader.
- *alarm*: An alarm is turned on, thereby requesting metro personnel.

Based on such an understanding of states, events, and actions, the meaning of the different *transitions* in Fig. 2.1 should be obvious by now. Consider, for example, the transition from the source state "locked" to the target state 'unlocked', which is annotated by "ticket/collect" to mean that the transition is triggered by the event of inserting a ticket and the transition causes the action of collecting the ticket.

The idea is now that architects and customers can validate their intuitions about turnstiles by starting from some input (a sequence of events) and determine the corresponding output (a sequence of actions), as illustrated below.

Illustration 2.1 (Sample input for the turnstile FSM)
The input is a sequence of the following events:

ticket   A ticket is inserted. (The turnstile is thus unlocked.)
ticket   Another ticket is inserted. (The superfluous ticket is ejected.)
pass   Someone passes through the turnstile. (This is OK.)
pass   Someone else passes through the turnstile. (This triggers an alarm.)
ticket   A ticket is inserted. (The ticket is ejected in the exceptional state.)
mute   The alarm is muted.
release   Metro personnel switch back to normal.

Illustration 2.2 (Sample output for the sample input of Illustration 2.1)
The output is a sequence of the following actions:

collect   *The inserted ticket is collected.*
eject   *A ticket inserted in the unlocked state is ejected.*
alarm   *An attempt to pass in the locked state triggers an alarm.*
eject   *A ticket inserted in the exceptional state is ejected.*

2.2 Internal DSL

Over the years, the *Acme* engineers increasingly appreciated the FSM notation. There was growing interest in handling FSMs as proper software engineering artifacts, as opposed to simply passing down whiteboard drawings from architects to developers.

DSL implementation efforts were sparked off within the company. One engineer implemented FSML as an *internal DSL* [5, 14, 1, 12] in Java. In this manner, a machine-checked and executable notation for FSMs was obtained without much effort, and also without the need for special tools.

In the internal style of DSL implementation, DSL programs are represented and their behavior is implemented in a host language. The idea is that the language concepts of the DSL are implemented as a library and the DSL programmer is provided with an API for manipulating DSL programs. We demonstrate the use of Java and Python as host languages for FSML here. We should mention that the details of internal DSL style depend significantly on the host language. If we were using C++, Scheme, Haskell, Scala, or some other language as the host language, additional or different techniques could be leveraged, for example, operator overloading, macros, or templates.

2.2.1 Baseline Object Model

Let us begin with a very simple object model for FSML. We assume classes Fsm, State, and Transition for the representation of FSMs, states, and transitions. Setter/getter-based Java code for FSM construction may take the form as shown below.

Note: Most "code snippets" (from Chapter 2 onwards) in this book are enclosed into "**Illustration**" blocks and contain a clickable URL so that the corresponding source file can be looked up in the underlying online repository. Many source files are shown with elisions and, thus, by following the link, one can inspect the complete file and also observe the context of the file in the repository. The following illustration contains the URL above the actual source code; see the underlined string.

Illustration 2.3 (Imperative style of constructing FSML objects)

Java source code org/softlang/fsml/ImperativeSample.java

```
turnstile = new Fsm();
State s = new State();
s.setStateid("locked");
s.setInitial(true);
turnstile.getStates().add(s);
s = new State();
s.setStateid("unlocked");
turnstile.getStates().add(s);
s = new State();
s.setStateid("exception");
turnstile.getStates().add(s);
Transition t = new Transition();
t.setSource("locked");
t.setEvent("ticket");
t.setAction("collect");
t.setTarget("unlocked");
turnstile.getTransitions().add(t);
t = new Transition();
...// add more transitions
```

That is, various objects are to be constructed and initialized with setters and other accessors. This style may be slightly improved if *functional constructors* are put to work as shown below.

Illustration 2.4 (Functional construction of FSML objects)

Java source code org/softlang/fsml/FunctionalSample.java

```
turnstile = new Fsm();
turnstile.getStates().add(new State("locked", true));
turnstile.getStates().add(new State("unlocked"));
turnstile.getStates().add(new State("exception"));
turnstile.getTransitions().add(new Transition("locked", "ticket", "collect", "unlocked"));
turnstile.getTransitions().add(new Transition("locked", "pass", "alarm", "exception"));
...// add more transitions
```

The code is still littered with object construction, container manipulation, and the repetition of source states for transitions. We will discuss below a more "fluent" API. As a baseline, we implement a simple baseline as follows.

Illustration 2.5 (Object model with functional constructors)

Java source code org/softlang/fsml/Fsm.java

```java
public class Fsm {
    private List<State> states = new LinkedList<>();
    private List<Transition> transitions = new LinkedList<>();
    public List<State> getStates() { return states; }
    public List<Transition> getTransitions() { return transitions; }
}
```

Java source code org/softlang/fsml/State.java

```java
public class State {
    private String id;
    private boolean initial;
    public String getStateid() { return id; }
    public void setStateid(String state) { this.id = state; }
    public boolean isInitial() { return initial; }
    public void setInitial(boolean initial) { this.initial = initial; }
    public State() { }
    public State(String id) { this.id = id; }
    public State(String id, boolean initial) { this.id = id; this.initial = initial; }
}
```

Java source code org/softlang/fsml/Transition.java

```java
public class Transition {
    private String source;
    private String event;
    private String action;
    private String target;
    ...// getters and setters omitted
    public Transition() { }
    public Transition(String source, String event, String action, String target) {
        this.source = source;
        this.event = event;
        this.action = action;
        this.target = target;
    }
}
```

Exercise 2.1 (Object model with references)   [Basic level]
Implement an alternative object model where the target state of a transition is modeled as a proper object reference to a state object, as opposed to the use of strings in the baseline model.

2.2.2 Fluent API

Let us aim at a more "fluent" API, which is focused on language concepts, elimi-
nates sources of redundancy, and hides the object-oriented representation, as shown
for the host languages Java and Python below.

Illustration 2.6 (Fluent style of representing an FSM in Java)

Java source code org/softlang/fsml/fluent/Sample.java

```
turnstile = fsm()
  .addState("locked")
    .addTransition("ticket", "collect", "unlocked")
    .addTransition("pass", "alarm", "exception")
  .addState("unlocked")
    .addTransition("ticket", "eject", "unlocked")
    .addTransition("pass", null, "locked")
  .addState("exception")
    .addTransition("ticket", "eject", "exception")
    .addTransition("pass", null, "exception")
    .addTransition("mute", null, "exception")
    .addTransition("release", null, "locked");
```

Illustration 2.7 (Fluent style of representing an FSM in Python)

Python module FsmlSample

```
turnstile = \
  Fsm() \
    .addState("locked") \
      .addTransition("ticket", "collect", "unlocked") \
      .addTransition("pass", "alarm", "exception") \
    .addState("unlocked") \
      .addTransition("ticket", "eject", "unlocked") \
      .addTransition("pass", None, "locked") \
    .addState("exception") \
      .addTransition("ticket", "eject", "exception") \
      .addTransition("pass", None, "exception") \
      .addTransition("mute", None, "exception") \
      .addTransition("release", None, "locked")
```

The construction of the FSM is expressed in a relatively concise and readable
manner. The choice of Java or Python as a host language does not influence the notation much. The fluent API style is achieved by applying a few simple techniques:

Factory methods   Rather than invoking regular constructors, any sort of DSL program fragment is constructed by appropriate factory methods. In this manner, we
effectively abstract from the low-level representation of DSL programs. Also,
the DSL concepts map more systematically to API members and the verbosity of
constructor invocation is avoided.

Method chaining   A DSL program is represented as a chain of object mutations
such that each step returns a suitable object on which to perform the next step. For
the simple DSL at hand, the returned object is the FSM to add transitions. In this
manner, DSL programs can be represented as expressions instead of statement
sequences on local variables.

Implicit parameters   The API for DSL program construction may maintain implicit parameters so that they do not need to be repeated explicitly. For FSML, it
is natural to group all transitions by source state and, thus, the API maintains a
"current" state.

Conventions (defaults)   Some details may be omitted by the programmer if reasonable defaults can be assumed, subject to conventions. For FSML, it makes
sense to assume that the first state is the initial state and, thus, the flag "initial"
can be omitted universally.

Let us illustrate the fluent API in Java.

Illustration 2.8 (A fluent Java API for FSMs)

Java source code org/softlang/fsml/fluent/Fsm.java

```
public interface Fsm {
    public Fsm addState(String state);
    public Fsm addTransition(String event, String action, String target);
    public String getInitial();
    public ActionStatePair makeTransition(String state, String event);
}
```

Java source code org/softlang/fsml/fluent/ActionStatePair.java

```
// Helper class for "makeTransition"
public class ActionStatePair {
    public String action;
    public String state;
}
```

The API does not just feature members for construction; it also provides access
to the initial state and the transitions, thereby preparing for the 'interpretation' of
FSMs, as discussed later in detail (Section 2.2.3). Let us illustrate one option of
implementing the fluent API such that we use a cascaded map to maintain states
and transitions as shown below.

Illustration 2.9 (A fluent API implementation for FSML in Java)

Java source code org/softlang/fsml/fluent/FsmImpl.java

```java
public class FsmImpl implements Fsm {
    private String initial; // the initial state
    private String current; // the "current" state
    // A cascaded map for maintaining states and transitions
    private HashMap<String, HashMap<String, ActionStatePair>> fsm =
        new HashMap<>();
    private FsmImpl() { }
    // Construct FSM object
    public static Fsm fsm() { return new FsmImpl(); }
    // Add state and set it as current state
    public Fsm addState(String id) {
        // First state is initial state
        if (initial == null) initial = id;
        // Remember state for subsequent transitions
        this.current = id;
        if (fsm.containsKey(id)) throw new FsmlDistinctIdsException();
        fsm.put(id, new HashMap<String, ActionStatePair>());
        return this;
    }
    // Add transition for current state
    public Fsm addTransition(String event, String action, String target) {
        if (fsm.get(current).containsKey(event)) throw new FsmlDeterministismException();
        ActionStatePair pair = new ActionStatePair();
        pair.action = action;
        pair.state = target;
        fsm.get(current).put(event, pair);
        return this;
    }
    // Getter for initial state
    public String getInitial() {
        return initial;
    }
    // Make transition
    public ActionStatePair makeTransition(String state, String event) {
        if (!fsm.containsKey(state)) throw new FsmlResolutionException();
        if (!fsm.get(state).containsKey(event)) throw new FsmlInfeasibleEventException();
        return fsm.get(state).get(event);
    }
}
```

The implementation makes the assumption that the first state corresponds to the initial state. Also, when a transition is added, the most recently added state (current) serves as the source state. The implementation also shields against some programming errors when describing an FSM; see the exceptions raised. We will discuss the related constraints later on (Section 2.2.4).

Exercise 2.2 (Fluent API on baseline object model)   [Basic level]
*Provide an alternative implementation of the fluent API such that the API is realized
on top of the baseline object model of Section 2.2.1.*

We also exercise Python as the host language for API implementation as follows.

Illustration 2.10 (A fluent API implementation for FSML in Python)

Python module FsmlModel

```python
class Fsm():
    def __init__(self):
        self.fsm = defaultdict(list)
        self.current = None
    def addState(self, id):
        return self.addStateNoDefault(self.current is None, id)
    def addStateNoDefault(self, initial, id):
        if id in self.fsm[id]: raise FsmlDistinctIdsException;
        self.stateObject = dict()
        self.stateObject['transitions'] = defaultdict(list)
        self.stateObject['initial'] = initial
        self.fsm[id] += [self.stateObject]
        self.current = id
        return self
    def addTransition(self, event, action, target):
        if event in self.stateObject['transitions']: raise FsmlDeterminismException;
        self.stateObject['transitions'][event] += \
            [(action, self.current if target is None else target)]
        return self
```

When comparing the Python implementation with the earlier Java implementation, we note that the Python class does not feature members for "observation"; remember the methods getInitial and makeTransition in Illustration 2.9. This is a matter of choice; we assume here that the programmer can simply access the dictionary-based representation of FSMs in the case of Python.

> **Note**: We summarize some important workflows in this book by means of "recipes" such as the one below. The frontmatter of the book features a list of recipes.

Recipe 2.1 (Development of a fluent API).

Samples   Pick some sample DSL "programs" and represent them as expressions in the host language. Strive for fluency by adopting techniques such as method chaining.

API   Extract the fluent API from the samples. You may represent the API literally as an interface or capture the API by starting the implementation of an object model with empty method bodies.

Implementation   Identify suitable representation types for the DSL "programs" (e.g., objects with suitable attributes or data structures such as maps). Implement the fluent API in terms of the representation types.

2.2.3 Interpretation

An obvious aspect of implementing a DSL for FSMs is the *simulation* of FSMs in the sense of processing some input (a sequence of events) to experience the resulting state transitions and to derive the corresponding output (a sequence of actions). At *Acme*, engineers appreciated the possibility of simulation because it would allow them to "play" with the FSMs and to document and verify traces of expected system behavior without yet implementing the FSMs proper on the target platform.

FSM simulation is an instance of what is generally referred to as *interpretation*. An interpreter processes a "program" (i.e., an FSM in the running example), it takes possibly additional input (namely a sequence of events in the running example), and it returns an output (namely a sequence of actions in the running example). We may also use streams to enable "interactive" as opposed to "batch-oriented" simulation.

Let us capture an expected "run" of the turnstile FSM as a (JUnit) testcase.

Illustration 2.11 (Test case for simulation of turnstile execution)

Java source code org/softlang/fsml/tests/FluentTest.java

```java
public class FluentTest {

    private static final String[] input =
        {"ticket", "ticket", "pass", "pass", "ticket", "mute", "release"};
    private static final String[] output =
        {"collect", "eject", "alarm", "eject"};

    @Test
    public void runSample() {
        assertArrayEquals(output, run(Sample.turnstile, input));
    }
}
```

In this test case, we invoke a run method with a sequence of events as input (i.e., as a method argument) and with a sequence of actions as output (i.e., as the method result). Both actual input and expected output are set up as string arrays accordingly. The run method (i.e., the FSML interpreter) can be implemented in Java as follows.

Illustration 2.12 (An interpreter for FSML hosted by Java)

Java source code org/softlang/fsml/fluent/FsmlInterpreter.java

```java
public class FsmlInterpreter {
  public static String[] run(Fsm fsm, String[] input) {
    ArrayList<String> output = new ArrayList<>();
    String state = fsm.getInitial();
    for (String event : input) {
      ActionStatePair pair = fsm.makeTransition(state, event);
      if (pair.action != null) output.add(pair.action);
      state = pair.state;
    }
    return output.toArray(new String[output.size()]);
  }
}
```

That is, the semantics of an FSM is essentially modeled by the API members getInitial and makeTransition so that it just remains to loop over the input and accumulate the output.

Let us implement an interpreter in Python.

Illustration 2.13 (An interpreter for FSML hosted by Python)

Python module FsmlInterpreter

```python
def run(fsm, input):
    # Determine initial state
    for id, [decl] in fsm.iteritems():
        if decl["initial"]:
            current = decl
            break
    # Consume input; produce output
    output = []
    while input:
        event = input.pop(0)
        if event not in current["transitions"]: raise FsmlInfeasibleEventException
        else:
            [(action, target)] = current["transitions"][event]
            if action is not None: output.append(action)
            if target not in fsm: raise FsmlResolutionException
            [current] = fsm[target]
    return output
```

In this implementation, the underlying data structure is accessed directly; this also entails an extra loop to identify the initial state.

The present section is summarized by means of a recipe.

Recipe 2.2 (Development of an interpreter).

Program representation *Set up representation types for the programs to be interpreted. For instance, you may rely on the representation types used by a more or less fluent API (Recipe 2.1).*

Arguments *Identify types of interpretation arguments. In the case of FSML, the interpreter takes a sequence of events, i.e., strings.*

Results *Identify types of interpretation results. In the case of FSML, the interpreter returns a sequence of actions, i.e., strings. The interpreter could also expose intermediate states encountered during the transitions – even though this was not demonstrated earlier.*

Test cases *Set up test cases for the interpreter. A positive test case consists of a program to be interpreted, additional arguments, and the expected result(s). A negative test case does not provide an expected result; instead it is marked with the expectation that interpretation terminates abnormally.*

Case discrimination *Implement interpretation as case discrimination on the syntactic constructs. The interpretation of compound constructs commences recursively or by list processing.*

Testing *Test the interpreter in terms of the test cases.*

We will refine the interpreter recipe in Chapter 5.

Exercise 2.3 (Irregular interpreter completion for FSML)   [Basic level]
Implement a test case which illustrates irregular completion. Hint: Design an event sequence such that simulation ends up in a state where a given event cannot be handled.

2.2.4 Well-Formedness

An FSM should meet certain well-formedness constraints to "make sense", i.e., so that we can expect interpretation of the FSM to be feasible. For instance, each target state mentioned in a transition of an FSM should also be declared in the FSM. Clearly, it is important that language users at *Acme* have a good understanding of these constraints so that they use the language correctly. New *Acme* employees attend an FSML seminar, where they are trained according to the principle "language by example", i.e., understanding the language by means of complementary, illustrative examples. This includes both well-formed (useful) examples and simple illustrations of constraint violation.

Here is a list of some conceivable constraints; we assign names to the constraints for later reference:

- *distinctStateIds*: The state ids of the state declarations must be distinct.
- *singleInitialState*: An FSM must have exactly one initial state.
- *deterministicTransitions*: The events must be distinct per state.
- *resolvableTargetStates*: The target state of each transition must be declared.
- *reachableStates*: All states must be reachable from the initial state.

Yet more constraints could be identified. For instance, we could require that all states offer transitions for all possible events; this constraint is not met by the turnstile FSM. Let us demonstrate violation of a constraint with an FSM. In the following code, we use the fluent Python API (Section 2.2.2).

Illustration 2.14 (A violation of the *resolvableTargetStates* constraint)

Python module FsmlResolutionNotOk

```
resolutionNotOk = \
  Fsm() \
    .addState("stateA") \
      .addTransition("eventI", "actionI", "stateB") \
      .addTransition("eventII", "actionII", "stateC") \
    .addState("stateB")
```

Exercise 2.4 (Violation of constraints)   [Basic level]
Construct an FSM which violates the distinctStateIds *constraint. Construct another FSM which violates the* reachableStates *constraint.*

FSMs exercising constraint violation can be turned into negative test cases for the implementation of the DSL. In implementing the fluent API (Section 2.2.2), we have already shielded against some problems related to the aforementioned constraints. That is, the addState method throws if the given state id has been added before, thereby addressing the constraint *distinctStateIds*. Also, the addTransition method throws if the given event has already occurred in another transition for the current state, thereby addressing the constraint *deterministicTransitions*. The constraints may be implemented by predicates as shown below.

Illustration 2.15 (Constraint checking for FSMs)

Python module FsmlConstraints

```
def ok(fsm):
    for fun in [
            distinctStateIds,
            singleInitialState,
            deterministicTransitions,
            resolvableTargetStates,
```

```
            reachableStates ] : fun(fsm)

def distinctStateIds(fsm):
    for state, decls in fsm.iteritems():
        if not len(decls) == 1: raise FsmlDistinctIdsException()

def singleInitialState(fsm):
    initials = [initial for initial, [decl] in fsm.iteritems() if decl["initial"]]
    if not len(initials) == 1: raise FsmlSingleInitialException()

def deterministicTransitions(fsm):
    for state, [decl] in fsm.iteritems():
        for event, transitions in decl["transitions"].iteritems():
            if not len(transitions) == 1: raise FsmlDeterminismException()

def resolvableTargetStates(fsm):
    for _, [decl] in fsm.iteritems():
        for _, transitions in decl["transitions"].iteritems():
            for (_, target) in transitions:
                if not target in fsm: raise FsmlResolutionException()

def reachableStates(fsm):
    for initial, [decl] in fsm.iteritems():
        if decl["initial"]:
            reachables = set([initial])
            chaseStates(initial, fsm, reachables)
    if not reachables == set(fsm.keys()): raise FsmlReachabilityException()

# Helper for recursive closure of reachable states
def chaseStates(source, fsm, states): ...
```

Arguably, some constraints do not need to be checked if we assume a fluent API implementation as discussed before, because some constraint violations may be caught during construction. However, we do not assume necessarily that all DSL samples are constructed by means of the fluent API. For instance, DSL samples may also be represented in interchange formats, thereby calling for well-formedness checking atop serialization.

We mention in passing that additional constraints apply, when all arguments are considered for interpretation. In the case of FSML, we must require that the events in the input can always be handled in the corresponding transition. This sort of problem is caught by the interpreter.

The present section is summarized by means of a recipe.

Recipe 2.3 (Development of a constraint checker).

Negative test cases   Designate one negative test case for each constraint that
    should be checked. Ideally, each such test case should violate just one con-
    straint and not several at once.
Reporting   Choose an approach to "reporting". The result of constraint vi-
    olation may be communicated either as a Boolean value, as a list of error
    messages, or by throwing an exception.
Modularity   Implement each constraint in a separate function, thereby sup-
    porting modularity and testing.
Testing   The constraint violations must be correctly detected for the negative
    test cases. The positive test cases, for example, those for the interpreter
    (Recipe 2.2), must pass.

2.3 External DSL

The developers at *Acme* were happy with the internal DSL implementation, as it
helped them to experiment with FSMs in a familiar programming language. However, the programming-language notation implied a communication barrier between
developers and other stakeholders, who could not discuss matters in terms of programs or did not want to.

An *Acme* developer with competence in language implementation therefore proposed a concise and machine-checkable domain-specific *textual syntax* for FSMs as
exercised below.

Illustration 2.16 (Turnstile FSM in textual syntax)

FSML resource languages/FSML/sample.fsml

```
initial state locked {
  ticket/collect -> unlocked;
  pass/alarm -> exception;
}
state unlocked {
  ticket/eject;
  pass -> locked;
}
state exception {
  ticket/eject;
  pass;
  mute;
  release -> locked;
}
```

In the textual notation, all state declarations group together the transitions with the given state as the source state. The target state of a transition appears to the right of the arrow "−>". If the arrow is missing, this is taken to mean that the target state equals the source state.

2.3.1 Syntax Definition

An *Acme* developer with competence in software language engineering suggested a *grammar*-based syntax definition as follows.

```
fsm : state+ EOF ;
state : 'initial'? 'state' stateid '{' transition* '}' ;
transition : event ('/' action)? ('−>' target=stateid)? ';' ;
stateid : NAME ;
event : NAME ;
action : NAME ;
NAME : ('a'..'z'|'A'..'Z')+ ;
```

A variation of the EBNF [7] notation for context-free grammars [6] is used here. The grammar rules define the syntactic categories ("nonterminals"): state machines (fsm), state declarations (state), transitions (transition), and more basic categories for state ids, events, and actions. Each rule consists of the name of the being defined (on the left), a separator (":"), and the actual definition (on the right) in terms of other grammar symbols. For instance, the rule defining fsm models the fact that an FSM consists of a non-empty sequence of state declarations followed by the EOF (end-of-file) character. The rule defining state models the fact that a state declaration starts with the optional keyword 'initial', followed by the keyword "state", followed by a state id, followed by a sequence of transitions enclosed in braces.

Let us provide a general recipe for authoring a grammar.

Recipe 2.4 (Authoring a grammar).

Samples *Sketch the intended language in terms of a few simple samples (i.e., strings) without trying to design a grammar at the same time. If you have carried out a domain analysis (Section 1.3), then your samples should cover the concepts identified by the analysis.*

Categories *Identify the syntactic categories exercised in your samples (and possibly suggested by your domain analysis), for example, state declarations and transitions in the case of FSML. Assign names to these categories. These names are referred to as* nonterminals, *to be defined by the grammar; they show up on the left-hand sides of grammar rules.*

Alternatives *Identify the alternatives for each category. (Again, a domain analysis may readily provide such details.) FSML is so simple that there is*

> only a single alternative per category, but think of different expression forms
> in a language with arithmetic and comparison expressions. Assign names
> to these alternatives; these names may be used to label grammar rules.
>
> **Structure**   Describe the structure of each alternative in terms of nontermi-
> nals, terminals (keywords and special characters), sequential composition
> (juxtaposition), repetition ("*" or "+"), and optionality ("?").
>
> **Validation**   Ultimately, check that the language samples comply with the au-
> thored grammar, as discussed later (Recipe 2.5).

2.3.2 Syntax Checking

A grammar can be used directly for implementing a *syntax checker* so that everyone
can easily check conformance of given text to the rules of the textual syntax. By implementing such a checker, the *Acme* engineers started a transition from an internal
to an *external DSL*. That is, there was a dedicated frontend for FSML to permit the
representation of FSMs in a language-specific notation without making any concessions to an existing programming language. The *Acme* developer in charge chose
the popular technology ANTLR[5] [11] for implementing the syntax checker. That
is, ANTLR includes a parser generator which generates code for syntax checking
(or parsing) from a given syntax definition (a grammar). The grammar, which was
shown above, can be trivially completed into actual ANTLR input so that most of
the code for a syntax checker can be generated by ANTLR, as shown below.

Illustration 2.17 (An ANTLR input for FSML)

ANTLR resource languages/FSML/Java/Fsml.g4

```
1   grammar Fsml;
2   @header {package org.softlang.fsml;}
3   fsm : state+ EOF ;
4   state : 'initial'? 'state' stateid '{' transition* '}' ;
5   transition : event ('/' action)? ('−>' target=stateid)? ';' ;
6   stateid : NAME ;
7   event : NAME ;
8   action : NAME ;
9   NAME : ('a'..'z'|'A'..'Z')+ ;
10  WS : [ \t\n\r]+ −> skip ;
```

The earlier grammar appears in lines 3–9. Otherwise, the ANTLR input features
the following details.

- The grammar is given a name: Fsml (line 1). This name is used in names of
  generated Java classes such as FsmlParser and FsmlLexer.

---

[5] http://www.antlr.org/

- By means of a header pragma, a Java package name is specified: org.softlang.fsml (line 2). The generated Java classes are put into this package.
- A special grammar symbol for white space is declared: WS (line 10). Such white space is to be skipped in the input, as controlled by the skip action.
- Two of the nonterminals use uppercase identifiers: NAME and WS (lines 9–10). This is a hint to ANTLR that these nonterminals model lexical syntax. That is, the input text is first converted into a sequence NAME and WS tokens as well as keywords or special tokens from the other rules, before parsing commences.

The present section is summarized by means of a recipe.

Recipe 2.5 (Development of a syntax checker).

Grammar *It is assumed that you have authored a grammar and samples according to Recipe 2.4.*

Approach *Choose an approach to grammar implementation. In this section, we favored the use of a parser generator (ANTLR). In Chapter 7, we will also discuss programmatic implementation (recursive descent and parser combinators).*

Driver *Develop driver code for applying the implemented grammar to input.*

Testing *Apply the syntax checker to language samples to confirm their conformance to the grammar. One should also author samples with syntax errors to test that the syntax checker catches the errors and communicates them appropriately.*

In the running example, we still need the driver code for applying the ANTLR-based checker to samples, as shown below.

Illustration 2.18 (Driver code for the generated syntax checker (parser))

Java source code org/softlang/fsml/FsmlSyntaxChecker.java

```
public class FsmlSyntaxChecker {
  public static void main(String[] args) throws IOException {
    FsmlParser parser =
      new FsmlParser(
        new CommonTokenStream(
          new FsmlLexer(
            new ANTLRFileStream(args[0])))));
    parser.fsm();
    System.exit(parser.getNumberOfSyntaxErrors()-Integer.parseInt(args[1]));
  }
}
```

The code is idiosyncratic to ANTLR; it entails the following steps:

- An ANTLRFileStream object is constructed and applied to a filename; this is essentially an input stream to process a text file.

- An FsmlLexer object is wrapped around the stream; this is a lexer (scanner) object as an instance of a class that was generated from the grammar.
- A CommonTokenStream object is wrapped around the lexer; thereby allowing the lexer to communicate with the parser in a standardized manner.
- An FsmlParser object is wrapped around the token stream; this is a parser object as an instance of a class that was generated from the grammar.
- The parser is invoked; in fact, the nonterminal (the method) fsm is selected. As a side effect, a parse tree (CST) is associated with the parser object and parse errors, if any, can be retrieved from the same object.
- Finally, there is an assertion to check for parse errors.

The driver code shown is used by a test suite. We have set up the main method in such a way that we can check positive and negative examples through a command-line interface. That is, two arguments are expected: the name of the input file and the expected number of syntax errors. The main method exits with "0", if the actual number of syntax errors equals the expected number, otherwise it exits with a nonzero code. Let us provide a sample for which syntax checking should fail.

Illustration 2.19 (A syntactically incorrect FSML sample)

FSML resource languages/FSML/tests/syntaxError.fsml

initial state stateA {

The ANTLR-based parser should report a syntax error as follows:

```
..line 2:0 missing '}' at '<EOF>'
```

For the sake of completeness, let us describe the build process of the ANTLR- and Java-based syntax checker, as it combines code generation and compilation. We may capture the involved steps by means of a Makefile[6], as shown below.

Illustration 2.20 (Makefile for the FSML syntax checker)

Makefile resource languages/FSML/Java/Makefile

```
 1  cp = −cp .:../../../lib/Java/antlr−4.5.3−complete.jar
 2  antlr = java ${cp} org.antlr.v4.Tool −o org/softlang/fsml
 3  fsmlSyntaxChecker = java ${cp} org.softlang.fsml.FsmlSyntaxChecker
 4
 5  all:
 6    make generate
 7    make compile
 8    make test
 9
10  generate:
11    ${antlr} Fsml.g4
```

---

[6] http://en.wikipedia.org/wiki/Makefile

```
12
13   compile:
14     javac ${cp} org/softlang/fsml/*.java
15
16   test:
17     ${fsmlSyntaxChecker} ../sample.fsml 0
18     ${fsmlSyntaxChecker} ../tests/syntaxError.fsml 1
```

That is:

- Java's classpath is adjusted to incorporate the ANTLR tool and runtime (line 1).
- The invocation of the ANTLR tool for parser generation boils down to running the main method of the Java class org.antlr.v4.Tool from the ANTLR jar with some option ("-o") for the output directory (line 2 for the command line and line 11 for the actual application).
- The invocation of the syntax checker for FSML boils down to running the main method of the Java class org.softlang.fsml.FsmlSyntaxChecker (line 3 for the command line and lines 17–18 for the actual application). Each invocation involves the input file to be checked and the number of expected syntax errors.

By performing syntax checking at *Acme*, some level of quality assurance regarding the DSL for FSMs was supported. Language users could make sure that their samples conformed to the intended syntax.

2.3.3 Parsing

Now let us suppose that we want to process the textual input on the basis of its grammar-based structure. Thus, we need to make a transition from syntax checking (or "acceptance") to parsing. Classically, the output of parsing is a parse tree or concrete syntax tree (CST), the structure of which is aligned with the underlying grammar. A parser may also perform abstraction to eliminate details that are not relevant for assigning semantics to the input. In this case, the output of parsing is an abstract syntax tree (AST) or an abstract syntax graph (ASG), if the parser additionally performs resolution to discover references in the otherwise tree-based syntactical structure. The output of parsing is also referred to as a "model" in the context of model-driven engineering (MDE). The term "text-to-model" (transformation) may be used instead of "parsing" in the MDE context.

At *Acme*, it was decided that the parser should construct ASTs such that an existing object model for FSMs was used for the representation of ASTs. In this manner, one would be able also to apply well-formedness checking and interpretation (indirectly) to FSMs that are represented as text. This gives rise to the notion of "text-to-objects". The grammar of the ANTLR-based syntax checker was reused. ANTLR support for so-called parse-tree listeners was leveraged to attach functionality to the grammar for the construction of suitable objects.

An ANTLR listener is a collection of programmer-definable handler methods that are invoked by the parsing process at well-defined points. There are, basically, methods for entering and exiting parse-tree nodes for any nonterminal of the grammar. In fact, the methods are invoked during a generic walk over a parse tree that ANTLR constructs during its generic parsing process. Given a grammar, ANTLR generates a suitable listener class (FsmlBaseListener in the present example) with empty handler methods. A programmer may extend the base listener by implementing handler methods that perform object construction. Let us present a listener which facilitates parsing FSMs into objects according to the baseline object model for FSML (Section 2.2.1). The corresponding Java code follows.

Illustration 2.21 (A parse-tree listener for text-to-objects)

Java source code org/softlang/fsml/FsmlToObjects.java

```java
public class FsmlToObjects extends FsmlBaseListener {
  private Fsm fsm;
  private State current;
  public Fsm getFsm() { return fsm; }
  @Override public void enterFsm(FsmlParser.FsmContext ctx) {
    fsm = new Fsm();
  }
  @Override public void enterState(FsmlParser.StateContext ctx) {
    current = new State();
    current.setStateid(ctx.stateid().getText());
    fsm.getStates().add(current);
  }
  @Override public void enterTransition(FsmlParser.TransitionContext ctx) {
    Transition t = new Transition();
    fsm.getTransitions().add(t);
    t.setSource(current.getStateid());
    t.setEvent(ctx.event().getText());
    if (ctx.action() != null) t.setAction(ctx.action().getText());
    t.setTarget(ctx.target != null ? ctx.target.getText() : current.getStateid());
  }
}
```

Thus, the listener extends FsmlBaseListener and it overrides enterFsm, enterState, and enterTransition – these are the events of entering parse-tree nodes rooted in the rules for the nonterminals fsm, state, and transition. The methods construct an FSM object, which is stored in the attribute fsm of the listener.

We also need driver code to compose syntax checking, parse-tree construction (done transparently by the ANTLR runtime), and parse-tree walking with the listener at hand, as shown below.

Illustration 2.22 (Parsing with an ANTLR listener)

Java source code org/softlang/fsml/tests/FsmlToObjectsTest.java

```
1   public Fsm textToObjects(String filename) throws IOException {
2       FsmlParser parser = new FsmlParser(
3           new CommonTokenStream(
4               new FsmlLexer(
5                   new ANTLRFileStream(filename))));
6       ParseTree tree = parser.fsm();
7       assertEquals(0, parser.getNumberOfSyntaxErrors());
8       FsmlToObjects listener = new FsmlToObjects();
9       ParseTreeWalker walker = new ParseTreeWalker();
10      walker.walk(listener, tree);
11      return listener.getFsm();
12  }
```

This process consists of these phases:

- We construct an FsmlParser object and thus also objects for a file stream, a lexer, and a token stream (lines 2–5). We use the same ANTLR grammar and the same generated code as for the syntax checker.
- We invoke the parser (line 6). During parsing the parse tree is constructed and is returned as the result of the method call parser.fsm().
- We check that parsing has completed without errors (line 7), as it would not be sound to access the parse tree otherwise.
- We construct an FsmlToObjects object for listening (line 8), as explained earlier.
- We construct a ParseTreeWalker object (line 9) and we invoke the walker's walk method while passing the listener and the parse tree as arguments (line 10).
- Ultimately, we can extract the constructed AST from the listener object (line 11).

Let us summarize the development steps for obtaining a parser (i.e., a text-to-model or text-to-objects transformation); the recipe given below mentions ANTLR and its listener-based approach while it characterizes the underlying steps also more generally.

Recipe 2.6 (Development of a parser).

Syntax checker   Develop a syntax checker for the language according to Recipe 2.5.

Representation   Design a representation for parse trees, unless a suitable representation is readily provided by the underlying technology such as a parser generator. The representation may be defined, for example, in terms of an object model, by means of JSON, or by other means of abstract syntax implementation (Recipe 4.1).

Parse trees   Implement functionality for the construction of parse trees, unless a suitable representation is readily constructed by the underlying tech-

> *nology. For instance, in the case where ANTLR is used, you may implement a listener for mapping generic ANTLR-specific parse trees to a designated object model.*
> **Driver**   *Generalize the driver code of the underlying syntax checker to perform parsing, i.e., mapping text to parse trees.*
> **Testing**   *Generalize the test suite of the underlying syntax checker to perform parsing, including the validation of the returned parse trees by comparison with baselines.*

Exercise 2.5 (Validation of text-to-objects)   [Intermediate level]
How would you validate that the parser obtained according to Recipe 2.6 constructs reasonable ASTs? To this end, assume that there are a large number of valid textual inputs available. You need to find a scalable approach that takes into account all these inputs.

2.4 DSL Services

Arguably, we have reached the "minimum" of a language implementation: representation (internal style and grammar-based textual syntax), parsing, interpretation, and well-formedness checking. In practice, a DSL is likely to call for yet other language-based components or "services". For the running example, we are going to discuss briefly an interchange format for serializing FSMs, a visual syntax for FSML, and (C) code generation to represent FSMs directly as executable code. Examples of yet other language services, which, however, are not discussed here, include these: a refactoring tool for FSMs (e.g., for renaming state ids), a generator tool for FSMs that could be used to test language services, a language-specific editor, other IDE services, and a verification tool that could be used to prove equivalence or subsumption for FSMs.

2.4.1 Interchange Format

At *Acme*, the developers wanted to implement language-based components in different programming languages while permitting integration of the services on the basis of an interchange format for serialization. For instance, it should be possible to use the output of a Java-based parser in a Python-based well-formedness checker. An interchange format would also make it possible to distribute the language implementation, for example, in a web application. The *Acme* developers agreed on a JSON[7]-based representation as follows.

---
[7] http://json.org/

Illustration 2.23 (A JSON-based model of the turnstile FSM)

JSON resource languages/FSML/Python/tests/baselines/sample.json

```
{"exception": [{
    "initial": false,
    "transitions": {
        "release": [[null, "locked"]],
        "ticket": [["eject", "exception"]],
    "mute": [[null, "exception"]],
    "pass": [[null, "exception"]]}}],
"locked": [{
    "initial": true,
    "transitions": {
        "ticket": [["collect", "unlocked"]],
        "pass": [["alarm", "exception"]]}}],
"unlocked": [{
    "initial": false,
    "transitions": {
        "ticket": [["eject", "unlocked"]],
        "pass": [[null, "locked"]]}}]}
```

JSON is suitable for language-agnostic representation of (nested) dictionary-like data with support for lists and some data types. JSON-based serialization is supported for most, if not all, popular programming languages. In the JSON-based representation of an FSM, as shown above, an FSM is a nested dictionary with the state ids as keys at the top, with keys "initial" and "transitions" per state, and with the events as keys per transition. For each event, a pair consisting of an action ("null" when missing) and a target state is maintained. In fact, each event is mapped to a list of action-state pairs; see the following exercise.

Exercise 2.6 (Lists of action-state pairs)   [Basic level]
What "expressiveness" is gained by mapping events to lists of action-state pairs? Hint: Think of the separation of parsing and well-formedness checking.

The rules underlying the JSON format may be understood as defining the abstract syntax of FSML. The engineers at *Acme* did not bother to define the format explicitly by means of a schema, but this would be possible; see the following exercise.

Exercise 2.7 (A JSON schema for FSML)   [Intermediate level]
Using the example model in Illustration 2.23 and the informal explanations of the format, define a schema in JSON Schema[8] for FSML. Perform schema-based validation on the example.

---

[8] http://json-schema.org/

Exercise 2.8 (A JSON exporter for Java objects)   [Intermediate level]
*Implement an object-to-JSON mapping in Java. Start from the baseline object model
for FSML (Section 2.2.1). Check that the mapping results in the expected JSON
output for the turnstile example.*

Exercise 2.9 (Integrating Java and Python components)   [Intermediate level]
*Use the Java-based parser of Illustration 2.22 to parse text into objects. Use the
Java-based JSON exporter of Exercise 2.8 to serialize objects as JSON. It turns out
that the JSON format, when deserialized into Python with the "standard" load function, fits exactly the representation type of the fluent API implementation in Illustration 2.7. Validate the suitability of the Python objects, thus obtained, by applying
the Python-based components for interpretation and well-formedness checking, as
discussed earlier.*

There are various alternatives to a JSON-based interchange format. Other possible options include XML[9] and ASN.1.[10]

2.4.2 Code Generation

In the recent past, *Acme* engineers discovered that they could use FSMs for generating part of the ultimate implementation. In fact, as FSMs are used at *Acme* for
many different purposes and on many different devices and platforms, several code
generators were developed over time. Prior to using *code generation*, FSMs were
manually implemented in a more or less idiomatic manner.

In principle, one could "execute" FSMs on the target platform by means of some
form of (interactive) interpretation. However, code generation complements interpretation in several ways:

Efficiency   The generated code may potentially be more efficient than interpretation, just in the same way as compiled code typically runs faster than interpreted
code. The execution of the compiled code may also require less runtime resources
than interpretation. In particular, the interpreter itself, including its data structures
would not be needed for running the generated code.

Pluggability   Developers may need to plug actual functionality into FSM execution. For instance, events and actions are merely "symbols" in FSML, but actual
functionality needs to be executed on the target platform so that FSM execution
interacts with sensors and actors. Such pluggability is also feasible with interpretation, but perhaps even more straightforward with generated code.

---

[9] http://www.w3.org/XML/
[10] http://en.wikipedia.org/wiki/Abstract_Syntax_Notation_One

Customizability The actual implementation of behavior, as specified by the FSM, may need customization in some way. For instance, specific conditions may need to be added on transitions and extra housekeeping may need to be arranged to this end. By representing FSMs within a programming language, the programmers may customize functionality in a familiar manner.

Let us develop a simple code generator. Let us assume here that neither Python nor Java is supported on the target platform, which may be a lower-level platform for embedded systems, but there exists a *C* compiler emitting code for the target platform. Thus, our code generator must generate *target code* in the C language (rather than in Java or Python). Before looking at the implementation of the generator, let us agree on a baseline for the generated code, as shown below.

Illustration 2.24 (Generated code for the turnstile FSM)

C resource languages/FSML/Python/generated/Turnstile.c

```
1   enum State { EXCEPTION, LOCKED, UNDEFINED, UNLOCKED };
2   enum State initial = LOCKED;
3   enum Event { RELEASE, TICKET, MUTE, PASS };
4   void collect() { }
5   void alarm() { }
6   void eject() { }
7   enum State next(enum State s, enum Event e) {
8    switch(s) {
9     case EXCEPTION:
10     switch(e) {
11      case RELEASE: return LOCKED;
12      case TICKET: eject(); return EXCEPTION;
13      case PASS: return EXCEPTION;
14      case MUTE: return EXCEPTION;
15      default: return UNDEFINED;
16     }
17    case LOCKED:
18     switch(e) {
19      case TICKET: collect(); return UNLOCKED;
20      case PASS: alarm(); return EXCEPTION;
21      default: return UNDEFINED;
22     }
23    case UNLOCKED:
24     switch(e) {
25      case TICKET: eject(); return UNLOCKED;
26      case PASS: return LOCKED;
27      default: return UNDEFINED;
28     }
29    default: return UNDEFINED;
30   }
31  }
```

The C code contains these elements:

- An enumeration type for the state ids (line 1).
- A declaration for the initial state (line 2).
- An enumeration type for the events (line 3).
- Functions for the actions with empty bodies (lines 4–6).
- A function next (lines 7–31) which takes the current state s and an event e, performs the corresponding action, if any, and returns the new state. This function is defined by a nested switch-statement that dispatches on s and e.

It is up to the developer of the embedded system to wire up the generated code to the functionality for accessing sensors (to observe events) and actors (to perform actions).

Exercise 2.10 (Representation options)   [Intermediate level]
There are several options for code-level representations of FSM transitions: (i) a cascaded switch-statement, as in Illustration 2.24; (ii) a data structure using appropriate data types for collections, as used in the Java-based implementation of the fluent API in Illustration 2.9; and (iii) an OO approach with an abstract base type for states and one concrete subtype per state so that a polymorphic method for state transitions takes the current event and selects an action as well as the target state. What are the tradeoffs of these options, when using the following dimensions for comparison: runtime efficiency, runtime adaptiveness, type safety for generated code, and simplicity of the code generator? (You may need to actually experiment with code generators for the options.)

Let us leverage *template processing* to generate the required C code. The pattern of the code to be generated is represented by a *template*. Template processing boils down to instantiation of templates, i.e., parameterized text, in a program.

One *Acme* developer decided to exercise template processing in Python and to leverage the template engine *Jinja2*[11]. The template is shown below.

Illustration 2.25 (Jinja2-based template for C code for FSM)

Jinja2/C resource languages/FSML/Python/templates/Fsm.jinja2

```
1   enum State { {{states|join(', ')|upper()}} };
2   enum State initial = {{initial|upper}};
3   enum Event { {{events|join(', ')|upper()}} };
4   {% for a in actions %}void {{a}}() { }
5   {% endfor %}
6   enum State next(enum State s, enum Event e) {
7     switch(s) {
8   {% for (s, ts) in transitions %}
9     case {{s|upper()}}:
```

---

[11] http://jinja.pocoo.org/

```
10      switch(e) {
11   {% for (e, a, t) in ts %}
12        case {{e|upper()}}: {% if a %}{{a}}(); {% endif %}return {{t|upper()}};
13   {% endfor %}
14      default: return UNDEFINED;
15      }
16   {% endfor %}
17      default: return UNDEFINED;
18      }
19   }
```

It is best to compare the template with an instance; see again Illustration 2.24. The following concepts are used:

- For as long as the template does not involve templating-specific constructs, the template's text is literally copied to the output. For instance, the header of the method next (line 6) is directly copied from the template to the output.
- A template is parameterized by (Python) data structures that the template may refer to. For instance, there are Jinja2-level for-loops (lines 8 and 11) in the template which loop over parameters such as actions and transitions to generate similar code for all elements of these collection-typed parameters.
- The text content of a parameter, say x, can be inlined by using the notation "$\{\{x\}\}$" where x is a parameter. Parameters either are directly passed to the template or are extracted from other parameters, for example, within for-loops.
- Some parameters are processed by so-called filters; see the occurrences of upper and join. In this manner, the raw text of parameters is manipulated. That is, join composes a list of strings by interspersing another string (here, a comma); upper turns a string into uppercase.

There is more expressiveness for template processing, but we omit a detailed discussion here. The only missing part of the code generator is the functionality for template instantiation as shown below.

Illustration 2.26 (Template instantiation)

Python module FsmICGenerator

```
def generateC(fsm):
        # Initialize data structures
        states = set()
        states.add("UNDEFINED")
        events = set()
        actions = set()
        transitions = list()
        # Aggregate data structures
        for source, [statedecl] in fsm.iteritems():
            ts = list()
            transitions.append((source, ts))
            states.add(source)
            if statedecl["initial"]:
```

```
                    initial = source
                for event, [(action, target)] in statedecl["transitions"].iteritems():
                    events.add(event)
                    if action is not None: actions.add(action)
                    ts.append((event, action, target))
            # Look up template
            env = Environment(loader=FileSystemLoader('templates'), trim_blocks=True)
            fsmTemplate = env.get_template('Fsm.jinja2')
            # Instantiate template
            return fsmTemplate.render(\
                    states = states,\
                    initial = initial,\
                    events = events,\
                    actions = actions,\
                    transitions = transitions)
```

Thus, the template parameters states, events, actions, and transitions are trivially synthesized from the Python objects. Other than that, the code for template instantiation loads the template and renders it.

Another *Acme* developer decided to exercise template processing in Java and to leverage the template engine *StringTemplate*[12] [10]. StringTemplate encourages the use of template *groups*, that is, templates that invoke each other, as shown for FSML below.

Illustration 2.27 (StringTemplate-based templates for C code for FSM)

StringTemplate/C resource languages/FSML/Java/templates/Fsm.stg

```
1   main(states, initial, events, actions, tgroups) ::= <<
2   enum State { <states; format="upper", separator=", "> };
3   enum State initial = <initial; format="upper">;
4   enum Event { <events; format="upper", separator=", "> };
5   <actions:action(); format="lower", separator="\n">
6   enum State next(enum State s, enum Event e) {
7       switch(s) {
8   <tgroups:tgroup(); separator="\n">
9           default: return UNDEFINED;
10      }
11  }>>
12
13  action(a) ::= "void <a>() { }"
14
15  tgroup(g) ::= <<
16          case <g.stateid; format="upper">:
17              switch(e) {
18                  <g.ts:transition(); separator="\n">
19                  default: return UNDEFINED;
20              }>>
21
22  transition(t) ::= <%
```

---

[12] http://www.stringtemplate.org/

```
23   case <t.event; format="upper">:
24   <if(t.action)><t.action; format="lower">(); <endif>
25   return <t.target; format="upper">;%>
```

Let us explain the StringTemplate notation.

- We use a definition form $templ(p) ::= "\dots"$ to define named templates with parameters (such as p) that can invoke each other, just like possibly recursive functions. There is a *main* template (lines 1–11) to start template processing with. There is an *action* template (line 13) for the C code for each action function. There is a *tgroup* template (lines 15–20) for the transitions grouped by source state. There is also a *transition* template (lines 22–25) for the code for a single transition.
- We use $< \%\dots\% >$ instead of "$\dots$" to define multi-line instead of single-line templates.
- We use $<< \dots >>$ instead to define multi-line templates. Compared to $< \%\dots\% >$, indentation and line breaks are transported from the template to the output.
- We use the form $< p >$ to refer to a parameter p, i.e., to inline it as text. We use the form $p : templ()$ to invoke a template *templ* and to pass the parameter p. We use the form $< p.x >$ to refer to the property x of p.
- There are also *format* and *separator* controls that are similar to the filters of Jinja2. There is also expressiveness (if ... endif) for conditional parts, just as in the case of Jinja2.

We omit the Java code for template instantiation; it is very similar to the Python code discussed earlier.

Exercise 2.11 (A more advanced code generator)   [Basic level]
Revise the code generator so that the generated methods for the FSM actions get access to the initiating event, the source state, and the target state. The idea here is that the plugged code for actions may use these additional parameters for richer behavior. This context should be passed by regular arguments to the methods for the actions.

Exercise 2.12 (An object model for C code)   [Intermediate level]
Set up an object model for the subset of C needed in the FSML example. Implement a template-processing component for rendering C code. Implement a mapping between the object models of FSML and C. In this manner, you could implement the code generator in an alternative manner.

The present section is summarized by means of a recipe.

Recipe 2.7 (Development of a code generator).

Test cases   Develop code samples to be generated and complete them into test cases by also listing the corresponding inputs (programs) from which the code samples are to be generated. Strive for simplicity – certainly in the beginning so that code generation is more easily set up. Test that the samples compile and run on the target platform.
Templates   Parameterize the code samples to obtain templates with appropriate parameters, loops, etc.
Data structure   Design the data structure for the template parameters. The basic assumption is that some existing representation types (e.g., an object model) may be appropriate.
Instantiation   Implement the template instantiation functionality such that the data structure for the template parameters is synthesized, templates are loaded, template parameters are assigned, and rendering is done.
Testing   Test the code generator to return the expected code according to the test cases. Some fine tuning of the templates or the expected output may be required, for example, if spaces, line breaks, and indentation are taken into account.

2.4.3 Visualization

While the *Acme* engineers agreed on using textual notation for maintaining FSMs throughout the development cycle, some *Acme* employees insisted that a visual notation would still be needed. In particular, several architects made the point that the visual notation was more suitable for meetings with customers. Accordingly, it was decided to provide visualization functionality such that FSMs could be rendered according to a visual syntax; see Fig. 2.2. The notation is inspired by the whiteboard notation of Section 2.1 (Fig. 2.1). It was also decided that no graphical editor was required, because just rendering FSMs would be sufficient. We mention in passing that some competitors of *Acme* use graphical editors for FSMs, as visual syntax is favored in those companies.

The *Acme* engineer in charge decided that the visualization should be based on the popular technology Graphviz.[13] Graphviz processes input which conforms to the so-called DOT language, with language elements for describing graphs in terms of nodes and edges, as well as various attributes that control details of appearance, as shown below.

---

[13] http://www.graphviz.org/

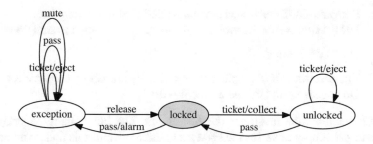

Fig. 2.2 A turnstile FSM in visual notation.

Illustration 2.28 (DOT representation of turnstile FSM)

DOT resource languages/FSML/Python/dot/sample.dot

```
digraph {
  graph [nodesep=0.5,
    rankdir=LR,
    tItle="Sample FSM"
  ];
  exception [shape=ellipse];
  exception -> exception [label="ticket/eject"];
  exception -> exception [label=pass];
  exception -> exception [label=mute];
  locked [shape=ellipse,
    style=filled];
  exception -> locked [label=release];
  locked -> exception [label="pass/alarm"];
  unlocked [shape=ellipse];
  locked -> unlocked [label="ticket/collect"];
  unlocked -> locked [label=pass];
  unlocked -> unlocked [label="ticket/eject"];
}
```

As FSMs are essentially also just node- and edge-labeled graphs, the visualization functionality should be straightforward. Nevertheless, this functionality is interesting in that it allows us to revisit some of the DSL concepts discussed earlier.

Different techniques may be employed for generating the Graphviz input for FSMs. An obvious option is to leverage templates (Section 2.4.2) such that the DOT graph is obtained by instantiating a template that represents the relevant DOT patterns. Another option is to leverage a DOT API, in fact, an implementation of DOT as an internal DSL such that the DOT graph is constructed by a sequence of API calls. Some pros ("+") and cons ("-") may be identified:

- Use template processing for DOT-graph construction:

    +   Relevant DOT constructs are clearly depicted in the template.
    −   DOT's syntax may be violated by the template or the instantiation.

- Use a DOT API instead:

    +   The resulting DOT graphs are syntactically correct by construction.
    −   One needs to understand a specific API.

The following code illustrates the API option. The functionality is straightforward in that it simply traverses the FSM representation and adds nodes and edges to a graph object.

Illustration 2.29 (A visualizer for FSML)

Python module FsmlVisualizer

```
import pygraphviz

def draw(fsm):
    # Create graph
    graph = pygraphviz.AGraph(title="Sample FSM", directed=True, strict=False, rankdir
        ='LR', nodesep=.5)
    # Create nodes
    for fromState, [stateDeclaration] in fsm.iteritems():
        if stateDeclaration["initial"]:
            graph.add_node(n=fromState, shape='ellipse', style='filled')
        else:
            graph.add_node(n=fromState, shape='ellipse')
    # Create edges
    for fromState, [stateDeclaration] in fsm.iteritems():
        for symbol, [(action, toState)] in stateDeclaration["transitions"].iteritems():
            graph.add_edge(fromState, toState, label=symbol + ("" if action is None else
                "/"+action))
    return graph
```

Exercise 2.13 (Template-based visualization)   [Basic level]
Reimplement the visualizer in Illustration 2.29 with template processing instead of using an API for DOT graphs.

Summary and Outline

We have developed the domain-specific language FSML for modeling, simulating, and otherwise supporting finite state machines. Several aspects of language design and implementation were motivated by reference to language users and implementers whom we envisaged, as well as possible changes to requirements over time. The implementation leveraged the programming languages Java, Python, and C as well as additional tools, namely the parser generator ANTLR, the template processors Jinja2 and StringTemplate, and Graphviz with its DOT language.

Clearly, FSML, or any other DSL for that matter, could be implemented in many other ways, within different technological spaces, leveraging different kinds of metaprogramming systems. The online resources of the book come with several alternative implementations. FSML is going to serve as a running example for the remainder of the book.

FSML's language design could be modified and enhanced in many ways. For instance, FSML is clearly related to statecharts in the widely adopted modeling language UML. The statecharts of UML are much more expressive. There is also existing support for statecharts, for example, in terms of code generators in the MDE context. This may suggest a critical discussion to identify possibly additional expressiveness that would also be useful at *Acme*. Also, perhaps, existing UML tooling could provide a more standardized replacement for *Acme*'s proprietary DSL.

In the remaining chapters of this book, we will study the foundations and engineering of syntax, semantics, types, and metaprogramming for software languages. FSML will show up as an example time and again, but we will also discuss other software languages.

References

1. Erdweg, S.: Extensible languages for flexible and principled domain abstraction. Ph.D. thesis, Philipps-Universität Marburg (2013)
2. Erdweg, S., van der Storm, T., Völter, M., Boersma, M., Bosman, R., Cook, W.R., Gerritsen, A., Hulshout, A., Kelly, S., Loh, A., Konat, G.D.P., Molina, P.J., Palatnik, M., Pohjonen, R., Schindler, E., Schindler, K., Solmi, R., Vergu, V.A., Visser, E., van der Vlist, K., Wachsmuth, G., van der Woning, J.: The state of the art in language workbenches – conclusions from the language workbench challenge. In: Proc. SLE, *LNCS*, vol. 8225, pp. 197–217. Springer (2013)
3. Erdweg, S., van der Storm, T., Völter, M., Tratt, L., Bosman, R., Cook, W.R., Gerritsen, A., Hulshout, A., Kelly, S., Loh, A., Konat, G.D.P., Molina, P.J., Palatnik, M., Pohjonen, R., Schindler, E., Schindler, K., Solmi, R., Vergu, V.A., Visser, E., van der Vlist, K., Wachsmuth, G., van der Woning, J.: Evaluating and comparing language workbenches: Existing results and benchmarks for the future. Comput. Lang. Syst. Struct. **44**, 24–47 (2015)
4. Fowler, M.: Refactoring: Improving the Design of Existing Code. Addison Wesley (1999)
5. Fowler, M.: Domain-Specific Languages. Addison-Wesley (2010)
6. Hopcroft, J., Motwani, R., Ullman, J.: Introduction to Automata Theory, Languages, and Computation. Pearson (2013). 3rd edition
7. ISO/IEC: ISO/IEC 14977:1996(E). Information Technology. Syntactic Metalanguage. Extended BNF. (1996). Available at http://www.cl.cam.ac.uk/~mgk25/iso-14977.pdf
8. Kats, L.C.L., Visser, E.: The Spoofax language workbench. In: Companion SPLASH/OOPSLA, pp. 237–238. ACM (2010)
9. Kats, L.C.L., Visser, E.: The Spoofax language workbench: rules for declarative specification of languages and IDEs. In: Proc. OOPSLA, pp. 444–463. ACM (2010)
10. Parr, T.: A functional language for generating structured text (2006). Draft. http://www.stringtemplate.org/articles.html
11. Parr, T.: The Definitive ANTLR 4 Reference. Pragmatic Bookshelf (2013). 2nd edition

12. Renggli, L.: Dynamic language embedding with homogeneous tool support. Ph.D. thesis, Universität Bern (2010)
13. Visser, E., Wachsmuth, G., Tolmach, A.P., Neron, P., Vergu, V.A., Passalaqua, A., Konat, G.: A language designer's workbench: A one-stop-shop for implementation and verification of language designs. In: Proc. SPLASH, Onward!, pp. 95–111. ACM (2014)
14. Voelter, M., Benz, S., Dietrich, C., Engelmann, B., Helander, M., Kats, L.C.L., Visser, E., Wachsmuth, G.: DSL Engineering – Designing, Implementing and Using Domain-Specific Languages. dslbook.org (2013)
15. Voelter, M., Ratiu, D., Kolb, B., Schätz, B.: mbeddr: instantiating a language workbench in the embedded software domain. Autom. Softw. Eng. **20**(3), 339–390 (2013)
16. Völter, M., Visser, E.: Language extension and composition with language workbenches. In: Companion SPLASH/OOPSLA, pp. 301–304. ACM (2010)
17. Wachsmuth, G., Konat, G.D.P., Visser, E.: Language design with the Spoofax language workbench. IEEE Softw. **31**(5), 35–43 (2014)

Chapter 3
Foundations of Tree- and Graph-Based Abstract Syntax

RICHARD PAIGE.[1]

Abstract A software language can be regarded as a set of structured elements with some associated meaning. A language's *syntax* defines its elements and their structure. We may speak of string, tree, and graph languages – to convey the nature of the elements' structure. One may distinguish two forms of syntax: *concrete* versus *abstract syntax*. The former is tailored towards processing (reading, writing, editing) by humans who are language users; the latter is tailored towards processing (parsing, analyzing, transforming, generating) by programs that are authored by language implementers. In this chapter, we cover the foundations of abstract syntax. This includes the notion of *conformance* of terms (trees) or models (graphs) to *signatures* or *metamodels*. The proposed notations for signatures and metamodels correspond to proper software languages in themselves, giving rise to a *metametalevel* that we develop as well. We defer implementation aspects of abstract syntax, coverage of concrete syntax, and semantics of languages to later chapters.

---

[1] The software language engineering community aims to integrate more specialized communities. Richard Paige is a modelware "stronghold"; he has contributed to pretty much everything modelware, for example, model merging and composition [6, 1], model evolution [9], model to text and vice versa [10, 5], and visual syntax [7]. Richard Paige definitely advances community integration in his work, as exemplified by his tutorial on metamodeling for grammar researchers [8] or his Twitter persona.

Artwork Credits for Chapter Opening: This work by Wojciech Kwasnik is licensed under CC BY-SA 4.0. This artwork quotes the artwork *DMT*, acrylic, 2006 by Matt Sheehy with the artist's permission. This work also quotes https://commons.wikimedia.org/wiki/File:Irises-Vincent_van_Gogh.jpg, subject to the attribution "Vincent van Gogh: Irises (1889) [Public domain], via Wikimedia Commons." This work artistically morphes an image, https://www.cs.york.ac.uk/people/paige, showing the person honored, subject to the attribution "Permission granted by Richard Paige for use in this book."

© Springer International Publishing AG, part of Springer Nature 2018
R. Lämmel, *Software Languages*,
https://doi.org/10.1007/978-3-319-90800-7_3

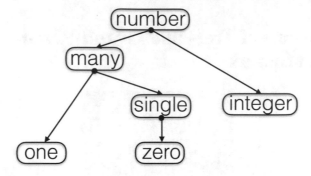

Fig. 3.1 The binary number "10" as a tree.

3.1 Tree-Based Abstract Syntax

The abstract syntax of a language is concerned with the tree- or graph-like structure of language elements. Abstract syntax definitions define languages as sets of trees or graphs. We need a *membership test* to decide whether a given tree or graph is actually an element of the language of interest. To this end, we also speak of conformance of a tree or a graph to a syntax definition, such as a signature or a metamodel. In this section, we focus on tree-based abstract syntax. In the next section, we focus on graph-based abstract syntax.

3.1.1 Trees versus Terms

Let us define the abstract syntax of binary numbers in the sense of a dedicated language: *BNL* (Binary Number Language). We begin by exercising the abstract syntactical representation of numbers; see Fig. 3.1 for a tree-based representation. That is, we use node-labeled rose trees, i.e., trees with any number of subtrees; symbols serve as infos of nodes. The symbols used in a such a tree classify the subtrees at hand. Each symbol has an associated arity (i.e., number of children). The following symbols (with the arity given next to each symbol) are used in the figure:

- *number/2*: The two children are the integer and fractional parts.
- *integer/0*: In fact, there is no fractional part.
- *many/2*: The first child is a digit; the second child is a sequence of digits.
- *single/1*: The child is a digit.
- *one/0*: The digit "1".
- *zero/0*: The digit "0".

For most of this book, we will prefer term-based representations of such trees, but we assume that it is obvious how to go back and forth between the term- and tree-based views. The term-based counterpart to Fig. 3.1 is shown below.

Illustration 3.1 (The binary number "10" as a term)

Term resource languages/BNL/samples/10.term

```
number(
  many(
    one,
    single(
      zero)),
  integer).
```

That is, a simple prefix notation is used here for terms. A function symbol serves as the prefix (e.g., number or many) and the arguments (say, subterms or subtrees) are enclosed in parentheses. Indentation is used here as a visual hint at the tree-like structure.

3.1.2 A Basic Signature Notation

One could use informal text to define (abstract) syntax. We prefer more formal means. We use (many-sorted algebraic) *signatures* [11, 4] for defining tree (term) languages. We propose a specific notation here: *BSL* (*B*asic *S*ignature *L*anguage). This is a "fabricated" language of this book, but similar notations are part of established languages for formal specification, algebraic specification, term rewriting, and functional programming. Let us apply BSL to BNL as follows.

Illustration 3.2 (Abstract syntax of BNL)

BSL resource languages/BNL/as.bsl

```
symbol number: bits × rest → number ; // A binary number
symbol single: bit → bits ; // A single bit
symbol many: bit × bits → bits ; // More than one bit
symbol zero: → bit ; // The zero bit
symbol one: → bit ; // The nonzero bit
symbol integer: → rest ; // An integer number
symbol rational: bits → rest ; // A rational number
```

A (BSL-based) many-sorted algebraic *signature* is a list of types of function symbols. Each *type* (or *profile*) consists of the function symbol, a list of argument sorts (say, argument types), and a result sort (say, the result type). A function symbol with zero argument sorts is also called a constant symbol. Sorts are not separately declared; they are implicitly introduced, as they appear in types of function symbols.

An abstract syntax abstracts from representational details that surface in a concrete syntax. That is, an abstract syntax definition does not necessarily cover all notational variations and details that may just be part of the concrete syntax for language users' convenience. In a very limited manner, such abstraction can be observed even in the trivial signature for BNL. That is, no separator between integer and fractional parts is expressed. We will consider more interesting forms of abstraction later, when we study concrete syntax (Chapter 6).

The intended interpretation of a signature is the set of terms that can be built recursively from the function symbols with the constants as base cases. Of course, such term construction must obey the types of the symbols.

Simply because we can switch back and forth between trees and terms, as illustrated above, we can also view a signature as a tree grammar [3], i.e., a grammar that defines (generates) a set of trees.

3.1.3 Abstract Syntax Trees

When terms are generated by a signature meant for abstract syntax definition, then we refer to these terms also as abstract syntax trees (ASTs). Given a signature and a term, there is a simple way to show that the term is indeed a valid AST with regard to the signature, i.e., a term "generated" by the signature. This is the case if each function symbol of the term is declared by the signature and it is used with the declared arity (i.e., number of subterms), and each subterm is built from a function symbol, with the result sort agreeing with the argument sort of the position in which the subterm occurs, as illustrated for binary numbers and their syntax below.

Illustration 3.3 (A term generated by a signature)
The term of Illustration 3.1 is a term generated by the signature of Illustration 3.2 in accordance with the following evidence:

- *number(*   symbol number: bits × rest → number ;

  - *many(*   symbol many: bit × bits → bits ;
    · *one,*   symbol one: → bit ;
    · *single(*   symbol single: bit → bits ;
      · *zero)),*   symbol zero: → bit ;
  - *integer).*   symbol integer : → rest ;

Exercise 3.1 (BNL with negative numbers)   [Basic level]
Extend the signature of Illustration 3.2 to enable negative binary numbers.

Exercise 3.2 (Redundancy in an abstract syntax) [Intermediate level]
The obvious solution to Exercise 3.1 would enable a redundant representation of "0" (i.e., zero) with a positive and a negative zero. Further, the initial abstract syntax definition in Illustration 3.2 permits a form of redundancy. That is, bit sequences with leading zeros before "." or bit sequences with trailing zeros after "." can be represented, for example, "0010" instead of just "10". Define an abstract syntax that avoids both forms of redundancy.

3.1.4 An Extended Signature Notation

Consider again the signature in Illustration 3.2. There are issues of conciseness. That is, optionality of the fractional part is encoded by the function symbols integer and rational, subject to an "auxiliary" sort rest. Sequences of bits are encoded by the function symbols single and many, subject to an "auxiliary" sort bits. These are recurring idioms which can be expressed more concisely in an extended signature notation. We propose a specific notation here: *ESL* (*E*xtended *S*ignature *L*anguage). This is a "fabricated" language of this book, but the notation is again inspired by established languages for algebraic specification, term rewriting, and functional programming. We begin by exercising a more concise representation of numbers. Let us apply ESL to BNL as follows.

Illustration 3.4 (More concise abstract syntactical representation of "10")

Term resource languages/BNL/ESL/samples/10.term

([one, zero], []).

We use standard notation for tuples ("$(\cdots)$") and lists ("$[\cdots]$"). Numbers are pairs of integer and fractional parts; both parts are simply sequences of bits, as captured by the following signature.

Illustration 3.5 (More concise abstract syntax of BNL)

ESL resource languages/BNL/ESL/as.esl

```
type number = bit+ × bit∗ ;
symbol zero: → bit ;
symbol one: → bit ;
```

These are all the constructs of ESL:

- symbol declarations as in BSL;

- type declarations to define (say, alias) types in terms of other types;
- list types $t*$ and $t+$ for a given type t;
- optional types t? for a given type t;
- tuple types $t_1 \times \ldots \times t_n$ for given types $t_1, \ldots, t_n$;
- primitive types:

  - boolean;
  - integer;
  - float;
  - string;
  - term ("all conceivable terms"; see Definition 3.3).

3.1.5 Illustrative Examples of Signatures

We define the tree-based abstract syntax of a few more languages here. We revisit ("fabricated") languages that were introduced in Chapter 1.

3.1.5.1 Syntax of Simple Expressions

Let us define the abstract syntax of the expression language BTL.

Illustration 3.6 (Abstract syntax of BTL)

BSL resource languages/BTL/as.bsl

```
symbol true :  → expr ; // The Boolean "true"
symbol false :  → expr ; // The Boolean "false"
symbol zero :  → expr ; // The natural number zero
symbol succ : expr → expr ; // Successor of a natural number
symbol pred : expr → expr ; // Predecessor of a natural number
symbol iszero : expr → expr ; // Test for a number to be zero
symbol if : expr × expr × expr → expr ; // Conditional
```

It may be interesting to reflect on the conceivable differences between abstract and concrete syntax. In particular, a concrete syntax may favor "mixfix" syntax "*if ... then ... else ...*" for the conditional form. In an abstract syntax, we use prefix notation universally.

3.1.5.2 Syntax of Simple Imperative Programs

Let us define the abstract syntax of the imperative programming language BIPL.

Illustration 3.7 (Abstract syntax of BIPL)

ESL resource languages/BIPL/as.esl

// Statements
symbol skip : → stmt ;
symbol assign : string × expr → stmt ;
symbol seq : stmt × stmt → stmt ;
symbol if : expr × stmt × stmt → stmt ;
symbol while : expr × stmt → stmt ;

// Expressions
symbol intconst : integer → expr ;
symbol var : string → expr ;
symbol unary : uop × expr → expr ;
symbol binary : bop × expr × expr → expr ;

// Unary operators
symbol negate : → uop ;
symbol not : → uop ;

// Binary operators
symbol or : → bop ;
symbol and : → bop ;
symbol lt : → bop ;
symbol leq : → bop ;
symbol eq : → bop ;
symbol geq : → bop ;
symbol gt : → bop ;
symbol add : → bop ;
symbol sub : → bop ;
symbol mul : → bop ;

Thus, there are symbols for the empty statement ("skip"), assignment, if-then-else, while-loops, and sequences of statements. There are symbols for expression forms and operator symbols. We use the primitive type integer for integer literals in the abstract syntax. We use the primitive type string for variable names in the abstract syntax.

3.1.5.3 Syntax of Simple Functional Programs

Let us define the abstract syntax of the functional programming language BFPL.

Illustration 3.8 (Abstract syntax of BFPL)

ESL resource languages/BFPL/as.esl

// Program = typed functions + main expression
type **program** = functions × expr ;
type **functions** = function* ;
type **function** = string × funsig × fundef ;
type **funsig** = simpletype* × simpletype ;
type **fundef** = string* × expr ;

// Simple types
symbol **inttype** : → simpletype ;
symbol **booltype** : → simpletype ;

// Expressions
symbol **intconst** : integer → expr ;
symbol **boolconst** : boolean → expr ;
symbol **arg** : string → expr ;
symbol **if** : expr × expr × expr → expr ;
symbol **unary** : uop × expr → expr ;
symbol **binary** : bop × expr × expr → expr ;
symbol **apply** : string × expr* → expr ;

// Unary and binary operators
...

3.1.5.4 Syntax of Finite State Machines

Let us define the abstract syntax of the domain-specific modeling language FSML.

Illustration 3.9 (Abstract syntax of FSML)

ESL resource languages/FSML/as.esl

type **fsm** = state* ;
type **state** = initial × stateid × transition* ;
type **initial** = boolean ;
type **transition** = event × action? × stateid ;
type **stateid** = string ;
type **event** = string ;
type **action** = string ;

Because FSMs have such a simple structure, we can define the abstract syntax solely in terms of lists, tuples, optional elements, and primitive types – without introducing any FSML-specific function symbols. We represent the familiar turnstile example according to this signature as follows.

Illustration 3.10 (Abstract syntactical representation of a turnstile FSM)

Term resource languages/FSML/sample.term

```
[
  (true,locked,[
    (ticket,[collect],unlocked),
    (pass,[alarm],exception)]),

  (false,unlocked,[
    (ticket,[eject],unlocked),
    (pass,[],locked)]),

  (false,exception,[
    (ticket,[eject],exception),
    (pass,[],exception),
    (mute,[],exception),
    (release,[],locked)])
].
```

3.1.6 Languages as Sets of Terms

We may complement the informal explanation of tree-based abstract syntax, given so far, with formal definitions.

Definition 3.1 ((Many-sorted algebraic) signature) *A signature Σ is a triple $\langle F, S, P \rangle$, where F is a finite set of function symbols, S is a finite set of sorts, and P is a finite set of types of function symbols ("profiles") as a subset of $F \times S^* \times S$. There are no distinct types $\langle f_1, a_1, s_1 \rangle$, $\langle f_2, a_2, s_2 \rangle \in P$ with $f_1 = f_2$. For any $\langle c, \langle \rangle, s \rangle \in P$ (i.e., a type with the empty sequence of argument sorts), we say that c is a constant symbol.*

Definition 3.2 (Terms of a sort) *Given a signature $\Sigma = \langle F, S, P \rangle$, the set of terms of a given sort $s \in S$, also denoted by Φ_s, is defined as the smallest set closed under these rules:*

- *If c is a constant symbol of sort $s \in S$, i.e., $\langle c, \langle \rangle, s \rangle \in P$, then $c \in \Phi_s$.*
- *If $\langle f, \langle s_1, \ldots, s_n \rangle, s \rangle \in P$, $n > 0$, s, s_1, $\ldots$, $s_n \in S$, $t_1 \in \Phi_{s_1}$, $\ldots$, $t_n \in \Phi_{s_n}$, then $f(t_1, \ldots, t_n) \in \Phi_s$.*

3.1.7 Conformance to a Signature

We will now set out the concept of conformance to decide whether a given term is actually an element of a certain sort for a given signature. To this end, we assume a possibly infinite set F^U of candidate function symbols, and we define a set $\Sigma(F^U)$ of all terms that can be built from F^U so that we can refer to $\Sigma(F^U)$ as the universe on which to define conformance. As the terms in $\Sigma(F^U)$ are constructed "before" distinguishing any sorts, we also call them pre-terms.

Definition 3.3 (Pre-terms) *Given a set F^U of candidate function symbols, the set of all pre-terms, also denoted by $\Sigma(F^U)$, is defined as the smallest set closed under these rules:*

- *$F^U \subset \Sigma(F^U)$.*
- *For all $f \in F^U, n > 0$, if $t_1, \ldots, t_n \in \Sigma(F^U)$, then $f(t_1,\ldots,t_n) \in \Sigma(F^U)$.*

Conformance is easily defined in an algorithmic manner.

Definition 3.4 (Conformance of a pre-term to a signature) *Given a set F^U of candidate function symbols, a pre-term $t \in \Sigma(F^U)$ and a signature $\Sigma = \langle F,S,P \rangle$ with $F \subseteq F^U$, we say that t is of sort $s \in S$ and conforms to Σ, also denoted by $\Sigma \vdash t : s$, if:*

- *$t \in F^U$ and $\langle t, \langle \rangle, s \rangle \in P$, or*
- *t is of the form $f(t_1,\ldots,t_n)$ such that*

  - *$f \in F^U$, and*
  - *$t_1,\ldots,t_n \in \Sigma(F^U)$, and*
  - *$\langle t, \langle s_1,\ldots,s_n \rangle, s \rangle \in P$ for some $s_1,\ldots,s_n \in S$, and*
  - *$\Sigma \vdash t_1 : s_1, \ldots, \Sigma \vdash t_n : s_n$.*

Operationally, given a pre-term, its sort is the result sort of the outermost function symbol, while the sorts of the subterms must be checked recursively to ensure that they are equal to the argument sorts of the function symbol.

3.2 Graph-Based Abstract Syntax

Many if not most software languages involve conceptual references in that one may want to refer in one position of a compound element to another position. Thus, one may need to model *reference relationships*. Tree-based abstract syntax is limited in this respect, as language elements are simply decomposed into parts in a tree-like manner; references need to be encoded and resolved programmatically. Graph-based abstract syntax distinguishes whole-part and referencing relationships. In this section, we use a simple *metamodeling* notation for defining graph languages.

3.2.1 Trees versus Graphs

We illustrate graph-based abstract syntax here with the Buddy Language (BL) for modeling persons with their names and buddy relationships. This is a "fabricated" language of this book, but it can be viewed as a simple variant of the popular example *FOAF* ("friends of a friend"). We begin with a tree-based variant of the Buddy Language, as illustrated below.

Illustration 3.11 (Two buddies as a term)

Term resource languages/BL/samples/small-world.term

[(joe, [bill]), (bill, [joe])].

Joe's buddy is Bill. Bill's buddy is Joe. Thus, the idea is that persons' names function as "ids" of persons. We use these ids in the term-based representation to refer to buddies. Arguably, names are not necessarily unique. Thus, in practice, we should use other means of identification, for example, social security numbers, but we will keep things simple here. Thus, the tree-based abstract syntax of the Buddy Language may be defined as follows.

Illustration 3.12 (Tree-based abstract syntax of BL)

ESL resource languages/BL/as.esl

type world = person* ;
type person = string × string? ;

The expected meaning of the names as acting as references is not captured by the signature. We may be able to define a separate analysis that checks names for consistent use, but such an analysis is not prescribed by the signature and not standardized as part of conformance.

Once we use a graph-based syntax we can model references explicitly. This is demonstrated now for a graph-based variant of the Buddy Language. The following illustration shows a graph rather than a tree for Joe and Bill's buddy relationships.

Illustration 3.13 (Two buddies as a graph)

Graph resource languages/BL/samples/small-world.graph

```
0 & { class : world,
   persons : [
     1 & { class : person, name : 'joe', buddy : [ #2 ] },
     2 & { class : person, name : 'bill', buddy : [ #1 ] } ] }.
```

Thus, a graph is essentially a container of potentially labeled sub-graphs with base cases for references (such as "#2") or primitive values (such as "joe"). In the example, the complete graph models a "world"; there are two subgraphs for persons. List brackets "[···]" are used here to deal with optionality of buddies. (In general, list brackets may also be used to deal with list cardinalities, i.e., "+" and "*".) In the example, the references to buddies are optional. A (sub-) graph is made referable by assigning an id to it, as expressed by the notation "1 & ..." above. The labels for sub-graphs (such as "name" or "buddy") can be thought of as selectors for those sub-graphs. We use a special label "class" to record the type of a sub-graph. Types are to be described eventually by a metamodel.

3.2.2 Languages as Sets of Graphs

Let us define the set of (resolvable) pre-graphs, i.e., all as yet "untyped" graphs, akin to the pre-terms of Definition 3.3 for tree-based abstract syntax. For simplicity, the definition does not cover primitive values and lists.

Definition 3.5 (Pre-graphs) *Given sets L^U and R^U, referred to as (universes of) labels (for sub-graphs) and ids (for referencing), the set of all pre-graphs, also denoted by $M(L^U, R^U)$, is defined as the smallest set closed under this rule:*

- *If $r \in R^U$ and*
  $g_1, \ldots, g_n \in M(L^U, R^U) \cup R^U$ *and*
  distinct $l_1, \ldots, l_n \in L^U$,
  then $\langle r, \{\langle l_1, g_1 \rangle, \ldots, \langle l_n, g_n \rangle\}\rangle \in M(L^U, R^U)$.

The component r of the pre-graph is referred to as its id.

Thus, pre-graphs are essentially sets of labeled pre-graphs with an id for the collection. There is the special case in which a sub-pre-graph is not a collection (not even an empty collection), but it is a reference, which is why the g_i may also be drawn from R^U in the definition.

We should impose an important constraint on pre-graphs: they should be resolvable, such that assigned ids are distinct, and, for each id used as a reference, there should be a sub-pre-graph with that assigned id. Let us first define sets of sub-pre-graphs and references of a given pre-graph which we need to refer to when formulating the constraint described above.

Definition 3.6 (Sub-pre-graphs and pre-graph references) *Given a pre-graph $g \in M(L^U, R^U)$, the multi-set of its sub-pre-graphs, also denoted by $SPG(g)$, is defined as the smallest multi-set closed under these rules:*

- $g \in SPG(g)$.
- *If $\langle r, \{\langle l_1, g_1 \rangle, \ldots, \langle l_n, g_n \rangle\}\rangle \in SPG(g)$ for appropriate r, $l_1, \ldots, l_n$, and $g_1, \ldots, g_n$, then $SPG(g_i) \subset SPG(g)$ for $1 \le i \le n$ and g_i is a pre-graph (and not a reference).*

The set of pre-graph references, also denoted by $PGR(g)$, is defined as the smallest set closed under this rule:

- *If $\langle r, \{\langle l_1, g_1 \rangle, \ldots, \langle l_n, g_n \rangle\}\rangle \in SPG(g)$ for appropriate r, $l_1, \ldots, l_n$, and $g_1, \ldots, g_n$, then $g_i \in PGR(g)$ for $1 \le i \le n$ and g_i is a reference (and not a pre-graph).*

We use a multi-set rather than a plain set when gathering sub-pre-graphs because, in this manner, we can "observe" identical sub-pre-graphs (with also the same id); see the following definition.

Definition 3.7 (Resolvable pre-graph) *A pre-graph $g \in M(L^U, R^U)$ is said to be resolvable if the following conditions hold:*

- *For all distinct $g_1, g_2 \in SPG(g)$, the ids of g_1 and g_2 are distinct.*
- *$SPG(g)$ is a set (rather than a proper multi-set).*
- *For all $r \in PGR(g)$, there exists a $g' \in SPG(g)$ such that its id equals r.*

The first condition condition requires that all sub-pre-graphs have a distinct id. Additionally, the second rules out (completely) identical sub-pre-graphs. The third condition requires that each reference used equals the id of one sub-pre-graph.

3.2.3 A Metamodeling Notation

On top of this basic formal model, we can define metamodels for describing sets of graphs in the same way as signatures describe sets of terms.

We propose a specific notation here: *MML* (MetaModeling Language). This is a "fabricated" language of this book, but the notation is inspired by established metamodeling frameworks such as *EMF*'s metamodeling language *Ecore*[2]. Let us

---

[2] https://eclipse.org/modeling/emf/

reapproach the Buddy Language; see the following metamodel for graph-based as opposed to tree-based abstract syntax.

Illustration 3.14 (Graph-based abstract syntax of BL)

MML resource languages/BL/gbl.mml

```
class world { part persons : person* ; }
class person {
  value name : string ;
  reference buddy : person? ;
}
datatype string ;
```

That is, a metamodel describes a set of classes with members for values, parts, and references with an associated cardinality ("?" for optional members, "*" and "+" for lists). In the metamodel shown, the persons of a world are modeled as parts, whereas the buddy of a person is modeled as a reference. While it is not demonstrated by the simple metamodel at hand, classes may also be related by inheritance so that a sub-class inherits all members from its super-class. Classes may also be abstract to express the fact that they cannot be instantiated.

Let us also show a metamodel for BL which does not involve references, but it encodes references by means of persons' names, just like in the case of the earlier signature-based model.

Illustration 3.15 (A metamodel for BL without references)

MML resource languages/BL/tbl.mml

```
class world { part persons : person* ; }
class person {
  value name : string ;
  value buddy : string? ;
}
datatype string ;
```

3.2.4 Conformance to a Metamodel

We omit the definition of conformance of a pre-graph to a metamodel; it is relatively straightforward and easy to define and implement; it is similar to conformance of a pre-term to a signature. In particular, each sub-graph would need to conform to its class in terms of the members of the class, as prescribed by the metamodel.

Exercise 3.3 (Pre-graph-to-metamodel conformance)   [Intermediate level]
Define pre-graph-to-metamodel conformance.

When graphs conform to a metamodel meant for abstract syntax definition, then we refer to these graphs as abstract syntax graphs (ASGs). We may also say "model" instead of "graph".

Exercise 3.4 (Metamodeling with EMF)   [Intermediate level]
Study the Eclipse Modeling Framework (EMF) and define an Ecore-based abstract syntax of BL.

3.2.5 Illustrative Examples of Metamodels

Many software languages involve references conceptually once we take into account the meaning of language elements or the assumed result of checking well-formedness.

3.2.5.1 Syntax of Finite State Machines

The target state ids in FSML's transitions may be viewed as references to states. Accordingly, we may also define a graph-based abstract syntax for FSML as shown below. We begin with a corresponding metamodel, followed by a model (a graph) for the turnstile FSM.

Illustration 3.16 (A metamodel for FSML with references)

MML resource languages/FSML/mm.mml

```
class fsm { part states : state* ; }
class state {
  value initial : boolean ;
  value stateid : string ;
  part transitions : transition* ;
}
class transition {
  value event : string ;
  value action : string? ;
  reference target : state ;
}
datatype boolean ;
datatype string ;
```

Illustration 3.17 (Graph-based representation of a turnstile FSM)

Graph resource languages/FSML/sample.graph

```
{
 class : fsm,
 states : [
  1 & {
   class : state,
   initial : true,
   stateid : 'locked',
   transitions : [
    {
     class : transition,
     event : 'ticket',
     action : ['collect'],
     target : #2
    },
    ...
   ]
  },
  2 & { ...
  },
  3 & { ...
  }
 ]
}.
```

3.2.5.2 Syntax of Simple Functional Programs

Exercise 3.5 (A metamodel for BFPL)   [Basic level]
Consider function applications in the functional language BFPL. The name in a function application can be understood as a reference to the corresponding function declaration. Accordingly, devise a graph-based abstract syntax for BFPL by turning the signature of Illustration 3.8 into a metamodel with references for functions used in function applications.

3.3 Context Conditions

The abstract syntax definitions discussed thus far do not capture all the constraints that one would want to assume for the relevant languages. Here are a few examples:

Imperative programs (BIPL) We may require that a program should only use a variable in an expression once the variable has been assigned a value. Also, when operators are applied to subexpressions, the types of the latter should agree with the operand types of the former. These are name binding or typing constraints that are not captured by BIPL's signature.

Functional programs (BFPL) We may require that the function name of a function application can actually be resolved to a function declaration with a suitable type. Again, when operators are applied to subexpressions, the types of the latter should agree with the operand types of the former. These are typing constraints that are not captured by BFPL's signature.

Finite state machines (FSML) We may require, for example, that, in a given state, for a given event, at most one transition is feasible. Also, each state id referenced as a target of a transition must be declared. These are well-formedness constraints that are not captured by FSML's signature. The consistent referencing of (target) states is modeled by FSML's metamodel.

Buddy relationships (BL) We may require that a buddy graph (i.e., a BL world) should not contain any person whose buddy is that person themselves. This is a well-formedness constraint that is not captured by BL's metamodel.

Typical formalisms used for syntax definition – such as those leveraged in this chapter, but also context-free grammars, as leveraged in the context of concrete syntax definition (Chapter 6) – do not permit the capture of all constraints that one may want to assume for software languages. It is not uncommon to differentiate between *context-free* and *context-sensitive syntax*. The former refers to the more structural part of syntax, as definable by signatures, metamodels, or context-free grammars (Chapter 6). The latter assumes a definition that includes constraints requiring "context sensitivity" in terms of, for example, using names. One can model such typing or well-formedness constraints either by a metaprogram-based analysis (Chapter 5, specifically Section 5.3) or by means of dedicated formalisms, for example, type systems (Chapter 9) and attribute grammars (Chapter 12).

3.4 The Metametalevel

The notations for syntax definition (BSL, ESL, and MML) correspond to proper software languages in themselves. In this section, tree- or graph-based syntaxes of these syntax definition languages are defined. Accordingly, we operate at the *metametalevel*. In this manner, we advise on a representation of syntax definitions and thereby prepare for metaprograms that operate on the representation. For instance, we will eventually be able to approach conformance checking as a simple metaprogramming problem (Section 4.2).

3.4.1 The Signature of Signatures

To facilitate understanding, we look at the basic signature notation first. Its abstract syntax is modeled in the extended signature notation, as specified below.

Specification 3.1 (The ESL signature of BSL signatures)

ESL resource languages/BSL/as.esl

type signature = profile* ;
type profile = sym × sort* × sort ;
type sym = string ;
type sort = string ;

Thus, any signature can be represented as a term, as illustrated below.

Illustration 3.18 (BNL's signature in abstract syntax)

Term resource languages/BNL/as.term

[(number, [bits, rest], number),
  (single, [bit], bits),
  (many, [bit, bits], bits),
  (zero, [], bit),
  (one, [], bit),
  (integer, [], rest),
  (rational, [bits], rest)].

BSL cannot be described in itself, i.e., there is no BSL signature of BSL signatures because BSL lacks ESL's strings needed for the representation of function symbols and sorts. However, ESL can be described in itself as shown below.

Specification 3.2 (The ESL signature of ESL signatures)

ESL resource languages/ESL/as.esl

type signature = decl* ;
symbol type : sort × typeexpr → decl ;
symbol symbol : fsym × typeexpr* × sort → decl ;
symbol boolean : → typeexpr ;
symbol integer : → typeexpr ;
symbol float : → typeexpr ;
symbol string : → typeexpr ;
symbol term : → typeexpr ;
symbol sort : sort → typeexpr ;
symbol star : typeexpr → typeexpr ;
symbol plus : typeexpr → typeexpr ;
symbol option : typeexpr → typeexpr ;
symbol tuple : typeexpr* → typeexpr ;

```
type sort = string ;
type fsym = string ;
```

The signature does not capture several constraints that we may want to assume for a signature to be well-formed:

- The function symbols of the declared function types are distinct.
- The names of declared types are distinct.
- There is no name that is declared both as a type and as a sort (i.e., as a result type of a function symbol).

One may also expect a constraint that all referenced type and sort names are actually declared. More strongly, one could require that all sorts are "reachable" from a designated top-level sort and that all sorts are "productive" in that there exist terms of each sort. We do not commit to these extra constraints, however, because we may want to deal with incomplete signatures or modules, which could, for example, reference names (types or sorts) that are not declared in the same file.

3.4.2 The Signature of Metamodels

We can devise a signature for the tree-based abstract syntax of metamodels.

Specification 3.3 (The ESL signature of MML metamodels)

ESL resource languages/MML/as.esl

```
type metamodel = classifier* ;
symbol class : abstract × cname × extends? × member* → classifier ;
symbol datatype : cname → classifier ;
type member = kind × mname × cname × cardinality ;
symbol value : → kind ;
symbol part : → kind ;
symbol reference : → kind ;
symbol one : → cardinality ;
symbol option : → cardinality ;
symbol star : → cardinality ;
symbol plus : → cardinality ;
type abstract = boolean ;
type extends = cname ;
type cname = string ;
type mname = string ;
```

3.4.3 The Metamodel of Metamodels

We can devise a metamodel for the graph-based abstract syntax of metamodels.

Specification 3.4 (The MML metamodel of MML metamodels)

MML resource languages/MML/mm.mml

```
abstract class base { value name : string; }
class metamodel { part classifiers : classifier*; }
abstract class classifier extends base { }
class datatype extends classifier { }
class class extends classifier {
    value abstract : boolean;
    reference super : class?;
    part members : member*;
}
abstract class member extends base { part cardinality : cardinality; }
class value extends member { reference type : datatype; }
class part extends member { reference type : class; }
class reference extends member { reference type : class; }
abstract class cardinality { }
class one extends cardinality { }
class option extends cardinality { }
class star extends cardinality { }
class plus extends cardinality { }
datatype string;
datatype boolean;
```

The metamodel of metamodels can also be represented as a model – in fact, as an instance of itself. This underlines its status as a metametamodel.

Specification 3.5 (Excerpt of the metametamodel)

Graph resource languages/MML/mm.graph

```
{ class:metamodel,
  classifiers:[
    ( base & { class:class, name:base,
        abstract:true,
        super:[],
        members:[{class:value, name:name, type: #string, cardinality:{class:one}}]}),
    ( metamodel & { class:class, name:metamodel, ...
    ( classifier & { class:class, name:classifier, ...
    ( class & { class:class, name:class, ...
    ( member & { class:class, name:member, ...
    ...
  ]}.
```

Just as in the case of the language of signatures, we may also impose constraints on the language of metamodels, such as that the names of declared classes should be distinct; we omit a discussion of these routine details.

Summary and Outline

Some of the content of this chapter can be summarized in a recipe as follows.

Recipe 3.1 (Authoring an abstract syntax definition).

Syntactic categories   *Identify the syntactic categories of the language such as state declarations and transitions in the case of FSML. Assign names to these categories. This identification process may also have been completed as part of a domain analysis (Section 1.3). The assigned names are also referred to as sorts in an algebraic signature or as classes in a metamodel.*

Trees versus graphs   *Make a choice as to whether tree- or graph-based abstract syntax should be defined. You may prefer trees if the metaprogramming approach at hand favors trees or if references within the software language artifacts are easily resolved on top of trees.*

Alternatives   *Identify the alternatives for each category. (Again, a domain analysis may readily provide such details.) Assign names to these alternatives; these names may be used as function symbols in a signature or as class names in a metamodel.*

Structure   *Describe the structure of each alternative in terms of, for example, part-whole relationships or reference relationships, while making appropriate use of cardinalities (optionality, repetition), as supported by the syntax definition formalism at hand.*

Validation   *Author samples so that the abstract syntax is exercised. Ultimately, you will want to check that the samples conform to the authored signature or metamodel, as discussed in a later recipe (Recipe 4.1).*

We have explained how trees and graphs may be used for abstract syntactical representation. We have also explained how signatures and metamodels may be used for modeling abstract syntax. The syntax definition formalisms described are inspired by notations used in practice, although some conveniences and expressiveness may be missing. In metamodeling, in particular, one may use a richer formalism with coverage of constraints (e.g., OCL constraints [2]).

In the next chapter, we will discuss the *implementation* of abstract syntax. Afterwards, we will engage in metaprogramming on top of abstract syntax. We are also prepared for metaprograms that process syntax definitions, since we have described the signature of signatures and other such metametalevel definitions in this chapter. A few chapters down the road, we will complement abstract syntax with concrete syntax for the purpose of defining, parsing, and formatting string languages.

References

1. Bézivin, J., Bouzitouna, S., Fabro, M.D.D., Gervais, M., Jouault, F., Kolovos, D.S., Kurtev, I., Paige, R.F.: A canonical scheme for model composition. In: Proc. ECMDA-FA, *LNCS*, vol. 4066, pp. 346–360. Springer (2006)
2. Clark, T., Warmer, J. (eds.): Object Modeling with the OCL, The Rationale behind the Object Constraint Language, *LNCS*, vol. 2263. Springer (2002)
3. Comon, H., Dauchet, M., Gilleron, R., Löding, C., Jacquemard, F., Lugiez, D., Tison, S., Tommasi, M.: Tree automata techniques and applications. Available at http://www.grappa.univ-lille3.fr/tata (2007)
4. Heering, J., Hendriks, P.R.H., Klint, P., Rekers, J.: The Syntax Definition Formalism SDF. reference manual. SIGPLAN Not. **24**(11), 43–75 (1989)
5. Herrera, A.S., Willink, E.D., Paige, R.F.: An OCL-based bridge from concrete to abstract syntax. In: Proc. International Workshop on OCL and Textual Modeling, *CEUR Workshop Proceedings*, vol. 1512, pp. 19–34. CEUR-WS.org (2015)
6. Kolovos, D.S., Paige, R.F., Polack, F.: Merging models with the Epsilon Merging Language (EML). In: Proc. MoDELS, *LNCS*, vol. 4199, pp. 215–229. Springer (2006)
7. Kolovos, D.S., Rose, L.M., bin Abid, S., Paige, R.F., Polack, F.A.C., Botterweck, G.: Taming EMF and GMF using model transformation. In: Proc. MODELS, *LNCS*, vol. 6394, pp. 211–225. Springer (2010)
8. Paige, R.F., Kolovos, D.S., Polack, F.A.C.: A tutorial on metamodelling for grammar researchers. Sci. Comput. Program. **96**, 396–416 (2014)
9. Paige, R.F., Matragkas, N.D., Rose, L.M.: Evolving models in model-driven engineering: State-of-the-art and future challenges. J. Syst. Softw. **111**, 272–280 (2016)
10. Rose, L.M., Matragkas, N.D., Kolovos, D.S., Paige, R.F.: A feature model for model-to-text transformation languages. In: Proc. MiSE, pp. 57–63. IEEE (2012)
11. Sannella, D., Tarlecki, A.: Foundations of Algebraic Specification and Formal Software Development (Monographs in Theoretical Computer Science. An EATCS Series). Springer (2011)

Chapter 4
Representation of Object Programs in Metaprograms

JEAN BÉZIVIN [1]

Abstract This chapter discusses different representation options for abstract syntax in the context of implementing programming languages or language-based software components. This is an important foundation for metaprogramming. That is, we assume that one language – the metalanguage – is used for writing programs that analyze, manipulate, translate, generate, or otherwise consume or produce programs in another language – the object language. In this context, abstract syntax thus plays the role of defining the object-program representation in metaprograms. This chapter also discusses other implementation aspects of abstract syntax: conformance checking, serialization, and resolution (AST-to-ASG mapping).

---

[1] Technological spaces are not dictated by natural laws, but once they are observed, named, and promoted, they add structure to the computer science landscape. Jean Bézivin has been prominent in observing, characterizing, and promoting the move from objects and components to models [3]. His projects have been aimed at practical and relevant languages and tools, for example, ATL [13]. He has mediated between academia and practice (such as OMG) in the field of model-driven engineering/architecture (MDE/MDA) [5]. He has helped to give birth to the very notion of technological space, explained the MDE instance [18, 4], integrated it into the broader software language engineering community, and pushed MDE to a more macroscopic level [7, 6, 2].

Artwork Credits for Chapter Opening: This work by Wojciech Kwasnik is licensed under CC BY-SA 4.0. This artwork quotes the artwork *DMT*, acrylic, 2006 by Matt Sheehy with the artist's permission. This work also quotes `https://commons.wikimedia.org/wiki/File:Vincent_van_Gogh_-_Almond_Blossom_-_VGM_F671.jpg`, subject to the attribution "Vincent van Gogh: Almond Blossom (1890) [Public domain], via Wikimedia Commons." This work artistically morphes an image, `https://plus.google.com/+JeanBezivin`, showing the person honored, subject to the attribution "Permission granted by Jean Bézivin for use in this book."

© Springer International Publishing AG, part of Springer Nature 2018
R. Lämmel, *Software Languages*,
https://doi.org/10.1007/978-3-319-90800-7_4

4.1 Representation Options

Terms (in the sense of tree-based abstract syntax) and graphs (in the sense of graph-based abstract syntax) can be represented more or less directly in programming languages. This is essential for programs that process or produce abstract syntactical representations. We use the term "object-program representation" because we view the representation problem from the perspective of metaprogramming, with a distinction between a metalanguage in which to write metaprograms and an object language for the representations processed or produced.

The term "object program" should be understood here broadly because the object language does not need to be a normal programming language; it could be any software language, for example, a specification language or a markup language. Object programs are essentially data from the metaprogram's point of view. To this end, we need a representation of object programs within metaprograms which is based on the object language's abstract syntax.

Terms are native to many languages, for example, Scheme, Haskell, and Prolog. Graphs can be easily represented in languages with "reference semantics" for data structures and objects, for example, C, Java, C#, Scala, Python, and JavaScript. We will discuss different representation options in the sequel. This also includes a discussion of interchange formats.

4.1.1 Untyped Representation

In most dynamically typed languages, arbitrary terms (or graphs) can be natively expressed directly – without dedicated, language-specific data structures. For instance, a (BTL) expression can be represented easily in Prolog as follows.

Illustration 4.1 (Untyped, Prolog-based representation of a BTL expression)

Term resource languages/BTL/sample.term

```
pred(if(iszero(zero), succ(succ(zero)), zero)).
```

Metaprogramming on untyped representations may be straightforward, except for the lack of static type checking, which could catch some metaprogramming errors early on.

In this context, the notion of a homoiconic language may be worth mentioning. A language is homoiconic when the concrete and abstract syntactical structures are essentially isomorphic. Examples include Prolog and Scheme (Lisp). A homoiconic language may easily access code of the same language – without any representation mappings.

4.1.2 Universal Representation

A data structure for "untyped" terms or graphs can be implemented in pretty much any general-purpose programming language – whether or not the language is statically typed. This can be demonstrated for Haskell as follows.

Illustration 4.2 (Universal term representation type)

Haskell module Data.TermRep

```
data TermRep = TermRep ConstrId [TermRep]
type ConstrId = String
```

Illustration 4.3 (Universal representation of a BTL expression)

Haskell module Language.BTL.Universal.Sample

```
sampleExpr :: TermRep
sampleExpr =
  TermRep "pred" [
    TermRep "if" [
      TermRep "iszero" [TermRep "zero" []],
      TermRep "succ" [TermRep "succ" [TermRep "zero" []]],
      TermRep "zero" [] ]]
```

Essentially, we encode arbitrary abstract syntactical representations as Haskell terms of a designed *TermRep* type for universal representation. We have only covered the expressiveness of the basic signature notation (BSL), but it would be straightforward to cover the extended notation (ESL) as well.

Exercise 4.1 (Universal representation in ESL)   [Basic level]
Revise the type TermRep to cover the expressiveness of ESL. Thus, you need to add cases for lists, tuples, and primitive types.

Exercise 4.2 (Universal representation in Java)   [Basic level]
Implement a type for universal representation so that Illustration 4.3 can be ported to Java. (You may also pick another statically typed object-oriented or a C-like programming language.)

Universal representation is used in metaprogramming when it is convenient to operate on a universal (i.e., generic, de facto untyped) representation as opposed to a language-specific representation. We refer to the ATerms library [8] as an example of universal representation in Java and C.

4.1.3 Typeful Representation

When the metalanguage is statically typed, static typing may also be used for object representation so that metaprograms can be type-checked in terms of accessing or constructing object-language constructs.

4.1.3.1 Algebraic Data Type-Based Representation

Let us focus here on tree-based abstract syntax first. We will look at graphs later. The expressiveness of signatures is available in many functional programming languages. We dedicate one "type" in the metalanguage to each sort of the object language's syntax. We dedicate one "variant" in the metalanguage to each function symbol of the object language's syntax.

Of course, it depends on the metalanguage what exactly constitutes a type and a variant. In Haskell, we model sorts as algebraic data types, with each function symbol corresponding to a data-type constructor, as illustrated below for BTL as the object language.

Illustration 4.4 (Types for BTL representation)

Haskell module Language.BTL.Syntax

```
data Expr
  = TRUE  -- True taken by Haskell Prelude
  | FALSE  -- False taken by Haskell Prelude
  | Zero
  | Succ Expr
  | Pred Expr
  | IsZero Expr
  | If Expr Expr Expr
```

We exercise the Haskell types for object-program representation as follows.

Illustration 4.5 (Typeful representation of a BTL expression)

Haskell module Language.BTL.Sample

```
sampleExpr :: Expr
sampleExpr = Pred (If (IsZero Zero) (Succ (Succ Zero)) Zero)
```

Exercise 4.3 (Reuse of primitive types)   [Basic level]
Revise the type Expr *in Illustration 4.4 to use Haskell's* Bool *type instead of the constructors* TRUE *and* FALSE.

Let us also look at more complex illustrations of typeful representation. That is, we will deal with abstract syntaxes that involve more than just one sort; also, we will exercise tuples, lists, and primitive types. The Haskell-based abstract syntaxes of BIPL (Basic Imperative Programming Language), BFPL (Basic Functional Programming Language), and FSML (Finite State Machine Language) are defined below; see Section 3.1.5 for the ESL-based abstract syntax definitions.

Illustration 4.6 (Types for BFPL representation)

Haskell module Language.BFPL.Syntax

```
-- Program = typed functions + main expression
type Program = (Functions, Expr)
type Functions = [Function]
type Function = (String, (FunSig, FunDef))
type FunSig = ([SimpleType], SimpleType)
type FunDef = ([String], Expr)

-- Simple types
data SimpleType = IntType | BoolType

-- Expressions
data Expr
  = IntConst Int
  | BoolConst Bool
  | Arg String
  | If Expr Expr Expr
  | Unary UOp Expr
  | Binary BOp Expr Expr
  | Apply String [Expr]

-- Unary and binary operators
data UOp = Negate | Not
data BOp = Add | Sub | Mul | Lt | Leq | Eq | Geq | Gt | And | Or
```

Illustration 4.7 (Types for BIPL representation)

Haskell module Language.BIPL.Syntax

```
-- Statements
data Stmt
  = Skip
  | Assign String Expr
  | Seq Stmt Stmt
  | If Expr Stmt Stmt
  | While Expr Stmt

-- Expressions
data Expr
  = IntConst Int
  | Var String
  | Unary UOp Expr
```

```
| Binary BOp Expr Expr
```

— — Unary and binary operators
```
data UOp = Negate | Not
data BOp = Add | Sub | Mul | Lt | Leq | Eq | Geq | Gt | And | Or
```

Illustration 4.8 (Types for FSML representation)

Haskell module Language.FSML.Syntax

```
data Fsm = Fsm { getStates :: [State] }
data State = State {
    getInitial :: Initial,
    getId :: StateId,
    getTransitions :: [Transition]
    }
data Transition = Transition {
    getEvent :: Event,
    getAction :: (Maybe Action),
    getTarget :: StateId
    }
type Initial = Bool
type StateId = String
type Event = String
type Action = String
```

4.1.3.2 Object-Based Representation

As a particular approach to typed representation, we may map an abstract syntax definition to an object model: sorts become abstract classes, and function symbols become concrete subclasses of the classes for the result sorts with attributes for the arguments. This option is illustrated below for Java as the metalanguage.

Illustration 4.9 (Classes for BTL representation)

Java source code org/softlang/btl/Syntax.java

```
public class Syntax {
    public static abstract class Expr { }
    public static class True extends Expr { }
    public static class False extends Expr { }
    public static class Zero extends Expr { }
    public static class Succ extends Expr {
        public Expr e;
        public Succ(Expr e) { this.e = e; }
    }
    public static class Pred extends Expr {
        public Expr e;
        public Pred(Expr e) { this.e = e; }
```

```
    }
    public static class IsZero extends Expr {
        public Expr e;
        public IsZero(Expr e) { this.e = e; }
    }
    public static class If extends Expr {
        public Expr e0;
        public Expr e1;
        public Expr e2;
        public If(Expr e0, Expr e1, Expr e2) {
            this.e0 = e0; this.e1 = e1; this.e2 = e2;
        }
    }
}
```

For the sake of convenience, we place all the classes in a single class Syntax. There are nondefault constructors so that instances can be populated conveniently by nested constructor application as opposed to just using setters, as illustrated below.

Illustration 4.10 (Object-based representation of a BTL expression)

Java source code org/softlang/btl/Sample.java

```
static final Expr sample =
    new Pred(
        new If(
            new IsZero(new Zero()),
            new Succ(new Succ(new Zero())),
            new Zero()));
```

There are various additional options regarding such object models, some of which we mention here briefly. One may want to provide getters and setters instead of permitting public access to attributes for phrases. One also may want to enrich the object model to provide a "fluent" interface so that object construction and access are more convenient (Section 2.2.2). Further, one faces several different options for authoring metaprograms on top of the object representation. That is, one may model such functionality as regular methods within the classes for object-program representation, as (static) methods outside the classes, or as a visitor subject to visitor support by the classes. The pros and cons of these options are relatively well understood; see, for example, the literature on visitors and the "expression problem" [26, 32, 10, 24].

4.1.3.3 Reference Relationships

When going from tree- to graph-based abstract syntax, an additional requirement for typeful representation arises: we may leverage the expressiveness of the metalanguage for references, for example, pointers or references, so that references in the abstract syntax correspond to references in the metalanguage.

TBL

```
package org.softlang.tbl;
public class Syntax {
    public static class World {
        public Person[] persons;
    }
    public static class Person {
        public String name;
        public String buddy;
    }
}
```

GBL

```
package org.softlang.gbl;
public class Syntax {
    public static class World {
        public Person[] persons;
    }
    public static class Person {
        public String name;
        public Person buddy;
    }
}
```

Fig. 4.1 Object models for tree- and graph-based BL in Java.

Graph-based abstract syntax can be encoded conveniently in an OO programming language with reference semantics. In Fig. 4.1, we show two Java-based object models for the Buddy Language. One object model assumes tree-shaped objects (**TBL**); another object model relies on proper object graphs (**GBL**). The difference is highlighted.

In contrast to BL's metamodel (Illustration 3.14), the Java types do not distinguish part-of from reference relationships, because Java does not cater for such a distinction. This may be a problem in metaprogramming because a Java-based object model allows us to construct objects that would not conform to a metamodel which distinguishes part-of from reference relationships.

The construction of a graph is illustrated below.

Illustration 4.11 (Object-based representation of BL example)

Java source code org/softlang/gbl/Sample.java

```
public class Sample {
    public World smallWorld() {
        World w = new World();
        Person p1 = new Person();
        Person p2 = new Person();
        w.persons = new Person[] {p1, p2};
        p1.name = "joe";
        p1.buddy = p2;
        p2.name = "bill";
        p2.buddy = p1;
        return w;
    }
}
```

That is, we first construct person objects and then we tie up the object graph with the setters for buddies. These two steps must be separated, because the references relationships are cyclic. More generally, objects must clearly exist before their ref-

TBL   **GBL**

```
newtype World = World {          newtype World = World {
  getPersons :: [Person]           getPersons :: [IORef Person]
}                                }


data Person = Person {           data Person = Person {
  getName :: String,               getName :: String,
  getBuddy :: Maybe String         getBuddy :: Maybe (IORef Person)
}                                }
```

Fig. 4.2 Data models for BL in Haskell.

erences can be assigned for the purpose of tying up the graph. This is a consequence of using an imperative metalanguage.

Graph-based abstract syntax can also be encoded in a language without native reference semantics. This is shown here for Haskell and its IO references as provided by the IO monad [27].

In Fig. 4.2, we show Haskell-based data models for the Buddy Language. In fact, there is one data model for tree-based abstract syntax (**TBL**) without use of the IO monad, and there is another data model for graph-based abstract syntax (**GBL**) which uses IORefs in two places. The differences are highlighted.

This data model is special in that the buddy component is of type Maybe (IORef Person). Hence, buddies are accessed by dereferencing IORefs. We have also set up the data type *World* with references to person terms. In this manner, programming on these graphs becomes more uniform (in Haskell).

The construction of a graph is illustrated below.

Illustration 4.12 (IORef-based representation of a BL graph)

Haskell module Language.GBL.Sample

```
mkSmallWorld :: IO World
mkSmallWorld = do
  r1 ← newIORef undefined
  r2 ← newIORef undefined
  writeIORef r1 Person { getName = "joe", getBuddy = Just r2 }
  writeIORef r2 Person { getName = "bill", getBuddy = Just r1 }
  return $ World [r1, r2]
```

The code above is similar to the earlier Java code. That is, we create references before we tie up the graph. The functional and OO approaches differ as follows. In the functional approach, the references are initialized with undefined persons to be modified eventually to refer to proper persons. In the OO approach, proper person objects are created right from the start, and setters are used to fill in all attributes.

Despite the ability in principle to represent references, this sort of representation is not too common. Functional programmers tend to prefer to operate on tree-based abstract syntactical representations, while using extra functionality (traversals) to look up and propagate bindings when necessary.

4.1.3.4 Smart Constructors

Object-program representation may be "opaque" in that functions of an abstract data type (ADT) or a library are used for object-program manipulation. This is helpful, for example, when the construction of object-program fragments may be subject to constraints that are to be enforced by ADT functions for construction as opposed to regular data-type constructors (Section 4.1.3.1). Constrained constructor functions are also referred to as *smart constructors*.

For instance, we may want to enforce the "type-correct" construction of (BTL) expressions evaluating to numbers or Booleans. Thus, we would need smart constructors which examine their arguments and wrap their results in a Maybe type so that they can detect and communicate unsatisfied constraints, as illustrated below.

Interactive Haskell session:

```
-- Construct 1
▶ zero >>=succ
Just (Succ Zero)
- - - - - - - - - - - - - - - - - - - - - - - - - - - - - - - - - - - - - - -
-- Fail at applying successor function to true
▶ true >>=succ
Nothing
- - - - - - - - - - - - - - - - - - - - - - - - - - - - - - - - - - - - - - -
-- Construct a well-typed If
▶ true >>=λ e1 → zero >>=λ e2 → ifthenelse e1 e2 e2
Just (If TRUE Zero Zero)
```

As it can be seen from the illustration above, the use of the Maybe monad makes us describe construction of compound phrases as a sequence. (One could also consider using applicative functors to better retain the structure of compound phrases.) The smart constructors are easily implemented as follows.

Illustration 4.13 (Smart constructors for BTL expressions)

Haskell module Language.BTL.SmartSyntax

```
true, false, zero :: Maybe Expr
true = Just TRUE
false = Just FALSE
zero = Just Zero
succ, pred, iszero :: Expr → Maybe Expr
succ e = if isNat e then Just (Succ e) else Nothing
pred e = if isNat e then Just (Pred e) else Nothing
iszero e = if isNat e then Just (IsZero e) else Nothing
ifthenelse :: Expr → Expr → Expr → Maybe Expr
ifthenelse e1 e2 e3 =
```

```
if isBool e1 && (isNat e2 && isNat e3 || isBool e2 && isBool e3)
then Just (If e1 e2 e3)
else Nothing

isNat, isBool :: Expr → Bool
isNat Zero = True
isNat (Succ _) = True
isNat (Pred _) = True
isNat (If _ e _) = isNat e
isNat _ = False
isBool = not . isNat
```

Thus, the smart constructors examine their arguments to "guess" at their types. To this end, two auxiliary functions, isNat and isBool, are used. These functions do not fully traverse ("type-check") arguments; they only look as deep into the term as it is necessary to distinguish the two types at hand. This sort of type derivation ("inference") for BTL terms is correct if terms are constructed exclusively by the smart constructors.

Strictly speaking, we are starting a transition from abstract syntax to type checking or semantic analysis, as we are modeling constraints that were not even present in the original abstract syntax definition. However, one may also take the position that the constraints should be part of the abstract syntax definition to start with. Type systems of programming languages and, most notably, those of advanced functional languages such as Haskell provide yet other means of imposing constraints on object-program representations (Chapter 9).

Exercise 4.4 (Advanced typeful representation)   [Intermediate level]
Study one of the following notions: generalized algebraic data types [33, 16], liquid types [28], or refinement types [31]. Exercise any of these notions for the purpose of modeling additional constraints like those discussed above.

Let us briefly mention another example of the use of smart constructors or an ADT for syntax manipulation. Template Haskell [29] (TH) is a Haskell extension for metaprogramming, with Haskell as both the metalanguage and the object language. In particular, TH can be used to analyze or synthesize Haskell code at compile time. To this end, there are Haskell data types for representing Haskell programs. Here is a fragment of an algebraic data type for representing Haskell expressions:

```
data Exp
  = VarE Name
  | LamE [Pat] Exp
  | ConE Name
  | LitE Lit
  | AppE Exp Exp
  | ...
```

TH assumes that these constructors are not used directly – especially not for constructing program fragments. Instead, one is supposed to use smart constructors as follows:

```
varE :: Name → Q Exp
lamE :: [Q Pat] → Q Exp → Q Exp
conE :: Name → Q Exp
litE :: Lit → Q Exp
appE :: Q Exp → Q Exp → Q Exp
...
```

The smart constructors use a so-called quotation monad Q. Among other things, this monad serves to enforce name hygiene [1] in the sense that names of constructed program fragments do not accidentally capture the enclosing program context. This is a concern, as TH is used in a context in which constructed program fragments contribute to (i.e., are "spliced" into) a given Haskell program. Thus, TH's smart constructors are not concerned with type checking, but they handle scopes for names.

4.1.4 Interchange Formats

Abstract syntax may also be encoded in interchange formats such as JSON[2] and XML.[3] Many programming languages may consume, produce, or directly operate on such formats; this opens up a path towards persistence of object programs and interchange (exchange) between metaprogram components, even if written in different languages. While we only discuss JSON and XML here, there are a myriad of other formats[4], for example, Protocol buffers[5] and Thrift.[6] For now, we only discuss the mere representation of object programs in JSON and XML, but later (Section 4.2.3) we will also discuss the transcription of abstract syntax definitions to JSON and XML schemas for appropriate forms of conformance checking.

4.1.4.1 JSON Representation

Let us begin with the turnstile FSM encoded in JSON.

---

[2] http://www.json.org/

[3] https://www.w3.org/XML/

[4] https://en.wikipedia.org/wiki/Comparison_of_data_serialization_formats

[5] https://developers.google.com/protocol-buffers/

[6] http://thrift.apache.org/

Illustration 4.14 (JSON representation of a BTL expression)

JSON resource languages/BTL/JSON/sample.json

```
{
  "pred": {
    "if": {
      "cond": { "iszero": { "zero": {}}},
      "then": { "succ": { "succ": { "zero": {}}}},
      "else": { "zero": {}}
    }
  }
}
```

JSON is tailored towards nested collections of labeled components as opposed to trees (terms) with positional arguments, which is what we assumed for tree-based abstract syntax before. The encoding is based on the following assumptions:

- Terms are mapped to JSON objects. We do not use JSON's lists (arrays) or primitive types, because the abstract syntax at hand also does not use such expressiveness.
- More precisely, terms are mapped to JSON objects, with one name/value pair with the name being the function symbol of the term and the JSON value v modeling the arguments of the term:
  - If the function symbol is, in fact, a constant, then v is the empty object "{ }".
  - If the function symbol is unary, i.e., there is one argument, then v is the JSON encoding of the argument term.
  - If the function symbol has more than one argument, then the argument positions are encoded by several name/value pairs. In the case of "if", we use the names *cond*, *then*, and *else*.

4.1.4.2 XML Representation

The turnstile FSM is encoded in XML as follows.

Illustration 4.15 (XML representation of a BTL expression)

XML resource languages/BTL/XML/sample.xml

```
<pred xmlns="http://www.softlang.org/BTL">
  <if>
    <iszero><zero/></iszero>
    <succ><succ><zero/></succ></succ>
    <zero/>
  </if>
</pred>
```

There is a good fit between XML trees and terms that what we assumed for tree-based abstract syntax before. The XML encoding is based on the following assumptions:

- Terms are mapped to XML elements. We do not use XML attributes because XML elements are generally sufficient in terms of expressiveness. We do not use elements of primitive types (i.e., elements with text content), because the abstract syntax at hand also does not use primitive types.
- More precisely, terms are mapped to XML elements with the element name being the function symbol of the term and the children elements corresponding to the arguments of the term. The order of arguments in the signature carries over into the order of XML children.

As an example of a metaprogramming technology based on an interchange format, we mention the srcML toolkit [9]; srcML is based on an XML representation of source code and it supports C/C++, C#, and Java.

4.2 Conformance Checking

When a typeful representation is employed, then, ideally, object program representations can be assumed to conform to the abstract syntax. Practically, the underlying mapping of signatures or metamodels to programming language types may be lossy [30, 22, 23], but we do not discuss this challenge here. When an untyped or a universal representation is employed, then it is worthwhile to implement conformance checking so that representations can be checked to be valid at runtime. For instance, a metaprogram may check conformance on arguments and results as pre- and post-conditions. We may also rely on existing means of schema-based validation when leveraging interchange formats. Let us discuss several options for conformance checking in detail.

4.2.1 Language-Specific Conformance Checking

We may encode an abstract syntax definition directly as *functionality* in a metalanguage so that the functionality is specific to the object language at hand. The following Haskell predicate tests terms to represent BTL expressions. We represent terms according to the Haskell data type *TermRep* that we introduced earlier (Illustration 4.2).

Illustration 4.16 (Conformance checking for the universal representation of BTL)

Haskell module Language.BTL.Dynamics

```
expr :: TermRep → Bool
expr (TermRep "true" []) = True
expr (TermRep "false" []) = True
expr (TermRep "zero" []) = True
expr (TermRep "succ" [e]) = expr e
expr (TermRep "pred" [e]) = expr e
expr (TermRep "iszero" [e]) = expr e
expr (TermRep "if" es@[_,_,_]) = and (map expr es)
expr _ = False
```

That is, we dedicate a function to each sort of the abstract syntax. (There is only one sort in the BTL example at hand.) There is one case (equation) for each function symbol of a sort; each such case checks the function symbol, including its arity, and it recursively checks arguments.

4.2.2 Generic Conformance Checking

We may implement the general notion of conformance (Definition 3.4) as a relation between pre-terms or pre-graphs and signatures or metamodels within the metalanguage. We focus here on pre-term-to-signature conformance. The implementation requires the following ingredients:

- a representation of pre-terms;
- a representation of signatures according to the signature of signatures;
- an implementation of actual conformance.

Let us develop a Haskell-based implementation of conformance checking. We choose a typeful representation for signatures (Section 4.1.3). That is, we provide Haskell data types that correspond to the signature of signatures (Section 3.4.1). We begin with a representation of signatures as follows.

Illustration 4.17 (Typeful representation of signatures)

Haskell module Language.BSL.Syntax

```
type Signature = [Profile]
type Profile = (Sym, [Sort], Sort)
type Sym = String
type Sort = String
```

Illustration 4.18 (The signature of BTL expressions)

Haskell module <u>Language.BTL.Universal.Signature</u>

```
btlSignature :: Signature
btlSignature =
  [ ("true", [], "expr"),
    ("false", [], "expr"),
    ("zero", [], "expr"),
    ("succ", ["expr"], "expr"),
    ("pred", ["expr"], "expr"),
    ("iszero", ["expr"], "expr"),
    ("if", ["expr", "expr", "expr"], "expr")
  ]
```

We assume the universal representation (Section 4.1.2) for pre-terms. To this end, we use the Haskell data type *TermRep* that we introduced earlier (Illustration 4.2). We expect to check for conformance with a Haskell predicate *termOfSort* as follows:

Interactive Haskell session:

▶ termOfSort btlSignature sampleExpr *"Expr"*
- -
True

Let us implement the predicate *termOfSort* for conformance checking as a recursive function which follows closely the formal definition of conformance (Definition 3.4).

Illustration 4.19 (Conformance checking for BSL)

Haskell module <u>Language.BSL.Conformance</u>

```
termOfSort :: [Profile] → TermRep → Sort → Bool
termOfSort ps (TermRep c ts) s =
    case [ ss | (c', ss, s') ← ps, c==c', s==s' ] of
    [ss] → and (map (uncurry (termOfSort ps)) (zip ts ss))
    _ → False
```

Exercise 4.5 (Conformance checking for ESL)   [Intermediate level]
Pick a programming language of your choice. Devise a representation of ESL signatures and pre-terms and implement conformance checking.

Exercise 4.6 (Conformance checking for MML)   [Intermediate level]
Pick a programming language of your choice. Devise a representation of MML metamodels and pre-graphs and implement conformance checking.

Incidentally, we have started to write metaprograms. In fact, a metaprogram for generic conformance checking can be viewed as an "interpreter", as it interprets signatures or metamodels in a manner which realizes the meaning of these syntax definitions in an operational manner. Here is the I/O behavior: the input of conformance checking is a signature (or a metamodel) and a pre-term (or a pre-graph); the output is a Boolean value stating whether conformance holds.

4.2.3 Schema-Based Conformance Checking

Interchange formats provide their own schema languages (say, type systems), for example, JSON Schema[7] for JSON and XML Schema[8] (XSD) for XML. Abstract syntax definitions may be mapped to schemas, as illustrated below. For what it matters, these schema languages are also subsets of the respective JSON and XML universes. There even exist corresponding schemas of schemas, thereby providing a metametalevel for the interchange formats. Given a JSON file and a JSON schema (or an XML file and an XML schema), we may leverage existing technologies for schema-based validation to provide conformance checking.

The JSON representation exercised in Illustration 4.14 can be modeled by a JSON schema as follows.

Illustration 4.20 (JSON Schema for BTL expressions)

JSON resource languages/BTL/JSON/schema.json

```
{
    "$schema": "http://json-schema.org/draft-04/schema#",
    "description": "schema for BTL syntax",
    "type": "object",
    "oneOf": [
      {
          "properties": { "true" : { "additionalProperties": false } },
          "additionalProperties": false
      },
      {
          "properties": { "false" : { "additionalProperties": false } },
          "additionalProperties": false
      },
      {
          "properties": { "zero" : { "additionalProperties": false } },
          "additionalProperties": false
      },
      {
          "properties": { "succ" : { "$ref": "" } },
          "additionalProperties": false
      },
```

---

[7] http://json-schema.org/

[8] https://www.w3.org/XML/Schema

```
{
    "properties": { "pred" : { "$ref": "" } },
    "additionalProperties": false
},
{
    "properties": { "iszero" : { "$ref": "" } },
    "additionalProperties": false
},
{
    "properties": {
        "if": {
            "properties": {
                "cond": { "$ref": "" },
                "then": { "$ref": "" },
                "else": { "$ref": "" }
            },
            "required": [ "x", "y", "z" ],
            "additionalProperties": false
        }
    },
    "additionalProperties": false
}
]
}
```

JSON Schema is sophisticated, and there exist different mapping options – even more so when one is handling the extended signature notation. Let us briefly characterize the schema encoding at hand. Each function symbol is mapped to a designated sub-schema. Each sort is mapped to a designated sub-schema, which combines the sub-schemas for the function symbols by means of JSON Schema's "oneOf". (There is only one sort in the BTL example at hand.) Argument positions are also mapped to sub-schemas; these are references (see "$ref") to the schema for the relevant sort. In the present example, with just one sort at hand, the references point to the top-level object type. The schema contains some elements that control optionality and rule out additional name/value pairs that are not explicitly declared; we omit a detailed discussion here.

The XML representation exercised in Illustration 4.15 can be modeled by an XML schema as follows.

Illustration 4.21 (XML Schema for BTL expressions)

XSD resource languages/BTL/XML/schema.xsd

```
<schema
        xmlns="http://www.w3.org/2001/XMLSchema"
        targetNamespace="http://www.softlang.org/BTL"
        xmlns:tns="http://www.softlang.org/BTL"
        elementFormDefault="qualified">
    <element name="true"><complexType/></element>
    <element name="false"><complexType/></element>
```

```
<element name="zero"><complexType/></element>
<element name="succ" type="tns:expr"/>
<element name="pred" type="tns:expr"/>
<element name="iszero" type="tns:expr"/>
<element name="if">
   <complexType>
      <group ref="tns:expr" minOccurs="3" maxOccurs="3"/>
   </complexType>
</element>
<complexType name="expr">
   <group ref="tns:expr"/>
</complexType>
<group name="expr">
   <choice>
     <element ref="tns:true"/>
     <element ref="tns:false"/>
     <element ref="tns:zero"/>
     <element ref="tns:succ"/>
     <element ref="tns:pred"/>
     <element ref="tns:iszero"/>
     <element ref="tns:if"/>
   </choice>
  </group>
</schema>
```

XML Schema is quite sophisticated, and there exist different mapping options – even more so when one is handling the extended signature notation. Let us briefly characterize the schema encoding at hand. Each function symbol is mapped to a designated root-element declaration. Each sort is mapped to a designated model group, which constructs a "choice" over the different elements for the sort. (There is only one sort in the BTL example at hand.) There is also a complex type for each sort, which simply refers to the aforementioned model group. This duplication allows us to refer to "sorts" in argument positions without wrapping arguments in extra element open/close tags.

Exercise 4.7 (Metamodeling with XML Schema) [Intermediate level]
Study the expressiveness for identity constraints,[9] as provided by XML Schema. Use identity constraints in an XML-based abstract syntax for the Buddy Language.

While interchange formats help with persistence and language interoperability, their use comes at a cost, especially when mapping is involved [30, 22, 23]: the mapping may be idiosyncratic, imprecise, and prone to round-tripping problems. The illustrations given above certainly involve issues of idiosyncrasies of mapping signatures to schemas; we would face yet other problems when mapping programming-language types to schemas or vice versa.

---

[9] https://www.w3.org/TR/xmlschema-1/#cIdentity-constraint_Definitions

4.3 Serialization

Universal representations are suited for interchange and storage, since one may provide the corresponding functionality once and for all for the universal representation type. By contrast, a typeful representation calls for type-specific support for serialization if data interchange and persistence are required. Programming language ecosystems routinely support some form of XML- or JSON-based serialization for programming language types. Let us briefly discuss serialization here.

We could target JSON or XML for serialization, but let us exercise a different, illustrative option here. That is, we provide a bidirectional mapping between universal and typeful representations. We assume that this mapping can be easily complemented by another bidirectional mapping between universal and JSON- or XML-based representations. Thus, we only consider the mapping between universal and typeful representations here. In Haskell, we capture such serialization with a type class as follows.

Illustration 4.22 (A type class for serialization)

Haskell module Data.Term

```
class Term a where
  toTermRep :: a → TermRep
  fromTermRep :: TermRep → a
```

Deserialization should be the inverse of serialization. Thus, the following law should hold:

```
fromTermRep (toTermRep x) = x
```

Serializing terms to term representations ("*toTermRep*") should always succeed; deserializing term representations to terms ("*fromTermRep*") necessarily entails conformance checking and, thus, may fail. We assume here that the function for de-serialization may be undefined, but we could use the Maybe monad too. Each typeful representation type needs to instantiate the type class Term, as illustrated for the representation type for BTL expressions below.

Illustration 4.23 (Serialization for BTL expressions)

Haskell module Language.BTL.Universal.Term

```
instance Term Expr where
  toTermRep TRUE = TermRep "true" []
  toTermRep FALSE = TermRep "false" []
  toTermRep Zero = TermRep "zero" []
  toTermRep (Succ e) = TermRep "succ" [toTermRep e]
  ...
  fromTermRep (TermRep "true" []) = TRUE
  fromTermRep (TermRep "false" []) = FALSE
```

```
fromTermRep (TermRep "zero" []) = Zero
fromTermRep (TermRep "succ" [t]) = Succ (fromTermRep t)
...
```

Incidentally, such a mapping between typeful and universal representations makes it possible for both representations to coexist in metaprogramming. The idea is that metaprograms use a typeful representation where possible and escape to a universal representation where necessary, for example, for serialization.

Exercise 4.8 (Generic serialization)   [Advanced level]
Consider again the difference between language-specific and generic conformance checking (Section 4.2). Applying this distinction to serialization suggests that the Haskell illustration, as given above, is language-specific, because the serialization function is specific to a language; it actually encodes the underlying signature in the equations of the fromTermRep function. Devise a generic serialization approach. Hint: If you pick Haskell as the metalanguage, then you may want to employ Haskell's "scrap your boilerplate" (SYB) approach to generic functional programming [19, 20, 21].

4.4 AST-to-ASG Mapping

In practice, mappings between different syntaxes are frequently needed. For instance, a language implementation may involve two abstract syntaxes: one which includes some extra constructs in the sense of syntactic sugar and another desugared one. Basic means of metaprogramming may be sufficient for such mappings. Later, we will also need to map from concrete to abstract syntax and vice versa (Chapter 7). In this section, we focus on a particular problem: *resolution*, i.e., mapping tree- to graph-based abstract syntax, i.e., from trees or terms (ASTs) to graphs (ASGs). Such mappings are not straightforward, which is why we discuss the problem here.

Resolution is based on the identification of encoded references (e.g., names) and their replacement by actual references. The techniques for resolution depend significantly on the metaprogramming and metamodeling approaches at hand. In the literature, the problem of resolution, which is also related to "name binding" [15, 12, 14, 17, 11, 25], is often discussed in the context of relatively specific setups for declarative language specification. Let us discuss resolution as a metaprogramming problem here.

We will demonstrate resolution for the Buddy Language as the object language and for Java and Haskell as metalanguages. We have already considered tree- and graph-based abstract syntax for the Buddy Language (Section 4.1.3.3). Thus, we face the problem of mapping persons with string-based encoding of buddies to persons with references to buddies.

Resolution can be implemented in Java as follows — we operate on the object models of Fig. 4.1.

Illustration 4.24 (Resolution of buddies)

Java source code org/softlang/gbl/Resolution.java

```
1   package org.softlang.gbl;
2   public class Resolution {
3       public static Syntax.World resolve(org.softlang.tbl.Syntax.World tree) {
4           Syntax.World graph = new Syntax.World();
5           graph.persons = new Syntax.Person[tree.persons.length];
6           for (int i=0; i<tree.persons.length; i++) {
7               graph.persons[i] = new Syntax.Person();
8               graph.persons[i].name = tree.persons[i].name;
9           }
10          for (int i=0; i<tree.persons.length; i++)
11              for (int j=0; j<tree.persons.length; j++)
12                  if (tree.persons[i].buddy==tree.persons[j].name) {
13                      graph.persons[i].buddy = graph.persons[j];
14                      break;
15                  }
16          return graph;
17      }
18  }
```

Thus, resolution is modeled as a mapping from a tree-based world of tree-based persons to a graph-based world of graph-based persons. The types of the mapping source (package ".…tbl" for trees) are qualified to avoid name clashes with the type of the mapping target ("….gbl" for graphs). The mapping consists of these steps:

- A world object graph is constructed (line 4).
- The persons array of graph is initialized by a new array, which is of the same length as the incoming persons array of tree (line 5).
- The individual persons are initialized with newly constructed person objects and each person's name is copied from the input (lines 6–9).
- In a separate loop, the buddy names are mapped to actual person references (lines 10–15); we perform a linear search on tree to find the right index and then assign the located object as the buddy.

The phases of initialization and lookup + assignment need to be separated for the same reasons as we had to separate the initial construction and the tying up of objects in object construction (Section 4.1.3.3).

Exercise 4.9 (Resolution with visitors)   [Intermediate level]
*Based on a metamodel for functional programs (BFPL) with function application
involving references to declared functions (Exercise 3.5), implement an object model
for both the tree-based and the graph-based syntax of BFPL. Further, implement
resolution as a mapping between the two syntaxes. Use the visitor design pattern to
make the mapping concise and structured.*

We also attempt resolution in Haskell. The Haskell-based mapping, as described
below, operates on the data models of Fig. 4.2. Overall, the Haskell approach is a
little tedious because of the purity of the language and the monadic types involving
IORefs.

Illustration 4.25 (Resolution of buddies)

Haskell module <u>Language.GBL.Resolution</u>

```
1   -- Helper types for resolution
2   type PersonRef = IORef GBL.Person
3   type PersonMap = Map String PersonRef
4
5   -- Map tree- to graph-based world
6   resolve :: TBL.World → IO GBL.World
7   resolve (TBL.World ps) = do
8       rs ← termsToRefs personToRef empty ps
9       return (GBL.World rs)
10    where
11      -- Store person as IORef
12      personToRef :: TBL.Person → PersonMap → IO (PersonRef, PersonMap)
13      personToRef p m = do
14          let n = TBL.getName p
15          let b = TBL.getBuddy p
16          (r, m') ← keyToRef n m
17          (b', m") ← (case b of
18            Nothing → return (Nothing, m')
19            (Just n') → do
20              (r', m") ← keyToRef n' m'
21              return (Just r', m"))
22          writeIORef r (
23            GBL.Person {
24              GBL.getName = n,
25              GBL.getBuddy = b' } )
26          return (r, m")
```

We use a map *PersonMap* to keep track of references that have been assigned to
person names. We use a reusable helper function *termsToRefs* for mapping over the
list of tree-based persons to derive a reference to a graph-based person according to
the function *personToRef*, subject to the following steps:

- We extract the person's name n and the optional buddy b (lines 14–15) .
- We retrieve or generate the reference r for n using the reusable helper function *keyToRef* (line 16). The reference may have been assigned already, if n has served as the name of a buddy of a person that was mapped earlier.
- We examine the optional buddy b so that we can retrieve or generate the reference for the buddy's name n', if present (lines 17–21). Thus, b' holds an optional reference for the buddy.
- We compose the person from the name and the optional buddy and write it to the IORef (lines 22–25).

The reusable helper functions are shown below.

Illustration 4.26 (Mini-framework for resolution)

Haskell module Data.Graph

```
-- Map list of terms to a list of refs
termsToRefs :: (a → s → IO (IORef b, s)) → s → [a] → IO [IORef b]
termsToRefs f z ts = termsToRefs' z ts
  where
    termsToRefs' _ [] = return []
    termsToRefs' _ (t:ts) = do
      (r, z') ← f t z
      rs ← termsToRefs' z' ts
      return (r:rs)

-- Map key to ref, use map for housekeeping
keyToRef :: Ord a => a → Map a (IORef b) → IO (IORef b, Map a (IORef b))
keyToRef k m =
  case lookup k m of
    Nothing → do
      r ← newIORef undefined
      return (r, insert k r m)
    Just r → return (r, m)
```

The function *termsToRefs* is little more than a monadic map, except that it also incorporates an "accumulator" which is used in our example for the map which keeps track of references for persons' names. The function *keyToRef* tries to look up a reference for a key (such as a name), and allocates a new reference if the key is not yet in the given map. When allocating a reference, undefined content is assigned; we assume that the content will eventually be overridden.

Summary and Outline

Some of the content of this chapter can be summarized in a recipe as follows.

Recipe 4.1 (Implementation of a conformance checker).

Abstract syntax   It is assumed that you have authored abstract syntax and samples according to Recipe 3.1.

Representation   Identify the representation that you plan to use for programming and serialization. Represent the samples accordingly. Consider JSON, XML, or code – the latter based on an assumed API or a concrete data type-based representation within a programming language.

Conformance   Implement conformance for the chosen representation. To this end, the authored abstract syntax may be used directly or it may need to be implemented in a different formalism or language, for example, as a JSON schema, an XML schema, or a suite of language-specific types. Serialization may be leveraged to apply the implemented syntax definition to the preferred representation of samples.

Testing   Apply the conformance checker to language samples to confirm their conformance to the rules of the signature or metamodel. One should also author samples that violate the abstract syntax to test that the conformance checker catches the errors and communicates them appropriately.

We have discussed various options for representing object programs according to an abstract syntax. In this manner, we are prepared for metaprogramming in different programming languages with more or less static typing and interchangeability. We have also demonstrated the implementation of the fundamental notion of conformance in different settings.

We will now engage in actual metaprogramming on top of abstract syntax. We will later cover concrete syntax for the purpose of defining, parsing, and formatting string languages.

References

1. Adams, M.: Towards the essence of hygiene. In: Proc. POPL, pp. 457–469. ACM (2015)
2. Barbero, M., Jouault, F., Bézivin, J.: Model driven management of complex systems: Implementing the macroscope's vision. In: Proc. ECBS 2008, pp. 277–286. IEEE (2008)
3. Bézivin, J.: On the unification power of models. SoSyM **4**(2), 171–188 (2005)
4. Bézivin, J.: Model driven engineering: An emerging technical space. In: GTTSE 2005, Revised Papers, *LNCS*, vol. 4143, pp. 36–64. Springer (2006)
5. Bézivin, J., Gerbé, O.: Towards a precise definition of the OMG/MDA framework. In: Proc. ASE, pp. 273–280. IEEE (2001)
6. Bézivin, J., Jouault, F., Rosenthal, P., Valduriez, P.: Modeling in the large and modeling in the small. In: European MDA Workshops MDAFA 2003 and MDAFA 2004, Revised Selected Papers, *LNCS*, vol. 3599, pp. 33–46. Springer (2005)

 7. Bézivin, J., Jouault, F., Valduriez, P.: On the need for megamodels. In: Proc. OOPSLA/GPCE: Best Practices for Model-Driven Software Development Workshop (2004)
 8. van den Brand, M., Klint, P.: ATerms for manipulation and exchange of structured data: It's all about sharing. Inf. Softw. Technol. **49**(1), 55–64 (2007)
 9. Collard, M.L., Decker, M.J., Maletic, J.I.: Lightweight transformation and fact extraction with the srcML toolkit. In: Proc. SCAM, pp. 173–184. IEEE (2011)
10. van Deursen, A., Visser, J.: Source model analysis using the JJTraveler visitor combinator framework. Softw., Pract. Exper. **34**(14), 1345–1379 (2004)
11. Fors, N., Cedersjö, G., Hedin, G.: JavaRAG: a Java library for reference attribute grammars. In: Proc. MODULARITY, pp. 55–67. ACM (2015)
12. Hedin, G.: An overview of door attribute grammars. In: Proc. CC, *LNCS*, vol. 786, pp. 31–51. Springer (1994)
13. Jouault, F., Allilaire, F., Bézivin, J., Kurtev, I.: ATL: A model transformation tool. Sci. Comput. Program. **72**(1-2), 31–39 (2008)
14. Jouault, F., Bézivin, J., Kurtev, I.: TCS: a DSL for the specification of textual concrete syntaxes in model engineering. In: Proc. GPCE, pp. 249–254. ACM (2006)
15. Kastens, U., Waite, W.M.: Modularity and reusability in attribute grammars. Acta Inf. **31**(7), 601–627 (1994)
16. Kennedy, A., Russo, C.V.: Generalized algebraic data types and object-oriented programming. In: Proc. OOPSLA, pp. 21–40. ACM (2005)
17. Konat, G.D.P., Kats, L.C.L., Wachsmuth, G., Visser, E.: Declarative name binding and scope rules. In: Proc. SLE 2012, *LNCS*, vol. 7745, pp. 311–331. Springer (2013)
18. Kurtev, I., Bézivin, J., Akşit, M.: Technological spaces: An initial appraisal. In: Proc. CoopIS, DOA 2002, Industrial track (2002)
19. Lämmel, R., Jones, S.L.P.: Scrap your boilerplate: a practical design pattern for generic programming. In: Proc. TLDI, pp. 26–37. ACM (2003)
20. Lämmel, R., Jones, S.L.P.: Scrap more boilerplate: reflection, zips, and generalised casts. In: Proc. ICFP, pp. 244–255. ACM (2004)
21. Lämmel, R., Jones, S.L.P.: Scrap your boilerplate with class: extensible generic functions. In: Proc. ICFP, pp. 204–215. ACM (2005)
22. Lämmel, R., Meijer, E.: Mappings make data processing go 'round. In: GTTSE 2005, Revised Papers, *LNCS*, vol. 4143, pp. 169–218. Springer (2006)
23. Lämmel, R., Meijer, E.: Revealing the X/O impedance mismatch – (changing lead into gold). In: Datatype-Generic Programming – International Spring School, SSDGP 2006, Revised Lectures, *LNCS*, vol. 4719, pp. 285–367. Springer (2007)
24. Lämmel, R., Ostermann, K.: Software extension and integration with type classes. In: Proc. GPCE, pp. 161–170. ACM Press (2006)
25. Neron, P., Tolmach, A.P., Visser, E., Wachsmuth, G.: A theory of name resolution. In: Proc. ESOP, *LNCS*, vol. 9032, pp. 205–231. Springer (2015)
26. Palsberg, J., Jay, C.B.: The essence of the Visitor pattern. In: Proc. COMPSAC, pp. 9–15. IEEE (1998)
27. Peyton Jones, S.: Tackling the awkward squad: monadic input/output, concurrency, exceptions, and foreign-language calls in Haskell. In: Engineering theories of software construction – Marktoberdorf Summer School 2000, NATO ASI Series, pp. 47–96. IOS Press (2001)
28. Rondon, P.M., Kawaguchi, M., Jhala, R.: Liquid types. In: Proc. PLDI, pp. 159–169. ACM (2008)
29. Sheard, T., Peyton Jones, S.L.: Template meta-programming for Haskell. SIGPLAN Not. **37**(12), 60–75 (2002)
30. Thomas, D.A.: The impedance imperative – Tuples + objects + infosets = too much stuff! J. Object Technol. **2**(5), 7–12 (2003)
31. Vazou, N., Seidel, E.L., Jhala, R., Vytiniotis, D., Jones, S.L.P.: Refinement types for Haskell. In: Proc. ICFP, pp. 269–282. ACM (2014)
32. Visser, J.: Visitor combination and traversal control. In: Proc. OOPSLA, pp. 270–282. ACM (2001)
33. Xi, H., Chen, C., Chen, G.: Guarded recursive datatype constructors. In: Proc. POPL, pp. 224–235. ACM (2003)

Chapter 5
A Suite of Metaprogramming Scenarios

JAMES CORDY.[1]

Abstract This chapter is a basic introduction to metaprogramming. A metaprogram is a program that processes (i.e., takes as input or produces as output) programs. Metaprogramming is at the heart of software language implementation and processing. The processed programs or artifacts are also referred to as *object programs*. The language in which the metaprograms are written is referred to as the *metalanguage*. The language of the processed programs or artifacts is referred to as the *object language*. The following are all important scenarios of metaprogramming: interpretation, compilation, transformation, analysis, and code generation. In this chapter, we exercise several metaprogramming scenarios using Haskell as the metalanguage.

---

[1] At its heart, this book focuses on metaprogramming in the sense of source-code analysis and manipulation (as opposed to run-time reflection or adaptive systems). James Cordy may be regarded as a representative of the discipline – he has developed languages and systems for metaprogramming (notably TXL [12]), and he has carried out or overseen major industrial projects, important case studies, or surveys in many application areas of metaprogramming [13, 45]. James Cordy started his career with influential work on language design and compiler technology, focused eventually on legacy systems [14], and is nowadays an authority on program comprehension, software transformation, code analysis (e.g., clone detection), and various other areas in empirical and automated software engineering.

Artwork Credits for Chapter Opening: This work by Wojciech Kwasnik is licensed under CC BY-SA 4.0. This artwork quotes the artwork *DMT*, acrylic, 2006 by Matt Sheehy with the artist's permission. This work also quotes https://commons.wikimedia.org/wiki/File:Sunset_at_Montmajour_1888_Van_Gogh.jpg, subject to the attribution "Vincent Van Gogh: Sunset at Montmajour (1888) [Public domain], via Wikimedia Commons." This work artistically morphes an image, https://en.wikipedia.org/wiki/James_Cordy, showing the person honored, subject to the attribution "By Cordyj (talk) (Uploads) - Own work, CC BY-SA 3.0, https://en.wikipedia.org/w/index.php?curid=31348050."

© Springer International Publishing AG, part of Springer Nature 2018
R. Lämmel, *Software Languages*,
https://doi.org/10.1007/978-3-319-90800-7_5

5.1 Interpretation

Interpretation means, essentially, program execution. An interpreter is a metaprogram which executes or evaluates a given object program. An interpreter returns
some result such as a value, a variable assignment, or a "reduced" (simplified) object program. An interpreter may take arguments in addition to the object program,
such as a stream of input values, and it may have access to the object program's
"environment", for example, the file system. In metaprogramming, in general, and
in interpretation, in particular, the metalanguage and the object language can be the
same language, in principle, but we will not specifically look at this case.

At this stage, we cover the topic of interpretation in a pragmatic manner. Later
on (starting with Chapter 8), we adopt a more formal approach towards interpretation and, in fact, semantics. We use Haskell as the metalanguage for the illustrative
implementation of interpreters of different languages. Functional programming is
indeed quite suited for interpreter implementation.

5.1.1 Basics of Interpretation

We will demonstrate interpretation for the trivial expression language BTL, the (abstract) syntax of which we introduced earlier. (See Illustration 4.4 for the Haskell-
based abstract syntax.) A BTL interpreter evaluates expressions and returns their
values. Let us set up an informal semantics for BTL which will guide us in implementing an interpreter. For each kind of BTL expression, we need to characterize
the corresponding value:

- TRUE and FALSE: These constant forms of expressions evaluate to the Boolean
  values True and False.
- Zero: This constant form evaluates to the natural number 0.
- Succ e: The subexpression e must evaluate to a natural number, say n. The evaluation result of the compound expression is then n+1.
- Pred e: The subexpression e must evaluate to a natural number, say n. The evaluation result of the compound expression is either 0, if n equals 0, or n−1 otherwise.
  This part of the semantics involves an element of choice, in that we could also
  assume that the operation is undefined if e evaluates to the natural number 0.
- IsZero e: The subexpression e must evaluate to a natural number, say n. The evaluation result of the compound expression is either True, if n equals 0, or False, if
  n is greater than 0.
- If e0 e1 e2: The subexpression e0 must evaluate to a Boolean value, say b. If b
  equals True, then e1 is evaluated as the result of the compound expression. If b
  equals False, then e2 is evaluated as the result of the compound expression.

Overall, the interpreter could return an Int or a Bool. In fact, the result could be
undefined too. To deal with the choice between Int and Bool, we model the result
type of interpretation as an Either type, as shown below.

Illustration 5.1 (Result type for BTL expression evaluation)

Haskell module Language.BTL.Value

```
-- Results of evaluation
type Value = Either Int Bool
```

Here is how we expect to use the interpreter:

Interactive Haskell session:

```
▶ evaluate (Pred (If (IsZero Zero) (Succ (Succ Zero)) Zero))
Left 1
```
- -
```
▶ evaluate (Pred TRUE)
Left *** Exception: ... Irrefutable pattern failed for pattern ...
```

The first example evaluates the expression to Left 1 because IsZero Zero is evaluated to True and thus the first branch of the "if" is selected, thereby applying "Pred" to Succ (Succ Zero) resulting in Succ Zero (i.e., "1"). The second example illustrates failing interpretation – the predecessor of a Boolean value is not defined. Failure is manifested here by run-time pattern-match failure.

The following interpreter directly implements the informal BTL semantics given above. The Haskell code shown below is completely straightforward.

Illustration 5.2 (A BTL interpreter)

Haskell module Language.BTL.Interpreter

```
evaluate :: Expr → Value
evaluate TRUE = Right True
evaluate FALSE = Right False
evaluate Zero = Left 0
evaluate (Succ e) = Left (n+1) where Left n = evaluate e
evaluate (Pred e) = Left (n − if n==0 then 0 else 1) where Left n = evaluate e
evaluate (IsZero e) = Right (n==0) where Left n = evaluate e
evaluate (If e0 e1 e2) = evaluate (if b then e1 else e2) where Right b = evaluate e0
```

Exercise 5.1 (Interpretation without throwing)   [Basic level]
The interpreter "throws" when the operand of Succ, Pred, *or* IsZero *does not evaluate to a number or when the first subterm of* If *does not evaluate to a Boolean value. Revise the interpreter so that it returns* Nothing *of Haskell's* Maybe *type in these cases.*

Let us refine an earlier (simpler) recipe for interpreters (Recipe 2.2).

Recipe 5.1 (Development of an interpreter (continued)).

Metalanguage   *Pick the metalanguage for the interpreter.*
Object-program representation   *Implement the abstract syntax of the inter-*
preted object language within the metalanguage (Recipe 4.1).
Semantic domains   *Define all types that are needed for additional inputs,*
and for the final and intermediate results of interpretation. We refer to these
types as semantic domains. Identify relevant operations on the semantic
domains, for example, arithmetic operations on number types or lookup
and update operations on maps.
Informal semantics   *Describe the semantics of interpretation informally.*
Cover each abstract language construct (i.e., each syntactical pattern) in-
dividually.
Test cases   *Set up test cases that explain how one expects to use the inter-*
preter. That is, provide object programs and interpretation results and all
additional details needed.
Case discrimination   *Implement interpretation as case discrimination on the*
syntactic constructs. There is going to be one code block per language con-
struct. There is a recursive function (procedure or method) per syntactic
category.
Testing   *Test the interpreter in terms of the test cases.*

Exercise 5.2 (Interpreter in an OO language)   [Basic level]
Implement the BTL interpreter in an OO language such as Java. You may use the
Interpreter Pattern or the Visitor Pattern [18].

Exercise 5.3 (Interpretation in a scripting language)   [Basic level]
Implement the BTL interpreter in a scripting language such as Python.

In the sequel, we apply the interpreter recipe to a few more languages. We will
encounter additional aspects of interpretation: stores, environments, and stepwise
interpretation.

5.1.2 Interpretation with Stores

Let us now discuss interpretation of imperative programs, thereby encountering concepts such as assignment and control flow. We pick the fabricated imperative programming language BIPL for this purpose. (See Illustration 4.7 for the Haskell-

based abstract syntax.) Consider the following sample program represented as a Haskell term; concrete syntax is shown for clarity in the Haskell comment.

Illustration 5.3 (An imperative program for Euclidean division)

Haskell module <u>Language.BIPL.Sample</u>

```
-- // Compute quotient q and remainder r for dividing x by y
-- q = 0; r = x; while (r >= y) { r = r - y; q = q + 1; }
euclideanDiv :: Stmt
euclideanDiv =
  Seq (Assign "q" (IntConst 0)) (Seq (Assign "r" (Var "x"))
    (While
        (Binary Geq (Var "r") (Var "y"))
        (Seq (Assign "r" (Binary Sub (Var "r") (Var "y")))
            (Assign "q" (Binary Add (Var "q") (IntConst 1))))))
```

An interpreter for an imperative language such as BIPL needs to maintain a store (i.e., a map from variable names to values). The execution of statements may modify the store, as assignment statements may be performed. The evaluation of expressions observes the store. The simple BIPL language does not permit side effects in the scope of expressions. The notion of a store is generally important in interpretation; it is needed whenever imperative programs are being interpreted. Here is the informal semantics for BIPL:

Statement execution:

- Skip: The given store is returned, as is.
- Assign x e: The right-hand-side expression e is evaluated to a value, which is then assigned to the variable x in the given store.
- Seq s1 s2: Statement s1 is interpreted first. Statement s2 is interpreted second. Thus, the effects are incurred from left to right.
- If e s1 s2: The expression e must evaluate to a Boolean value, say b. If b equals True, then statement execution proceeds with s1; if b equals False, then statement execution proceeds with s2.
- While e s: The while-loop is executed as If e (Seq s (While e s)) Skip. That is, if the condition e holds, then the body s is executed, followed by the same while-loop again. If the condition does not hold, then a skip-statement is executed.

Expression evaluation:

- IntConst i: The literal i is returned as an integer value.
- Var x: The given store must map the variable name x to a value; this value is the result of evaluation.
- Unary o e and Binary o e1 e2: The operands must be evaluated to values of suitable types and the symbol o is interpreted as an operation of the metalanguage that is applied to the operands' values.

To this end, we need semantic domains as follows.

Illustration 5.4 (Semantic domains of a BIPL interpreter)

Haskell module <u>Language.BIPL.Domains</u>

```
-- Results of expression evaluation
type Value = Either Int Bool
-- Stores as maps from variable names to values
type Store = Map String Value
```

Thus, we use Haskell's library type Map to model stores as maps (say, dictionaries) from variable names to values. Here is how we expect to use the interpreter:

Interactive Haskell session:

▶ execute euclideanDivision (fromList [("x", Left 13), ("y", Left 4)])
fromList [("q", Left 3), ("r", Left 2), ("x", Left 14), ("y", Left 4)]

Thus, we start from a store with suitable arguments "x" and "y" for division; interpretation returns a store with "x" and "y" unchanged and with "q" and "r" bound to the computed quotient and remainder. We are ready to present the interpreter.

Illustration 5.5 (A BIPL interpreter)

Haskell module <u>Language.BIPL.Interpreter</u>

```
-- Execution of statements
execute :: Stmt → Store → Store
execute Skip m = m
execute (Assign x e) m = insert x (evaluate e m) m
execute (Seq s1 s2) m = execute s2 (execute s1 m)
execute (If e s1 s2) m = execute (if b then s1 else s2) m where Right b = evaluate e m
execute (While e s) m = execute (If e (Seq s (While e s)) Skip) m

-- Evaluation of expressions
evaluate :: Expr → Store → Value
evaluate (IntConst i) _ = Left i
evaluate (Var x) m = m!x
evaluate (Unary o e) m = uop o (evaluate e m)
evaluate (Binary o e1 e2) m = bop o (evaluate e1 m) (evaluate e2 m)

-- Interpretation of unary operators
uop :: UOp → Value → Value
uop Negate (Left i) = Left (negate i)
uop Not (Right b) = Right (not b)

-- Interpretation of binary operators
bop :: BOp → Value → Value → Value
bop Add (Left i1) (Left i2) = Left (i1+i2)
...
```

Exercise 5.4 (Interpretation without throwing)   [Basic level]
The interpreter "throws" when (i) a variable is used in an expression without a
value in the current store, (ii) a unary or binary operation finds an operand of
an unexpected type, or (iii) a condition of an if-statement does not evaluate to a
Boolean value. Revise the interpreter so that it uses Haskell's Maybe *type instead.*

Exercise 5.5 (Parameterless procedures)   [Basic level]
Extend the BIPL interpreter of Section 5.1.2 to incorporate procedures without pa-
rameters. A procedure is a named abstraction of a statement. There is a new state-
ment form for calling a procedure. For simplicity, assume that procedures can only
be declared at the top level of a program.

5.1.3 Interpretation with Environments

Let us now discuss the interpretation of functional programs, thereby encountering
function application or, more generally, application of a named and parameterized
abstraction, as a concept. We pick the fabricated functional programming language
BFPL for this purpose. (See Illustration 4.6 for the Haskell-based abstract syntax.)
Consider the following sample program represented as a Haskell term; concrete
syntax is shown for clarity in the Haskell comment.

Illustration 5.6 (A BFPL program for the factorial)

Haskell module *Language.BFPL.Samples.Factorial*

```
-- factorial :: Int -> Int
-- factorial x = if ((==) x 0) then 1 else ((*) x (factorial ((-) x 1)))
-- main = print $ factorial 5
factorial :: Program
factorial = ([(
  "factorial",
  (([IntType], IntType),
  (["x"],
    If (Binary Eq (Arg "x") (IntConst 0))
        (IntConst 1)
        (Binary Mul
            (Arg "x")
            (Apply "factorial" [Binary Sub (Arg "x") (IntConst 1)]))))))],
  (Apply "factorial" [IntConst 5]))
```

An interpreter for a functional language such as BFPL may maintain an environment for binding function arguments to values. Thus, we expect that BFPL expressions will be evaluated in the presence of an environment and function application

will set up an environment on the basis of actual arguments. The notion of an environment is generally important in interpretation; it is needed whenever names will need to bound within a scope of interpretation. Here is the informal semantics for BFPL:

- IntConst i: The literal i is returned as an integer value.
- BoolConst b: The literal b is returned as a Boolean value.
- Arg x: The binding of the argument x is looked up in the environment.
- If e0 e1 e2: The subexpression e0 must evaluate to a Boolean value, say b. If b equals True, then e1 is evaluated as the result of the compound expression. If b equals False, then e2 is evaluated as the result of the compound expression.
- Apply fn es: In the program with its collection of functions, the function of name fn is looked up – specifically the formal arguments xs and the body. The actual arguments es are evaluated, resulting in a list vs of values. A new environment is formed as a list of pairs, with elements drawn from xs and vs. The body is ultimately evaluated in the new environment.
- Evaluation of the main expression starts from an empty environment.

To this end, we need semantic domains as follows.

Illustration 5.7 (Semantic domains of a BFPL interpreter)

Haskell module Language.BFPL.Domains

```
-- Results of expression evaluation
type Value = Either Int Bool
-- Environments as maps from argument names to values
type Env = Map String Value
```

When defining the type Env, we again use Haskell's library type Map to model environments as maps (say, dictionaries) from argument names to values. Here is how we expect to use the interpreter:

Interactive Haskell session:

```
▶ evaluate factorial
Left 120
```

Thus, in the main function, we apply the factorial function to 5, thereby computing 120. We are ready to present the interpreter.

Illustration 5.8 (A BFPL interpreter)

Haskell module Language.BFPL.Interpreter

```
-- Evaluation of a program's main expression
evaluate :: Program → Value
evaluate (fs, e) = f e empty
  where
    -- Evaluation of expressions
    f :: Expr → Env → Value
    f (IntConst i) _ = Left i
    f (BoolConst b) _ = Right b
    f (Arg x) m = m!x
    f (If e0 e1 e2) m = f (if b then e1 else e2) m where Right b = f e0 m
    f (Unary o e) m = uop o (f e m)
    f (Binary o e1 e2) m = bop o (f e1 m) (f e2 m)
    f (Apply x es) m = f body m'
      where
        Just (_, (xs, body)) = lookup x fs
        vs = map (flip f m) es
        m' = fromList (zip xs vs)

-- Interpretation of unary operators
uop :: UOp → Value → Value
uop Negate (Left i) = Left (negate i)
uop Not (Right b) = Right (not b)

-- Interpretation of binary operators
bop :: BOp → Value → Value → Value
bop Add (Left i1) (Left i2) = Left (i1+i2)
...
```

Exercise 5.6 (Parameterized procedures)   [Intermediate level]
*Exercise 5.5 is extended to go beyond parameterless procedures. That is, a proce-
dure declares variables for formal parameters and the statement form for calling
a procedure includes a list of expressions as actual arguments. Extend the BIPL
interpreter to incorporate such procedures.*

5.1.4 Stepwise Interpretation

Let us now discuss interpretation for finite state machines according to the fabricated
language FSML; as introduced earlier. (See Illustration 4.8 for the Haskell-based
abstract syntax.) In contrast to the previous examples, FSML is a modeling language
rather than a programming language. Perhaps more importantly, interpretation of
FSMs intrinsically calls for stepwise execution, as we will see in a second. Here is
the recurring turnstile FSM represented as a Haskell term.

Illustration 5.9 (An FSM for a turnstile in a metro system)

Haskell module Language.FSML.Sample

```
turnstileFsm :: Fsm
turnstileFsm = Fsm [
  State True "locked" [
    (Transition "ticket" (Just "collect") "unlocked"),
    (Transition "pass" (Just "alarm") "exception") ],
  State False "unlocked" [
    (Transition "ticket" (Just "eject") "unlocked"),
    (Transition "pass" Nothing "locked") ],
  State False "exception" [
    (Transition "ticket" (Just "eject") "exception"),
    (Transition "pass" Nothing "exception"),
    (Transition "mute" Nothing "exception"),
    (Transition "release" Nothing "locked") ] ]
```

We expect that interpretation will consume events one by one. In each step, the corresponding action, if any, is produced as output and the machine makes a transition to the next state. Here is the informal semantics:

- To start the simulation, we need to determine the initial state of the FSM.
- For a given state and a given event, we need to look up the applicable transition, if any. We assume here that the FSM is deterministic, i.e., there is at most one applicable transition. The transition identifies the optional action to contribute to the output and the new state.
- The process of looking up transitions is to be repeated "step by step" until the input has been consumed, if possible. If there is no applicable transition at any point, then the FSM "gets stuck" and the remaining input is not consumed.

To this end, we need semantic domains as follows.

Illustration 5.10 (Semantic domains of an FSML interpreter)

Haskell module Language.FSML.Domains

```
-- Input of FSM simulation
type Input = [Event]
-- Output of FSM simulation
type Output = [Action]
```

The sample FSM can be exercised with input and output as follows.

Illustration 5.11 (Input and expected output for the turnstile FSM)

Haskell module Language.FSML.SampleIO

```
-- Sample input for sample FSM
sampleInput :: Input
sampleInput =
  [
    "ticket", -- Regular insertion of a ticket in locked state
    "ticket", -- Irregular insertion of a ticket in unlocked state
    "pass", -- Regular passage through turnstile in unlocked state
    "pass", -- Irregular attempt to pass through turnstile in locked state
    "ticket", -- Irregular insertion of a ticket in exceptional state
    "mute", -- Mute exceptional state alarm
    "release" -- Return from exceptional to locked state
  ]

-- Expected output
sampleOutput :: Output
sampleOutput = ["collect", "eject", "alarm", "eject"]
```

We assume a top-level function simulate which takes an FSM as well as a sequence of events and returns the corresponding sequence of actions. Here is how we expect to use the interpreter:

Interactive Haskell session:

```
▶ simulate turnstileFsm sampleInput == sampleOutput
True
```

We limit ourselves to a "batch-oriented" interpretation here. That is, we assume the complete input to be available upfront and that the complete output will become available at once. One may also think of "interactive" interpretation such that we would consume an input stream, event by event, and we would produce an output stream, action by action. The simple batch-oriented interpreter follows.

Illustration 5.12 (An FSML interpreter)

Haskell module Language.FSML.Interpreter

```
1   -- FSM simulation starting from initial state
2   simulate :: Fsm → Input → Output
3   simulate (Fsm ss) xs = snd (foldl makeTransition (getInitial, []) xs)
4     where
5       -- Look up initial state
6       getInitial :: StateId
7       getInitial = ini
8         where [State _ ini _] = [ s | s@(State initial _ _) ← ss, initial ]
9
10      -- Process event; extent output
```

```
11   makeTransition :: (StateId, Output) → Event → (StateId, Output)
12   makeTransition (source, as) x = (target, as ++ maybeToList a)
13     where (Transition _ a target) = getTransition source x
14
15   -- Look up transition
16   getTransition :: StateId → Event → Transition
17   getTransition sid x = t
18     where
19       [t] = [ t | t@(Transition x' _ _) ← ts, x == x' ]
20       [(State _ _ ts)] = [ s | s@(State _ sid' _) ← ss, sid == sid' ]
```

The interpreter folds over the entire input (line 3). We use list comprehensions to identify the initial state ini (line 8), the transition t for the given event (line 19), and the transitions ts of a state identified by its id (line 20).

Exercise 5.7 (Interpretation without throwing)   [Basic level]
The interpreter "throws" when a transition to an undeclared state is attempted, when a given event is not handled in a given state, or it is not handled deterministically. Revise the interpreter so that it uses Haskell's Maybe type instead.

Exercise 5.8 (A more abstract FSML syntax)   [Intermediate level]
There is an opportunity for a more abstract syntax for FSML. Note that the ids of the declared states must be distinct. Further, assume that only deterministic FSMs are to be represented, which implies that the events for the transitions of each state are distinct too. Thus, collections of both declared states and transitions per state can be modeled as maps. Revise FSML's Haskell-based abstract syntax (Illustration 4.8) and interpreter (Illustration 5.12) accordingly.

Exercise 5.9 (An interactive FSML interpreter)   [Intermediate level]
Implement an interactive FSML interpreter, as discussed above. For instance, you may represent the input and output as streams or message queues so that events are handled and actions are communicated as they become available.

5.2 Compilation

Compilation is alternative form of language implementation. In contrast to interpretation, programs are not "directly" executed, but are translated first. Thus, a compiler is a metaprogram which translates one language into another language. More generally, a translation is a description of a mapping (or the execution thereof) from one software language to another software language. The translation of a compiler is assumed to be semantics-preserving, that is, if we had interpreters (semantics) for the input and output languages of the translation, then interpretation of the input and output would return the same result.

The topic of compilation will be covered here only superficially. There is no shortage of good textbooks on compilation (e.g., [1, 32, 3]). We will briefly summarize the architecture of a "classic" compiler and develop a simple, two-phase compiler for translating imperative programs first to an assembly language and second to a machine language.

5.2.1 Architecture of a Compiler

A compiler breaks down into a frontend and a backend with subordinate phases or components as follows:

Frontend

Syntactic analysis This phase, which is also referred to as *parsing*, essentially determines the syntactical structure of the input. To this end, parsing is typically guided by a grammar which defines the input language.

Preprocessing A preprocessor may be applied prior to actual parsing. This is, for example, the case for the C and C++ languages. Other languages may use more syntax-aware macro mechanisms which are readily integrated with parsing.

Lexical analysis Parsing may involve an extra phase, scanning, for processing text at the level of lexical syntax for units such as white space, comments, identifiers, and literals. There are scannerless and non-scannerless parsers.

Semantic analysis Name-binding and typing rules are checked. Appropriate data structures (i.e., a symbol table or an attributed parse tree) are built to represent semantic information about program identifiers that is also to be used in subsequent phases.

Backend

Program analysis The control and data flow in the program are analyzed to find nontrivial problems (such as dead code), and to enable optimizations (such as dead-code elimination) and efficient code generation. An extended development of the topic can be found in a dedicated textbook [37]; textbooks on compiler construction also cover the topic to some extent.

Optimization The code is optimized, for example, by dead-code elimination, constant folding, common-subexpression elimination, or loop unfolding. Optimizations may be applied at different levels of abstraction, i.e., at the level of parse trees, intermediate representations (abstracting from input syntax), dedicated representations provided by program analysis (e.g., control-flow graphs), or target code (assembly or machine code).

Code generation   The source language or some language for intermediate representation is translated into a target language such as a virtual machine language. This translation is also referred to as code generation. The translation may be described in different ways, for example, by simple rules or by a recursive function that composes target code from parts of source code. Code generation may also use constraints on the size of the target code or other "cost functions" on code [38]. Further, code generation can also commence in phases, for example, a phase of translation from a high-level language to bytecode, followed by a phase completing translation to machine code.

Among all these components of a real compiler, we focus below on the core component for code generation. Parsing (syntactic analysis) is covered separately (Chapter 7) because it is such a recurring phase in many metaprogramming scenarios. Some other components will be touched upon later, i.e., semantic analysis (Section 5.3) and optimization (Section 5.4); these aspects are also relevant beyond the scope of compilation.

5.2.2 Translation to Assembly Code

We use a fabricated assembly language: *BAL* (*B*asic *A*ssembly *L*anguage). BAL is stack-based, as far as primitive operations (Add, Not, ...) are concerned; it is symbol-based, as far as addressing memory cells is concerned; and it is jump- and label-based in terms of control flow (i.e., there are labels, and unconditional and conditional jumps, but no structured if-statements or while-loops). Let us illustrate the language with the following sample program for Euclidean division; the underlying imperative code is shown in the Haskell comments.

Illustration 5.13 (Euclidean division in assembly code)

Haskell module Language.BAL.Sample

```
euclideanDiv = [
    Const 14, Store "x",  -- x = 14;
    Const 4, Store "y",  -- y = 4;
    Const 0, Store "q",  -- q = 0;
    Load "x", Store "r",  -- r = x;
    Label "0",  -- Beginning of while loop
    Load "r", Load "y", Geq,  -- (r >= y)
    Not, CJump "1",  -- Skip while loop
    Load "r", Load "y", Sub, Store "r",  -- r = r - y;
    Load "q", Const 1, Add, Store "q",  -- q = q + 1;
    Jump "0",  -- Next iteration of loop
    Label "1"  -- Label to goto when skipping loop
    ]
```

The type for BAL instructions is defined as follows.

Illustration 5.14 (Abstract syntax of BAL assembly code)

Haskell module Language.BAL.Syntax

```
data Instr
  = Const Int -- Push a constant onto the stack
  | Store String -- Store TOS in storage and pop TOS
  | Load String -- Push a storage cell's content onto stack
  | Label String -- Place a label as an address for jumps
  | Jump String -- Jump to a label
  | CJump String -- Jump to a label, if TOS is nonzero; also pop TOS
  | Not -- Apply negation to TOS and replace it by result
  | Add -- Apply addition to the two topmost stack elements; pop them; push result
  ...
```

For each BAL instruction form, we have also included its informal semantics as a comment. We have elided several primitive operations for brevity. Importantly, there are instruction forms for accessing the memory in a symbol-based (i.e., name-based) manner. There are instruction forms for jumping both conditionally and unconditionally to a label.

The translation of imperative programs (BIPL) to assembly code (BAL) is a function which maps each statement or expression to a corresponding sequence of assembly instructions, as shown below.

Illustration 5.15 (Translation to assembly code)

Haskell module Language.BIPL.Compiler

```
compile :: Stmt → [Instr]
compile s = fst (stmt s 0)

stmt :: Stmt → Int → ([Instr], Int)
stmt Skip l = ([], l)
stmt (Assign x e) l = (expr e ++ [Store x], l)
stmt (Seq s1 s2) l0 =
  let
    (zs1, l1) = stmt s1 l0
    (zs2, l2) = stmt s2 l1
  in (zs1 ++ zs2, l2)
stmt (If e s1 s2) l0 =
  let l1 = l0+1
      (zs1, l2) = stmt s1 (l1+1)
      (zs2, l3) = stmt s2 l2
  in (expr e
      ++ (CJump (show l0) : zs2)
      ++ (Jump (show l1) : (Label (show l0) : zs1))
      ++ [Label (show l1)], l3)
stmt (While e s) l0 =
  let l1 = l0+1
      (zs, l2) = stmt s (l1+1)
```

```
in ([Label (show l0)] ++ expr e
    ++ (Not : (CJump (show l1) : zs))
    ++ [Jump (show l0), Label (show l1)], l2)

expr :: Expr → [Instr]
expr (IntConst i) = [Const i]
expr (Var x) = [Load x]
expr (Unary BIPL.Negate e) = expr (Binary BIPL.Sub (IntConst 0) e)
expr (Unary BIPL.Not e) = expr e ++ [BAL.Not]
expr (Binary o e1 e2) = expr e1 ++ expr e2 ++
  [ case o of
      BIPL.Add → BAL.Add
      ...
```

The function above models a recursive walk over BIPL's syntactical patterns such that the resulting BAL instruction sequences are composed from recursive results. Labels need to be introduced along the way, subject to some housekeeping. That is, an Int is passed around to represent the next "available" label.

We explain the translation rules for the statement forms as follows:

- Skip: The empty instruction sequence "[]" is returned with the unmodified label counter.
- Assign x e: A Store x instruction is added to the instruction sequence for the expression e; the label counter is not modified, as *e* cannot involve control flow.
- Seq s1 s2: The instruction sequences for the two statements s1 and s2 are simply concatenated; the label counter is threaded through the two recursive applications of the translation function.
- If e s1 s2: Two labels are used: label l0 is for the instructions of the else-branch; and label l1 is for the end of the if-statement, as the then-branch needs to skip over the else-branch. The overall instruction sequence is obtained by concatenating the sequences for the condition, then-branch, and else-branch with appropriate insertions for labels and jumping.
- While e s: This case is similar to the one for if-statements, as it involves label placement and jumps.

The translation of expressions is even more straightforward and will not be explained here further for brevity. To summarize, each statement and each expression are mapped to zero, one, or more instructions while recursing into compound statements and expressions and composing the recursively computed instruction sequences in appropriate ways. Along the way, house keeping is done so that labels can be introduced consistently.

Exercise 5.10 (Compilation of functional programs)   [Intermediate level]
The translation of function applications requires stack-based subroutines and parameter passing. Extend BAL to provide enough expressiveness and devise a translation from BFPL to the extended assembly language.

5.2.3 Translation to Machine Code

The assembly language, as discussed above, makes some assumptions that necessitate another phase of translation if we want to arrive at the low level of a machine language. Firstly, in BAL, labels are explicitly placed and arbitrary names can be assigned to labels. In a low-level language, there are no labels, but instead one needs to deal with instruction addresses. Secondly, in BAL, memory access is symbol-based. In a low-level language, one needs to deal with addresses of memory cells.

We use a fabricated machine language: *BML* (*B*asic *M*achine *L*anguage). BML is very similar to BAL, but memory access leverages integers for addresses, and jumping leverages integers for the instruction pointer; there is no label operation. Here is a sample program.

Illustration 5.16 (Euclidean division in machine code)

Haskell module Language.BML.Sample

```
euclideanDiv = [Const 14,Store 0,Const 4,Store 1,Const 0,Store 2,Load 0,Store 3,Load
    3,Load 1,Geq,Not,CJump 22,Load 3,Load 1,Sub,Store 3,Load 2,Const 1,Add,Store
    2,Jump 8]
```

The type for BML instructions is defined as follows.

Illustration 5.17 (Abstract syntax of BML machine code)

Haskell module Language.BML.Syntax

```
data Instr
  = Const Int -- Push a constant onto the stack
  | Store Int -- Store TOS in storage and pop TOS
  | Load Int -- Push a storage cell's content onto stack
  | Jump Int -- Jump to an address
  | CJump Int -- Jump to an address, if TOS is nonzero; also pop TOS
  | Not -- Apply negation to TOS and replace it by result
  | Add -- Apply addition to the two topmost stack elements; pop them; push result
  ...
```

A translator from BAL to BML may also be referred to as an assembler. The following translator essentially translates BAL instruction sequences to BML instruction sequences, one by one.

Illustration 5.18 (BAL to BML assembler)

Haskell module Language.BAL.Assembler

```
assemble :: [BAL.Instr] → [BML.Instr]
assemble zs = concat (map f zs)
  where
    f (BAL.Const i) = [BML.Const i]
    f (BAL.Store x) = [BML.Store (cell x)]
    f (BAL.Load x) = [BML.Load (cell x)]
    f (BAL.Label x) = []
    f (BAL.Jump x) = [BML.Jump (instruction x)]
    f (BAL.CJump x) = [BML.CJump (instruction x)]
    f BAL.Not = [BML.Not]
    f BAL.Add = [BML.Add]
    ...

    -- Map symbol to memory cell
    cell :: String → Int
    cell x = fromJust (findIndex (==x) symbols)
      where
        symbols = nub (concat (map symbol zs))
        symbol (BAL.Store x) = [x]
        symbol _ = []

    -- Map label to instruction address
    instruction :: String → Int
    instruction x = instruction' 0 zs
      where
        instruction' i (BAL.Label x' : zs) = if x==x' then i else instruction' i zs
        instruction' i (_ : zs) = instruction' (i+1) zs
```

The translation is largely trivial because the instruction forms of BAL and BML are so similar. However, we need to take a closer look at the instructions for memory access, label placement, and jumps. We explain the corresponding translation rules in detail as follows:

- BAL.Label x: No corresponding BML instruction is generated. The label is only used when resolving jumps; see the helper function instruction.
- BAL.Store x: A corresponding BML.Store instruction is generated, where the symbol x is mapped to an address for the memory cell; see the helper function cell which collects all symbols, "nubs" them (i.e., makes them unique), and determines a symbol's address as the position in the resulting list.
- BAL.Load x: A corresponding BML.Load instruction is generated. The symbol x is mapped in the same way as in the case of BAL.Store x.
- BAL.Jump x: A corresponding BML.Jump instruction is generated. The symbol x is mapped to an address for an instruction; see the helper function instruction, which determines the position of x in the input sequence zs while not counting label instructions, as they will not end up in the machine code.

- BAL.CJump x: A corresponding BML.CJump instruction is generated. The symbol x is mapped in the same way as in the case of BAL.Jump x.

For the sake of completeness, we need to provide an interpreter for the BML language, thereby making sure that we fully understand the translation in terms of the semantics of the languages involved. The interpreter is illustrated by applying it to the instructions for Euclidean division:

Interactive Haskell session:

▶ run Language.ML.Sample.euclideanDivision
(fromList [(0,14),(1,4),(2,3),(3,2)],[])

This result is basically a "memory dump"; the key "0" corresponds to the original variable *"x"*, the key "1" to *"y"*, and so on. The underlying interpreter uses a stack for operands and a map for the memory as shown below.

Illustration 5.19 (Interpretation of BML machine code)

Haskell module Language.BML.Machine

```
1   type Memory = Map Int Int
2   type Stack = [Int]
3
4   run :: [Instr] → (Memory, Stack)
5   run zs0 = run' zs0 empty []
6     where
7       run' :: [Instr] → Memory → Stack → (Memory, Stack)
8       run' [] sto sta = (sto, sta)
9       run' (z:zs) sto sta = let (zs', sto', sta') = step z in run' zs' sto' sta'
10        where
11          step :: Instr → ([Instr], Memory, Stack)
12          step (Const i) = (zs, sto, i : sta)
13          step (Store i) = (zs, insert i (head sta) sto, tail sta)
14          step (Load i) = (zs, sto, sto!i : sta)
15          step (Jump i) = (drop i zs0, sto, sta)
16          step (CJump i) = (if head sta /= 0 then drop i zs0 else zs, sto, tail sta)
17          step Not = (zs, sto, uop (λ i → if i == 0 then 1 else 0) sta)
18          step Add = (zs, sto, bop (+) sta)
19          ... -- other operations omitted
20
21   -- Apply unary operation on ints on stack
22   uop :: (Int → Int) → Stack → Stack
23   uop f (i1:sta) = f i1 : sta
24
25   -- Apply binary operation on ints on stack
26   bop :: (Int → Int → Int) → Stack → Stack
27   bop f (i2:i1:sta) = f i1 i2 : sta
```

Thus, the run function takes an instruction sequence and returns a memory and a stack; the initial memory is assumed to be the "empty" map from Ints to Ints; and the initial stack is empty. The function uses a tail-recursive helper function run' to execute instruction sequences until the empty sequence is left (line 8). When facing a nonempty sequence (line 9), the helper function step is used to execute the heading instruction. Most of the cases of step return the remaining instruction sequence zs, while the cases for jump instructions (lines 15–16) identify an alternative "continuation", that is, the instruction sequence corresponding to the jump address. (We will discuss continuations again in Section 11.3.)

Exercise 5.11 (Compilation to Java bytecode)   [Intermediate level]
Implement a translation from BIPL to Java bytecode. To this end, you may use ASM,[2] a framework for Java bytecode analysis and manipulation.

5.3 Analysis

We are concerned here with the static analysis of software artifacts such as source code. We are not concerned with the analysis of programs at runtime or with traces of program execution. We use the term "(static) analysis" here in a broad sense to include well-formedness checking, type checking, other forms of program checking and analysis [44], type inference, and fact or model extraction, thereby encompassing areas as different as language implementation, program verification, software quality assurance, and software reverse engineering.

We develop analyses here as more or less disciplined metaprograms without much discussion of the underlying foundations of type systems [40] and (formal) program analysis [37], and also without employing specification languages such as attribute grammars [25, 2] or Object Constraint Language (OCL) [11].

There are several different kinds of analysis results. In the basic case, an analysis may consist of a predicate checking for constraint satisfaction, as in well-formedness or type checking. In other cases, an analysis computes a data structure such as a collection of metrics or facts for program abstractions. Ultimately, an analysis may return nontrivial software language artifacts, for example, a recovered architectural model. We cover such diversity only in a sketchy manner.

5.3.1 Type Checking

A type checker is a metaprogram which checks that all language constructs are used correctly in terms of the types of operands or arguments. Along the way, a type checker also checks that each name used (e.g., for variables) can be associated with a declaration (e.g., a variable declaration). We demonstrate type checking here for

---

[2] asm.ow2.org

the trivial expression language BTL. This language features natural numbers and
Boolean values, as well as operations on these types of values.

Here is how we expect to use BTL's type checker:

Interactive Haskell session:

▶ wellTyped (Succ Zero)
True

- -

▶ wellTyped (Succ TRUE)
False

That is, the expression Succ Zero is well-typed because the Succ operation is correctly applied to an expression that is of the type of natural numbers. In contrast,
the expression Succ TRUE is ill-typed because the Succ operation is incorrectly applied to an expression that is of the type of Boolean values. The type checker is
implemented as follows.

Illustration 5.20 (A type checker for BTL expressions)

Haskell module Language.BTL.TypeChecker

```
1   -- Types of expressions
2   data Type = NatType | BoolType
3
4   -- Well-typedness of expressions
5   wellTyped :: Expr → Bool
6   wellTyped e = isJust (typeOf e)
7
8   -- Types of expressions
9   typeOf :: Expr → Maybe Type
10  typeOf TRUE = return BoolType
11  typeOf FALSE = return BoolType
12  typeOf Zero = return NatType
13  typeOf (Succ e) = do { NatType ← typeOf e; return NatType }
14  typeOf (Pred e) = do { NatType ← typeOf e; return NatType }
15  typeOf (IsZero e) = do { NatType ← typeOf e; return BoolType }
16  typeOf (If e0 e1 e2) = do
17      BoolType ← typeOf e0
18      t1 ← typeOf e1
19      t2 ← typeOf e2
20      guard (t1==t2)
21      return t1
```

Thus, the type checker is a simple syntax-driven metaprogram with one equation
per syntactical pattern and the use of recursion for checking types of subexpressions.
In this sense, metaprograms for type checking and interpretation (Section 5.1) leverage a similar program structure. The type checker designates the type Type (lines
1–2) to represent the different types of BTL expressions. The type checker returns
a Boolean value (lines 4–6) to report whether or not a BTL expression is well-
typed, i.e., the type of the expression can be determined. The central function of

the type checker is typeOf (lines 8-21), which maps expressions to types; the result is wrapped in the Maybe monad so that type-checking failure is communicated gracefully. We consider all the equations of the type checker:

- TRUE, FALSE, and Zero (lines 10–12): These cases of constant forms of expressions simply return the corresponding type of the constant.
- Succ e, Pred e, and IsZero e (lines 13–15): These cases of unary operations check the type of the operand by a monadic bind and return the result type of the operation.
- If e0 e1 e2 (lines 16–21): The first operand must be of type Bool. The second and third operands must be of the same type – this common type is also returned as the type of the if-expression.

The complexity of type checking obviously increases with the complexity of the object language. For instance, a type checker for a functional programming language (e.g., BFPL) would need to check that the types of the actual arguments in function applications agree with the declared types of the formal arguments. In Chapter 9, we will see several more interesting type checkers.

Exercise 5.12 (Graceful failure)   [Basic level]
We decided to wrap the result of type checking in the Maybe *monad (Illustration 5.20), whereas we did not wrap the result of interpretation (Illustration 5.2). Argue why it is more "important" to deal gracefully with failure in type checking than in interpretation.*

5.3.2 Well-Formedness Checking

A *well-formedness checker* is a metaprogram which checks language-specific constraints on top of the abstract syntax of object programs. In fact, a type checker, as discussed before, can also be referred to as a well-formedness checker – except that well-formedness is also applicable without direct reference to types. A well-formedness checker may be implemented as a predicate modeling the underlying constraints.

We demonstrate well-formedness checking here for the domain-specific modeling language FSML. For instance, it makes sense to check that all referenced state ids (i.e., ids appearing as targets of transitions) are actually declared by a state declaration – no types are involved here. Such matching of name references and declarations is also referred to as *name binding*. Here is how we expect to use a well-formedness checker for FSML:

Interactive Haskell session:

▶ check turnstileFsm
True

- -

▶ check (Fsm [State False *"x"* []])
False

In the first check, we confirm that the turnstile FSM is well-formed. In the second check, we face an FSM without an initial state and it is thus confirmed to be ill-formed. We are ready to present the well-formedness checker.

Illustration 5.21 (Well-formedness for finite state machines)

Haskell module <u>Language.FSML.BoolChecker</u>

```
check :: Fsm → Bool
check fsm = and (map ($ fsm) [
    distinctStateIds,
    singleInitialState,
    resolvableTargetStates,
    deterministicTransitions,
    reachableStates ] )

distinctStateIds :: Fsm → Bool
distinctStateIds (Fsm ss) = sids == nub sids
  where sids = [ sid | (State _ sid _) ← ss ]

singleInitialState :: Fsm → Bool
singleInitialState (Fsm ss) = length inis == 1
  where inis = [ sid | s@(State initial sid _) ← ss, initial ]

resolvableTargetStates :: Fsm → Bool
resolvableTargetStates (Fsm ss) = and (map (λ (State _ _ ts) → and (map f ts)) ss)
  where f (Transition _ _ target) =
        not (null [ s | s@(State _ source _) ← ss, source == target ])

deterministicTransitions :: Fsm → Bool
deterministicTransitions (Fsm ss) = and (map (λ (State _ _ ts) → f ts) ss)
  where f ts = events == nub events
        where events = [ event | (Transition event _ _) ← ts ]

reachableStates :: Fsm → Bool
reachableStates (Fsm ss) = ...
```

The analysis (i.e., the checker) combines several constraints (*distinctStateIds*, *singleInitialState*, etc.) by conjunction – meaning that all the individual constraints must hold for an FSM to be well-formed. We describe the constraints and their implementation in Haskell in some detail as follows:

- distinctStateIds: The state ids of the different state declarations which an FSM consists of need to be distinct. This is checked by extracting the state ids from all the declarations and checking that the result is a proper set (by means of nub).

- singleInitialState: There is supposed to be exactly one initial state. A list comprehension is used to extract the list of initial states, which is then checked to ensure that it is of length 1.
- resolvableTargetStates: All the target state ids are supposed to be resolvable to declared states. This is checked for each target state id by trying to find the corresponding state declaration by means of a list comprehension.
- deterministicTransitions: The per-state transitions are supposed to involve distinct events. This is checked for each state by extracting the events from the transitions and checking that the result is a proper set (by means of nub).
- reachableStates: All states are supposed to be reachable from the initial state. We omit a description of the implementation of this constraint for brevity.

Exercise 5.13 (Resolution of target states)   [Basic level]
Consider the implementation of resolvableTargetStates *and identify an aspect of unnecessarily inefficient implementation; improve the implementation accordingly.*

When an analysis is supposed to check artifacts and thus potentially identify problems, then it may be practically important to return errors or warnings that will be helpful for better understanding and locating problems. Thus, we should make a transition from predicates to functions that return collections of error messages. Here is how we expect to use an accordingly revised well-formedness checker for FSML:

Interactive Haskell session:

▶ check turnstileFsm
[]
- -
▶ check (Fsm [State False *"x"* []])
[*"Missing initial state"*,*"Unreachable state x"*]

In the first check, we confirm that the turnstile FSM is well-formed; an empty list of error messages proxies for well-formedness. In the second check, we face an FSM without an initial state. Ill-formedness is explained in terms of two error messages: the initial state is missing, and the declared state is unreachable, as a consequence of the missing initial state. The revised checker looks as follows.

Illustration 5.22 (Analysis with error messages)

Haskell module Language.FSML.StringChecker

```
1  check :: Fsm → [String]
2  check fsm = concatMap ($ fsm) [
3      distinctStateIds,
4      singleInitialState,
5      resolvableTargetStates,
6      deterministicTransitions,
```

```
7      reachableStates ]
8
9    distinctStateIds :: Fsm → [String]
10   distinctStateIds (Fsm ss) = map ("Multiple declarations of state " ++) doubles
11     where
12       doubles = (\\) sids (nub sids)
13       sids = [ sid | (State _ sid _) ← ss ]
14   ...
```

The error messages returned by the individual constraints are concatenated together (line 2). Compare the Boolean version of the *distinctStateIds* constraint with
the version returning error messages. In the former case, there is simply a test for
whether there are any doubles. In the latter case, the set of doubles is precisely
determined (lines 12–13) and then we map over the doubles to generate one error
message per double (line 10).

Exercise 5.14 (Avoiding duplicate error messages)   [Basic level]
*Analyze the above checker and identify potential sources of duplicate error mes-
sages; revise the checker so that duplicates are never returned to the user.*

5.3.3 Fact Extraction

A fact extractor is a metaprogram which extracts certain "facts" from given software
artifacts. The idea is that a fact is essentially a property of a well-defined part of the
input or a relationship between parts; see [35, 31, 6] for many scenarios and fact
extraction techniques. Fact extraction is often used in the context of software reverse
engineering. We may take the view that collections of facts, as extracted by a fact
extractor, form elements of a dedicated software language.

We use trivial metric-like examples to illustrate fact extraction. Let us consider
the problem of determining the number of inbounds and outbounds for each state
in an FSM — this may be viewed as some sort of "complexity metric". A state is
an inbound for another state if there is a transition from the former to the latter.
Likewise, a state is an outbound for another state if there is a transition from the
latter to the former. Such fact extraction is implemented as a function inouts, which
we use as follows.

Interactive Haskell session:

```
▶ inouts turnstileFsm
fromList [("exception",(1,1)),("locked",(2,2)),("unlocked",(1,1))]
```

For instance, there is only one state with a transition to *exception*; there is also
just one state that is directly reachable by a transition from *exception*. In both cases,
we do not count "self-transitions". The implementation of inouts follows.

Illustration 5.23 (Counting inbound and outbound states for FSMs)

Haskell module Language.FSML.Extraction

```
inouts :: Fsm → Map StateId (Int, Int)
inouts (Fsm ss) = fromList (map f ss)
   where
      −− Per−state fact extraction
      f (State _ sid ts) = (sid, (ins, outs))
         where
            −− Number of states from which sid is reached directly
            ins = length (filter g ss)
               where g (State _ sid' ts') =
                        elem sid [ sid" | Transition _ _ sid" ← ts', sid" /= sid' ]
            −− Number of states reached directly from sid
            outs = length (nub [ sid' | Transition _ _ sid' ← ts, sid /= sid' ])
```

That is, list comprehensions are used to collect states ins from which a given state sid is reached directly, and states out which are reached directly from sid. The collection is performed per state, and the per-state results are combined into a map from state ids to inbounds and outbounds.

As another example of fact extraction, let us consider the problem of measuring the frequency of unary and binary operator usage in a program — this may be viewed as some sort of "language-usage analysis". We apply such fact extraction to imperative BIPL programs. We assume that this fact extraction is implemented as a function ops, which we expect to use as follows:

Interactive Haskell session:

```
▶ ops euclideanDiv
fromList [("Add",1),("Geq",1),("Sub",1)]
```

That is, addition, comparison ("$\geq$"), and subtraction are all used once in the sample program; no other operators are used. The implementation of ops follows.

Illustration 5.24 (Counting operator applications in BIPL programs)

Haskell module Language.BIPL.Extraction

```
ops :: Stmt → Map String Int
ops s = foldr (λ o m → insertWith (+) o 1 m) empty os
   where
      os = everything (++) ([] `mkQ` f) s
      f (Unary o _) = [showConstr (toConstr o)]
      f (Binary o _ _) = [showConstr (toConstr o)]
      f _ = []
```

In the code above, we use a generic functional programming scheme everything to go over a BIPL program and extract operator uses; we rely on Haskell's "scrap your boilerplate" (SYB) approach to generic functional programming [28, 29, 30]. We use the traversal scheme everything in such a manner that we reach each and every expression – including those statements – and we extract all operators (their string representations) from unary and binary expressions. Each occurrence counts as one when we build up the frequency map for operator usage; see the use of insertWith.

Exercise 5.15 (Function application graph)   [Basic level]
In a functional program, functions can of course apply other functions and they may be directly and indirectly recursive. Devise a fact extraction for BFPL which results in a graph with a node for each function and with an edge between functions f and g if there is an application of g within the definition of f.

5.4 Transformation

We are concerned here with the static transformation of software artifacts such as source code. We are not concerned with the transformation (adaptation) of programs at runtime, for example, in the sense of self-adaptive systems. The term "transformation" is highly overloaded in software engineering. We assume here that a transformation is a description of changes or replacements to be applied to elements of a given software language. The result may be in the same or a different software language; see also the established classifiers for endogenous versus exogenous transformations [33].

We use the term "(static) transformation" here in a broad sense to include program optimization, program refactoring, model transformation, and technological space mapping, thereby encompassing areas as different as language implementation, model-driven engineering, and software re-engineering. Arguably, translation and analysis, as discussed above, can be viewed as exogenous transformations [33], i.e., the source and target languages differ. We focus below on endogenous transformations, i.e., transformations with the same source and target language.

In practice, especially in the areas of software re-engineering, reverse engineering, and model-driven engineering, transformations may be implemented with the help of dedicated frameworks or even metaprogramming systems or transformation languages (e.g., ASF+SDF [49], TXL [12, 13], Stratego [10], Rascal [23, 22], or ATL [21]). We will continue to use Haskell for illustration here; we do not use any advanced frameworks at this point.

5.4.1 Optimization

Optimization is a recurring issue in language implementation. For instance, a compiler performs optimizations at various stages on the basis of different program representations. A DSL implementation may provide good performance compared with a general-purpose language because of domain-specific optimizations.

Let us consider expression simplification as a simple instance of optimization here. More specifically, we will deal with the expression forms that are common to the fabricated imperative and functional programming languages BIPL and BFPL, as used throughout this book. We refer to these shared expression forms as EL (*Expression Language*) with the abstract syntax defined as follows.

Illustration 5.25 (Abstract syntax of EL expressions)

Haskell module Language.EL.Syntax

```
-- Expressions
data Expr =
  IntConst Int | BoolConst Bool | Var String | Unary UOp Expr | Binary BOp Expr Expr
-- Unary operators
data UOp = Negate | Not
-- Binary operators
data BOp = Add | Sub | Mul | Lt | Le | Eq | Geq | Gt | And | Or
```

One can think of various simplification rules that cater for optimization. For instance, the algebraic units of addition and multiplication can be used for simplification. We assume a function simplify to this end:

Interactive Haskell session:

```
▶ simplify (Binary Add (Var "a") (IntConst 0))
Just (Var "a")
- - - - - - - - - - - - - - - - - - - - - - - - - - - - - - - - - - - - -
▶ simplify (IntConst 42)
Nothing
```

An application of the function simplify succeeds only if a rule is applicable. The first application succeeds because "0" is a (right) unit of addition and thus we can simplify the addition expression to the remaining (left) operand. The second application fails because no simplification rule is applicable. The simplify function collects a number of simplification rules together as shown below.

Illustration 5.26 (Simplification rules for expressions)

Haskell module <u>Language.EL.Rules.Simplify</u>

```
simplify :: Expr → Maybe Expr
simplify (Binary Add x (IntConst 0)) = Just x
simplify (Binary Mul x (IntConst 1)) = Just x
simplify (Binary Mul x (IntConst 0)) = Just (IntConst 0)
simplify _ = Nothing
```

In order to fully define the intended optimization, a little more work is needed because our simplification rules are encoded in such a way that, so far, they only apply at the top of the input term. Consider the following failing attempt of simplification:

Interactive Haskell session:

▶ simplify (Binary Add (Var *"a"*) (Binary Add (Var *"b"*) (IntConst 0)))
Nothing

That is, the application fails despite a simplification opportunity in a subterm position; see the right operand of the outermost binary expression. Let us devise a normalization function for expressions which exhaustively applies a given function to a term and all its subterms recursively, as many times as needed for this process to arrive at a fixed point, as shown below.

Illustration 5.27 (Normalization of expressions)

Haskell module <u>Language.EL.Normalizer</u>

```
normalize :: (Expr → Maybe Expr) → Expr → Expr
normalize f e _ let e' _ pass e in if e__e' then e else normalize f e'
  where
    —— Apply one pass of normalization
    pass e = sub (maybe e id (f e))
    —— Push normalization into subexpressions
    sub (Unary o e) = Unary o (pass e)
    sub (Binary o e1 e2) = Binary o (pass e1) (pass e2)
    sub e = e
```

The function recursively traverses into the given expression and applies the argument f to the root and all subexpressions. When f fails, then we maintain the input term as is; see the application of maybe. Careful inspection suggests that normalization commences in a top-down manner, as f is applied to an expression e before recursive application. Recursive passes are performed until the term does not change anymore. Thus, we can apply the higher-order function normalize to the function simplify to perform exhaustive simplification:

Interactive Haskell session:

▶ normalize simplify (Binary Add (Var *"a"*) (Binary Add (Var *"b"*) (IntConst 0)))
Binary Add (Var *"a"*) (Var *"b"*)

More effort would be needed to be able also to optimize expressions that are part of bigger program phrases, for example, imperative statements. The normalize function at hand can only deal with expressions. Ultimately, we need a more powerful metaprogramming technique: *term rewriting* [15, 24, 16], as discussed later in this book (Section 12.1).

Exercise 5.16 (Positive test cases for optimization)   [Basic level]
State positive test cases for all of the simplification rules in Illustration 5.26 which have not yet been tested above.

5.4.2 Refactoring

A refactoring is a transformation that changes a program's "design" without changing its behavior [17, 34]. A very simple example of a refactoring in an object-oriented program is renaming of classes or methods. Refactorings can be automated (see Opdyke's seminal work [39]), and they make sense across all kinds of software languages [27]. For instance, some form of renaming can be applied to abstractions in different kinds of programming languages or other kinds of software languages, as we will demonstrate in this section.

Let us demonstrate renaming for the FSML language. In particular, we may want to rename state ids in finite state machines. The FSML instance is illustrated in Fig. 5.1; the illustration provides a positive test case for renaming such that the state id "*locked*" is renamed to "*closed*" and "*unlocked*" is renamed to "*open*".

Before discussing the actual transformation, let us identify the precondition and the postcondition for a "proper" renaming, as described below.

Illustration 5.28 (Pre/postconditions for state-id renaming)

Haskell module Language.FSML.Rename.Condition

```
pre, post :: StateId → StateId → Fsm → Bool
pre i i' x = elem i (states x) && not (elem i' (states x))
post i i' y = not (elem i (states y)) && elem i' (states y)
states :: Fsm → [StateId]
states fsm =
  concatMap (λ s →
    getId s : map getTarget (getTransitions s))
      (getStates fsm)
```

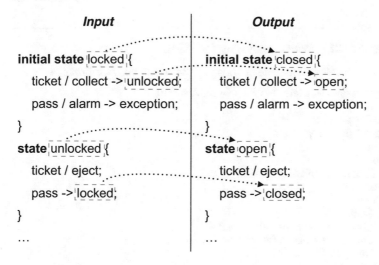

Fig. 5.1 Illustration of rename refactoring for FSML's state ids: the input and the output of the transformation are shown; the related state ids are highlighted by edges.

That is, the precondition for renaming state id i to i' in an FSM x is that i must be in use in x and i' must not be in use in x. The postcondition is that i must not be in use in the resulting FSM y (anymore) and i' must be (now) in use in y.

In implementing pre/postconditions, we interpret the notion of a state id being "in use" in an FSM as meaning that the id occurs either as the name assigned to a state (a declaration thereof) or in the target location of a transition.

Exercise 5.17 (Postcondition for state-id renaming)   [Basic level]
Argue that the postcondition stated above is not as strong as possible. Attempt a stronger formulation.

Exercise 5.18 (Negative test cases for state-id renaming)   [Basic level]
Devise negative test cases for the precondition stated above.

For any transformation, it is useful to understand the laws obeyed by the transformation. As far as renaming is concerned, we may state that renaming can be reverted as follows; we gloss over the detail here that renaming returns a "maybe".

```
rename i' i . rename i i' = id
```

We are ready to present the actual transformation.

Illustration 5.29 (State-id renaming for FSML)

Haskell module Language.FSML.Rename.Transformation

```
rename :: StateId → StateId → Fsm → Maybe Fsm
rename i i' x = do
    guard $ pre i i' x
    guard $ post i i' y
    return y
  where
    y = Fsm (map perState (getStates x))
    perState s =
      State
        (getInitial s)
        (if getId s == i then i' else getId s)
        (map perTransition (getTransitions s))
    perTransition t =
      Transition
        (getEvent t)
        (getAction t)
        (if getTarget t == i then i' else getTarget t)
```

Thus, the code describes a traversal over the structure of an FSM while replacing state ids systematically.

Let us consider another instance of renaming, i.e., renaming variables in an imperative program. This is a much simplified variation on what IDEs provide for mainstream programming languages. The pre/postconditions are similar to the FSML instance – except that "names in use" are determined differently, as shown below.

Illustration 5.30 (Pre/postconditions for variable renaming)

Haskell module Language.BIPL.Rename.Condition

```
pre, post :: String → String → Stmt → Bool
pre i i' x = elem i (vars x) && not (elem i' (vars x))
post i i' y = not (elem i (vars y)) && elem i' (vars y)
vars :: Data a => a → [String]
vars z = nub (everything (++) (const [] `extQ` f `extQ` g) z)
  where
    f (Assign i _) = [i]
    f _ = []
    g (Var i) = [i]
    g _ = []
```

That is, we leverage Haskell's "scrap your boilerplate" (SYB) approach to generic functional programming [28, 29, 30] to collect variables in statements and expressions. The traversal scheme everything extracts names from each and every subterm – either the empty list or a singleton list for a variable which appears on the left-hand side of an assignment (see the helper function f) or as a variable in the sense of the corresponding expression form (see the helper function g).

We are ready to present the actual transformation.

Illustration 5.31 (Variable renaming for BIPL)

Haskell module Language.BIPL.Rename.Transformation

```
rename :: String → String → Stmt → Maybe Stmt
rename i i' x = do
    guard $ pre i i' x
    guard $ post i i' y
    return y
  where
    y = everywhere (id `extT` f `extT` g) x
      where
        f (Assign i" e) | i" == i = Assign i' e
        f s = s
        g (Var i") | i" == i = Var i'
        g e = e
```

Thus, the code uses the traversal scheme everywhere to reach each and every subterm and to possibly replace variable names in patterns of the same kind as those from which we extracted variable names in implementing pre/postconditions.

The two instances of the rename refactoring, as discussed above, are deliberately simple, but it should be clear that even renaming can be much more involved, for instance, when the object language features possibly nested scopes. Still, renaming is a rather simple refactoring; we refer to the literature for the correctness challenges for refactoring more generally [5, 46, 47].

Generally, the development (the design and implementation) of a software transformation, in the sense of a transformational program for optimization, refactoring, or yet other purposes, breaks down into the steps summarized by the following recipe.

Recipe 5.2 (Development of a software transformation).

Positive test cases   *Devise one or more examples of input-output pairs that demonstrate the expected input/output behavior of the intended transformation in a meaningful way. These examples can be used as positive test cases eventually. In the earlier optimization scenario, a test case consisted of an expression and the predicted result of its optimization. A test case may encompass additional arguments, for example, the old and new names in the case of renaming.*

Negative test cases   *A transformation's applicability and correctness may depend on a precondition to be met. Devise inputs that violate the precondition. Assuming that the implementation should check the precondition, these inputs form test cases with the expected behavior that the transformation will reject them. For instance, in the case of renaming, the transformation is superfluous, and thus worth rejecting, if the "old" name is not in use in the input artifact. More obviously, renaming must not cause name clashes, and thus the "new" name must not be in use in the input.*

Pre/postconditions *Formulate the precondition (see above) and the postcondition (i.e., condition to hold for the output of the transformation).*

Laws *Identify transformation laws which may be helpful for better understanding the transformation. For instance, one may identify the inverse of a transformation. Renaming is obviously reversible, while optimizations generally are not, but other laws may be relevant, for example, idempotence.*

Implementation *Implement the actual transformation including the pre/postconditions. In fact, an implementation of the postcondition is not necessary if the transformation "guarantees" that the postcondition will hold. In principle, the precondition can always be set up in a strong enough manner that no postcondition checking is needed. In practice, it is sometimes convenient to leave the precondition underspecified and to constrain the output instead. Also, postcondition checking may be helpful during debugging. For instance, the issue of superfluous renaming, as mentioned above, could be checked either by the precondition or by a comparison of the input and output to show that they are different.*

Testing *Test the transformation in terms of the test cases. Test the validity of the laws for some inputs, such as those from the positive test cases.*

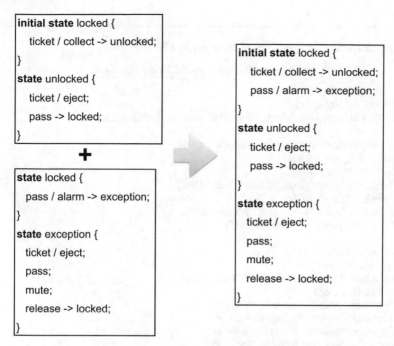

```
initial state locked {
    ticket / collect -> unlocked;
}
state unlocked {
    ticket / eject;
    pass -> locked;
}
```

+

```
state locked {
    pass / alarm -> exception;
}
state exception {
    ticket / eject;
    pass;
    mute;
    release -> locked;
}
```

```
initial state locked {
    ticket / collect -> unlocked;
    pass / alarm -> exception;
}
state unlocked {
    ticket / eject;
    pass -> locked;
}
state exception {
    ticket / eject;
    pass;
    mute;
    release -> locked;
}
```

Fig. 5.2 Illustration of the merging of FSMs. On the left-hand side, the two operands (FSMs) for merging are shown; on the right-hand side, the result of merging is shown – this is the recurring turnstile FSM. The upper operand shows the non-exceptional behavior, whereas the lower operand shows the exceptional behavior.

5.5 Composition

A (software) composition combines multiple input artifacts into one. Any composition is essentially a transformation, except that multiple inputs are transformed into one output. In particular, modularity mechanisms [19] and forms of specialization and overriding [9, 8] for programs may be considered instances of composition; see [4, 43] for a broad discussion of software composition concepts. We also refer to related notions such as *invasive software composition* [4], *aspect weaving* [41, 20], *stepwise enhancement* and related metaprogramming extension or composition techniques [36, 26], and *feature-oriented programming* [42, 48]. The notion of composition is by no means restricted to programming languages, but it applies rather generally to software languages; we mention model composition [7] as an example.

We demonstrate composition here for finite state machines by merging (think of "adding" or "combining") two FSMs; see Fig. 5.2 for an illustration. The actual composition, in the sense of the input for a positive test case, is shown in code form below.

Illustration 5.32 (Composition of the sample FSM)

Haskell module Language.FSML.Merge.Sample

```
turnstileFsm :: Maybe Fsm
turnstileFsm = sampleFsmRegular `merge` sampleFsmException

sampleFsmRegular, sampleFsmException :: Fsm
sampleFsmRegular = Fsm [
  State True "locked" [
    (Transition "ticket" (Just "collect") "unlocked") ],
  State False "unlocked" [
    (Transition "ticket" (Just "eject") "unlocked"),
    (Transition "pass" Nothing "locked") ]
  ]
sampleFsmException = Fsm [
  State True "locked" [
    (Transition "pass" (Just "alarm") "exception") ],
  State False "exception" [
    (Transition "ticket" (Just "eject") "exception"),
    (Transition "pass" Nothing "exception"),
    (Transition "mute" Nothing "exception"),
    (Transition "release" Nothing "locked") ]
  ]
```

Just as in the case of transformation, we need to identify the pre/postconditions for a composition. This is slightly involved for the merging of FSMs. We begin by pointing out that the composition at hand does not involve any additional inputs other than the FSMs themselves. Thus, it appears to make sense to consider well-formedness of FSMs (Section 5.3.2) as a starting point for both pre/postconditions. However, well-formedness would be both too weak and too strong in practice. Here are some considerations:

- When two or more FSMs are composed, the well-formedness constraint singleInitialState is arguably too weak. Even if each of the operands has exactly one initial state, the operands may still fail to share the ultimate initial state. Thus, we may need to actually check the constraint with the postcondition, unless we strengthen the precondition so that the operands, in combination, have at most one initial state.
- The well-formedness constraint singleInitialState is also too strong if we assume that operands and intermediate results of merging are acceptable without an initial state. Along the same lines, the well-formedness constraint reachableStates should not be part of the pre/postconditions.
- We should include the well-formedness constraint resolvableTargetStates in the pre/postconditions because each operand, as much as the result, should never describe a transition to a state that is not explicitly declared in the FSM at hand. (One may argue differently.)

We are ready to implement the pre/postconditions. In fact, we define one predicate, ok, which models both the precondition and the postcondition.

Illustration 5.33 (Pre/postconditions for merging of FSMs)

Haskell module Language.FSML.Merge.Condition

```
ok :: Fsm → Bool
ok fsm = and $ map ($fsm) [
  zeroOrOneInitialState,
  distinctStateIds,
  resolvableTargetStates,
  deterministicTransitions ]

zeroOrOneInitialState :: Fsm → Bool
zeroOrOneInitialState fsm = ...
    length inis < 2
  where
    inis = [ getId s | s ← getStates fsm, getInitial s ]

...
```

The actual composition is implemented as a union-like operation at several levels as shown below.

Illustration 5.34 (FSM composition)

Haskell module Language.FSML.Merge.Transformation

```
merge :: Fsm → Fsm → Maybe Fsm
merge x y = do
    guard $ ok x && ok y
    let z = fromMap (unionWith f (toMap x) (toMap y))
    guard $ ok z
    return z
  where
    −− Per−state composition
    f sx sy = State
        (getInitial sx || getInitial sy)
        (getId sx)
        (getTransitions sx ++ getTransitions sy)
    toMap = fromList . map (λ s → (getId s, s)) . getStates
    fromMap = Fsm . map snd . toList
```

That is:

- We represent FSMs as "maps" from state ids to the actual state declarations, i.e., groups of transitions with the same source state.
- In this manner, we can use a unionWith operation on maps which is parameterized by a helper f that combines two state declarations for the same state id.

- A composed state is initial if it is initial in at least one operand. The composed transitions are obtained by concatenating the operands' transitions.

In terms of laws, we may commit to associativity and commutativity of the merge composition:

```
x `merge` (y `merge` z) = x `merge` (y `merge` z)
x `merge` y = y `merge` x
```

Here, we gloss over the detail here that merge returns a "maybe". More interestingly, for these laws to hold, we need to "normalize" FSMs in such a way that the order of states and transitions does not need to matter, as modeled by the following function.

Illustration 5.35 (Normalization of FSMs)

Haskell module <u>Language.FSML.Normalization</u>

```
normalize :: Fsm → Fsm
normalize =
    Fsm
  . sortOn getId
  . map (λ s → State (getInitial s) (getId s) (sort (getTransitions s)))
  . getStates
```

We may also define equality on FSMs in such a manner that normalization precedes testing for plain structural equality.

Illustration 5.36 (Equality of FSMs)

Haskell module <u>Language.FSML.Eq</u>

```
instance Eq Fsm where
  x == y = getStates (normalize x) == getStates (normalize y)
```

Such aspects of normalization and relaxed equality are not uncommon in implementing software transformations.

Exercise 5.19 (Precondition for merging of FSMs)   [Intermediate level]
If the operands define different initial states, then the postcondition does not hold, and thus it needs to be checked. Identify all remaining issues of underspecification and implement a stronger precondition so that no postcondition would be needed.

Summary and Outline

We have discussed a number of metaprogramming scenarios: interpretation, compilation, analysis, transformation, and composition. We have exercised instances of these scenarios ("problems") with Haskell as the metalanguage and simple object languages for illustration.

All of the metaprograms operated on top of abstract syntax. In the next two chapters, we will describe the foundations and implementation of concrete syntax. In this manner, we will also be able to use concrete object syntax in metaprograms. Afterwards, we will discuss semantics and types of software languages, thereby contributing to the foundations of metaprogramming in general, and of interpretation and analysis in particular. Towards the end of the book, in Chapter 12, we will discuss a few metaprogramming techniques that could also be used in addressing the scenarios of the present chapter in a more advanced manner.

References

1. Aho, A., Monica S., Sethi, R., Ullman, J.: Compilers: Principles, Techniques, and Tools. Addison Wesley (2006). 2nd edition
2. Alblas, H., Melichar, B. (eds.): Attribute Grammars, Applications and Systems, International Summer School SAGA, 1991, Proceedings, *LNCS*, vol. 545. Springer (1991)
3. Appel, A., Palsberg, J.: Modern Compiler Implementation in Java. Cambridge University Press (2002). 2nd edition
4. Aßmann, U.: Invasive software composition. Springer (2003)
5. Bannwart, F., Müller, P.: Changing programs correctly: Refactoring with specifications. In: Proc. FM, *LNCS*, vol. 4085, pp. 492–507. Springer (2006)
6. Basten, H.J.S., Klint, P.: DeFacto: Language-parametric fact extraction from source code. In: Proc. SLE 2008, *LNCS*, vol. 5452, pp. 265–284. Springer (2009)
7. Bézivin, J., Bouzitouna, S., Fabro, M.D.D., Gervais, M., Jouault, F., Kolovos, D.S., Kurtev, I., Paige, R.F.: A canonical scheme for model composition. In: Proc. ECMDA-FA, *LNCS*, vol. 4066, pp. 346–360. Springer (2006)
8. Bracha, G., von der Ahé, P., Bykov, V., Kashai, Y., Maddox, W., Miranda, E.: Modules as objects in Newspeak. In: Proc. ECOOP, *LNCS*, vol. 6183, pp. 405–428. Springer (2010)
9. Bracha, G., Lindstrom, G.: Modularity meets inheritance. In: Proc. ICCL, pp. 282–290. IEEE (1992)
10. Bravenboer, M., Kalleberg, K.T., Vermaas, R., Visser, E.: Stratego/XT 0.17. A language and toolset for program transformation. Sci. Comput. Program. 72(1-2), 52–70 (2008)
11. Clark, T., Warmer, J. (eds.): Object Modeling with the OCL, The Rationale behind the Object Constraint Language, *LNCS*, vol. 2263. Springer (2002)
12. Cordy, J.R.: The TXL source transformation language. Sci. Comput. Program. 61(3), 190–210 (2006)
13. Cordy, J.R.: Excerpts from the TXL cookbook. In: GTTSE 2009, Revised Papers, *LNCS*, vol. 6491, pp. 27–91. Springer (2011)
14. Dean, T.R., Cordy, J.R.: A syntactic theory of software architecture. IEEE Trans. Softw. Eng. 21(4), 302–313 (1995)
15. Dershowitz, N.: A taste of rewrite systems. In: Functional Programming, Concurrency, Simulation and Automated Reasoning: International Lecture Series 1991-1992, McMaster University, Hamilton, Ontario, Canada, *LNCS*, vol. 693, pp. 199–228. Springer (1993)

16. Dershowitz, N., Jouannaud, J.P.: Rewrite systems. In: Handbook of Theoretical Computer Science B: Formal Methods and Semantics, pp. 243–320. North-Holland (1990)
17. Fowler, M.: Refactoring: Improving the Design of Existing Code. Addison Wesley (1999)
18. Gamma, E., Helm, R., Johnson, R., Vlissides, J.: Design Patterns: Elements of Reusable Object-Oriented Software. Addison-Wesley (1994)
19. Henriksson, J., Johannes, J., Zschaler, S., Aßmann, U.: Reuseware – Adding modularity to your language of choice. J. Object Technol. **6**(9), 127–146 (2007)
20. Hilsdale, E., Hugunin, J.: Advice weaving in AspectJ. In: Proc. AOSD, pp. 26–35. ACM (2004)
21. Jouault, F., Allilaire, F., Bézivin, J., Kurtev, I.: ATL: A model transformation tool. Sci. Comput. Program. **72**(1-2), 31–39 (2008)
22. Klint, P., van der Storm, T., Vinju, J.J.: RASCAL: A domain specific language for source code analysis and manipulation. In: Proc. SCAM, pp. 168–177. IEEE (2009)
23. Klint, P., van der Storm, T., Vinju, J.J.: EASY meta-programming with Rascal. In: GTTSE 2009, Revised Papers, *LNCS*, vol. 6491, pp. 222–289. Springer (2011)
24. Klop, J.W.: Term rewriting systems. In: Handbook of Logic in Computer Science, pp. 1–117. Oxford University Press (1992)
25. Knuth, D.E.: Semantics of context-free languages. Mathematical Systems Theory **2**(2), 127–145 (1968)
26. Lämmel, R.: Declarative aspect-oriented programming. In: Proc. PEPM, pp. 131–146. University of Aarhus (1999)
27. Lämmel, R.: Towards generic refactoring. In: Proc. RULE, pp. 15–28. ACM (2002)
28. Lämmel, R., Jones, S.L.P.: Scrap your boilerplate: a practical design pattern for generic programming. In: Proc. TLDI, pp. 26–37. ACM (2003)
29. Lämmel, R., Jones, S.L.P.: Scrap more boilerplate: reflection, zips, and generalised casts. In: Proc. ICFP, pp. 244–255. ACM (2004)
30. Lämmel, R., Jones, S.L.P.: Scrap your boilerplate with class: extensible generic functions. In: Proc. ICFP, pp. 204–215. ACM (2005)
31. Lin, Y., Holt, R.C.: Formalizing fact extraction. ENTCS **94**, 93–102 (2004)
32. Louden, K.: Compiler Construction: Principles and Practice. Cengage Learning (1997)
33. Mens, T., Gorp, P.V.: A taxonomy of model transformation. ENTCS **152**, 125–142 (2006)
34. Mens, T., Tourwé, T.: A survey of software refactoring. IEEE Trans. Softw. Eng. **30**(2), 126–139 (2004)
35. Murphy, G.C., Notkin, D.: Lightweight lexical source model extraction. ACM Trans. Softw. Eng. Methodol. **5**(3), 262–292 (1996)
36. Naish, L., Sterling, L.: Stepwise enhancement and higher-order programming in Prolog. J. Funct. and Log. Program. **2000**(4) (2000)
37. Nielson, F., Nielson, H.R., Hankin, C.: Principles of Program Analysis, corrected 2nd printing edn. Springer (2004)
38. Nymeyer, A., Katoen, J., Westra, Y., Alblas, H.: Code generation = A* + BURS. In: Proc. CC, *LNCS*, vol. 1060, pp. 160–176. Springer (1996)
39. Opdyke, W.F.: Refactoring object-oriented frameworks. Ph.D. thesis, University of Illinois at Urbana-Champaign (1992)
40. Pierce, B.: Types and Programming Languages. MIT Press (2002)
41. Popovici, A., Alonso, G., Gross, T.R.: Just-in-time aspects: efficient dynamic weaving for java. In: Proc. AOSD, pp. 100–109. ACM (2003)
42. Prehofer, C.: Feature-oriented programming: A fresh look at objects. In: Proc. ECOOP, *LNCS*, vol. 1241, pp. 419–443. Springer (1997)
43. Pulvermüller, E., Goos, G., Aßmann, U.: New software composition concepts. Sci. Comput. Program. **56**(1-2), 1–4 (2005)
44. Renggli, L., Ducasse, S., Gîrba, T., Nierstrasz, O.: Domain-specific program checking. In: Proc. TOOLS, *LNCS*, vol. 6141, pp. 213–232. Springer (2010)
45. Roy, C.K., Cordy, J.R., Koschke, R.: Comparison and evaluation of code clone detection techniques and tools: A qualitative approach. Sci. Comput. Program. **74**(7), 470–495 (2009)

46. Schäfer, M., Ekman, T., de Moor, O.: Challenge proposal: Verification of refactorings. In: Proc. PLPV, pp. 67–72. ACM (2009)
47. Soares, G., Gheyi, R., Massoni, T.: Automated behavioral testing of refactoring engines. IEEE Trans. Softw. Eng. **39**(2), 147–162 (2013)
48. Trujillo, S., Batory, D.S., Díaz, O.: Feature oriented model driven development: A case study for portlets. In: Proc. ICSE, pp. 44–53. IEEE (2007)
49. van den Brand, M., Sellink, M.P.A., Verhoef, C.: Generation of components for software renovation factories from context-free grammars. Sci. Comput. Program. **36**(2-3), 209–266 (2000)

Chapter 6
Foundations of Textual Concrete Syntax

AVRAM NOAM CHOMSKY.[1]

Abstract In this chapter, we consider the notion of *concrete syntax* of software languages thereby complementing the earlier discussion of *abstract syntax* (Chapters 3and 4). Concrete syntax is tailored towards processing (reading, writing, editing) by humans who are language users, while abstract syntax is tailored towards processing by programs that are authored by language implementers. In this chapter, we focus on the concrete syntax of *string languages* as defined by *context-free grammars* (CFGs). In fact, we cover only textual concrete syntax; we do not cover visual concrete syntax. We introduce the algorithmic notion of *acceptance* for a membership test for a language. We also introduce the algorithmic notion of parsing for recovering the grammar-based structure of input. We defer the implementation aspects of concrete syntax, including actual parsing approaches, to the next chapter.

---

[1] There is clearly nothing wrong with the notion of a Turing machine – after all it is Turing-complete, but the way it is described and discussed is clearly very reminiscent of how we think of actual (early) computing machines working operationally, if not mechanically. Personally, I have always felt more attracted to the lambda calculus, with its high level of abstraction, much more focused on computation than on operation. Likewise, I admire the Chomsky hierarchy [4], as it defines grammars in a fundamental manner, including a semantics that makes no operational concessions. There is a need for well-engineered grammar forms, such as parsing expression grammars [5], but all such work stands on the shoulders of Chomsky.

Artwork Credits for Chapter Opening: This work by Wojciech Kwasnik is licensed under CC BY-SA 4.0. This artwork quotes the artwork *DMT*, acrylic, 2006 by Matt Sheehy with the artist's permission. This work also quotes https://commons.wikimedia.org/wiki/File:Van_Gogh_-_Starry_Night_-_Google_Art_Project.jpg, subject to the attribution "Vincent van Gogh: The Starry Night (1889) [Public domain], via Wikimedia Commons." This work artistically morphes an image, https://en.wikipedia.org/wiki/Noam_Chomsky, showing the person honored, subject to the attribution "By culturaargentinai - This file has been extracted from another file: Noam Chomsky .jpg, CC BY-SA 2.0, https://commons.wikimedia.org/w/index.php?curid=48394900."

© Springer International Publishing AG, part of Springer Nature 2018
R. Lämmel, *Software Languages*,
https://doi.org/10.1007/978-3-319-90800-7_6

6.1 Textual Concrete Syntax

A *grammar* is a collection of rules defining the syntax of a language's syntactic categories such as statements and expressions. We introduce a basic grammar notation and a convenient extension here. We also show that a grammar can be understood in a "generative" sense, i.e., a grammar derives ("generates") language elements as strings.

6.1.1 A Basic Grammar Notation

Let us study the concrete syntax of *BNL* (*B*inary *N*umber *L*anguage). This is the language of unsigned binary numbers, possibly with decimal places, for example, "10" (2 as a decimal number) and "101.01" (5.25 as a decimal number). Let us define the concrete syntax of BNL. To this end, we use "fabricated" grammar notation: *BGL* (*B*asic *G*rammar *L*anguage).

Illustration 6.1 (Concrete syntax of BNL)

BGL resource languages/BNL/cs.bgl

[number] number : bits rest ; // *A binary number*
[single] bits : bit ; // *A single bit*
[many] bits : bit bits ; // *More than one bit*
[zero] bit : '0' ; // *The zero bit*
[one] bit : '1' ; // *The nonzero bit*
[integer] rest : ; // *An integer number*
[rational] rest : '.' bits ; // *A rational number*

BGL is really just a notational variation on the classic *Backus-Naur form* (BNF) [1]. A grammar is a collection of rules (say, productions). Each rule consists of a label such as *[number]* for better reference, a left-hand side which is a grammar symbol such as *number* in the first rule, and a right-hand side which is a sequence of grammar symbols. There are two kinds of grammar symbols:

Terminals   These are quoted symbols such as "0" and "1"; they must not appear on the left-hand side of context-free rules. The terminals constitute the "alphabet" from which to build strings.

Nonterminals   These are alphabetic symbols such as *number*, *bits*, and *rest*; they may appear on both the left- and the right-hand side of rules. In fact, the left-hand side of a context-free rule is a single nonterminal. Nonterminals correspond to syntactic categories.

6.1.2 Derivation of Strings

The intended meaning of a grammar is that rules can be applied from left to right to derive (say, "generate") strings composed of terminals such that nonterminals are replaced by right-hand sides of rules and terminals remain. We often assume that a grammar identifies a distinguished nonterminal – the *start symbol* – from which to start derivation. We may also just assume that the left-hand side of the first production is simply the start symbol. Derivation is illustrated below for a binary number.

Illustration 6.2 (Derivation of a string)
The following sequence of steps derives the terminal string "10" from the nonterminal number:

• *number*	*Apply rule [number]*
• *bits rest*	*Apply rule [integer] to rest*
• *bits*	*Apply rule [many] to bits*
• *bit bits*	*Apply rule [zero] to bit*
• *'1' bits*	*Apply rule [single] to bits*
• *'1' bit*	*Apply rule [zero] to bit*
• *'1' '0'*	

We assume that a "well-formed" grammar must permit derivation of terminal sequences for each of its nonterminals and that each nonterminal should be exercised by some of the derivations, starting from the start symbol. Such well-formedness is meant to rule out "nonsensical" grammars.

Exercise 6.1 (An alternative derivation) [Basic level]
There is actually more than one way to derive the terminal sequence in Illustration 6.2. Identify an alternative derivation.

Exercise 6.2 (Derivation of a string) [Basic level]
Present the derivation sequence for "101.01" in the style of Illustration 6.2.

Exercise 6.3 (BNL with signed numbers) [Basic level]
Extend the grammar in Illustration 6.1 to enable signed binary numbers.

6.1.3 An Extended Grammar Notation

Consider again the grammar in Illustration 6.1. Optionality of the fractional part is encoded by the rules *[integer]* and *[rational]*, subject to an "auxiliary" nonterminal *rest*. Sequences of bits are encoded by the rules *[single]* and *[many]*, subject to an "auxiliary" nonterminal *bits*. These are recurring idioms which can be expressed more concisely in the *extended Backus-Naur form* [7] (EBNF). We propose a related grammar notation here: *EGL* (*E*xtended *G*rammar *L*anguage). Let us illustrate EGL here with a concise syntax definition for BNL.

Illustration 6.3 (EBNF-like concrete syntax of BNL)

EGL resource languages/BNL/EGL/cs.egl

[number] number : { bit }+ { '.'{ bit }+ }? ;
[zero] bit : '0' ;
[one] bit : '1' ;

Optionality of a phrase is expressed by the form "{ ... }?". Repetition zero, one, or more times is expressed by the form "{ ... }∗". Repetition one or more times is expressed by the form "{ ... }+". Rule labels are optional in EGL. In particular, we tend to leave out labels for nonterminals with only one alternative.

The extended notation (EGL) can be easily reduced ("desugared") to the basic notation (BGL) by modeling the EGL-specific phrases through additional rules, also subject to extra (fresh) nonterminals. There are these cases:

- Given one or more occurrences of a phrase $\{s_1 \cdots s_n\}$? with grammar symbols $s_1, \ldots, s_n$ and a fresh nonterminal x, each occurrence is replaced by x and two rules are added:

  - $x : ;$
  - $x : s_1 \cdots s_n ;$

- Given one or more occurrences of a phrase $\{s_1 \cdots s_n\}∗$ and a fresh nonterminal x, each such occurrence is replaced by x and two rules are added:

  - $x : ;$
  - $x : s_1 \cdots s_n x ;$

- Given one or more occurrences of a phrase $\{s_1 \cdots s_n\}+$ and a fresh nonterminal x, each such occurrence is replaced by x and two rules are added:

  - $x : s_1 \cdots s_n ;$
  - $x : s_1 \cdots s_n x ;$

Exercise 6.4 (Grammar notation translation)   [Intermediate level]
The full EBNF notation [7] supports nested groups of alternatives. If such grouping was expressible in (an extended) EGL, then we could use grammar rules such as "s : a { b | c }? d ;" where the group of alternatives is "b | c". Reduce ("desugar") this group form to the basic notation.

6.1.4 Illustrative Examples of Grammars

We define the concrete syntax of a few more languages here. We revisit ("fabricated") languages for which we already defined the abstract syntax in Chapter 3.

6.1.4.1 Syntax of Simple Expressions

Let us define the concrete syntax of the expression language BTL.

Illustration 6.4 (Concrete syntax of BTL)

BGL resource languages/BTL/cs.bgl

```
[true] expr : "true" ;
[false] expr : "false" ;
[zero] expr : "zero" ;
[succ] expr : "succ" expr ;
[pred] expr : "pred" expr ;
[iszero] expr : "iszero" expr ;
[if] expr : "if" expr "then" expr "else" expr ;
```

That is, we assume "curried" notation (juxtaposition) for function application, i.e., for applying the operators *'pred'*, *'succ'*, and *'iszero'*. That is, we write succ zero instead of succ(zero). Curried notation is also used, for example, in the functional programming language Haskell.

6.1.4.2 Syntax of Simple Imperative Programs

Let us define the concrete syntax of the imperative programming language BIPL.

Illustration 6.5 (Concrete syntax of BIPL)

EGL resource languages/BIPL/cs.egl

// Statements
[skip] stmt : ';' ;
[assign] stmt : name '=' expr ';' ;
[block] stmt : '{' { stmt }* '}' ;
[if] stmt : 'if' '(' expr ')' stmt { 'else' stmt }? ;
[while] stmt : 'while' '(' expr ')' stmt ;

// Expressions
[or] expr : bexpr { '||' expr }? ;
[and] bexpr : cexpr { '&&' bexpr }? ;
[lt] cexpr : aexpr { '<' aexpr }? ;
[leq] cexpr : aexpr { '<=' aexpr }? ;
[eq] cexpr : aexpr { '==' aexpr }? ;
[geq] cexpr : aexpr { '>=' aexpr }? ;
[gt] cexpr : aexpr { '>' aexpr }? ;
[add] aexpr : term { '+' aexpr }? ;
[sub] aexpr : term { '−' aexpr }? ;
[mul] term : factor { '*' term }? ;
[negate] factor : '−' factor ;
[not] factor : '!' factor ;
[intconst] factor : integer ;
[var] factor : name ;
[brackets] factor : '(' expr ')' ;

There are several different statement and expression forms. For instance, the first rule ([skip]) defines the syntax of an empty statement; the second rule ([assign]) defines the syntax of assignment with a variable to the left of "=" and an expression to the right of "=". The rule for if-statements makes the 'else' branch optional, as in the C and Java languages.

The rules for expression forms are layered with extra nonterminals *bexpr* (for "Boolean expressions"), *cexpr* (for "comparison expressions"), etc. to model operator priorities such as that "*" to bind more strongly than "+". We note that the syntax of names and integers is left unspecified here.

Exercise 6.5 (Priorities of alternatives)   [Intermediate level]
Practical grammar notations and the corresponding parsing approaches support a more concise approach to the modeling of priorities, not just of operators but possibly of alternatives (rules) in general. Study some grammar notation, for example, YACC [8], SDF [12], or ANTLR [11], with regard to priorities and sketch a possible extension of EGL, illustrated with a revision of the BIPL grammar.

6.1.4.3 Syntax of Simple Functional Programs

Let us define the concrete syntax of the functional programming language BFPL.

Illustration 6.6 (Concrete syntax of BFPL)

EGL resource languages/BFPL/cs.egl

```
// Program = functions + main expression
program : { function }* main ;
function : funsig fundef ;
funsig : name '::' funtype ;
fundef : name { name }* '=' expr ;
funtype : simpletype { '->' simpletype }* ;
main : 'main' '=' 'print' '$' expr ;

// Simple types
[inttype] simpletype : 'Int' ;
[booltype] simpletype : 'Bool' ;

// Expressions
[unary] expr : uop subexpr ;
[binary] expr : '(' bop ')' subexpr subexpr ;
[subexpr] expr : subexpr ;
[apply] expr : name { subexpr }+ ;
[intconst] subexpr : integer ;
[brackets] subexpr : '(' expr ')' ;
[if] subexpr : 'if' expr 'then' expr 'else' expr ;
[arg] subexpr : name ;

// Unary and binary operators
[negate] uop : '-' ;
[not] uop : 'not' ;
[add] bop : '+' ;
...
```

The syntax of BFPL is focused on expression forms. There are further syntactic categories for programs (as lists of functions combined with a "main" expression) and function signatures. The central expression form is that of function application. Curried notation is assumed. Operators are applied in (curried) prefix notation too. Thus, operator priorities are not modeled. We note that the syntax of names and integers is left unspecified here.

6.1.4.4 Syntax of Finite State Machines

Let us define the concrete syntax of the DSML FSML.

Illustration 6.7 (Concrete syntax of FSML)

EGL resource languages/FSML/cs.egl

```
fsm : {state}* ;
state : {'initial'}? 'state' stateid '{' {transition}* '}' ;
transition : event {'/' action}? {'->' stateid}? ';' ;
stateid : name ;
event : name ;
action : name ;
```

That is, an FSM is a collection of *state* declarations, each of which groups state transitions together. Each transition identifies an *event* (say, an input symbol), an optional *action* (say, an output symbol), and an optional target *stateid*. An omitted target state is taken to mean that the target state equals the source state. We note that the syntax of names is left unspecified here.

Exercise 6.6 (EGL to BGL reduction)   [Basic level]
Apply the EGL-to-BGL reduction to the definition of the syntax of FSML in Illustration 6.7.

6.2 Concrete versus Abstract Syntax

The definitions of concrete and abstract syntax differ in that they model text-based versus tree- or graph-based languages. In addition, concrete and abstract syntax also differ in terms of intention – they are targeted towards the language user and the language implementer, respectively. This difference in intention affects the level of abstraction in the definitions. Abstraction potential arises from constructs that have a rich concrete syntax, but where fewer details or variations are sufficient to ultimately assign meaning to the constructs. We look at such differences in the sequel.

At the most basic level, concrete and abstract syntax differ just in terms of representation or notation. Here are some definition fragments of the expression language BTL:

```
-- Concrete syntax of BTL
[zero] expr : "zero" ;
[succ] expr : "succ" expr ;
```

```
-- Abstract syntax of BTL
symbol zero : -> expr ;
symbol succ : expr -> expr ;
```

In the concrete syntax, "succ" is modeled as a prefix symbol because it precedes its operand in the grammar rule. In the abstract syntax, succ is a prefix symbol simply because *all* symbols are prefix symbols in such a basic, signature-based abstract syntax. In the concrete syntax, we have full control over the notation. For instance, the rule [succ] favors curried notation for function application, i.e., using juxtaposition instead of parentheses and commas. Again, however, in the abstract syntax, uncurried notation is cemented into the formalism as the assumed representation of terms (trees).

Exercise 6.7 (Uncurried notation for BTL expressions) [Basic level]
Revise the concrete syntax of BTL to use uncurried notation instead.

Let us also consider the differences between concrete and abstract syntax for the imperative language BIPL. We have already pointed out earlier (Section 6.1.4.2) that the grammar of BIPL models expression forms with a dedicated nonterminal for each operator priority. Such layering makes no sense in the tree-based abstract syntax and it is indeed missing from the earlier signature (Section 3.1.5.2). Another difference concerns the if-statement:

```
−− Concrete syntax of BIPL
[if] stmt : 'if' '(' expr ')' stmt { 'else' stmt }? ;
```

```
−− Abstract syntax of BIPL
symbol if : expr × stmt × stmt → stmt ;
```

That is, the else-part is optional in the concrete syntax, whereas it is mandatory in the abstract syntax. An optional else-part is convenient for the language user because no empty statement ("skip") needs to be filled in to express the absence of an else-part. A mandatory else-part is convenient for the language implementer because only one pattern of the if-statement needs to be handled.

There is another major difference we should point out:

```
−− Concrete syntax of BIPL
[block] stmt : '{' { stmt }* '}' ;
```

```
−− Abstract syntax of BIPL
symbol seq : stmt × stmt → stmt ;
```

That is, in the concrete syntax, sequences of statements are formed as statement blocks with enclosing braces. This notation was chosen to resemble the syntax of C and Java. In the abstract syntax, there is a binary combinator for sequential composition. This simple model is convenient for the language implementer. For this correspondence between concrete and abstract syntax to be sound, we must assume that statement blocks have here no meaning other than sequential composition. By contrast, in C and Java, statement blocks actually define scopes with regard to local variables.

Exercise 6.8 (Abstraction for FSML)   [Basic level]
Identify the differences between the concrete and the abstract syntax of FSML.

Exercise 6.9 (Abstraction for BFPL)   [Basic level]
Identify the differences between the concrete and the abstract syntax of BFPL.

We mention in passing that some metaprogramming systems, for example, Rascal [10, 9] and Stratego XT [13, 3], advertise the view that, under certain conditions, there may not even be an abstract syntax for a language; all language processing is implemented on top of the concrete syntax, subject to suitable support for concrete object syntax, as we will discuss later (Section 7.5). The assumption is here that a metaprogrammer may prefer using the familiar, concrete syntactical patterns of the object language as opposed to the more artificial patterns according to an abstract syntax definition.

6.3 Languages as Sets of Strings

Let us complement the informal explanations of concrete syntax definitions given so far with formal definitions drawn from formal language theory [6]. In particular, we will define the meaning of grammars in a set-theoretic sense, i.e., a grammar "generates" a language as a set of strings.

6.3.1 Context-Free Grammars

BGL (or BNF) and EGL (or EBNF) are grammar notations for the fundamental formalism of context-free grammars (CFGs).

Definition 6.1 (Context-free grammar) *A CFG G is a quadruple $\langle N, T, P, s \rangle$ where N is a finite set of nonterminals, T is a finite set of terminals, with $N \cap T = \emptyset$, P is a finite set of rules (or productions) as a subset of $N \times (N \cup T)^*$, and $s \in N$ is referred to as the start symbol.*

As noted before, in the BGL and EGL grammar notations, we use the convention that the left-hand side of a grammar's first rule is considered the start symbol. Also, we note that BGL and EGL rules may be labeled whereas no labels are mentioned in the formal definition. Labels are simply to identify rules concisely.

6.3.2 The Language Generated by a Grammar

Rules can be applied in a "generative" sense: replace a nonterminal by a corresponding right-hand side. By many such replacements, one may eventually derive terminal strings. This is the foundation for interpreting a grammar as the definition of a language, namely the set of all terminal strings that are derivable from the grammar's start symbol.

Definition 6.2 (Context-free derivation) *Given a CFG $G = \langle N,T,P,s \rangle$ and a sequence $p\, n\, q$ with $n \in N$, $p,q \in (N \cup T)^*$, the sequence $p\, r\, q$ with $r \in (N \cup T)^*$ is called a derivation, as denoted by $p\, n\, q \Rightarrow p\, r\, q$, if there is a production $\langle n, r \rangle \in P$.*

The transitive closure of "$\Rightarrow$" is denoted by "$\Rightarrow^+$". The reflexive closure of "$\Rightarrow^+$" is denoted by "$\Rightarrow^*$".

Definition 6.3 (Language generated by a CFG) *Given a CFG $G = \langle N,T,P,s \rangle$, the language $L(G)$ generated by G is defined as the set of all the terminal sequences that are derivable from s. That is:*

$$L(G) = \left\{ w \in T^* \mid s \Rightarrow^+ w \right\}$$

6.3.3 Well-Formed Grammars

Well-formedness constraints on grammars for ruling out nonsensical grammars are defined formally as follows.

Definition 6.4 (Well-formed CFG)
A CFG $G = \langle N,T,P,s \rangle$ is called well-formed if the following two conditions hold for each $n \in N$:

Productivity   There exists $w \in T^*$ such that $n \Rightarrow^+ w$.
Reachability   There exist $p,q \in (N \cup T)^*$ such that $s \Rightarrow^* p\, n\, q$.

Exercise 6.10 (Productivity of CFG)   [Basic level]
Give a simple grammar that violates productivity defined in Definition 6.4.

Exercise 6.11 (Reachability of CFG)   [Basic level]
Give a simple grammar that violates reachability defined in Definition 6.4.

Exercise 6.12 (Well-formed signature)   [Intermediate level]
Consider again Definition 6.4 for well-formed CFGs. Transpose this definition, with its components for productivity and reachability, to signatures as used in abstract syntax definition (Chapter 3).

6.3.4 The Notion of Acceptance

Suppose we want to decide whether a given terminal string is an element of $L(G)$. We cannot perform a direct membership test because the set $L(G)$ is infinite for any nontrivial syntax definition. We need a computable kind of membership test instead. To this end, we introduce the algorithmic notion of acceptance. The term "recognition" is also used instead. Further, we may speak of an "acceptor" or "recognizer" instead, when we want to refer to the actual functionality for acceptance.

Definition 6.5 (Acceptor) *Given a CFG $G = \langle N, T, P, s \rangle$, an acceptor for G is a computable predicate a_G on T^* such that for all $w \in T^*$, $a_G(w)$ holds iff $s \Rightarrow^+ w$.*

The process of applying an acceptor is referred to as acceptance. In practice, we are interested in "descriptions" of such predicates. For instance, the grammar itself may serve as a description and the predicate may be obtained by "interpreting" the grammar. It is known from formal language theory that the membership problem for CFGs is decidable and, thus, a computable predicate such as the one in the definition can be assumed to exist. We will discuss some options later (Section 7.2).

6.4 Languages as Sets of Trees

An acceptor only answers the question whether a given string w is an element of the language generated by some grammar G. A parser, in addition, reports on the structure of w based on the rules of G. The structure is represented as a concrete syntax tree (CST). We may also say "parse tree" instead of "CST". Success of parsing means that at least one CST is returned. Failure of parsing means that no CST is returned. In this manner, we assign meaning to grammars in a second manner.

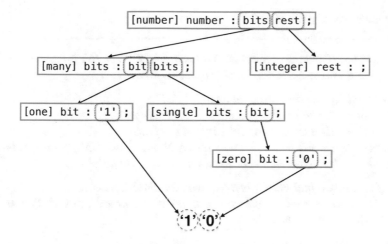

Fig. 6.1 CST for the binary number "10".

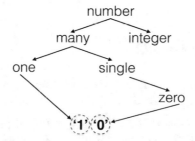

Fig. 6.2 Alternative CST representation.

6.4.1 Concrete Syntax Trees

A CST for a terminal string w contains the terminals of w as leaf nodes in the same order. Each CST node with its subtrees represents the application of a grammar rule except for some leaf nodes that simply represent terminals. The root node corresponds to a rule application for the start symbol. Before formalizing this intuition, let us look at some examples.

CSTs can be represented or visualized in different ways. The representation in Fig. 6.1 uses rules as node infos. In the figure, we circled right-hand side grammar symbols to better emphasize the correspondence between them and the subtrees. The visualization in Fig. 6.2 is more concise. BGL's rule labels are used as node infos here.

We are ready to define the CST notion formally.

Definition 6.6 (Concrete syntax tree) *Given a CFG $G = \langle N,T,P,s \rangle$ and a string $w \in T^*$, a CST for w according to G is a tree as follows:*

- *Nodes hold a rule or a terminal as info.*
- *The root holds a rule with s on the left-hand side as info.*
- *If a node holds a terminal as info, then it is a leaf.*
- *If a node holds rule $n \to v_1 \cdots v_m$ with $n \in N$, $v_1, \ldots, v_m \in N \cup T$ as info, then the node has m branches with subtrees t_i for $i = 1, \ldots, m$ as follows:*

  - *If v_i is a terminal, then t_i is a leaf with terminal v_i as info.*
  - *If v_i is a nonterminal, then t_i is a tree with a rule as info such that v_i is the left-hand side of the rule.*

- *The concatenated terminals at the leaf nodes equal w.*

6.4.2 The Notion of Parsing

Let us make the transition from acceptance to parsing.

Definition 6.7 (Parser) *Given a CFG $G = \langle N,T,P,s \rangle$, a parser for G is a partial function p_G from T^* to CSTs such that for all $w \in L(G)$, $p_G(w)$ returns a CST of w and for all $w \notin L(G)$, $p_G(w)$ is not defined.*

The process of applying a parser is referred to as parsing. A parser returns no CST for a given input exactly in the same cases as when an acceptor fails.

6.4.3 Ambiguous Grammars

If a parser has a choice of what CST to return, then this means that the grammar is ambiguous, as formalized by the following definition.

Definition 6.8 (Ambiguous grammar) *A CFG $G = \langle N,T,P,s \rangle$ is called ambiguous, if there exists a terminal string $w \in T^*$ with multiple CSTs.*

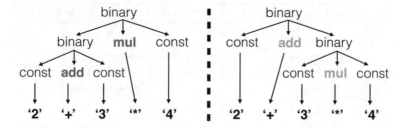

Fig. 6.3 Alternative CSTs for an arithmetic expression.

Let us consider a simple example for ambiguities.

Illustration 6.8 (Ambiguous grammar for arithmetic expressions)

EGL resource languages/EGL/samples/ambiguity.egl

[binary] expr : expr bop expr ;
[const] expr : integer ;
[add] bop : '+' ;
[mul] bop : '*' ;

In the grammar shown above, the syntax of binary expression is defined ambiguously. This is demonstrated in Fig. 6.3 by showing two CSTs for the expression "2 + 3 * 4". The tree on the right meets our expectation that "*" binds more strongly than "+". The grammar for BIPL (Illustration 6.5) addresses this problem by describing layers of expressions with dedicated nonterminals for the different priorities.

We mention in passing that Definition 6.7 could be revised to make a parser possibly return a collection of CSTs, i.e., a parse-tree forest. This may be useful in practice and may require an extra phase of filtering to identify a preferred tree eventually [2].

Exercise 6.13 (Ambiguous grammar)   [Basic level]
Consider the rule for if-statements taken from Illustration 6.5:

[if] stmt : 'if' '(' expr ')' stmt { 'else' stmt }? ;

Demonstrate that this rule implies an ambiguous grammar.

While both concrete and abstract syntax, as discussed thus far, provide a tree-based definition of a software language, there is an important difference. In the case of concrete syntax, the trees arise as a secondary means: to represent the derivation of language elements, which are strings. In the case of abstract syntax, the trees correspond to the language elements themselves.

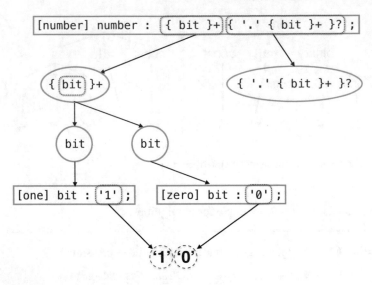

Fig. 6.4 A CST with extra nodes due to EGL expressiveness.

Definition 6.6 (CST) applies to the basic grammar notation of BGL only. CSTs for the extended grammar notation of EGL require extra nodes:

- Each occurrence of "?", "*", and "+" within a rule is subject to an extra node with 0, 1, or more branches.
- Each branch of these extra nodes is rooted in an extra node with the list of symbols that are optional or to be repeated.

These extra nodes are visualized by ellipses in Fig. 6.4. The example in the figure is a variation on Fig. 6.1.

6.5 Lexical Syntax

In the illustrative grammars presented earlier, we left out some details: the syntax of names (FSML, BIPL, and BFPL) and integers (BIPL and BFPL). Such details are usually considered to be part of what is called the *lexical syntax*. That is, the lexical syntax covers the syntactic categories that correspond to syntactical units without any "interesting" tree-based structure. The approach of defining a separate lexical syntax is something of a dogma, but we give in on this dogma for now.

Let us define the lexical syntax of FSML. The earlier grammar contained rules for redirecting several nonterminals for different kinds of names or symbols to the nonterminal name. Thus:

stateid : name ;
event : name ;
action : name ;

The nonterminal name can be defined by a rule as follows:

name : { alpha }+ ;

Here, alpha is a predefined nonterminal for uppercase and lowercase letters[2]. Thus, FSML's name is defined as nonempty sequences of letters. Generally, the lexical syntax of a language can be defined by grammar rules too. In practice, different grammar notations of varying expressiveness are used for this purpose.

There is a pragmatic reason for not having included the above rule in the earlier grammar. In one way (by separation, as done here) or another, we need to describe the indivisible lexical units of the language as opposed to divisible syntactical units that may contain white space (space, tab, newline, line feed) or comments. In the case of FSML, we want to admit white space everywhere – except, of course, within names or the terminals such as *'state'* and *'->'*. Further, we may also want to declare the lexical syntax of white space and comments. To this end, we define a special nonterminal layout, which, by convention, defines the lexical syntax of strings to be skipped anywhere in the input between (but not within) lexical units. Let us provide the complete lexical syntax of FSML.

Illustration 6.9 (Lexical syntax of finite state machines (FSML))

EGL resource languages/FSML/ls.egl

name : { alpha }+ ;
layout : { space }+ ;

Here, space is a "predefined" nonterminal which subsumes "white space", i.e., space, tab, newline, and line feed. Thus, FSML's layout is defined as a non-empty sequence of such white space characters.

Let us consider another example.

Illustration 6.10 (Lexical syntax of imperative programs (BIPL))

EGL resource languages/BIPL/ls.egl

```
1   name : { alpha }+ ;
2   integer : { digit }+ ;
3   layout : { space }+ ;
4   layout : '//' { { end_of_line }~ }* end_of_line ;
```

---

[2] In the rules for the lexical syntax, we assume predefined nonterminals for common character classes such as *alpha*, *space*, *digit*, and *end_of_line*.

BIPL's name is defined in the same way as in FSML (line 1). BIPL's integer is defined as nonempty sequence of digits (line 2). There are two rules for layout. The first one models white space in the same way as in FSML (line 3); the second one models C/Java-style line comments (line 4). In the last rule, we use negation "~" to express that no "end-of line" character is admitted in a given position.

Let us consider yet another example.

Illustration 6.11 (Lexical syntax of functional programs (BFPL))

EGL resource languages/BFPL/ls.egl

```
name : lower { alpha }* ;
integer : { digit }+ ;
layout : { space }+ ;
layout : '−−'{ { end_of_line }~ }* end_of_line ;
```

BFPL's name is defined as non-empty sequence of letters starting in lowercase. BFPL's integer is defined in the same way as in BIPL. There are two rules for layout. The first one captures white space in the same way as before; the second one models Haskell-style line comments.

Exercise 6.14 (Primitive types in syntax definitions)   [Intermediate level]
Provide a convincing hypothesis that explains why the extended signature notation (ESL) features primitive types such as string *and* integer *whereas EGL does not.*

6.6 The Metametalevel

The grammar notations BGL and EGL correspond to proper software languages in themselves. In this section, the concrete and abstract syntaxes of these syntax definition languages are defined. Accordingly, we operate at the metametalevel. This development enables, for example, a systematic treatment of acceptance and parsing. We also revisit the abstract syntax definition languages BSL, ESL, and MML and define their concrete syntaxes, as we have only defined their abstract syntaxes previously (Section 3.4).

6.6.1 The Signature of Grammars

Let us define the abstract syntax of concrete syntaxes. In this manner, concrete syntaxes can be processed programmatically, for example, when implementing ("generating") parsers. To make the presentation more approachable, the basic grammar notation (BGL) is covered first.

Specification 6.1 (The ESL signature of BGL grammars)

ESL resource languages/BGL/as.esl

```
type grammar = rule* ;
type rule = label × nonterminal × gsymbols ;
type gsymbols = gsymbol* ;
symbol t : terminal → gsymbol ;
symbol n : nonterminal → gsymbol ;
type label = string ;
type terminal = string ;
type nonterminal = string ;
```

The abstract syntactical representation of grammars can be illustrated as follows.

Illustration 6.12 (BNL's grammar in abstract syntax)

Term resource languages/BNL/cs.term

```
[
  (number,number,[n(bits),n(rest)]),
  (single,bits,[n(bit)]),
  (many,bits,[n(bit),n(bits)]),
  (zero,bit,[t('0')]),
  (one,bit,[t('1')]),
  (integer,rest,[]),
  (rational,rest,[t('.'),n(bits)])
].
```

Let us now provide the signature for the extended grammar notation.

Specification 6.2 (The ESL signature of EGL grammars)

ESL resource languages/EGL/as.esl

```
type grammar = rule* ;
type rule = label? × nonterminal × symbols ;
type symbols = symbol* ;
symbol t : terminal → symbol ;
symbol n : nonterminal → symbol ;
symbol star : symbols → symbol ;
symbol plus : symbols → symbol ;
symbol option : symbols → symbol ;
symbol not : symbols → symbol ;
type label = string ;
type terminal = string ;
type nonterminal = string ;
```

We should impose constraints on the language of grammars, such as that the rule labels are distinct and that the conditions of productivity and reachability (Definition 6.4) are met, but we omit a discussion of these routine details.

6.6.2 The Signature of Concrete Syntax Trees

On top of the signature of grammars, we can also define a signature for CSTs, which is useful, for example, as a fundamental representation format for parsing results. We cover only the basic grammar notation (BGL) here. We introduce a corresponding language: *BCL* (*BGL CST Language*).

Specification 6.3 (Signature of BGL-based CSTs)

ESL resource languages/BCL/as.esl

symbol **leaf** : terminal → ptree ;
symbol **fork** : rule × ptree∗ → ptree ;
// Rules as in BGL
...

Thus, there is a *leaf* symbol for a terminal, and there is a *fork* symbol which combines a rule and a list of subtrees for the nonterminals on the right-hand side of the rule. An actual CST, which conforms to the signature, is shown below.

Illustration 6.13 (CST for the binary number "10")

Term resource languages/BNL/samples/10.tree

```
fork(
  (number,number,[n(bits),n(rest)]), % rule
  [ % list of branches
    fork( % 1st branch
      (many,bits,[n(bit),n(bits)]), % rule
      [ % list of branches
        fork( % 1st branch
    (one,bit,[t('1')]), % rule
    [leaf('1')]), % leaf
  fork( % 2nd branch
    (single,bits,[n(bit)]), % rule
    [ % list of branches
      fork( % 1st branch % rule
        (zero,bit,[t('0')]),
        [leaf('0')])])]), % leaf
  fork( % 2nd branch
    (integer,rest,[]), % rule
    [])]). % empty list of branches
```

Exercise 6.15 (CSTs for EGL)   [Basic level]
Devise a signature for CSTs for the extended grammar notation EGL.

The signature as stated above is underspecified. For a CST to be well-formed, it must use only rules from the underlying grammar and it must combine them in a correct manner, as constrained by Definition 6.6.

6.6.3 The Grammar of Grammars

We can also devise a grammar of grammars, which is useful, for example, for parsing grammars. To make the presentation more approachable, the basic grammar notation (BGL) is covered first.

Specification 6.4 (The EGL grammar of BGL grammars)

EGL resource languages/BGL/cs.egl

```
grammar : {rule}* ;
rule : '[' label ']' nonterminal ':' gsymbols ';' ;
gsymbols : {gsymbol}* ;
[t] gsymbol : terminal ;
[n] gsymbol : nonterminal ;
label : name ;
terminal : qstring ;
nonterminal : name ;
```

Let us now provide the grammar for the extended grammar notation.

Specification 6.5 (The EGL grammar of EGL grammars)

EGL resource languages/EGL/cs.egl

```
grammar : {rule}* ;
rule : {'[' label ']'}? nonterminal ':' gsymbols ';' ;
gsymbols : {gsymbol}* ;
[t] gsymbol : terminal ;
[n] gsymbol : nonterminal ;
[star] gsymbol : '{' gsymbols '}' '*' ;
[plus] gsymbol : '{' gsymbols '}' '+' ;
[option] gsymbol : '{' gsymbols '}' '?' ;
[not] gsymbol : '{' gsymbols '}' '~' ;
label : name ;
terminal : qstring ;
nonterminal : name ;
```

We also provide a separate grammar for the lexical syntax.

Illustration 6.14 (Lexical syntax of EGL)

EGL resource languages/EGL/ls.egl

```
qstring : quote { { quote }~ }+ quote ;
name : { csymf }+ ;
layout : { space }+ ;
layout : '//' { { end_of_line }~ }* end_of_line ;
```

6.6.4 The Grammar of Signatures

Let us also define the concrete syntax of tree-based abstract syntaxes, as useful, for
example, for parsing signatures. The basic signature notation (BSL) is covered first.

Specification 6.6 (The EGL grammar of BSL signatures)

EGL resource languages/BSL/cs.egl

```
signature : { symbol ';' }* ;
symbol : 'symbol' name ':' args '->' name ;
args : { name { '#' name }* }? ;
```

Let us now provide the grammar for the extended signature notation.

Specification 6.7 (The EGL grammar of ESL signatures)

EGL resource languages/ESL/cs.egl

```
signature : { decl ';' }* ;
[type] decl : 'type' name '=' typeexprs ;
[symbol] decl : 'symbol' name ':' { typeexprs }? '->' name ;
typeexprs : typeexpr { '#' typeexpr }* ;
typeexpr : factor cardinality ;
[boolean] factor : 'boolean' ;
[integer] factor : 'integer' ;
[float] factor : 'float' ;
[string] factor : 'string' ;
[term] factor : 'term' ;
[tuple] factor : '(' typeexpr { '#' typeexpr }+ ')' ;
[sort] factor : name ;
[star] cardinality : '*' cardinality ;
[plus] cardinality : '+' cardinality ;
[option] cardinality : '?' cardinality ;
[none] cardinality : ;
```

We also provide a separate grammar for the lexical syntax.

Illustration 6.15 (Lexical syntax of ESL)

EGL resource languages/ESL/ls.egl

```
name : { csymf }+ ;
layout : { space }+ ;
layout : '//'{ { end_of_line }~ }* end_of_line ;
```

6.6.5 The Grammar of Metamodels

It remains to provide the grammar of metamodels (MML) which is useful, for example, for parsing metamodels.

Specification 6.8 (The EGL grammar of MML metamodels)

EGL resource languages/MML/cs.egl

```
metamodel : { classifier }* ;
[datatype] classifier : 'datatype' name ';' ;
[enum] classifier : 'enum' name '{' name { ',' name }* '}' ;
[class] classifier : abstract 'class' name super members ;
super : { 'extends' name }? ;
[abstract] abstract : 'abstract' ;
[concrete] abstract : ;
members : '{' { member }* '}' ;
member : kind name ':' type ';' ;
[value] kind : 'value' ;
[part] kind : 'part' ;
[reference] kind : 'reference' ;
type : name cardinality ;
[plus] cardinality : '+' ;
[star] cardinality : '*' ;
[option] cardinality : '?' ;
[one] cardinality : ;
```

We also provide a separate grammar for the lexical syntax.

Illustration 6.16 (Lexical syntax of MML)

EGL resource languages/MML/ls.egl

```
name : { csymf }+ ;
layout : { space }+ ;
layout : '//'{ { end_of_line }~ }* end_of_line ;
```

Summary and Outline

We have explained how (context-free) grammars (or different notations for them) may serve for modeling string-based concrete syntax. We have defined two different semantics of grammars: (i) a set-theoretic semantics, defining a software language as a set of strings; and (ii) a tree-oriented semantics, defining the structure of language elements in terms of the productions of a grammar. Further, we have defined the fundamental notions of acceptance and parsing, which ultimately have to be complemented by algorithms for parsing.

In the next chapter, we will discuss the implementation of concrete syntax, including basic parsing algorithms and practical approaches to parsing, formatting, and mapping between concrete and abstract syntax, as well as the use of concrete syntax in metaprograms.

References

1. Backus, J.W., Bauer, F.L., Green, J., Katz, C., McCarthy, J., Perlis, A.J., Rutishauser, H., Samelson, K., Vauquois, B., Wegstein, J.H., van Wijngaarden, A., Woodger, M.: Revised report on the Algorithm Language ALGOL 60. Commun. ACM **6**(1), 1–17 (1963)
2. van den Brand, M., Scheerder, J., Vinju, J.J., Visser, E.: Disambiguation filters for scannerless generalized LR parsers. In: Proc. CC 2002, *LNCS*, vol. 2304, pp. 143–158. Springer (2002)
3. Bravenboer, M., Kalleberg, K.T., Vermaas, R., Visser, E.: Stratego/XT 0.17. A language and toolset for program transformation. Sci. Comput. Program. **72**(1-2), 52–70 (2008)
4. Chomsky, N.: Three models for the description of language. IRE Transactions on Information Theory **2**(3), 113–124 (1956)
5. Ford, B.: Parsing expression grammars: A recognition-based syntactic foundation. In: Proc. POPL, pp. 111–122. ACM (2004)
6. Hopcroft, J., Motwani, R., Ullman, J.: Introduction to Automata Theory, Languages, and Computation. Pearson (2013). 3rd edition
7. ISO/IEC: ISO/IEC 14977:1996(E). Information Technology. Syntactic Metalanguage. Extended BNF. (1996). Available at `http://www.cl.cam.ac.uk/~mgk25/iso-14977.pdf`
8. Johnson, S.C.: YACC—Yet Another Compiler Compiler. Computer Science Technical Report 32, AT&T Bell Laboratories (1975)
9. Klint, P., van der Storm, T., Vinju, J.J.: RASCAL: A domain specific language for source code analysis and manipulation. In: Proc. SCAM, pp. 168–177. IEEE (2009)
10. Klint, P., van der Storm, T., Vinju, J.J.: EASY meta-programming with Rascal. In: GTTSE 2009, Revised Papers, *LNCS*, vol. 6491, pp. 222–289. Springer (2011)
11. Parr, T.: The Definitive ANTLR 4 Reference. Pragmatic Bookshelf (2013). 2nd edition
12. Visser, E.: Syntax definition for language prototyping. Ph.D. thesis, University of Amsterdam (1997)
13. Visser, E.: Stratego: A language for program transformation based on rewriting strategies. In: Proc. RTA, *LNCS*, vol. 2051, pp. 357–362. Springer (2001)

Chapter 7
Implementation of Textual Concrete Syntax

PAUL KLINT.[1]

Abstract This chapter discusses implementation aspects of textual concrete syntax: parsing, abstraction, formatting, and the use of concrete as opposed to abstract object syntax in metaprograms. We focus on how parsers, formatters, etc. are actually implemented in practice, subject to using appropriate libraries, tools, and metaprogramming techniques.

---

[1] Paul Klint's contributions to computer science are not limited to the implementation (or the practice or the application) of concrete syntax, but this is an area in which he has continuously driven the state of the art over the years. Some of his work on concrete syntax has focused on supporting it in interactive programming environments and language workbenches such as ASF+SDF and Rascal [21, 55, 31, 30]. In other work, he has been addressing practical challenges regarding parsing, for example, in terms of scannerless parsing and ambiguity detection in generalized (LR) parsing [13, 3]. Paul Klint loves grammars [29].

Artwork Credits for Chapter Opening: This work by Wojciech Kwasnik is licensed under CC BY-SA 4.0. This artwork quotes the artwork *DMT*, acrylic, 2006 by Matt Sheehy with the artist's permission. This work also quotes https://commons.wikimedia.org/wiki/File:Sunset_at_Montmajour_1888_Van_Gogh.jpg, subject to the attribution "Vincent van Gogh: Sunset at Montmajour (1888) [Public domain], via Wikimedia Commons." This work artistically morphes an image, http://homepages.cwi.nl/~paulk, showing the person honored, subject to the attribution "Permission granted by Paul Klint for use in this book."

© Springer International Publishing AG, part of Springer Nature 2018
R. Lämmel, *Software Languages*,
https://doi.org/10.1007/978-3-319-90800-7_7

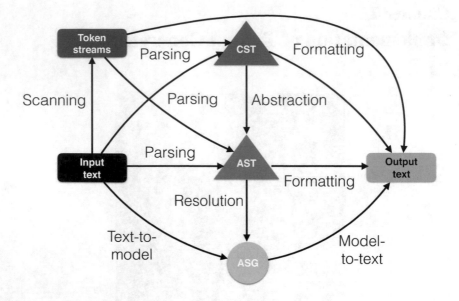

Fig. 7.1 Mappings (edges) between different representations (nodes) of language elements. For instance, "parsing" is a mapping from text or tokens to CSTs or ASTs.

7.1 Representations and Mappings

The big picture of concrete syntax implementation, as covered by this chapter, is shown in Fig. 7.1 with the exception of the special topic of concrete object syntax (Section 7.5). The nodes in the figure correspond to different representations of language elements; these representations have already been discussed, to some extent, but we summarize them here for clarity:

Text (String)   Text is an important format for representing language elements. Text may serve as input or may arise as the output of language-processing activities. We do not discuss visual languages in this chapter.

Token stream   Parsing may involve an extra phase, scanning, for processing text at the level of lexical syntax for units such as white space, comments, identifiers, and literals. The resulting units are referred to as tokens (or, more precisely, token-lexeme pairs). That is, a token is a classifier of a lexical unit. For instance, in FSML, we are concerned with "name" tokens as well as tokens for special characters, operators, and keywords (e.g., "/" and "state"). We use the term "lexeme" to refer to the string (text) that makes up a lexical unit. For instance, we may encounter the lexemes "locked", "unlocked", etc. in the input; we classify them as "name" tokens. In practice, the term "token" is also used to include lexemes.

CST   Concrete syntax trees typically arise as the result of parsing text. These trees follow the structure of the underlying grammar; each node, with its subtrees, represents the application of a grammar rule, except for some leaf nodes that simply represent terminals.

AST Abstract syntax trees may arise as the result of abstraction, i.e., a mapping from concrete to abstract syntax trees; they may also arise as the result of metaprograms such as transformers and generators.

ASG Abstract syntax graphs may be used to directly represent references on top of ASTs. In metamodeling, references are commonly used in models. Text-to-model transformations may also map text directly to graphs (models), without going through CSTs or ASTs explicitly. In other contexts, the explicit use of graphs is less common. For instance, in term rewriting, references are expressed only indirectly, for example, by means of traversals that look up subtrees or by an extra data structure for an environment.

The edges in the figure correspond to common forms of mapping:

Parsing This is a mapping from text or token streams to CSTs or ASTs.

Scanning This is a mapping from text to token streams, as an optional phase of parsing. It is the process of recognizing tokens. Scanning is like parsing, but at the level of lexical syntax. The input of scanning is text; the output is a token stream (to be precise, a stream of token-lexeme pairs), possibly enriched by position information. Scanning is performed by a scanner (a lexer). The underlying lexical syntax may be defined by regular or context-free grammars; see the examples in Section 6.1.4.

Abstraction This is a mapping from concrete to abstract syntax, i.e., from CSTs to ASTs.

Resolution This is a mapping from tree- to graph-based abstract syntax, i.e., from ASTs to ASGs.

Text-to-model This is about mapping from text that is an element of a language generated by a grammar to a model that conforms to a metamodel. Here, the grammar and metamodel are viewed as alternative syntax definitions for the same language.

Formatting This is a mapping from ASTs to text. We may expect that unparsing will produce textual output that follows some formatting conventions in terms of adding space, indentation, line breaks, and appropriate use of parentheses. As indicated in the figure, formatting can also be taken to mean that CSTs are mapped to text, in which case we may also speak of unparsing. Such a mapping should be straightforward because the leaf nodes of a CST should represent the text except that space, indentation, line breaks, and comments may be missing. Formatting may also operate at a lexical level such that token streams are mapped to text. Generally, we may also speak of "pretty printing" instead of formatting.

Model-to-text This is the opposite of "text-to-model". In different terms, if "text-to-model" is the metamodeling-centric variation on parsing, then "model-to-text" is the metamodeling-centric variation on formatting or pretty printing.

7.2 Parsing

A parser maps text to concrete or possibly abstract syntax trees or graphs. Parsing is a prerequisite for metaprogramming on object programs with a textual syntax. We will discuss different approaches to the implementation of parsers; we assume that parsers are systematically, if not mechanically, derived from context-free grammars. To this end, we illustrate mainstream parsing technologies: ANTLR [46] and Parsec [37]. We also discuss parsing algorithms briefly.

7.2.1 Basic Parsing Algorithms

A grammar can be interpreted in a systematic, algorithmic manner so that one obtains an acceptor (Definition 6.5) or a parser (Definition 6.7) directly. We discuss here some simple, fundamental algorithms for top-down and bottom-up parsing. There are many options and challenges associated with parsing [20]; we only aim to convey some basic intuitions here.

7.2.1.1 Top-Down Acceptance

In top-down acceptance (or parsing), we maintain a stack of grammar symbols, which we initialize with the start symbol; we process the input from left to right. In each step, we either "consume" or "expand". In the "consume" case, we consume a terminal from the input if it is also at the top of the stack. In the "expand" case, we replace a nonterminal on the stack by a corresponding right-hand side.

Definition 7.1 (Algorithm for top-down acceptance)

Input:

- *a well-formed context-free grammar $G = \langle N, T, P, s \rangle$;*
- *a string (i.e., a list) $w \in T^*$.*

Output:

- *a Boolean value.*

Variables:

- *a stack z maintaining a sequence of grammar symbols;*
- *a string (i.e., a list) i maintaining the remaining input.*

Steps:

1. *Initialize z with s (i.e., the start symbol) as the top of the stack.*
2. *Initialize i with w.*

3. *If both i and z are empty, then return* **true**.
4. *If z is empty and i is nonempty, then return* **false**.
5. *Choose an action:*
   Consume: *If the top of z is a terminal, then:*
       a.   *If the top of z equals the head of i, then:*
           i.   *Remove the head of i.*
           ii. *Pop the top of z.*
       b.   *Return* **false** *otherwise.*
   Expand: *If the top of z is a nonterminal, then:*
       a.   *Choose a $p \in P$ with the top of z on the left-hand side of p.*
       b.   *Pop the top of z.*
       c.   *Push the symbols of the right-hand side of p onto z.*
6. *Go to 3.*

Table 7.1 Illustration of top-down acceptance

Step	Remaining input	Stack (TOS left)	Action
1	'1', '0'	*number*	Expand rule [*number*]
2	'1', '0'	*bits rest*	Expand rule [*many*]
3	'1', '0'	*bit bits rest*	Expand rule [*one*]
4	'1', '0'	'1' *bits rest*	Consume terminal '1'
5	'0'	*bits rest*	Expand rule [*single*]
6	'0'	*bit rest*	Expand rule [*zero*]
7	'0'	'0' *rest*	Consume terminal '0'
8	–	*rest*	Expand rule [*integer*]
9	–	–	–

In the strict sense, the description is not a proper algorithm owing to nondeterminism (see the choice of action) and nontermination (think of infinite expansion for grammars with left recursion, as we will discuss more in detail below). Actual acceptance algorithms arise as refinements that constrain the choice or the grammar. In the sequence of steps shown in Table 7.1, we assume an oracle which tells us the "right" choice.

Exercise 7.1 (Nondeterminism of top-down acceptance)   [Basic level]
Identify the steps in Table 7.1 that make a choice, and identify alternative actions. How do these alternatives reveal themselves as inappropriate?

Let us implement top-down acceptance based on the pseudo-algorithm in Definition 7.1. We aim only at a very basic implementation, meant to be useful for understanding parsing conceptually. We implement top-down acceptance in Haskell.

Assuming a suitable representation of BNL's BGL grammar, we expect to perform acceptance for binary numbers as follows:

Interactive Haskell session:

▶ accept bnlGrammar *"101.01"*
True
- -
▶ accept bnlGrammar *"x"*
False

We assume a typeful representation (Section 4.1.3) of the signature of BGL grammars (Section 6.6.1) as Haskell data types, as shown below.

Illustration 7.1 (Datatypes for grammar representation)

Haskell module Language.BGL.Syntax

```
type Grammar = [Rule]
type Rule = (Label, Nonterminal, [GSymbol])
data GSymbol = T Terminal | N Nonterminal
type Label = String
type Terminal = Char
type Nonterminal = String
```

Illustration 7.2 (The grammar of BNL represented in Haskell)

Haskell module Language.BGL.Sample

```
bnlGrammar :: Grammar
bnlGrammar = [
  ("number", "number", [N "bits", N "rest"]),
  ("single", "bits", [N "bit"]),
  ("many", "bits", [N "bit", N "bits"]),
  ("zero", "bit", [T '0']),
  ("one", "bit", [T '1']),
  ("integer", "rest", []),
  ("rational", "rest", [T '.', N "bits"])
  ]
```

Top-down acceptance is implemented in Haskell as follows.

Illustration 7.3 (Implementation of top-down acceptance)

Haskell module Language.BGL.TopDownAcceptor

```
1   accept :: [Rule] → String → Bool
2   accept g = steps g [N s]
3     where
4        -- Retrieve start symbol
5        ((_, s, _):_) = g
6
7   steps :: [Rule] → [GSymbol] → String → Bool
8   -- Acceptance succeeds (empty stack, all input consumed)
9   steps _ [] [] = True
10  -- Consume terminal at top of stack from input
11  steps g (T t:z) (t':i) | t==t' = steps g z i
12  -- Expand a nonterminal; try different alternatives
13  steps g (N n:z) i = or (map (λ rhs → steps g (rhs++z) i) rhss)
14    where
15       rhss = [ rhs | (_, n', rhs) ← g, n == n' ]
16  -- Otherwise parsing fails
17  steps _ _ _ = False
```

The implementation is based on these ideas:

- The start symbol is determined within the main function accept as the left-hand side of the first rule (line 5).
- The program maintains a parser stack, which is represented simply as a list of grammar symbols. The head of the list is the top of the stack. The stack is initialized with the start symbol (line 2).
- The regular termination case is that both the input and the stack are empty and, thus, True is returned (line 9).
- The case where a terminal t is the top of stack requires that the input starts with the same terminal (see the guard t==t'), in which case the terminal is removed from both the stack and the input before continuing with the remaining stack and input (line 11).
- The case where a nonterminal n is the top of stack forms a disjunction over all the possible right-hand sides for n; these options are collected in a list comprehension; and the right-hand sides replace n in the different attempts (lines 13–15).
- In all other cases, acceptance fails (line 17), i.e., when the terminal at the top of the stack is not met by the head of the input, or the stack is empty while the input is not empty.

This implementation is naive because it tries all alternatives without considering the input. More seriously, the implementation may exhibit nonterminating behavior if applied to a *left-recursive grammar*. Instead of defining left recursion here formally, let us just look at an example. The BNL grammar does not involve left recursion, but consider the following syntax of simple arithmetic expressions:

Illustration 7.4 (A left-recursive grammar for arithmetic expressions)

EGL resource languages/EGL/samples/left-recursion.egl

[add] expr : expr '+' expr ;
[const] expr : integer ;

The grammar is left-recursive owing to the first rule because, if we apply the first rule, then expr is replaced by a sequence of grammar symbols that again starts with expr. Thus, such a derivation or expansion process could go on forever without consuming any input. There are various techniques for dealing with or removing left recursion (see, e.g., [20, 1, 42, 38, 18, 19, 43]).

Thanks to the way in which alternatives are handled in the Haskell code for top-down acceptance, we do not commit to a particular choice, but all alternatives are potentially tried. In principle, there are two major options for combining the alternatives:

Local backtracking   When a nonterminal is being expanded, the different alternatives are tried in the grammar-specified order; we commit to the first alternative for which acceptance succeeds, if there is any.

Global backtracking   There is no commitment to an alternative. That is, we may consider yet other alternatives even after successful completion of an alternative triggered by failure in the enclosing scope.

These two options differ in terms of efficiency and completeness. An incomplete acceptor corresponds to the situation where some proper language elements would not be accepted. Local backtracking is more efficient, but less complete than global backtracking. The Haskell-based implementation in Illustration 7.3, as discussed above, facilitates global backtracking because the disjunction does not just model choice over alternatives; rather it models choice over all possible continuations of acceptance.

Exercise 7.2 (Backtracking variations)   [Intermediate level]
Implement top-down acceptance with local backtracking.

The incompleteness of local backtracking can easily be observed on the basis of the BNL example. That is, consider the order of the rules [single] and [many] in Illustration 7.2. Local backtracking would commit us [single] even for the case of an input string with more than one digit. The rules [integer] and [rational] expose the same kind of order issue. Local backtracking is sufficient once we reorder the rules as follows.

Illustration 7.5 (BNL grammar for which local backtracking suffices)

<u>Haskell module *Language.BGL.SampleWithGreediness*</u>

```
bnlGrammar :: Grammar
bnlGrammar = [
  ("number", "number", [N "bits", N "rest"]),
  ("many", "bits", [N "bit", N "bits"]),
  ("single", "bits", [N "bit"]),
  ("zero", "bit", [T '0']),
  ("one", "bit", [T '1']),
  ("rational", "rest", [T '.', N "bits"]),
  ("integer", "rest", [])
]
```

There are various algorithms and grammar classes that cater for efficient top-down parsing without the issues at hand [20, 1].

7.2.1.2 Bottom-Up Acceptance

In bottom-up acceptance (or parsing), we maintain a stack of grammar symbols, starting from the empty stack; we process the input from left to right. In each step, we either "shift" or "reduce". In the "shift" case, we move a terminal from the input to the stack. In the "reduce" case, we replace a sequence of grammar symbols on the stack with a nonterminal, where the removed sequence must form the right-hand side and the added nonterminal must be the left-hand side of some grammar rule.

Definition 7.2 (Algorithm for bottom-up acceptance)

Input:

- *a well-formed context-free grammar $G = \langle N, T, P, s \rangle$;*
- *a string (i.e., a list) $w \in T^*$.*

Output:

- *a Boolean value.*

Variables:

- *a stack z maintaining a sequence of grammar symbols;*
- *a string (i.e., a list) i maintaining the remaining input.*

Steps:

1. *Initialize z with the empty stack.*
2. *Initialize i with w.*
3. *If i is empty and z consists of s alone, then return* true.

4.   *Choose an action:*
     Shift: *Remove the head of i and push it onto z.*
     Reduce:
         a.   *Pop a sequence x of symbols from z.*
         b.   *Choose a p ∈ P such that x equals the right-hand side of p.*
         c.   *Push the left-hand side of p onto z.*
     Return **false**, *if no action is feasible.*
5.   *Go to 3.*

Table 7.2 Illustration of bottom-up acceptance

Step	Remaining input	Stack (TOS right)	Action
1	'1', '0'	–	Shift terminal '1'
2	'0'	'1'	Reduce rule [*one*]
3	'0'	*bit*	Reduce rule [*single*]
4	'0'	*bits*	Shift terminal '0'
5	–	*bits* '0'	Reduce rule [*one*]
6	–	*bits bit*	Reduce rule [*many*]
7	–	*bits*	Reduce rule [*integer*]
8	–	*bits rest*	Reduce rule [*number*]
9	–	*number*	–

It is insightful to notice how top-down acceptance (Table 7.1) and bottom-up acceptance (Table 7.2) are opposites of each other in some sense. The top-down scheme starts with s on the stack; the bottom-up scheme ends with s on the stack. The top-down scheme ends with an empty stack; the bottom-up scheme starts from an empty stack.

Exercise 7.3 (Nondeterminism of bottom-up acceptance)   [Basic level]
Identify the steps in Table 7.2 that make a choice, and identify alternative actions. How does the inappropriateness of the options reveal itself?

Let us implement bottom-up acceptance based on the pseudo-algorithm in Definition 7.2. We aim again at a very basic implementation, meant to be useful for understanding parsing conceptually. We implement bottom-up acceptance in Haskell as follows.

Illustration 7.6 (Implementation of bottom-up acceptance)

Haskell module <u>Language.BGL.BottomUpAcceptor</u>

```
1   accept :: [Rule] → String → Bool
2   accept g = steps g [] —— Begin with empty stack
3
4   steps :: [Rule] → [GSymbol] → String → Bool
5   —— Acceptance succeeds (start symbol on stack, all input consumed)
6   steps g [N s] [] | s == s' = True
7     where
8       —— Retrieve start symbol
9       ((_, s', _):_) = g
10  —— Shift or reduce
11  steps g z i = shift || reduce
12    where
13      —— Shift terminal from input to stack
14      shift = not (null i) && steps g (T (head i) : z) (tail i)
15      —— Reduce prefix on stack to nonterminal
16      reduce = not (null zs) && or (map (λ z → steps g z i) zs)
17        where
18          —— Retrieve relevant reductions
19          zs = [ N n : drop l z
20               | (_, n, rhs) ← g,
21                 let l = length rhs,
22                 take l z == reverse rhs ]
```

The implementation is based on these ideas:

- The program maintains a parser stack, which is represented simply as a list of grammar symbols. The head of the list is the top of the stack. We start from the empty stack (line 2).
- The regular termination case is that the input is empty and the start symbol is the sole element on the stack and, thus, True is returned (line 6). The start symbol is assumed here to be the left-hand side of the first rule (line 9).
- Otherwise, shift and reduce actions are tried and combined by "||" (line 11). The shift action is tried first (line 14) and all possible reduce actions are tried afterwards (line 16), as encoded in the order of the operands of "||".
- Possible reduce actions are determined by trying to find (reversed) right-hand sides of rules on the stack; see the list comprehension computing zs (lines 19–22). The options are combined by "or".

This implementation is naive, just as much as the earlier implementation of top-down acceptance. For one thing, the options for shift and reduce are tried in a way that a huge search space is explored. More seriously, we face the potential of nontermination again. Left recursion is not a problem this time around, but nontermination may be caused by *epsilon productions* – this is when a rule has an empty right-hand side. Nontermination can arise because any stack qualifies for application of a reduce action with an empty list of grammar symbols. The original grammar for BNL does indeed contain an epsilon production [integer]. The following variation is needed to be able to use the naive implementation of bottom-up acceptance.

Illustration 7.7 (BNL grammar without epsilon productions)

Haskell module Language.BGL.SampleWithoutEpsilon

```
bnlGrammar :: Grammar
bnlGrammar = [
  ("integer", "number", [N "bits", N "rest"]),
  ("integer", "number", [N "bits", T '.', N "bits"]),
  ("single", "bits", [N "bit"]),
  ("many", "bits", [N "bit", N "bits"]),
  ("zero", "bit", [T '0']),
  ("one", "bit", [T '1'])
  ]
```

There are various algorithms and grammar classes that cater for efficient bottom-up parsing without termination issues [20, 1].

7.2.1.3 Top-Down Parsing

We move now from acceptance to parsing. Thus, we need to construct CSTs during acceptance. CSTs are represented in Haskell as follows.

Illustration 7.8 (CSTs for BGL)

Haskell module Language.BGL.CST

```
type Info = Either Char Rule
type CST = Tree Info
```

We use Haskell's library type Tree for node-labeled rose trees, i.e., trees with any number of subtrees. The labels (infos) are either characters for the leaf nodes or grammar rules for inner nodes. Top-down parsing is implemented in Haskell as follows.

Illustration 7.9 (Implementation of top-down parsing)

Haskell module Language.BGL.TopDownParser

```
parse :: [Rule] → String → Maybe CST
parse g i = do
    (i', t) ← tree g (N s) i
    guard (i'==[])
    return t
  where
    -- Retrieve start symbol
```

```
    ((_, s, _):_) = g
tree :: [Rule] → GSymbol → String → Maybe (String, CST)
-- Consume terminal at top of stack from input
tree _ (T t) i = do
  guard ([t] == take 1 i)
  return (drop 1 i, Node (Left t) [])
-- Expand a nonterminal
tree g (N n) i = foldr mplus mzero (map rule g)
  where
      -- Try different alternatives
    rule :: Rule → Maybe (String, CST)
    rule r@(_, n', rhs) = do
      guard (n==n')
      (i', cs) ← trees g rhs i
      return (i', Node (Right r) cs)

-- Parse symbol by symbol, sequentially
trees :: [Rule] → [GSymbol] → String → Maybe (String, [CST])
trees _ [] i = return (i, [])
trees g (s:ss) i = do
  (i', c) ← tree g s i
  (i'', cs) ← trees g ss i'
  return (i'', c:cs)
```

In this implementation, we do not model the parser stack explicitly, but we leverage Haskell's stack for function applications. This happens to imply that we are limited here to local backtracking. Thus, the parser is less complete than the acceptor implemented earlier (Section 7.2.1.1).

7.2.1.4 Bottom-Up Parsing

Exercise 7.4 (Bottom-up parsing in Haskell)   [Intermediate level]
Implement bottom-up parsing in Haskell.

7.2.2 Recursive Descent Parsing

Grammars can be implemented programmatically in a systematic manner. Recursive descent parsing [1, 20] is a popular encoding scheme where grammars are implemented as recursive "procedures". Recursive descent parsing is relatively popular, as (some form of) it is often used, when a handwritten parser is implemented. Further, the overall scheme is also insightful, as it may be used for program generation – this is when the code for a top-down parser implementation is generated directly from a grammar (Section 7.2.3).

In Java, some grammar rules for numbers in the BNL language would be represented by procedures (methods) as follows:

```
// [number] number : bits rest ;
void number() {
  bits();
  rest();
}
// [zero] bit : '0' ;
// [one] bit : '1' ;
void bit() {
  if (next == '0') match('0'); else match('1');
}
...
```

That is, there is a method for each nonterminal. Occurrences of nonterminals on right-hand sides of grammar rules are mapped to method calls. Occurrences of terminals are mapped to "match" actions on the input. When selecting alternatives (see bit), we may look ahead into the input.

Here is a more detailed description:

- Each nonterminal of the grammar is implemented as a possibly recursive procedure (a function). Success or failure of parsing may be communicated by the return value or by means of an exception. (The exception-based approach is assumed in the illustrative Java source code shown above.)
- A sequence of grammar symbols is mapped to a sequence of "actions" as follows.

  - A terminal is mapped to a "match" action to examine the head of the input stream. If the terminal is present, then it is removed and the action completes successfully. If the terminal is not present, then parsing fails.
  - A nonterminal is mapped to a procedure call (a function application). This call (application) may succeed or fail in the same sense as matching may succeed or fail.

- It remains to deal with alternatives.

  - *Parsing with look-ahead*: The procedures contain conditions on the prefix of the input stream to select the alternative to be tried. This technique can be used, for example, with $LL(k)$ [20] or $LL(*)$ [47] grammars.
  - *Parsing with backtracking*: The different alternatives are tried until one succeeds, if any does; the pointer in the input stream is reset to where it was when a failing branch was entered.

The following Haskell code represents a recursive descent parser for BNL where backtracking is supported with the help of the Maybe monad. The original grammar rules are shown as Haskell comments next to the corresponding Haskell functions.

Illustration 7.10 (Recursive descent with backtracking for BNL)

Haskell module Language.BNL.BacktrackingAcceptor

```
-- Accept and enforce complete input consumption
accept :: String → Bool
accept i = case number i of
   Just [] → True
   _ → False

-- Functions for nonterminals
number, bits, bit, rest :: String → Maybe String

-- [number] number : bits rest ;
number i = bits i >>=rest

-- [single] bits : bit ;
-- [many] bits : bit bits ;
bits i = many `mplus` single
   where
      single = bit i
      many = bit i >>=bits

-- [zero] bit : '0' ;
   [one] bit : '1' ;
bit i = zero `mplus` one
   where
      zero = match '0' i
      one = match '1' i

-- [integer] rest : ;
-- [rational] rest : '.' bits ;
rest i = rational `mplus` integer
   where
      integer = Just i
      rational = match '.' i >>=bits

-- Match a terminal (a character)
match :: Char → String → Maybe String
match t (t':i) | t == t' = Just i
match _ _ = Nothing
```

The parser can be used as follows:

Interactive Haskell session:

▶ accept *"101.01"*
True

The encoding is based on just a few ideas:

- Each nonterminal is modeled as a function that takes the input string and returns, maybe, the remaining input string. If a function returns Nothing, then this models failure of parsing.
- Sequential composition of grammar symbols, as prescribed by the grammar rules, is modeled by the bind combinator ">>=" of the Maybe monad; in this manner, input strings are processed from left to right.
- There is a general match function which just tries to match a given terminal with the head of the input and either succeeds or fails, as described earlier for the terminal case in recursive descent parsing.
- Different alternatives for a nonterminal are combined by the mplus combinator of the Maybe monad; this implies left-biased choice, i.e., the left operand is tried first and the right operand is tried only in the case of failure for the left operand.

The implementation, as it stands, is limited to local backtracking because alternatives are combined by mplus. As noted before (Section 7.2.1.1), acceptance may be thus incomplete depending on the order of the rules. For comparison, let us also look at an acceptor that uses look-ahead instead of backtracking.

Illustration 7.11 (Recursive descent with look-ahead for BNL)

Haskell module <u>Language.BNL.LookAheadAcceptor</u>

```
-- [single] bits : bit ;
-- [many] bits : bit bits ;
bits i = if lookahead 2 (flip elem ['0','1']) i
            then many
            else single
   where
      single = bit i
      many = bit i >>=bits

-- [zero] bit : '0' ;
-- [one] bit : '1' ;
bit i = if lookahead 1 ((==) '0') i
            then zero
            else one
   where
      zero = match '0' i
      one = match '1' i

-- [integer] rest : ;
-- [rational] rest : '.' bits ;
rest i = if lookahead 1 ((==) '.') i then rational else integer
   where
      integer = Just i
      rational = match '.' i >>=bits

-- Look ahead in input; avoid looking beyond end of input
lookahead :: Int → (Char → Bool) → String → Bool
lookahead l f i = length i >= l && f (i!!(l−1))
```

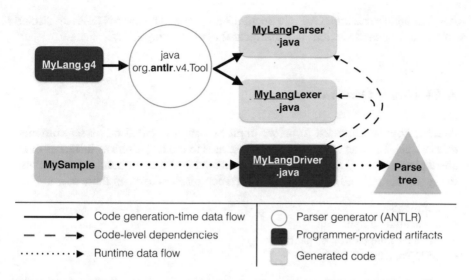

Fig. 7.2 Parser generation with ANTLR with Java as the target language: the data flow at parser-generation time and at runtime of a generated parser is shown.

That is, the functions use an additional function lookahead to perform tests on the input, thereby guarding the different branches for nonterminals with multiple alternatives.

7.2.3 Parser Generation

A popular approach to parser implementation is parser generation. The overall idea is to generate code or data structures from a (possibly enriched) grammar such that the generation process can perform some amount of grammar checking and manipulation, for example, with regard to grammar-class restrictions. Also, extra services may be provided, for example, handling parser errors by means of error messages and error recovery. We briefly discuss ANTLR here as an example of a parser generator. In Chapter 2, we have already applied ANTLR to FSML, thereby deriving a syntax checker and a parser based on walking ANTLR's CST with a listener.

Figure 7.2 summarizes the data flow for generating a parser with ANTLR [46] and using the generated parser. We focus here on Java as the target language for code generation; ANTLR also provides other backends. The input for parser generation is an ANTLR grammar (see the ".g4" file in the figure). Parser generation returns several files; we only care here about the parser and lexer files (see the ".java" files marked as generated code in the figure). Subject to some routine driver code to be provided by the developer, the generated code can be used to parse text into an

ANTLR-style parse tree (CST). In Section 7.3.2, we will revisit ANTLR and discuss how to add semantic actions to a grammar for constructing ASTs.

7.2.4 Parser Combinators

Another popular approach to parser implementation is based on parser combinators [52, 26, 24]. The simple (intriguing) idea is to model parsers as instances of an abstract data type (ADT) with function combinators that correspond to "constructs" for syntax definition. In particular, we need combinators to cover these cases:

- Terminals
- Sequential composition
- Choice (composition of alternatives)
- EBNF constructs ("?", "*", "+")

Nonterminals are modeled as (possibly recursive) functions – pretty much in the same way as in the case of recursive descent parsing (Section 7.2.2).

Let us demonstrate the use of the popular parser-combinator library *Parsec*[2] [37] in the Haskell context. Here is an acceptor for the FSML language.

Illustration 7.12 (A parser combinator-based acceptor for FSML)

Haskell module <u>Language.FSML.Acceptor</u>

```
fsm = many state
state =
      optional (reserved "initial")
   >> reserved "state"
   >> stateid
   >> braces (many transition)
transition =
      event
   >> optional (op "/" >> action)
   >> optional (op "->" >> stateid)
   >> semi
stateid = name
event = name
action = name
```

These combinators are used in the example:

- >>: Sequential composition
- many: EBNF's "*";
- optional: EBNF's "?";
- reserved: reserved keywords (provided by scanner);

---

[2] https://wiki.haskell.org/Parsec

- braces: constructs enclosed in { ··· };
- op: operator symbols (provided by scanner);
- semi: ";" (provided by scanner);
- name: names or identifiers (provided by scanner).

Choice (composition of alternatives) is not present in this simple example, but there is, of course, a corresponding binary combinator "<|>" for left-biased choice.

In the case of Parsec, scanners (lexers) are also just parsers, in terms of the underlying ADT. Technically, scanning and parsing are separated. This simplifies the process of skipping white space, recognizing (and skipping) comments, and handling reserved keywords and special characters in a special manner – also in the interest of enabling "good" error messages. The lexer for FSML is derived from a default lexer as follows.

Illustration 7.13 (A lexer for FSML)

Haskell module Language.FSML.Lexer

```
fsmlDef :: Token.LanguageDef ()
fsmlDef = emptyDef
    { Token.commentStart = "/*"
    , Token.commentEnd = "*/"
    , Token.commentLine = "//"
    , Token.identStart = letter
    , Token.identLetter = alphaNum
    , Token.nestedComments = True
    , Token.reservedNames = ["initial", "state"]
    , Token.reservedOpNames = ["/", "->"]
    }

lexer :: Token.TokenParser ()
lexer = Token.makeTokenParser fsmlDef

braces :: Parser p → Parser p
braces = Token.braces lexer

semi :: Parser String
semi = Token.semi lexer

reserved :: String → Parser ()
reserved = Token.reserved lexer

op :: String → Parser ()
op = Token.reservedOp lexer

name :: Parser String
name = Token.identifier lexer
```

Thus, the definition of the lexer entails the provision of certain parameters such as the start and end sequences for comments, the initial characters of an identifier, and the list of reserved names. Thereby, several lexical categories are readily defined, such as those used in the earlier acceptor.

The ADT for parsing provides a special operation, runParser, for applying the parser to an actual input string. This is demonstrated here at the lexical level:

Interactive Haskell session:

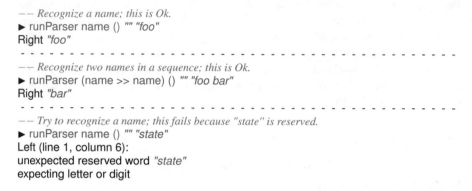

```
-- Recognize a name; this is Ok.
▶ runParser name () "" "foo"
Right "foo"
- - - - - - - - - - - - - - - - - - - - - - - - - - - - - - - - - - - - - - -
-- Recognize two names in a sequence; this is Ok.
▶ runParser (name >> name) () "" "foo bar"
Right "bar"
- - - - - - - - - - - - - - - - - - - - - - - - - - - - - - - - - - - - - - -
-- Try to recognize a name; this fails because "state" is reserved.
▶ runParser name () "" "state"
Left (line 1, column 6):
unexpected reserved word "state"
expecting letter or digit
```

The function runParser takes four arguments of which we are only interested here in the first one (i.e., the actual parser) and the last one (the input string). Running a parser returns either an error message (see Left ···) or a parse tree (see Right ···) such as a string in the two examples above.

In Section 7.3.3, we will return to the parser-combinator approach and discuss how the construction of ASTs can be accomplished with this approach. Until now we have limited ourselves to acceptance.

Exercise 7.5 (Layout in practice)   [Intermediate level]
Study some grammar notation, for example, YACC/LEX [25], SDF [57], or ANTLR [46], with regard to the definition of lexical units and the handling of layout (white space and comments). Explain and illustrate your findings.

7.3 Abstraction

We turn now to the problem of how to construct appropriate ASTs during parsing. In this manner, we effectively model relationships between concrete and abstract syntax, as discussed earlier (Section 6.2). To this end, we will revisit the grammar implementation approaches that we have seen above and enhance them accordingly. Such a mapping is a diverse and complex topic in software language engineering (see, e.g., [28, 27, 48, 62, 22]).

7.3.1 Recursive Descent Parsing

Here we generalize the scheme presented in Section 7.2.2. The key idea is that "procedures" (in our case, "functions") are assumed to construct and return ASTs of the appropriate type. In our Haskell-based approach, we capture a type constructor for the signature of functions that model nonterminals:

type Parser a = String → Maybe (a, String)

That is, the input string is mapped either to Nothing or to a pair consisting of an AST (of type a) and the remaining input string. Here is the parser for FSML.

Illustration 7.14 (A recursive descent parser for BNL in Haskell)

Haskell module Language.BNL.Parser

```
-- [number] number : bits rest ;
number :: Parser Number
number i = do
  (bs, i') ← bits i
  (r, i") ← rest i'
  Just (Number bs r, i")

-- [single] bits : bit ;
-- [many] bits : bit bits ;
bits i = many `mplus` single
  where
    single = do (b, i') ← bit i; Just (Single b, i')
    many = do (b, i') ← bit i; (bs, i") ← bits i'; Just (Many b bs, i")

-- [zero] bit : '0' ;
-- [one] bit : '1' ;
bit i = zero `mplus` one
  where
    zero = do i' ← match '0' i; Just (Zero, i')
    one = do i' ← match '1' i; Just (One, i')

-- [integer] rest : ;
-- [rational] rest : '.' bits ;
rest i = rational `mplus` integer
  where
    integer = Just (Integer, i)
    rational = do
      i' ← match '.' i
      (bs, i") ← bits i'
      Just (Rational bs, i")
```

The differences between a parser and an acceptor (Section 7.2.2) can be summarized as follows. A parser may return an AST; an acceptor is just a predicate. In the parser, we use "do" notation for convenience of sequential composition of actions.

In particular, we bind intermediate ASTs in this way. The encoding of each rule ends in an expression of the form "Just ···" to explicitly compose and return the AST of interest. For instance, consider this:

```
−− [number] number : bits rest ;
number :: Parser Number
number i = do
  (bs, i') ← bits i
  (r, i") ← rest i'
  Just (Number bs r, i")
```

That is, the rule for the nonterminal is encoded by a sequential composition so that we bind ASTs bs and r and construct the AST "Number bs r". Along the way, we thread the input (see i, i', and i").

Exercise 7.6 (A parser monad)   [Intermediate level]
Define an appropriate parser monad (or an applicative functor for parsing) which includes tracking of input and potential failure. Rewrite the recursive descent parser in Illustration 7.14 to use this monad. In this manner, we should arrive at more factored code so that the functions for the nonterminals do not need to pass the input explicitly; this would be taken care of by the bind operation of the monad.

7.3.2 Semantic Actions

In Section 2.3.3, we have already discussed the use of object-oriented listeners for walking a CST such that functionality for AST construction can be defined. We adopted ANTLR accordingly. It is common that parser generators also provide the option of injecting so-called semantic actions into a grammar so that computations can be performed during parsing. A major use case of semantic actions is indeed AST construction. A semantic action is basically some statement of the target language for parser generation; the statement is to be executed when parsing reaches the position of the semantic action within the grammar rule.

Let us inject Java code for AST construction into an ANTLR-based syntax definition.

Illustration 7.15 (An ANTLR-based parser description for FSML)

ANTLR resource languages/FSML/Java/FsmlToObjects.g4

```
1  grammar FsmlToObjects;
2  @header {package org.softlang.fsml;}
3  @members {public Fsm fsm = new Fsm();}
4
5  fsm : state+ EOF ;
6  state :
```

```
7    { boolean initial = false; }
8    ('initial' { initial = true; })?
9    'state' stateid
10   { fsm.getStates().add(new State($stateid.text, initial)); }
11   '{' transition* '}'
12   ;
13   transition :
14   { String source = fsm.getStates().get(fsm.getStates().size()-1).getStateid(); }
15   event
16   { String action = null; }
17   ('/' action { action = $action.text; })?
18   { String target = source; }
19   ('->' stateid { target = $stateid.text; })?
20   { fsm.getTransitions().add(new Transition(source, $event.text, action, target)); }
21   ';'
22   ;
23   stateid : NAME ;
24   event : NAME ;
25   action : NAME ;
26   NAME : ('a'..'z'|'A'..'Z')+ ;
27   WS : [ \t\n\r]+ -> skip ;
```

ANTLR's semantic actions can be briefly explained as follows:

- Semantic actions are injected into the grammar by escaping them with braces. For instance, the semantic action {boolean initial=true;} (line 7) declares and initializes a local Java variable (local to the generated code for the state rule).
- Nonterminals are associated with the text consumed by parsing. If n is a nonterminal in a given rule, then $n.text can be used to access the text within semantic actions; see, for example, {...$stateid.text ...} (line 10).

The semantic actions in the example build objects of a basic, influent object model for FSML (Section 2.2.1). The following members are used in the semantic actions:

- The constructor for Fsm is invoked to construct an FSM object and keep track of it through an attribute fsm that is injected into the generated class (line 3).
- The observer members getStates and getTransitions are invoked to access collections of states and transitions (lines 10 and 20).
- The constructors for State and Transition are invoked to construct objects for states and transitions and to add them to the FSM object (line 10 and line 20).

ANTLR and other parser generators have more sophisticated mechanisms for semantic actions. In particular, ANTLR makes it possible to declare arguments and results for nonterminals. These mechanisms are inspired by the attribute grammar paradigm [32, 40] which we discuss in Section 12.2.

7.3.3 *Parser Combinators*

Parser combinators, as discussed in Section 7.2.4, can be used to represent grammars as systems of recursive functions for parsing. The body of each function is basically an expression over parser combinators for sequential composition, choice (composition of alternatives), EBNF operators for optionality and iteration, and constants for scanning.

Let us demonstrate the use of the popular parser-combinator library Parsec [37] in the Haskell context. Parsers composed by combinators are of an abstract data type Parser a, where a is the type of representation (AST) constructed by the parser. The Parser type constructor is a monad [60] and the bind operator ">>=" is immediately the parser combinator for sequential composition.

AST construction basically boils down to the application of appropriate data constructors to "smaller" ASTs. In basic monadic style, this means that the ASTs for phrases are bound via ">>=" or monadic do-notation with a final return to compose an AST, as shown below.

Illustration 7.16 (A monadic style parser for FSML)

Haskell module Language.FSML.MonadicParser

```
fsm :: Parser Fsm
fsm = many state >>=return . Fsm

state :: Parser State
state = do
  ini ← option False (reserved "initial" >> return True)
  source ← reserved "state" >> stateid
  ts ← braces (many (transition source))
  return (State ini source ts)

transition :: StateId → Parser Transition
transition source = do
  e ← event
  a ← optionMaybe (op "/" *> action)
  t ← option source (op "->" *> stateid)
  semi
  return (Transition e a t)
```

The functions fsm, state, and transition are parsers with corresponding algebraic data types Fsm, State, and Transition for the ASTs. The function Transition is parameterized by a state id for the source state to which the transition belongs; the state id is used as the target state id if the id was omitted in the FSM.

We may also use the more restrained applicative functor style [41] where applicable. That is, we leverage the fact that the parser monad is also an applicative functor and thus, an AST constructor can essentially be applied to the computations for the phrases. Arguably, this leads to more "functional" code as shown below.

Illustration 7.17 (An applicative functor style parser for FSML)

Haskell module Language.FSML.ApplicativeParser

```
fsm :: Parser Fsm
fsm = Fsm <$> many state

state :: Parser State
state = do
  ini ← option False (reserved "initial" >> return True)
  source ← reserved "state" >> stateid
  ts ← braces (many (transition source))
  return (State ini source ts)

transition :: StateId → Parser Transition
transition source =
  Transition
    <$> event
    <*> optionMaybe (op "/" *> action)
    <*> option source (op "−>" *> stateid)
    <* semi
```

The functions fsm and transition are defined in applicative functor style whereas we resort to monadic style (do-notation) in the case of state because we need to intercept the state id so that it can be passed as an argument to transition.

7.3.4 Text-to-Model

For brevity, we will not discuss in any detail the problem of text-to-model transformations [27, 22], a parsing-like phase in the MDE. Conceptually, a text-to-model transformation can be viewed as consisting of parsing followed by abstraction and resolution (AST-to-ASG mapping), as discussed previously (Section 4.4). Technically or technologically, this is an involved and interesting problem.

Exercise 7.7 (Text-to-model with Xtext)   [Intermediate level]
Study Xtext[3] [4] and implement a mapping from text-based syntax for the Buddy Language to a graph-based representation.

---

[3] http://www.eclipse.org/Xtext/

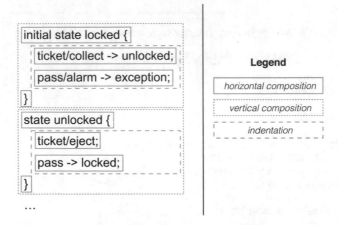

Fig. 7.3 Formatting with pretty-printer combinators: the FSM on the left-hand side is readily formatted. The boxes explain how the format has emerged from the composition of boxes by horizontal and vertical alignment and by indentation.

7.4 Formatting

We now switch from parsing to the opposite direction: formatting (or unparsing or pretty printing). Formatting is needed in the context of code generation, for example, in web programming; it also shows up as part of source-code transformation if we assume that the actual transformation is implemented at the level of ASTs and, thus, the transformation is complemented by parsing and formatting.

We describe two overall options for formatting: the combinator- versus the template-based approach. Both of these approaches are syntax-driven: formatting is essentially accomplished by recursing into an AST-like data structure. We do not discuss more lexical approaches to formatting any further here (see, e.g., [44, 2]). We also omit coverage of the interesting notion of invertible syntax descriptions such that parsing and formatting (pretty printing) can be unified [49].

7.4.1 Pretty Printing Combinators

The overall idea of the combinator-based approach is to view the output as a document that is composed from smaller documents, down to the level of pieces of text, by means of combinators for horizontal and vertical composition as well as indentation [5]; see Fig. 7.3 for an illustration. This approach is fundamentally different from the more ad hoc approach where a programmer takes care of line breaks and indentation in, say, an imperative manner, i.e., by maintaining the indentation level in a variable and producing textual output by means of "printf".

Let us demonstrate such pretty printing in Haskell with the help of a suitable combinator library [23]. There are combinators such as this:

Interactive Haskell session:

```
▶ −− Switch to the module for formatting
▶ :m Text.PrettyPrint.HughesPJ
- - - - - - - - - - - - - - - - - - - - - - - - - - - - - - - - - - - - - - - -
▶ −− The empty box
▶ :t empty
empty :: Doc
- - - - - - - - - - - - - - - - - - - - - - - - - - - - - - - - - - - - - - - -
▶ −− A box exactly containing some given text
▶ :t text
text :: String → Doc
- - - - - - - - - - - - - - - - - - - - - - - - - - - - - - - - - - - - - - - -
▶ −− Horizontal composition of two boxes
▶ :t (<>)
(<>) :: Doc → Doc → Doc
- - - - - - - - - - - - - - - - - - - - - - - - - - - - - - - - - - - - - - - -
▶ −− Space−separated horizontal composition
▶ :t (<+>)
(<+>) :: Doc → Doc → Doc
- - - - - - - - - - - - - - - - - - - - - - - - - - - - - - - - - - - - - - - -
▶ −− Vertical composition of two boxes
▶ :t ($$)
($$) :: Doc → Doc → Doc
- - - - - - - - - - - - - - - - - - - - - - - - - - - - - - - - - - - - - - - -
▶ −− Vertical composition of a list of boxes
▶ :t vcat
vcat :: [Doc] → Doc
- - - - - - - - - - - - - - - - - - - - - - - - - - - - - - - - - - - - - - - -
▶ −− Indentation of a box by a number of spaces
▶ :t nest
nest :: Int → Doc → Doc
```

The type Doc is an abstract data type; one may turn documents into text:

Interactive Haskell session:

```
▶ show $ text "hello"
"hello"
```

The combinators satisfy some convenient algebraic laws. For instance, an empty box is a left and right unit of (even space-separated) horizontal composition. Thus:

```
empty <> x = x
x <> empty= x
empty <+> x = x
x <+> empty = x
```

We are ready to present a formatter (a pretty printer) for FSML. In the following Haskell code, we assume that an FSM is given in the abstract syntactical representation, as introduced earlier.

Illustration 7.18 (Formatting FSML with pretty printer combinators)

Haskell module Language.FSML.CombinatorFormatter

```
1   fsm :: Fsm → Doc
2   fsm (Fsm ss) = vcat (map state ss)
3
4   state :: State → Doc
5   state (State initial source ts) =
6     (if initial then text "initial" else empty)
7     <+> text "state"
8     <+> text source
9     <+> text "{"
10    $$ nest 2 (vcat (map (transition source) ts))
11    $$ text "}"
12
13  transition :: String → Transition → Doc
14  transition source (Transition ev ac target) =
15    text ev
16    <> maybe empty (λ ac'→ text "/" <> text ac') ac
17    <+> (if source == target
18          then empty
19          else text "->" <+> text target)
20    <> text ";"
```

Thus, we designate a function for each type of the abstract syntax. The states are formatted independently and the resulting boxes are vertically composed; see the use of vcat in the function fsm (line 2). Each state is formatted by a mix of horizontal and vertical composition. The vertically composed transitions are indented; see the use of nest in the function state (line 10). The function transition is parameterized by the source state id so that it can leave out the target state id if it equals the source state id (lines 17–19).

7.4.2 Template Processing

A template is essentially a parameterized text (a string). Several related templates may be organized into groups of named templates so that they can invoke each other along with parameter passing. More abstractly, a group of templates can be viewed as a mutually recursive system of functions that map parameter data to text on the basis of filling parameters or projections thereof into "holes" in the templates. This process may also be controlled by conditions and may involve "loops" to iterate over parameters that represent lists. In Section 2.4.2s, we already discussed the use of template processing for code generation, i.e., mapping one language (e.g., FSML) to another language (e.g., C). In the present section, we discuss the use of template processing for formatting, i.e., mapping the abstract syntax of a language to the concrete syntax of the same language.

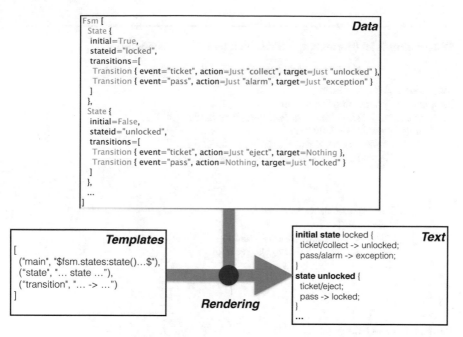

Fig. 7.4 I/O behavior of template processing for FSML.

A template processing-based formatter for FSML is illustrated in Fig. 7.4. Let us make some assumptions about the template-processing problem at hand:

- We assume the abstract syntactical representation for FSMs, as introduced earlier. This abstract representation provides the initial parameter for template processing.
- We need templates for the FSM as a whole, for states, and for transitions, as an FSM breaks down into many states, each of which breaks down into many transitions.
- Lines breaks and indentation are captured by the templates. Alternatively, a lexical formatter [44, 2] could be applied for postprocessing.
- Template parameters should be set up in such a way that no computations need to be performed during formatting, thereby separating the concerns of computation and formatting.

We are going to leverage the template processor *HStringTemplate*[4] for Haskell; this is a Haskell port of the well-known template processor *StringTemplate*[5] [45] which we used in Section 2.4.2.

---

[4] https://hackage.haskell.org/package/HStringTemplate

[5] http://www.stringtemplate.org/

Illustration 7.19 (Formatting FSML with template processing)

Haskell module <u>Language.FSML.TemplateFormatter</u>

```
1   templates :: STGroup String
2   templates = groupStringTemplates [
3       ("main", newSTMP "$fsm.states:state(); separator='\n'$"),
4       ("state", newSTMP $ unlines [
5           "$if(it.initial)$initial $endif$state $it.stateid$ {",
6           "$it.transitions:transition(); separator='\n'$",
7           "}"
8           ]
9       ),
10      ("transition", newSTMP (
11          " $it.event$\
12          \$if(it.action)$/$it.action$$endif$\
13          \$if(it.target)$ -> $it.target$$endif$\
14          \;"
15          )
16      )
17  ]
18
19  format :: Fsm -> String
20  format fsm =
21      let Just t = getStringTemplate "main" templates
22      in render $ setAttribute "fsm" fsm t
```

The formatter captures the template group (lines 1–17) as a list of name-value pairs. The values are strings which are spread out over multiple lines for readability (see the multiline strings in the "state" template in line 4) or for insertion of line breaks (see the use of unlines in the "transition" template in lines 10–15). The format function retrieves the "main" template, sets the "fsm" attribute, and starts rendering (lines 19-22). Within the templates, the following idioms are used:

- Parameter references and template invocations are included within "$···$".
- Components of parameters are selected by member-like access; see the use of "·".
- A template t is invoked by the idiom "$...t(···)$"; parameters, if any, are passed between the parentheses.
- Lists can be processed by an idiom "$l:t(···); separator = ···$" where l denotes access to a list-typed parameter, t is the name of the template to be invoked on each element, and the separator declaration can be used for injecting line breaks or other separators between the rendered elements. Within the template t, the element is referable to as the parameter "it"; see the uses of "it" in the templates.
- Conditional text may be modeled by the "$if(···)$···$endif$" idiom. There are these forms of condition: test of a Boolean parameter, test for the presence of an "optional" parameter (a Maybe in Haskell), and possibly others.

A general discussion of the features of template processing can be found elsewhere [50]; the discussion is systematic and technology-neutral, but it assumes the perspective of model-to-text transformation.

A valuable property of templates is that they encourage a separation between "model" and "view" (say, computation and formatting) by means of a simple mapping of a data structure, passed as a parameter, to text – as opposed to performing "arbitrary" computations along with text generation. A problematic property of (mainstream) template processing is that there is no static guarantee that the resulting text will be syntactically correct, and even less so that the result will be well-typed. Syntactic correctness can be achieved by constraining template systems in such a manner that templates are derived from a given grammar in a systematic manner [59].

7.5 Concrete Object Syntax

So far, we have basically assumed that metaprograms operate at the level of abstract syntactical object program representations. In this setting, if the concrete syntax of the object language is to be used, then metaprograms need to be complemented by parsing and formatting. Alternatively, subject to suitable metaprogramming support, metaprograms can operate directly at the level of concrete object syntax. In this case, the metaprogrammer can use the patterns of the object language in metaprograms. For instance, a translator from metamodels to database schemas would directly use metamodeling and SQL syntax. Likewise, the implementation of a refactoring suite for a given programming language such as Java would directly use programming language syntax of that language.

The notion of concrete object syntax has been developed in specialized metaprogramming systems over the last 30+ years (see [55, 58, 9, 10] for somewhat more recent accounts).

There is a poor man's approach towards using concrete object syntax in which object programs are encoded as strings in the metalanguage. This approach is used, for instance, in low-level database APIs such as JDBC for Java. Consider this illustration, quoted from [6, 7]; the Java code runs an SQL query to check a username/-password pair:

```
String userName = getParam("userName");
String password = getParam("password");
String query = "SELECT id FROM users "
            + "WHERE name = '" + userName + "' "
            + "AND password = '" + password + "'";
if (executeQuery(query).size() == 0)
    throw new Exception("bad user/password");
```

An obvious drawback of this poor man's approach is that the proper use of the object language's syntax is not checked at compile time. Syntax errors and issues with conformance of the query to the underlying database schema would only be found at runtime. Perhaps a less obvious consequence of such poor checking is that programs become vulnerable to injection attacks [6, 7].

In this section, we focus on proper syntax-aware embedding of the object language into the metalanguage. In an extended Java language with SQL embedded, the above example may look as follows; this code is again adopted from [6, 7]:

```
SQL q = <| SELECT id FROM users WHERE
    name = ${userName} AND password = ${password} |>;
if (executeQuery(q.toString()).size() == 0) ...
```

The key idea is that, within the metalanguage (here: Java), we can embed object program fragments (here: SQL) by means of an appropriate escaping or quoting mechanism (see the brackets "<| ··· |>") and we can escape back to the metalanguage to fill in details computed in the metaprogram (see the access to Java variables such as "${userName}". Thus, the syntax of the object language and the metalanguage are amalgamated in a certain manner.

7.5.1 Quotation

We will discuss here an approach to concrete object syntax which combines so-called quasi-quotation and language or syntax embedding [39, 53, 61]. We begin with a trivial example. Consider the following Haskell code which exercises embedding FSML syntax into Haskell.

Illustration 7.20 (Embedding of FSML into Haskell)

Haskell module <u>Language.FSML.QQ.Sample</u>

```
turnstileFsm :: Fsm
turnstileFsm = [fsml|
        initial state locked {
                ticket / collect → unlocked;
                pass / alarm → exception;
        }
        state unlocked {
                ticket / eject;
                pass → locked;
        }
        state exception {
                ticket / eject;
                pass;
                mute;
                release → locked;
        }
|]
```

We use so-called quasi-quote brackets "[fsml| ⋯ |]" (or Oxford brackets) to *quote* an FSM within the Haskell code. Quasi-quotation is realized (in Haskell) such that the quoted text is actually parsed at compile time. What happens underneath is that the parser synthesizes an AST based on the algebraic data type-based, abstract syntactical representation of the parsed language and the resulting expression is then mapped to a Haskell expression (AST) and inserted into the AST of the module. Thus, the shown binding has exactly the same meaning as if we had written Haskell code for FSM construction instead. This can be compared with storing the FSM in a file and parsing it at runtime – except that quasi-quotation allows us to embed the FSM directly into the Haskell code and parsing (syntax checking) happens transparently at compile time.

The quasi-quote brackets specify the language to be used; this is fsml in the example. The name is, in fact, the name of a binding of type QuasiQuoter, subject to Haskell's extension for quasi-quotation [39] based also on Template Haskell [51]. A quasi-quoter essentially describes how to map strings to Haskell expressions or elements of other categories of Haskell's syntax. We are ready to present the quasi-quote for FSML.

Illustration 7.21 (A quasi-quoter for FSML)

Haskell module Language.FSML.QuasiQuoter

```
1   fsml :: QuasiQuoter
2   fsml = QuasiQuoter
3       { quoteExp = quoteFsmlExp
4       , quotePat = undefined
5       , quoteType = undefined
6       , quoteDec = undefined
7       }
8
9   quoteFsmlExp :: String → Q Exp
10  quoteFsmlExp str = do
11      x ← parseQ fsm str
12      case check x of
13          [] → dataToExpQ (const Nothing) x
14          errs → error $ unlines errs
```

Thus, the quasi-quoter (lines 1–7) is a record with four components, each one applying to a different syntactic category. We are only concerned with expressions here (see quoteExp = ⋯ in line 3) and we leave the components for patterns, types, and declarations undefined. Let us describe the actual binding for quoteFsmlExp (lines 9–14) in terms of three phases:

Parsing   The expression parseQ fsm str (line 11) parses the string str between the quasi-quote brackets; it uses a standard parser fsm (Section 7.3.3). The function parseQ is a convenience wrapper around the normal run function of the parser monad; it sets up location and error reporting in a uniform manner.

Analysis   The expression check x (line 12) checks that the parsed FSM satisfies
the usual constraints that we set up for the FSML language earlier. If the check
returns any error messages, then they are communicated to the user by the invocation of the error function. Such checking is performed inside the quotation
monad and, thus, errors will be communicated to the language user in the same
way as type errors for the metalanguage.

Quoting   The expression dataToExp (const Nothing) x (line 13) maps an FSM (represented in the established abstract syntax) to a Haskell expression, which constructs a Haskell AST. The function dataToExp is a generic function in that it
can be applied to the different types that are used in an FSM representation. The
always-failing component const Nothing expresses that the generic behavior is
appropriate for all relevant types.

The first two phases, *parsing* and *analysis*, are relatively obvious. The last phase,
quoting, may require some extra reflection. That is, one may expect that the quasi-
quoter should somehow be able to use the AST representation of the FSM directly,
as this is exactly the AST that we want to process in a metaprogram anyway. Instead, we seem to detour through Haskell expressions only to recover the same AST
at runtime. This approach is appropriate because it is more general and uniform. The
uniformity assumption here is that the contents of the quasi-quote brackets denote
Haskell code (expressions, patterns, types, or declarations) as opposed to ASTs of
another language. Thus, the object language is integrated by translation to the metalanguage. We will demonstrate generality in a moment with another quasi-quotation
experiment.

Exercise 7.8 (Parsing FSMs into Haskell expressions)   [Intermediate level]
*Implement an FSML parser which directly constructs Haskell expressions as op-
posed to the present separation of parsing FSMs into FSM ASTs and converting
those ASTs into Haskell expressions.*

7.5.2 Antiquotation

When quasi-quoted phrases escape back to the metalanguage, then we also speak
of antiquotation. Let us consider program optimization for EL expressions again.
In contrast to the earlier discussion (Section 5.4.1), we would like to use concrete
object syntax to author simplification rules for EL in Haskell. In Fig. 7.5, we show
some simplification rules (or laws), we recall the encoding of rules as functions on
abstract syntax, and we show a new encoding which relies on concrete object syntax
for EL in Haskell.

Between the quasi-quote brackets, we use antiquotation in terms of "$"-prefixed
identifiers to denote metavariables of the metalanguage (i.e., Haskell). For instance,

```
-- Laws on expressions
x + 0 = x
x * 1 = x
x * 0 = 0
```

```
-- Implementation based on abstract object syntax
simplify :: Expr -> Maybe Expr
simplify (Binary Add x (IntConst 0)) = Just x
simplify (Binary Mul x (IntConst 1)) = Just x
simplify (Binary Mul x (IntConst 0)) = Just $ IntConst 0
simplify _ = Nothing
```

```
-- Implementation based on concrete object syntax
simplify :: Expr -> Maybe Expr
simplify [el| $x + 0 |] = Just [el| $x |]
simplify [el| $x * 1 |] = Just [el| $x |]
simplify [el| $x * 0 |] = Just [el| 0 |]
simplify _ = Nothing
```

Fig. 7.5 Comparison of simplification rules (or laws) with an encoding as a function on abstract syntax and an encoding as a function on concrete syntax based on quasi-quotation.

the regular Haskell pattern Binary Add x (IntConst 0) is written in concrete object syntax as [el| $x + 0|] with $x as a metavariable (i.e., Haskell variable). We need this special syntax for metavariables because, without the "$" sign, we would denote an object variable, i.e., a variable of the expression language EL according to its concrete syntax. Thus, we need an extended syntax for EL with a new case for metavariables, as defined below.

Illustration 7.22 (EL syntax extension for metavariables)

Haskell module Language.EL.QQ.Syntax

data Expr
  = ... *−− The same syntax as before*
  | MetaVar String *−− An additional constructor for the abstract syntax*

Haskell module Language.EL.QQ.Parser

factor :: Parser Expr
factor
  = ... *−− The same syntax as before*
  <|> (MetaVar <$> (op "$" >> identifier)) *−− An additional choice in parsing*

In the quasi-quoter, metavariables need to be mapped from the EL representation to proper Haskell variables as shown below.

Illustration 7.23 (A quasi-quoter for EL)

Haskell module Language.EL.QuasiQuoter

```
 1  el :: QuasiQuoter
 2  el = QuasiQuoter
 3      { quoteExp = quoteElExp
 4      , quotePat = quoteElPat
 5      , quoteType = undefined
 6      , quoteDec = undefined
 7      }
 8
 9  quoteElExp :: String → Q Exp
10  quoteElExp str = do
11      x ← parseQ expr str
12      dataToExpQ (const Nothing `extQ` f) x
13    where
14      f :: Expr → Maybe (Q Exp)
15      f (MetaVar v) = Just $ varE (mkName v)
16      f _ = Nothing
17
18  quoteElPat :: String → Q Pat
19  quoteElPat str = do
20      x ← parseQ expr str
21      dataToPatQ (const Nothing `extQ` f) x
22    where
23      f :: Expr → Maybe (Q Pat)
24      f (MetaVar v) = Just $ varP (mkName v)
25      f _ = Nothing
```

We point out the following aspects of the quasi-quoter:

- The quasi-quoter instantiates the components for both Haskell expressions (line 3) and patterns (line 4) because, as demonstrated in Fig. 7.5, we would like to use concrete EL syntax in the positions of both pattern matching and the right-hand sides of equations. Accordingly, the component quoteElExp returns an expression (Exp) within the quotation monad, whereas the component quoteElPat returns a pattern (Pat).
- Both of the quasi-quotation components (lines 9–25) use the same convenience function parseQ as before.
- When mapping ("quoting") the EL AST, the generic mapping functions dataToExpQ and dataToPatQ are properly customized (lines 15 and 24) so that EL's metavariables are mapped to Haskell variables. We use the constructor VarE for names in an expression context and the constructor VarP in a pattern context.

The situation at hand is more general than that for FSML above because we have properly amalgamated the syntaxes of Haskell and EL. That is, one can use EL within Haskell and one can also use Haskell (its variables) within EL. See the following exercise for a generalized amalgamation.

Exercise 7.9 (Comprehensive antiquotation) [Intermediate level]
Extend the quasi-quoter so that antiquotation can be used with arbitrary Haskell expressions as opposed to just metavariables. To this end, you need to replace the case for metavariables with one for arbitrary Haskell expressions; the Haskell parser needs to be invoked from within the EL parser.

Exercise 7.10 (Automated object syntax embedding) [Advanced level]
Metaprogramming systems such as ASF+SDF [54], TXL [10, 11], Stratego [8], the Sugar* line of systems [14, 15, 16], and Rascal [31, 30] support metaprogramming with concrete object syntax without the efforts of setting up (the equivalent of) a quasi-quoter. Develop a related infrastructure on top of Haskell's quasi-quotation on the basis of the following ideas:

- *The grammar of the object language is extended automatically to accomplish splicing according to Exercise 7.9. To this end, an alternative for meta-expressions (patterns) has to be added for each nonterminal.*
- *The grammar is interpreted by a generic component to construct a uniform, Haskell-based CST presentation. Alternatively, Template Haskell-based metaprogramming could be used to generate a parser. A parser combinator library would be used underneath.*
- *The actual quasi-quoter is essentially boilerplate code, as demonstrated for EL. One may define it as a generic abstraction that is refined into a language-specific quasi-quote by simple parameter passing for the language name and the grammar.*

Test your development by implementing simple metaprograms for different languages.

Summary and Outline

We have catalogued the different representations and mappings that arise in dealing with concrete syntax in language-based software components. We have described practical techniques for scanning, parsing, abstraction, and formatting. The list of techniques included parser generation, parser combinators, pretty printing combinators, and template processing. We have also described the quasi-quotation technique for integrating the concrete syntax of an object language into the metalanguage. The topic of parsing, in particular, could only be covered in a selective manner. There exist many different parsing approaches and technologies and they all come with their specific peculiarities. The topic of formatting was also not covered completely. In particular, lexical formatting [44, 2] was not exercised. The topic of concrete object syntax was also covered in just one specific manner. We have not covered several aspects of concrete syntax implementation, for example, grammar-based testing [34, 35, 17] and grammar transformation, for example, in the context of language evolution [33, 12, 56, 36].

We will now turn away from syntax and discuss semantics and types. For what it matters, we are going to use abstract object syntax again in most of what follows.

References

1. Aho, A., Monica S., Sethi, R., Ullman, J.: Compilers: Principles, Techniques, and Tools. Addison Wesley (2006). 2nd edition
2. Bagge, A.H., Hasu, T.: A pretty good formatting pipeline. In: Proc. SLE, *LNCS*, vol. 8225, pp. 177–196. Springer (2013)
3. Basten, H.J.S., Klint, P., Vinju, J.J.: Ambiguity detection: Scaling to scannerless. In: Proc. SLE 2011, *LNCS*, vol. 6940, pp. 303–323. Springer (2012)
4. Bettini, L.: Implementing Domain-Specific Languages with Xtext and Xtend. Packt Publishing (2013)
5. van den Brand, M., Visser, E.: Generation of formatters for context-free languages. ACM Trans. Softw. Eng. Methodol. **5**(1), 1–41 (1996)
6. Bravenboer, M., Dolstra, E., Visser, E.: Preventing injection attacks with syntax embeddings. In: Proc. GPCE, pp. 3–12. ACM (2007)
7. Bravenboer, M., Dolstra, E., Visser, E.: Preventing injection attacks with syntax embeddings. Sci. Comput. Program. **75**(7), 473–495 (2010)
8. Bravenboer, M., Kalleberg, K.T., Vermaas, R., Visser, E.: Stratego/XT 0.17. A language and toolset for program transformation. Sci. Comput. Program. **72**(1-2), 52–70 (2008)
9. Bravenboer, M., Visser, E.: Concrete syntax for objects: Domain-specific language embedding and assimilation without restrictions. In: Proc. OOPSLA, pp. 365–383. ACM (2004)
10. Cordy, J.R.: The TXL source transformation language. Sci. Comput. Program. **61**(3), 190–210 (2006)
11. Cordy, J.R.: Excerpts from the TXL cookbook. In: GTTSE 2009, Revised Papers, *LNCS*, vol. 6491, pp. 27–91. Springer (2011)
12. Dean, T.R., Cordy, J.R., Malton, A.J., Schneider, K.A.: Grammar programming in TXL. In: SCAM, pp. 93–104. IEEE (2002)
13. Economopoulos, G., Klint, P., Vinju, J.J.: Faster scannerless GLR parsing. In: Proc. CC, *LNCS*, vol. 5501, pp. 126–141. Springer (2009)
14. Erdweg, S.: Extensible languages for flexible and principled domain abstraction. Ph.D. thesis, Philipps-Universität Marburg (2013)
15. Erdweg, S., Rendel, T., Kästner, C., Ostermann, K.: SugarJ: Library-based syntactic language extensibility. In: Proc. OOPSLA, pp. 391–406. ACM (2011)
16. Erdweg, S., Rieger, F., Rendel, T., Ostermann, K.: Layout-sensitive language extensibility with SugarHaskell. In: Proc. Haskell, pp. 149–160. ACM (2012)
17. Fischer, B., Lämmel, R., Zaytsev, V.: Comparison of context-free grammars based on parsing generated test data. In: Proc. SLE 2011, *LNCS*, vol. 6940, pp. 324–343. Springer (2012)
18. Frost, R.A., Hafiz, R.: A new top-down parsing algorithm to accommodate ambiguity and left recursion in polynomial time. SIGPLAN Not. **41**(5), 46–54 (2006)
19. Frost, R.A., Hafiz, R., Callaghan, P.: Parser combinators for ambiguous left-recursive grammars. In: Proc. PADL, *LNCS*, vol. 4902, pp. 167–181. Springer (2008)
20. Grune, D., Jacobs, C.: Parsing Techniques: A Practical Guide. Monographs in Computer Science. Springer (2007). 2nd edition
21. Heering, J., Hendriks, P.R.H., Klint, P., Rekers, J.: The Syntax Definition Formalism SDF. reference manual. SIGPLAN Not. **24**(11), 43–75 (1989)

22. Herrera, A.S., Willink, E.D., Paige, R.F.: An OCL-based bridge from concrete to abstract syntax. In: Proc. International Workshop on OCL and Textual Modeling, *CEUR Workshop Proceedings*, vol. 1512, pp. 19–34. CEUR-WS.org (2015)

23. Hughes, J.: The design of a pretty-printing library. In: Spring School on Advanced Functional Programming Techniques, Båstad, Sweden, May 24-30, 1995, Tutorial Text, *LNCS*, vol. 925, pp. 53–96. Springer (1995)

24. Izmaylova, A., Afroozeh, A., van der Storm, T.: Practical, general parser combinators. In: Proc. PEPM, pp. 1–12. ACM (2016)

25. Johnson, S.C.: YACC—Yet Another Compiler Compiler. Computer Science Technical Report 32, AT&T Bell Laboratories (1975)

26. Jonnalagedda, M., Coppey, T., Stucki, S., Rompf, T., Odersky, M.: Staged parser combinators for efficient data processing. In: Proc. OOPSLA, pp. 637–653. ACM (2014)

27. Jouault, F., Bézivin, J., Kurtev, I.: TCS: a DSL for the specification of textual concrete syntaxes in model engineering. In: Proc. GPCE, pp. 249–254. ACM (2006)

28. Kadhim, B.M., Waite, W.M.: Maptool – supporting modular syntax development. In: Proc. CC, *LNCS*, vol. 1060, pp. 268–280. Springer (1996)

29. Klint, P., Lämmel, R., Verhoef, C.: Toward an engineering discipline for grammarware. ACM Trans. Softw. Eng. Methodol. **14**(3), 331–380 (2005)

30. Klint, P., van der Storm, T., Vinju, J.J.: RASCAL: A domain specific language for source code analysis and manipulation. In: Proc. SCAM, pp. 168–177. IEEE (2009)

31. Klint, P., van der Storm, T., Vinju, J.J.: EASY meta-programming with Rascal. In: GTTSE 2009, Revised Papers, *LNCS*, vol. 6491, pp. 222–289. Springer (2011)

32. Knuth, D.E.: Semantics of context-free languages. Mathematical Systems Theory **2**(2), 127–145 (1968)

33. Lämmel, R.: Grammar adaptation. In: Proc. FM, *LNCS*, vol. 2021, pp. 550–570. Springer (2001)

34. Lämmel, R.: Grammar testing. In: Proc. FASE, *LNCS*, vol. 2029, pp. 201–216. Springer (2001)

35. Lämmel, R., Schulte, W.: Controllable combinatorial coverage in grammar-based testing. In: Proc. TestCom, *LNCS*, vol. 3964, pp. 19–38. Springer (2006)

36. Lämmel, R., Zaytsev, V.: Recovering grammar relationships for the Java language specification. Softw. Qual. J. **19**(2), 333–378 (2011)

37. Leijen, D.: Parsec, a fast combinator parser. Tech. Rep. 35, Department of Computer Science, University of Utrecht (RUU) (2001)

38. Lohmann, W., Riedewald, G., Stoy, M.: Semantics-preserving migration of semantic rules during left recursion removal in attribute grammars. ENTCS **110**, 133–148 (2004)

39. Mainland, G.: Why it's nice to be quoted: quasiquoting for Haskell. In: Proc. Haskell, pp. 73–82. ACM (2007)

40. Maluszynski, J.: Attribute grammars and logic programs: A comparison of concepts. In: Proc. SAGA, *LNCS*, vol. 545, pp. 330–357. Springer (1991)

41. McBride, C., Paterson, R.: Applicative programming with effects. J. Funct. Program. **18**(1), 1–13 (2008)

42. Moore, R.C.: Removing left recursion from context-free grammars. In: Proc. ANLP, pp. 249–255 (2000)

43. Nederhof, M.: A new top-down parsing algorithm for left-recursive DCGs. In: Proc. PLILP, *LNCS*, vol. 714, pp. 108–122. Springer (1993)

44. Oppen, D.C.: Prettyprinting. ACM Trans. Program. Lang. Syst. **2**(4), 465–483 (1980)

45. Parr, T.: A functional language for generating structured text (2006). Draft. http://www.stringtemplate.org/articles.html

46. Parr, T.: The Definitive ANTLR 4 Reference. Pragmatic Bookshelf (2013). 2nd edition

47. Parr, T., Fisher, K.: LL(*): The foundation of the ANTLR parser generator. In: Proc. PLDI, pp. 425–436. ACM (2011)

48. Quesada, L., Berzal, F., Talavera, J.C.C.: A domain-specific language for abstract syntax model to concrete syntax model mappings. In: Proc. MODELSWARD, pp. 158–165. SciTePress (2014)

49. Rendel, T., Ostermann, K.: Invertible syntax descriptions: Unifying parsing and pretty print-
    ing. In: Proc. Haskell, pp. 1–12. ACM (2010)
50. Rose, L.M., Matragkas, N.D., Kolovos, D.S., Paige, R.F.: A feature model for model-to-text
    transformation languages. In: Proc. MiSE, pp. 57–63. IEEE (2012)
51. Sheard, T., Peyton Jones, S.L.: Template meta-programming for Haskell. SIGPLAN Not.
    37(12), 60–75 (2002)
52. Swierstra, S.D.: Combinator parsing: A short tutorial. In: International LerNet ALFA Summer
    School 2008, Piriapolis, Uruguay, February 24 – March 1, 2008, Revised Tutorial Lectures,
    LNCS, vol. 5520, pp. 252–300. Springer (2009)
53. Tratt, L.: Domain specific language implementation via compile-time meta-programming.
    ACM Trans. Program. Lang. Syst. **30**(6) (2008)
54. van den Brand, M., Sellink, M.P.A., Verhoef, C.: Generation of components for software reno-
    vation factories from context-free grammars. Sci. Comput. Program. **36**(2-3), 209–266 (2000)
55. van den Brand, M., van Deursen, A., Heering, J., de Jong, H., de Jonge, M., Kuipers, T., Klint,
    P., Moonen, L., Olivier, P.A., Scheerder, J., Vinju, J.J., Visser, E., Visser, J.: The ASF+SDF
    Meta-Environment: A component-based language development environment. ENTCS **44**(2),
    3–8 (2001)
56. Vermolen, S., Visser, E.: Heterogeneous coupled evolution of software languages. In: Proc.
    MoDELS, *LNCS*, vol. 5301, pp. 630–644. Springer (2008)
57. Visser, E.: Syntax definition for language prototyping. Ph.D. thesis, University of Amsterdam
    (1997)
58. Visser, E.: Meta-programming with concrete object syntax. In: Proc. GPCE, *LNCS*, vol. 2487,
    pp. 299–315. Springer (2002)
59. Wachsmuth, G.: A formal way from text to code templates. In: Proc. FASE, *LNCS*, vol. 5503,
    pp. 109–123. Springer (2009)
60. Wadler, P.: The essence of functional programming. In: Proc. POPL, pp. 1–14. ACM (1992)
61. Wielemaker, J., Hendricks, M.: Why it's nice to be quoted: Quasiquoting for Prolog. CoRR
    abs/1308.3941 (2013)
62. Zaytsev, V., Bagge, A.H.: Parsing in a broad sense. In: Proc. MODELS, *LNCS*, vol. 8767, pp.
    50–67. Springer (2014)

Chapter 8
A Primer on Operational Semantics

Isabelle Attali.[1]

Abstract The *semantics* of a software language assigns meanings to the elements of the language. The field of *programming language theory* provides rigorous techniques for the definition of semantics which are based on mathematical and logical tools. In this chapter, we introduce the method of *operational semantics*: inference rules are used to model the stepwise computation of a program. We do not go into the details of the underlying theoretical underpinnings, but the level of formality may help in developing and reasoning about interpreters and other semantics-aware language processing components (e.g., analyzers, optimizers, or refactorings) more systematically. We demonstrate the implementation of operational semantics in Haskell.

---

[1] The 2004 tsunami took Isabelle Attali and her sons Ugo and Tom from her family and friends. She was in Sri Lanka at the time. Isabelle Attali may be credited with helping launch the field of software languages as she was working on making formal and declarative language definitions – in particular, attribute grammars and operational semantics – practically useful by addressing issues of scalability, tool support, integration, and case studies [1, 3, 4, 2, 5]. She was involved in WAGA (Workshop on Attribute Grammars and Applications) and LDTA (Language Descriptions, Tools, and Applications) – both predecessors of the SLE conference. Isabelle, you are missed (http://www.labri.fr/perso/chaumett/attalicaromel/).

Artwork Credits for Chapter Opening: This work by Wojciech Kwasnik is licensed under CC BY-SA 4.0. This artwork quotes the artwork *DMT*, acrylic, 2006 by Matt Sheehy with the artist's permission. This work also quotes https://commons.wikimedia.org/wiki/File:Wheat_Stacks_with_Reaper_1888_Vincent_van_Gogh.jpg, subject to the attribution "Vincent Van Gogh: Wheat Stacks with Reaper (1888) [Public domain], via Wikimedia Commons." This work artistically morphes an image, http://www-sop.inria.fr/oasis/personnel/Isabelle.Attali/images/ia2002.jpg, showing the person honored, subject to the attribution "Permission granted by Isabelle Attali's husband Denis Caromel for use in this book."

© Springer International Publishing AG, part of Springer Nature 2018
R. Lämmel, *Software Languages*,
https://doi.org/10.1007/978-3-319-90800-7_8

8.1 Big-step Operational Semantics

The general idea underlying operational semantics is to model the stepwise *computation* (or execution or evaluation) of *program phrases*, for example, statements and expressions. Specifications of operational semantics leverage *inference rules* for *natural deduction*, as common in logic and proof theory.

Depending on how the steps are "exposed" by the rules, there are two major styles – *big-step* versus *small-step* operational semantics. In big-step style, the inference rules model complete execution or evaluation of a given program phrase, while the intermediate steps are implicit in the *proof trees* for applying inference rules. In small-step style, the inference rules model single computational steps.

We begin with a detailed discussion of big-step style. We introduce the basic concepts of operational semantics and exercise big-step style for a number of languages. We also demonstrate how operational semantics specifications can be implemented as interpreters in Haskell. Later we will cover small-step style.

8.1.1 Metavariables

In the context of semantics specifications, it is common practice to declare (short) *metavariables* to range over syntactic categories and other types needed in the specification. The use of these metavariables (possibly with subscripts or quotes) helps with conciseness and clarity; it also adds a simple typing discipline, as we will clarify in a second. We are ready to present the metavariables for the semantics of the simple expression language BTL:

- expressions *e* according to the abstract syntax;
- natural numbers *n*, i.e., *zero*, *succ*(*zero*), ...;
- Boolean values *b*, i.e., *true* and *false*;
- values *v*, i.e., Boolean values and natural numbers.

The type of expressions was readily defined according to the abstract syntax of BTL. The remaining types are subsets of expressions and we will define them shortly.

8.1.2 Judgments

In operational semantics, we are concerned with *relations* over program phrases (statements, expressions, etc.) and other data structures such as values (i.e., results of evaluation) and stores (i.e., maps from variable names to values). In operational semantics specifications, claims of relationships are referred to as *judgments*. That is, a judgment is a basic formula – a claim to be proved on the basis of the operational semantics specification. A judgment is thus formed from a relation symbol and some arguments. An argument is either a metavariable or an "instance" thereof such as a syntactical pattern. For instance:

- *evaluate*(e, v): a judgment about the evaluation of an expression e to a value v;
- *execute*(s, m, m'): a judgment about the execution of an imperative statement s for an initial store m and a resulting store m'; a store is viewed as a map from variable names to values;
- *evaluate*(fs, m, e, v): a judgment about the evaluation of an expression e in a functional program to a value v relative to a given collection of defined functions fs and an environment m (i.e., a map from argument names to values).

In the literature, as a matter of convention, relation symbols are often not alphabetical, nor are they applied in prefix fashion. Instead, some infix or mixfix notation is used instead. For instance:

- $e \rightsquigarrow v$ instead of *evaluate*(e, v);
- $m \vdash s \rightsquigarrow m'$ instead of *execute*(s, m, m');
- $fs, m \vdash e \rightsquigarrow v$ instead of *evaluate*(fs, m, e, v).

8.1.3 Inference Rules

An operational semantics specification, at its heart, consists of *inference rules*, as known from natural deduction in logic and proof theory. These rules are of the following format:

$$\frac{P_1 \quad \cdots \quad P_n}{C} \qquad [\mathsf{l}]$$

$P_1, \ldots, P_n$, and C are judgments and l is simply a label of the rule that can be used to refer to the rule conveniently. We refer to $P_1, \ldots, P_n$ as *premises* and to C as the *conclusion* because the idea is that the rules can be applied to perform proofs of judgments such that the truth of C can be concluded, once the truth of $P_1, \ldots, P_n$ has been established. For $n = 0$, we speak of an axiom and omit the separator line. Thus:

$$C \qquad [\mathsf{l}]$$

The rules of an operational semantics are syntax-driven. That is, the conclusion applies to a specific syntactic construct (or pattern), while the premises may apply to subterms of the conclusion's construct or terms formed over it.

Here is an axiom for the evaluation of the expression form zero:

$$\mathsf{zero} \rightsquigarrow \mathsf{zero} \qquad [\mathsf{ZERO}]$$

Here is the inference rule for the successor construct:

$$\frac{e \looparrowright n}{\mathsf{succ}(e) \looparrowright \mathsf{succ}(n)} \quad \text{[SUCC]}$$

This rule models that if e evaluates to a natural number n, then the compound expression evaluates to the successor of n, i.e., $\mathsf{succ}(n)$. Note that we are relying on metavariables being constrained in terms of type. That is, n is a placeholder for natural numbers rather than arbitrary evaluation results. This is the kind of typing discipline provided by the use of metavariables.

We are ready to discuss the rules for all expression forms.

Specification 8.1 (Operational semantics of BTL (big-step style))

$$\mathsf{true} \looparrowright \mathsf{true} \qquad \text{[TRUE]}$$

$$\mathsf{false} \looparrowright \mathsf{false} \qquad \text{[FALSE]}$$

$$\mathsf{zero} \looparrowright \mathsf{zero} \qquad \text{[ZERO]}$$

$$\frac{e \looparrowright n}{\mathsf{succ}(e) \looparrowright \mathsf{succ}(n)} \qquad \text{[SUCC]}$$

$$\frac{e \looparrowright \mathsf{zero}}{\mathsf{pred}(e) \looparrowright \mathsf{zero}} \qquad \text{[PRED1]}$$

$$\frac{e \looparrowright \mathsf{succ}(n)}{\mathsf{pred}(e) \looparrowright n} \qquad \text{[PRED2]}$$

$$\frac{e \looparrowright \mathsf{zero}}{\mathsf{iszero}(e) \looparrowright \mathsf{true}} \qquad \text{[ISZERO1]}$$

$$\frac{e \looparrowright \mathsf{succ}(n)}{\mathsf{iszero}(e) \looparrowright \mathsf{false}} \qquad \text{[ISZERO2]}$$

$$\frac{e_0 \looparrowright \mathsf{true} \quad e_1 \looparrowright v_1}{\mathsf{if}(e_0, e_1, e_2) \looparrowright v_1} \qquad \text{[IF1]}$$

$$\frac{e_0 \looparrowright \text{false} \quad e_2 \looparrowright v_2}{\text{if}(e_0, e_1, e_2) \looparrowright v_2} \qquad \text{[IF2]}$$

That is, there are three axioms, [TRUE], [FALSE], and [ZERO], for all the constant forms of expressions. There is one rule, [SUCC], to construct the successor of a given natural number. There are two rules, [PRED1] and [PRED2], to cover the zero and nonzero argument options for the predecessor. There are also two rules, [ISZERO1] and [ISZERO2], to cover the zero and nonzero argument options for the test for zero. Finally, there are two rules, [IF1] and [IF2], to cover selection of the then- and the else-branch, respectively.

Exercise 8.1 (A BTL extension) [Basic level]
Define the syntax and semantics of the operations odd *and* even *to determine whether a given argument expression evaluates to an odd or an even number and to return a Boolean value accordingly.*

We mention in passing that inference rules can also be applied to formalize abstract syntax. We do not really need such a formalization, because the earlier signature-based definition is perfectly sufficient for our purposes, but this alternative style of definition of abstract syntax may help to explain the notion of inference rules. Thus, let us provide a judgment $u \in expr$ for testing whether a given term u is an expression. Here we assume that the metavariable u ranges over the "universe" of prefix terms (Section 3.1.7), i.e., terms with arbitrary function symbols and any number of argument terms.

Specification 8.2 (Inference rules defining the abstract syntax of BTL)

$$\text{true} \in expr \qquad \text{[expr1]}$$

$$\text{false} \in expr \qquad \text{[expr2]}$$

$$\text{zero} \in expr \qquad \text{[expr3]}$$

$$\frac{u \in expr}{\text{succ}(u) \in expr} \qquad \text{[expr4]}$$

$$\frac{u \in expr}{\text{pred}(u) \in expr} \qquad \text{[expr5]}$$

$$\frac{u \in expr}{\text{iszero}(u) \in expr} \qquad \text{[expr6]}$$

$$\frac{u_0 \in expr \quad u_1 \in expr \quad u_2 \in expr}{\text{if}(u_0, u_1, u_2) \in expr} \qquad \text{[expr7]}$$

Likewise, we can define the precise (trivial) meaning of the types for number and Boolean values as subsets of *expr*, subject to judgments $e \in nat$, $e \in bool$, and $e \in value$ as follows.

Specification 8.3 (Inference rules for BTL's values)

$$\text{zero} \in nat \qquad \text{[nat1]}$$

$$\frac{e \in nat}{\text{succ}(e) \in nat} \qquad \text{[nat2]}$$

$$\text{true} \in bool \qquad \text{[bool1]}$$

$$\text{false} \in bool \qquad \text{[bool2]}$$

$$\frac{e \in nat}{e \in value} \qquad \text{[value1]}$$

$$\frac{e \in bool}{e \in value} \qquad \text{[value2]}$$

8.1.4 Derivation Trees

The proof of a (big-step) judgment commences in a tree-like shape. These trees are referred to as *derivation trees*. Figure 8.1 shows a derivation tree for a judgment related to the evaluation of a BTL expression.

Each node in a derivation tree is an instance of a conclusion of an inference rule. The subtrees of a node are instances of the premises of the same rule. The leaf nodes of the tree are instances of axioms. By "instance" we mean that metavariables in the rules applied are consistently replaced by phrases or data structures of the appropriate sort.

$$
\cfrac{\cfrac{\text{zero} \looparrowright \text{zero} \quad [\text{ZERO}]}{\text{iszero(zero)} \looparrowright \text{true}}\ [\text{ISZERO1}] \qquad \cfrac{\text{zero} \looparrowright \text{zero} \quad [\text{ZERO}]}{\text{succ(zero)} \looparrowright \text{succ(zero)}}\ [\text{SUCC}]}{\cfrac{\text{if}(\text{iszero(zero)},\text{succ(zero)},\text{zero}) \looparrowright \text{succ(zero)}}{\text{pred}(\text{if}(\text{iszero(zero)},\text{succ(zero)},\text{zero})) \looparrowright \text{zero}}\ [\text{PRED2}]}\ [\text{IF1}]
$$

Fig. 8.1 A derivation tree for evaluating a BTL expression (see at the bottom).

8.1.5 Big-Step Style Interpreters

Operational semantics specifications can be implemented as programs that serve the purpose of interpretation. Depending on any additional notational constraints that may be imposed on the operational semantics, and also depending on the choice of metalanguage, such an implementation can be more or less straightforward. In fact, there exist executable metalanguages that are essentially dedicated to inference rule systems for operational semantics and, possibly, type systems, for example, TYPOL [7] and RML [14]. Further, operational semantics can also be represented and thereby executed well in various logics in theorem provers or proof assistants, for example, Agda [13], Coq [6], Isabelle/HOL [12], and Twelf [15].

8.1.5.1 Aspects of Implementation

Implementing operational semantics specifications in declarative programming languages is relatively straightforward, as we will demonstrate with Haskell as implementation language. Regardless of the concrete metalanguage or paradigm, implementation of operational semantics specifications involves several aspects giving rise to a recipe as follows:

Recipe 8.1 (Implementation of inference rules).
The following explanation is tailored towards the implementation of big-step operational semantics, but we will see later that about the same scheme applies also to the implementation of small-step operational semantics, type checking, and potentially other applications of inference rule-based specifications.

Abstract syntax *Implement abstract syntax, as discussed previously (Recipe 4.1).*

> ***Semantic domains***   *Define semantic domains such as values and stores – in the same way as such domains are needed for any interpreter implementation (Recipe 2.2).*
>
> ***Judgments***   *Given a metalanguage, pick a primary abstraction form for modeling judgments. In functional programming, pick functions. In OO programming, pick methods.*
>
> ***I/O***   *An operational semantics defines mathematical relations. In contrast, an interpreter needs to be computationally effective with well-defined I/O behavior. Classify and implement the argument positions of judgments as either input or output positions. For instance, in a functional programming encoding, the input positions become function arguments and the output positions become function results.*
>
> ***Inference rules***   *Map each inference rule to a well-defined program phrase of the metalanguage, thereby supporting modularity and clarity. For instance, inference rules can be modeled as equations in functional programming.*
>
> ***Conjunctions***   *Logically, the premises of inference rules correspond to conjunctions. Computationally, these conjunctions correspond to sequences of subcomputations with some potential data flow from the conclusion to the premises, among the premises, and again from the premises back to the conclusion. Model such a sequence of computations and the corresponding data flow in the metalanguage accordingly. For instance, in functional programming, the premises can be arranged in a nested let-expression.*
>
> ***Failure and backtracking***   *Inference rules "fail" when the premises "fail". Such failures may be "fatal" meaning that proof derivation (interpretation) must be aborted or may be "recoverable" meaning that other inference rules should be tried. Model failure and recovery from it in the implementation. (To this end, backtracking may be leveraged.)*

Let us instantiate this recipe to interpret the expression language BTL in the functional programming language Haskell. We have already implemented BTL's abstract syntax in Haskell (Section 4.1.3.1) and thus, we move immediately to defining value forms of expressions that correspond to results of interpretation. We do not use algebraic data types here, because these value forms correspond to subsets of the existing type Expr. Instead, we leverage predicates on Expr.

Illustration 8.1 (Value forms of expressions)

Haskell module Language.BTL.ValueExpr

```
−− Boolean values
isBool :: Expr → Bool
isBool TRUE = True
isBool FALSE = True
isBool _ = False

−− Natural numbers
```

```
isNat :: Expr → Bool
isNat Zero = True
isNat (Succ e) = isNat e
isNat _ = False
```

-- Values
```
isValue :: Expr → Bool
isValue e = isBool e || isNat e
```

The judgment for expression evaluation can be modeled as a function with Expr both as the domain and the range:

```
evaluate :: Expr → Expr
```

The assumption is here that undefinedness of Haskell functions is used to model failure of derivation. Here is how we expect to use the interpreter.

Interactive Haskell session:

▶ evaluate Pred (If (IsZero Zero) (Succ Zero) Zero)
Zero

- -

▶ evaluate (Pred TRUE)
*** Exception: ... Irrefutable pattern failed for pattern ...

The first example evaluates the expression to Zero because IsZero Zero is evaluated to True and thus, the first branch of the if is selected, thereby applying Pred to Succ Zero, resulting in Zero. The second example illustrates failing interpretation – the predecessor of a Boolean value is not defined. Failure is manifested here by runtime pattern-match failure.

We are ready to present the Haskell equations corresponding to the inference rules for the big-step semantics of BTL.

Illustration 8.2 (Interpretation of expressions)

Haskell module Language.BTL.BigStep

```
1   evaluate :: Expr → Expr
2   evaluate TRUE = TRUE
3   evaluate FALSE = FALSE
4   evaluate Zero = Zero
5   evaluate (Succ e) =
6     let n = evaluate e in
7       if isNat n then Succ n else undefined
8   evaluate (Pred e) =
9     case evaluate e of
10      Zero → Zero
11      (Succ n) → if isNat n then n else undefined
12  evaluate (IsZero e) =
13    case evaluate e of
14      Zero → TRUE
```

```
15        (Succ n) → if isNat n then FALSE else undefined
16   evaluate (If e0 e1 e2) =
17     case evaluate e0 of
18        TRUE → evaluate e1
19        FALSE → evaluate e2
```

That is:

- Failure of derivation (proof) is readily modeled by Haskell's undefined. For instance, the evaluation Succ e fails with undefined if e does not evaluate to a result n for which the predicate isNat holds (lines 5–7).
- The use of metavariables is encoded by additional type tests such as the application of the predicate isNat, as just discussed above.
- A mapping is applied for now such that there is one equation per expression form of BTL, as opposed to one equation per inference rule. For instance, the two inference rules for the predecessor construct are combined in one equation with a case-expression (lines 8–11). This mapping is simple in terms of functional programming style, but it slightly obfuscates the correspondence between the formal semantics and the interpreter. We will revisit this decision in Section 8.1.5.3.

8.1.5.2 Explicit Model of Failure

Let us provide a variation such that we model the potential for *failure* explicitly in the type of the function for expression evaluation by means of applying the type constructor Maybe to the result:

evaluate :: Expr → Maybe Expr

Here is how we expect to use the interpreter:

Interactive Haskell session:

▶ evaluate Pred (If (IsZero Zero) (Succ Zero) Zero)
Just Zero
- -
▶ evaluate (Pred TRUE)
Nothing

That is, the first evaluation is successful; it returns Just Zero. The second evaluation fails with Nothing because Pred cannot be applied to TRUE. The mapping of inference rules to equations contains dedicated cases to explicitly return Nothing in the case of inappropriate intermediate results or failing premises.

Illustration 8.3 (Explicit model of failure in encoding big-step rules)

Haskell module Language.BTL.BigStepMaybe

```
evaluate :: Expr → Maybe Expr
evaluate TRUE = Just TRUE
evaluate FALSE = Just FALSE
evaluate Zero = Just Zero
evaluate (Succ e) =
  case evaluate e of
    (Just n) →
      if isNat n
        then Just (Succ n)
        else Nothing
    Nothing → Nothing
evaluate (Pred e) =
  case evaluate e of
    (Just Zero) → Just Zero
    (Just (Succ n)) →
      if isNat n
        then Just n
        else Nothing
    _ → Nothing
evaluate (IsZero e) =
  case evaluate e of
    (Just Zero) → Just TRUE
    (Just (Succ n)) →
      if isNat n
        then Just FALSE
        else Nothing
    _ → Nothing
evaluate (If e0 e1 e2) =
  case evaluate e0 of
    (Just TRUE) → evaluate e1
    (Just FALSE) → evaluate e2
    _ → Nothing
```

Exercise 8.2 (Distinguished result types) [Basic level]
The interpreters so far use value forms of expressions in the result position. However, the metalanguage readily provides primitive types for numbers and Booleans. Revise the previous interpreter to use Either Int Bool *instead of* Expr.

8.1.5.3 Rule-by-Rule Mapping

Let us now strive for a 1:1 correspondence between inference rules and function equations, as opposed to mapping multiple rules for one construct to a single equation. Such a rule-by-rule mapping arguably better conveys the structure of the formal definition in the implementation.

To this end, we may leverage Haskell 2010's *pattern guards*, which allow us to constrain equations more than by pattern matching and regular guards. That is, a regular guard is simply a Boolean expression over variables bound in the left-hand side patterns. By contrast, a pattern guard can perform more matching based on the results computed for the guard's expression. Consider this code pattern:

```
f (C x) | D y ← g x = h x y
```

This equation will be selected for an argument that is of the form C x, but only if the application g x returns a result that can be matched with D y. This expressiveness is sufficient to achieve a 1:1 correspondence between inference rules and function equations, as shown below.

Illustration 8.4 (Rule-by-rule mapping for big-step style)

Haskell module <u>*Language.BTL.BigStepWithGuards*</u>

```
evaluate :: Expr → Expr
evaluate TRUE = TRUE
evaluate FALSE = FALSE
evaluate Zero = Zero
evaluate (Succ e)
  | n ← evaluate e
  , isNat n
  = Succ n
evaluate (Pred e)
  | Zero ← evaluate e
  = Zero
evaluate (Pred e)
  | Succ n ← evaluate e
  , isNat n
  = n
evaluate (IsZero e)
  | Zero ← evaluate e
  = TRUE
evaluate (IsZero e)
  | Succ n ← evaluate e
  , isNat n
  = FALSE
evaluate (If e0 e1 e2)
  | TRUE ← evaluate e0
  = evaluate e1
evaluate (If e0 e1 e2)
  | FALSE ← evaluate e0
  = evaluate e2
```

For instance, the first equation for the pattern Pred e applies only if the evaluation of e results in Zero, whereas the second equation for the same pattern applies if the evaluation of e matches the pattern Succ n and isNat n holds.

8.1.6 More Examples of Big-Step Style

Let us define the semantics of a few more "fabricated" languages.

8.1.6.1 Semantics of Simple Imperative Programs

Let us define the semantics of the imperative programming language BIPL.

Specification 8.4 (Big-step operational semantics of BIPL)

Metavariables:

- *statements s according to abstract syntax;*
- *expressions e according to abstract syntax;*
- *unary operators uo according to abstract syntax;*
- *binary operators bo according to abstract syntax;*
- *variable names x;*
- *integer values i;*
- *Boolean values b;*
- *integer and Boolean values v;*
- *stores m as collections of variable name-value pairs.*

Judgments:

- $m \vdash s \leadsto m'$: *execution of statement s with m and m' as the stores before and after execution, respectively;*
- $m \vdash e \leadsto v$: *evaluation of expression e with v as the evaluation result and m as the observed store;*
- $\underline{unary(uo, v) \leadsto v'}$: *interpretation of unary operator uo on an argument value v with the result value v';*
- $\underline{binary(bo, v_1, v_2) \leadsto v'}$: *interpretation of binary operator bo on argument values v_1 and v_2 with the result value v'.*

Statement execution

$$m \vdash \mathsf{skip} \leadsto m \hspace{4cm} \text{[SKIP]}$$

$$\frac{m \vdash e \leadsto v}{m \vdash \mathsf{assign}(x, e) \leadsto m[x \mapsto v]} \hspace{2cm} \text{[ASSIGN]}$$

$$\frac{m_0 \vdash s_1 \leadsto m_1 \quad m_1 \vdash s_2 \leadsto m_2}{m_0 \vdash \mathsf{seq}(s_1, s_2) \leadsto m_2} \hspace{2cm} \text{[SEQ]}$$

$$\frac{m \vdash e \leadsto \mathsf{true} \quad m \vdash s_1 \leadsto m'}{m \vdash \mathsf{if}(e,s_1,s_2) \leadsto m'} \qquad \text{[IF1]}$$

$$\frac{m \vdash e \leadsto \mathsf{false} \quad m \vdash s_2 \leadsto m'}{m \vdash \mathsf{if}(e,s_1,s_2) \leadsto m'} \qquad \text{[IF2]}$$

$$\frac{m \vdash \mathsf{if}(e,\mathsf{seq}(s,\mathsf{while}(e,s)),\mathsf{skip}) \leadsto m'}{m \vdash \mathsf{while}(e,s) \leadsto m'} \qquad \text{[WHILE]}$$

Expression evaluation

$$m \vdash \mathsf{intconst}(i) \leadsto i \qquad \text{[INTCONST]}$$

$$\frac{m(x) \mapsto v}{m \vdash \mathsf{var}(x) \leadsto v} \qquad \text{[VAR]}$$

$$\frac{m \vdash e \leadsto v \quad \underline{unary}(uo,v) \leadsto v'}{m \vdash \mathsf{unary}(uo,e) \leadsto v'} \qquad \text{[UNARY]}$$

$$\frac{m \vdash e_1 \leadsto v_1 \quad m \vdash e_2 \leadsto v_2 \quad \underline{binary}(bo,v_1,v_2) \leadsto v'}{m \vdash \mathsf{binary}(bo,e_1,e_2) \leadsto v'} \qquad \text{[BINARY]}$$

The inference rules leverage some special notation:

- $m(x) \mapsto v$: This form of premise, as exercised in rule [VAR], applies a store m in the sense of function application. The premise fails, if the store does not map the given variable identifier x to any value v.
- $m[x \mapsto v]$: This form of argument, as exercised in rule [ASSIGN], denotes the store m updated in the position x to associate with value v while being identical to m in all other positions.

The inference rules can be explained as follows:

- [SKIP]: The "empty" statement is executed without any effect on the store.
- [ASSIGN]: The right-hand side expression is evaluated to a value v and the store m is updated in the left-hand position x to map to v.
- [SEQ]: The statements s_1 and s_2 of the sequential composition are executed in the given order, which is expressed by "threading" the store via the variables m_0, m_1, and m_2.

- [IF1]: If the condition e of the if-statement evaluates to true, then the then-branch s_1 is executed.
- [IF2]: If the condition e of the if-statement evaluates to false, then the else-branch s_2 is executed.
- [WHILE]: The statement $\mathsf{if}(e, \mathsf{seq}(s, \mathsf{while}(e,s)), \mathsf{skip})$ is executed instead. Thus, the condition is tested by an if-statement with a then-branch for the sequential composition of the loop's body s and the entire loop again; the else-branch is the empty statement.
- [INTCONST]: An integer constant i evaluates to an integer, as is.
- [VAR]: A variable identifier x evaluates to the value v if the given store m associates x with v.
- [UNARY]: The operand e is evaluated to v and we assume that the result v of the operation's application is computed by a judgment of the form $\underline{unary(uo, v)} \looparrowright \underline{v'}$; the routine rules for $\underline{unary}$ are omitted here.
- [BINARY]: This is similar to [UNARY].

Illustration 8.5 (Derivation tree for a BIPL statement)   *Consider the following statement, which computes the maximum c of two values a and b:*

$$\mathsf{if}(\mathsf{binary}(\mathsf{geq}, \mathsf{var}(a), \mathsf{var}(b)), \mathsf{assign}(c, \mathsf{var}(a)), \mathsf{assign}(c, \mathsf{var}(b)))$$

In the derivation tree shown in Fig. 8.2, m is a store such that $\langle a, 7 \rangle \in m$ and $\langle b, 42 \rangle \in m$. Thus, the statement given above should result in a store m' such that $\langle c, 42 \rangle \in m'$.

Exercise 8.3 (Implementation of derivation trees)   [Intermediate level]
Devise an object program representation of inference rules and derivation trees. Implement a metaprogram for mechanically verifying the conformance (correctness) of a derivation tree with regard to a set of inference rules. Your implementation should be tested with the examples in this chapter.

Exercise 8.4 (Expression-oriented imperative language)   [Basic level]
Define the big-step semantics of a variation of BIPL such that the syntactic category for expressions incorporates all statement forms. This requires a reasonable hypothesis as to what the evaluation result should be for any given "morphed" statement form. For instance, in the language C, assignments can be used in expression positions. It may happen that some statement form fails to return a proper value. For instance, skip cannot possibly return a proper value. Thus, the semantic domain for values should be extended to be able to express the "lack of value".

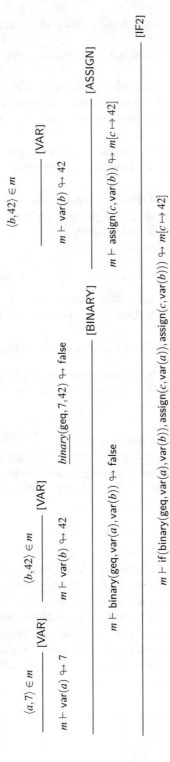

Fig. 8.2 A derivation tree for statement execution.

8.1.6.2 Semantics of Simple Functional Programs

Let us define the big-step operational semantics of the functional programming language BFPL.

Specification 8.5 (Big-step operational semantics of BFPL)

Metavariables:

- *programs p according to abstract syntax;*
- *function collections fs according to abstract syntax;*
- *function signatures sig according to abstract syntax;*
- *expressions e according to abstract syntax;*
- *unary operators uo according to abstract syntax;*
- *binary operators bo according to abstract syntax;*
- *function and argument names x;*
- *integer values i;*
- *Boolean values b;*
- *integers and Boolean values v;*
- *collections m of argument name-value pairs.*

Judgments:

- $fs, m \vdash e \leadsto v$: *expression evaluation with e as the expression to be evaluated, v as the evaluation result, fs as the list of defined functions, and m as the current argument binding ("environment");*
- $p \leadsto v$: *evaluation of the main expression of a program p.*

$$\textbf{\textit{Evaluation of programs}}$$

$$\frac{fs, \emptyset \vdash e \leadsto v}{\langle fs, e \rangle \leadsto v} \qquad \text{[PROG]}$$

$$\textbf{\textit{Evaluation of expressions}}$$

$$fs, m \vdash \mathsf{intconst}(i) \leadsto i \qquad \text{[INTCONST]}$$

$$fs, m \vdash \mathsf{boolconst}(b) \leadsto b \qquad \text{[BOOLCONST]}$$

$$\frac{\langle x, v \rangle \in m}{fs, m \vdash \mathsf{arg}(x) \leadsto v} \qquad \text{[ARG]}$$

$$\frac{fs, m \vdash e_0 \leadsto \mathsf{true} \quad fs, m \vdash e_1 \leadsto v}{fs, m \vdash \mathsf{if}(e_0, e_1, e_2) \leadsto v} \qquad \text{[IF1]}$$

$$\frac{fs,m \vdash e_0 \looparrowright \text{false} \quad fs,m \vdash e_2 \looparrowright v}{fs,m \vdash \text{if}(e_0,e_1,e_2) \looparrowright v} \quad \text{[IF2]}$$

$$\frac{fs,m \vdash e \looparrowright v \quad unary(uo,v) \looparrowright v'}{fs,m \vdash \text{unary}(uo,e) \looparrowright v'} \quad \text{[UNARY]}$$

$$\frac{fs,m \vdash e_1 \looparrowright v_1 \quad fs,m \vdash e_2 \looparrowright v_2 \quad binary(bo,v_1,v_2) \looparrowright v'}{fs,m \vdash \text{binary}(bo,e_1,e_2) \looparrowright v'} \quad \text{[BINARY]}$$

$$\frac{\begin{array}{c} fs,m \vdash e_1 \looparrowright v_1 \quad \cdots \quad fs,m \vdash e_n \looparrowright v_n \\ \langle x, sig, \langle\langle x_1,\ldots,x_n\rangle,e\rangle\rangle \in fs \\ fs,[x_1 \mapsto v_1,\ldots,x_n \mapsto v_n] \vdash e \looparrowright v \end{array}}{fs,m \vdash \text{apply}(x,\langle e_1,\ldots,e_n\rangle) \looparrowright v} \quad \text{[APPLY]}$$

The first rule concerns the evaluation of a program's main expression; "$\emptyset$" denotes the empty (initial) environment. The rule of particular interest is the one for function application ([APPLY]). The premises model the following aspects of function application. The actual arguments (expressions) $e_1, \ldots, e_n$ are evaluated to values $v_1, \ldots, v_n$. For the given function name x of the function application, a function is looked up from the collection fs; the function signature sig is not used any further, but the list of formal arguments (names) $x_1, \ldots, x_n$ and the body e of the definition are of interest. That is, a new environment is assembled from the formal arguments and the values of the actual arguments and the body is evaluated in this environment, thereby defining the value v of the function application.

Exercise 8.5 (A derivation tree for BFPL)   [Basic level]
Construct a derivation tree for an expression with a function application.

8.2 Small-Step Operational Semantics

We turn now to *small-step style*. For comparison, in big-step style, judgments relate program phrases directly to final "results". By contrast, in small-step style, judgments relate program phrases to intermediate results, as they arise from performing "one step" of computation. For clarity, we use different arrows in judgments:

- "→": small-step semantics;
- "⇥": big-step semantics.

We mention in passing that an operational semantics specification in general, and perhaps more specifically one in small-step style, can also be viewed as a model of the semantics of programs as computations in terms of steps of a formal machine with its *transition relation* specified by the inference rules. The different conceivable inputs of a judgment, such as program phrases combined with additional data structures, form the set of states ("configurations") of the machine.

8.2.1 Big- versus Small-Step Judgments

Let us illustrate small-step style for the expression language BTL. The two contrasting judgments for BTL are these:

- big step: $e \looparrowright v$;
- small step: $e \to e'$.

In the first case, an expression is associated with a value, which cannot be evaluated any further. In the second case, an expression is associated with another expression, which may or may not be a value.

Consider this valid big-step judgment:

$$\mathsf{pred}(\mathsf{if}(\mathsf{iszero}(\mathsf{zero}), \mathsf{succ}(\mathsf{zero}), \mathsf{zero})) \looparrowright \mathsf{zero}$$

The small-step judgment covers only one step:

$$\mathsf{pred}(\mathsf{if}(\mathsf{iszero}(\mathsf{zero}), \mathsf{succ}(\mathsf{zero}), \mathsf{zero})) \to \mathsf{pred}(\mathsf{if}(\mathsf{true}, \mathsf{succ}(\mathsf{zero}), \mathsf{zero}))$$

That is, the condition has been reduced from $\mathsf{iszero}(\mathsf{zero})$ to true, but the if has still to be reduced further in subsequent steps.

Let us complement the big-step semantics of BTL, as shown above in Specification 8.1, with its small-step counterpart, as shown below. (We use lowercase labels such as [if1] for the rules in small-step style as opposed to uppercase labels such as [IF1] for the rules in big-step style.)

Specification 8.6 (Operational semantics of BTL (small-step style))

$$\frac{e \to e'}{\mathsf{succ}(e) \to \mathsf{succ}(e')} \qquad [\mathsf{succ}]$$

$$\frac{e \to e'}{\mathsf{pred}(e) \to \mathsf{pred}(e')} \qquad [\mathsf{pred1}]$$

$$\text{pred}(\text{zero}) \rightarrow \text{zero} \qquad\qquad [\text{pred2}]$$

$$\text{pred}(\text{succ}(n)) \rightarrow n \qquad\qquad [\text{pred3}]$$

$$\frac{e \rightarrow e'}{\text{iszero}(e) \rightarrow \text{iszero}(e')} \qquad\qquad [\text{iszero1}]$$

$$\text{iszero}(\text{zero}) \rightarrow \text{true} \qquad\qquad [\text{iszero2}]$$

$$\text{iszero}(\text{succ}(n)) \rightarrow \text{false} \qquad\qquad [\text{iszero3}]$$

$$\frac{e_0 \rightarrow e_0'}{\text{if}(e_0,e_1,e_2) \rightarrow \text{if}(e_0',e_1,e_2)} \qquad\qquad [\text{if1}]$$

$$\text{if}(\text{true},t_1,t_2) \rightarrow t_1 \qquad\qquad [\text{if2}]$$

$$\text{if}(\text{false},t_1,t_2) \rightarrow t_2 \qquad\qquad [\text{if3}]$$

8.2.2 Normal Form

We say that e is in *normal form* if no further small-step inference rules are applicable. That is, there is no e' such that $e \rightarrow e'$ holds. This notion of normal form is easily generalized to other forms of judgments, for example, judgments of the form $\Gamma \vdash p \rightarrow p'$ with Γ being some context used by the judgment and p, p' standing for any sort of program phrases. In such a case, we say that p is in normal form for context Γ if there is no p' such that $\Gamma \vdash p \rightarrow p'$.

Illustration 8.6 (Normal form for BTL expressions)

- true, false, zero, succ(zero), succ(succ(zero)), ... *are in normal form. These values indicate the successful completion of expression evaluation.*
- if(zero, e, e') *for all expressions e and e' is in normal form because there is no rule that applies to* zero *in the condition position of an* if. *The semantics assumes that the expression in the condition position must be evaluated to a Boolean value.*

As the illustration shown above reveals, there are basically two kinds of normal forms:

Proper results   The derivation sequence ends in a program phrase that we consider a proper (final) result. For instance, in the case of an expression-oriented language, we would consider a value a proper result.

Stuck phrases   The derivation sequence ends in a program phrase that we consider not to be a proper result, but no step is feasible. In the case of BTL, the pattern if(zero, e, e'), as discussed above, is a stuck expression. There are more stuck expressions; see the following exercise.

Exercise 8.6 (Stuck expressions)   [Basic level]
Provide a complete description of all "stuck" expressions for BTL.

8.2.3 Derivation Sequences

In small-step style, stepwise computation is represented as a *derivation sequence*, where each step is a ("small") derivation tree. We speak of a *complete* derivation sequence if the sequence ends in normal form, as demonstrated below.

Illustration 8.7 (A complete derivation sequence for an expression)

Step 1

$$\cfrac{\cfrac{\mathsf{iszero(zero)} \to \mathsf{true} \quad [\mathsf{iszero2}]}{\mathsf{if(iszero(zero), succ(zero), zero)} \to \mathsf{if(true, succ(zero), zero)}} \; [\mathsf{if1}]}{\mathsf{pred(if(iszero(zero), succ(zero), zero))} \to \mathsf{pred(if(true, succ(zero), zero))}} \; [\mathsf{pred1}]$$

Step 2

$$\cfrac{\mathsf{if(true, succ(zero), zero)} \to \mathsf{succ(zero)} \quad [\mathsf{if2}]}{\mathsf{pred(if(true, succ(zero), zero))} \to \mathsf{pred(succ(zero))}} \; [\mathsf{pred1}]$$

Step 3

$$\text{pred}(\text{succ}(\text{zero})) \rightarrow \text{zero} \quad [\text{pred3}]$$

Summary of all steps

$$\text{pred}(\text{if}(\text{iszero}(\text{zero}), \text{succ}(\text{zero}), \text{zero}))$$

$$\rightarrow \text{pred}(\text{if}(\text{true}, \text{succ}(\text{zero}), \text{zero}))$$

$$\rightarrow \text{pred}(\text{succ}(\text{zero}))$$

$$\rightarrow \text{zero}$$

We may also take the reflexive, transitive closure of the one-step relation so that we can reduce a program phrase to normal form, just as in the case of big-step style. In the case of BTL, we may use a judgment as follows:

$$e \hookrightarrow^* e'$$

However, we may not be interested in arbitrary normal forms e'. Instead, we may prefer to look only at complete derivation sequences which end in proper results. Thus, the following judgment is more appropriate and also better in line with the big-step judgment:

$$e \hookrightarrow^* v$$

The difference between small- and big-step operational semantics can be visualized very well. Let us consider small-step style first with a sequence of multiple derivation trees, starting from an initial program phrase p_1, going through intermediate phrases $p_2, \ldots, p_{n-1}$, and ending in a proper result such as a value v:

$$\frac{\cdots}{p_1 \rightarrow p_2} \; [\text{I}_1] \qquad \cdots \qquad \frac{\cdots}{p_{n-1} \rightarrow v} \; [\text{I}_n]$$

In the case of big-step style, we face a single derivation tree mapping a phrase p to a proper result such as a value v; the steps are subsumed by the subtrees of the derivation tree; subterms and other constituent phrases $p_1, \ldots, p_m$ are evaluated in subtrees to intermediate values $v_1, \ldots, v_m$, ultimately contributing to the final value symbolized as a term $f(v_1, \ldots, v_m)$:

$$\frac{\cdots}{p_1 \looparrowright v_1} \; [\mathsf{L_1}] \qquad \cdots \qquad \frac{\cdots}{p_m \looparrowright v_m} \; [\mathsf{L_m}]$$

$$\frac{}{p \looparrowright f(v_1, \ldots, v_m)} \; [\mathsf{L_0}]$$

Small-step style is intrinsically more versatile than big-step style. That is, there are language constructs that are conveniently modeled in small-step style but with no obvious model in big-step style. For instance, the semantics of jump constructs or interleaving parallel execution can be modeled conveniently only in small-step style [10]. However, as long as we are facing no "challenging" constructs, big-step style appears to be more straightforward than small-step style.

8.2.4 Small-Step Style Interpreters

Everything we have said about the implementation of big-step operational semantics (Section 8.1.5) remains valid for small-step style. However, two additional aspects arise:

* A reflexive, transitive closure of the single-step relation should be implemented so that a small-step semantics can be still used to reduce a program phrase to a normal form, in fact, a proper (final) result.
* When the inference rules are applied computationally, they will fail intentionally on any input in normal form. Failure due to reaching a value should not be mapped to abnormal program termination.

Let us implement the small-step operational semantics for BTL's expressions in Haskell. We commit to a rule-by-rule mapping, as discussed in Section 8.1.5.3.

Illustration 8.8 (Rule-by-rule mapping for small-step style)

Haskell module Language.BTL.SmallStepWithGuards

```
step :: Expr → Maybe Expr
step (Succ e) | Just e' ← step e = Just (Succ e')
step (Pred e) | Just e' ← step e = Just (Pred e')
step (Pred Zero) = Just Zero
step (Pred (Succ n)) | isNat n = Just n
step (IsZero e) | Just e' ← step e = Just (IsZero e')
step (IsZero Zero) = Just TRUE
step (IsZero (Succ n)) | isNat n = Just FALSE
step (If e0 e1 e2) | Just e0' ← step e0 = Just (If e0' e1 e2)
step (If TRUE e1 e2) = Just e1
step (If FALSE e1 e2) = Just e2
step _ = Nothing
```

The Maybe monad is used systematically so that the step function may communicate failure due to reaching a normal form. Pattern guards model premises. The reflexive, transitive closure of the one-step relation is easily expressed as a dedicated function steps as follows.

Illustration 8.9 (Reflexive, transitive closure of one-step relation)

Haskell module Language.BTL.Closure

```
steps :: (Expr → Maybe Expr) → Expr → Maybe Expr
steps f e =
  if isValue e
    then Just e
    else case f e of
          Just e' → steps f e'
          Nothing → Nothing
```

We mention in passing that the steps function is actually parameterized by a function f for making single steps. Thus, the closure could be also applied to alternative implementations of the one-step relation. The closure fails with Nothing if a stuck phrase, as opposed to a proper result, is encountered.

Exercise 8.7 (Small steps for values)   [Basic level]
The definition of the steps *function in Illustration 8.9 does not attempt the argument* f *in case where the argument* e *is a value. Argue rigorously that no steps are feasible anyway in this case.*

8.2.5 More Examples of Small-Step Style

Let us define the small-step operational semantics of a few more "fabricated" languages.

8.2.5.1 Semantics of Simple Imperative Programs

Let us define the small-step operational semantics of the imperative programming language BIPL. The metavariables are the same as in the case of big-step style (Section 8.1.6.1). As far as expression evaluation is concerned, we also adopt the big-step judgment and the corresponding inference rules. That is, expression evaluation remains in big-step style; we apply small-step style to statement execution only. Thus, we use the following arrows for judgments below:

- "$\rightarrow$": small-step semantics (used for statements here);
- "$\rightsquigarrow$": big-step semantics (used for expressions here).

There is the following small-step judgment:

$$\langle m, s \rangle \rightarrow \langle m', s' \rangle$$

Given a store m, statement s is executed in one step, resulting in statement s' and store m'. For instance, if s was a sequence of two assignments, then s' would be the second assignment because the first assignment is performed in one step. The desired normal form is $\langle m, \text{skip} \rangle$ for any store m. Obviously, there is no rule for skip.

Specification 8.7 (Small-step operational semantics of BIPL)

Statement execution

$$\frac{m \vdash e \rightsquigarrow v}{\langle m, \text{assign}(x, e) \rangle \rightarrow \langle m[x \mapsto v], \text{skip} \rangle} \qquad \text{[assign]}$$

$$\langle m, \text{seq}(\text{skip}, s) \rangle \rightarrow \langle m, s \rangle \qquad \text{[seq1]}$$

$$\frac{\langle m, s_1 \rangle \rightarrow \langle m', s_1' \rangle}{\langle m, \text{seq}(s_1, s_2) \rangle \rightarrow \langle m', \text{seq}(s_1', s_2) \rangle} \qquad \text{[seq2]}$$

$$\frac{m \vdash e_0 \rightsquigarrow \text{true}}{\langle m, \text{if}(e_0, s_1, s_2) \rangle \rightarrow \langle m, s_1 \rangle} \qquad \text{[if1]}$$

$$\frac{m \vdash e_0 \rightsquigarrow \text{false}}{\langle m, \text{if}(e_0, s_1, s_2) \rangle \rightarrow \langle m, s_2 \rangle} \qquad \text{[if2]}$$

$$\langle m, \text{while}(e, s) \rangle \rightarrow \langle m, \text{if}(e, \text{seq}(s, \text{while}(e, s))), \text{skip}) \rangle \qquad \text{[while]}$$

We now explain the inference rules one by one:

- [assign]: This is essentially the same semantics as in the big-step case because an assignment is not a composed statement form and we continue to evaluate the right-hand side expression in big-step style. The modified store and the normal form skip are returned.
- [seq1]: A sequential composition with an empty statement in front can be simplified to just the second statement of the sequence; the store remains unchanged.

- [seq2]: A sequential composition may perform one step of computation by performing one step with the statement in front, possibly changing the store.
- [if1]: If the condition e of the if-statement evaluates to true, the statement s_1 of the then-branch combined with the unaffected store m is the result of the step. In contrast to big-step style, s_1 is not immediately executed.
- [if2]: Likewise for false and the else-branch.
- [while]: Just as in the big-step semantics, the semantics of a while-loop is redirected to $if(e, seq(s, while(e,s)), skip)$, except that the composed statement is not immediately executed; rather, it is combined with the unaffected store m and returned as the result of the step.

Exercise 8.8 (A derivation sequence for a BIPL statement)   [Basic level]
Consider the derivation tree in Fig. 8.2 which illustrated the computational process for big-step style. Provide the small-step counterpart, i.e., a complete derivation sequence for the same initial statement and store.

Exercise 8.9 (Expression-oriented imperative language)   [Intermediate level]
This is the small-step variation of Exercise 8.4. That is, define a small-step semantics for the same language.

Exercise 8.10 (Nondeterminism)   [Intermediate level]
Add the statement form $choose(s_1, s_2)$ for nondeterministic statement execution to BIPL. The expectation is that either of the two statements s_1 and s_2 is executed. This form of nondeterminism for an imperative language is developed in some detail in [11].

Exercise 8.11 (Parallelism)   [Advanced level]
Add a statement form $par(s_1, s_2)$ for parallel statement execution to BIPL. The expectation is that the possibly compound statements s_1 and s_2 are executed in an interleaving manner. That is, any step performed by s_1 could be followed by a step performed by s_2 or vice versa. Either of the two statements could actually perform any number of steps before the other statement proceeds. Consider the following compound statement; we use an infix operator "par" for the sake of readability:

$$x = 1; \ par \ x = 2; \ x = x + 2$$

The interleaving semantics would assign either of these final results to x. We can explain these results by presenting the assumed sequential order of statements for each interleaving order:

Result = 1; Order: $x = 2; x = x+2; x = 1$
Result = 3; Order: $x = 2; x = 1; x = x+2$

Result = 4; Order: $x = 1$; $x = 2$; $x = x + 2$

This form of parallelism for an imperative language is developed in some detail in [11].

8.2.5.2 Semantics of Simple Functional Programs

Let us define the small-step operational semantics of the functional programming language BFPL. The small-step judgment takes this form:

$$fs \vdash e \rightarrow e'$$

That is, a one-step computation is performed starting from expression e, resulting in expression e' while possibly making use of the collection fs of defined functions. In contrast to big-step style, there is no component for the current argument binding because we leverage the notion of *substitution* instead. That is, formal argument names are consistently replaced by actual argument values as part of the semantics of function application.

We are ready to present the inference rules.

Specification 8.8 (Small-step operational semantics of BFPL)

$$\textit{\textbf{Evaluation of expressions}}$$

$$\frac{fs \vdash e_0 \rightarrow e_0'}{fs \vdash \mathsf{if}(e_0, e_1, e_2) \rightarrow \mathsf{if}(e_0', e_1, e_2)} \qquad \text{[if1]}$$

$$fs \vdash \mathsf{if}(\mathsf{boolconst}(\mathsf{true}), e_1, e_2) \rightarrow e_1 \qquad \text{[if2]}$$

$$fs \vdash \mathsf{if}(\mathsf{boolconst}(\mathsf{false}), e_1, e_2) \rightarrow e_2 \qquad \text{[if3]}$$

$$\frac{fs \vdash e \rightarrow e'}{fs \vdash \mathsf{unary}(uo, e) \rightarrow \mathsf{unary}(uo, e')} \qquad \text{[unary1]}$$

$$\frac{\underline{unary}(uo, v) \rightarrow v'}{fs \vdash \mathsf{unary}(uo, v) \rightarrow v'} \qquad \text{[unary2]}$$

$$\frac{fs \vdash e_1 \rightarrow e_1'}{fs \vdash \mathsf{op}(bo, e_1, e_2) \rightarrow \mathsf{binary}(bo, e_1', e_2)} \qquad \text{[binary1]}$$

$$\frac{\mathit{fs} \vdash e_2 \rightarrow e_2'}{\mathit{fs} \vdash \mathsf{op}(\mathit{bo}, v_1, e_2) \rightarrow \mathsf{binary}(\mathit{bo}, v_1, e_2')} \qquad \text{[binary2]}$$

$$\frac{\mathit{binary}(\mathit{bo}, v_1, v_2) \rightarrow v'}{\mathit{fs} \vdash \mathsf{binary}(\mathit{bo}, v_1, v_2) \rightarrow v'} \qquad \text{[binary3]}$$

$$\frac{\mathit{fs} \vdash e_{i+1} \rightarrow e_{i+1}'}{\mathit{fs} \vdash \mathsf{apply}(x, \langle v_1, \ldots, v_i, e_{i+1}, \ldots, e_n \rangle) \rightarrow \mathsf{apply}(x, \langle v_1, \ldots, v_i, e_{i+1}', \ldots, e_n \rangle)} \qquad \text{[apply1]}$$

$$\frac{\langle x, \mathit{sig}, \langle \langle x_1, \ldots, x_n \rangle, e \rangle \rangle \in \mathit{fs}}{\mathit{fs} \vdash \mathsf{apply}(x, \langle v_1, \ldots, v_n \rangle) \rightarrow [v_1/x_1, \ldots, v_n/x_n] e} \qquad \text{[apply2]}$$

New notation for substitution is used in the last rule ([apply2]). The phrase $[v_1/x_1, \ldots, v_n/x_n] e$ means that all the occurrences of $x_1, \ldots, x_n$ within e are simultaneously replaced by $v_1, \ldots, v_n$, respectively.

Overall, the rules follow a common scheme. There are rules that bring subexpressions into value form. For some constructs, there are rules to perform the final step once all subexpressions are in value form. There are no rules for the constant forms of expressions, because they are readily in value form. Rule [apply1] models the evaluation of arguments of function applications by performing steps for the argument expressions. Rule [apply2] applies once all arguments are in value form; the formal argument names are then substituted by the actual argument values within the body of the function.

Exercise 8.12 (Argument substitution for BFPL)   [Basic level]
Define substitution as a recursive function over expressions such that names are replaced by expressions (in fact, values).

Exercise 8.13 (Simultaneous substitution)   [Basic level]
Demonstrate that simultaneous substitution of multiple names by expressions cannot be trivially represented by a sequence of substitutions such that each name/expression replacement is performed individually.

Exercise 8.14 (Context versus substitution)   [Intermediate level]
In small-step style, we leveraged substitution. In contrast, in big-step style, we leveraged an argument context. Argue why it would be hard to replace the use of substitution by the use of a context in small-step style.

8.2.5.3 Semantics of Finite State Machines

Let us define the small-step operational semantics of FSML – the domain-specific modeling language for finite state machines. FSML is quite different from imperative and functional programming languages. In particular, FSML is a language without statement- and expression-based constructs. In fact, the one-step relation consists of only two axioms: one with an action, and another one without an action for the applicable transition.

Specification 8.9 (Small-step operational semantics of FSML)

Metavariables:

- *FSMs f according to abstract syntax;*
- *state declarations s according to abstract syntax;*
- *Boolean values b (status of states to be initial);*
- *state ids x;*
- *transitions t according to abstract syntax;*
- *events e (input symbols);*
- *actions a (output symbols);*
- *inputs in (event sequences);*
- *outputs out (action sequences).*

Judgments:

- $f \vdash \langle x, e \rangle \rightarrow \langle x', out \rangle$: *the FSM f is interpreted ("simulated") to make a transition from a state with id x to a state with id x' while handling an event e, and possibly producing some output out (zero or one actions);*
- $f \vdash \langle in \rangle \rightarrow^* \langle x, out \rangle$: *the reflexive, transitive closure starting from the initial state and an input in, consuming the complete input, and ending in a state with id x and the output out.*

Interpretation of FSMs *(one-step relation)*

$$\langle \ldots, \langle b, x, \langle \ldots, \langle e, \langle a \rangle, x' \rangle, \ldots \rangle \rangle, \ldots \rangle \vdash \langle x, e \rangle \rightarrow \langle x', \langle a \rangle \rangle \qquad \text{[action]}$$

$$\langle \ldots, \langle b, x, \langle \ldots, \langle e, \langle \rangle, x' \rangle, \ldots \rangle \rangle, \ldots \rangle \vdash \langle x, e \rangle \rightarrow \langle x', \langle \rangle \rangle \qquad \text{[no−action]}$$

In both axioms, we simply decompose the FSM from the context to locate a suitable transition, i.e., one with event e within a suitable state declaration, i.e., the one for the current state x. The located transition provides the new state id x' and, optionally, an action a.

Exercise 8.15 (Closure for FMSL)   [Basic level]
Using the notation of inference rules, define the closure for FSML's small-step judgment. Further, explain how interpretation could get stuck.

Summary and Outline

We have described the established operational semantics approach to defining the semantics of programs. This approach is based on inference rules for modeling the stepwise computation of programs in two different styles – big- and small-step style. These styles differ in terms of how the computational steps are exposed when the inference rules are applied. We have focused on the basics of operational semantics, but we mention in passing that there exist refinements and variations such as reduction semantics [8] and modular operational semantics [9].

In the next chapter, we will discuss type systems which enable static typing of programs, thereby ruling out "programs that go wrong" from even being considered for assigning semantics to them or, in fact, running them. Type systems are modeled by inference rules, just like operational semantics. Afterwards, we consider an alternative, more functional (less operational) approach to defining semantics, that is, denotational semantics.

References

1. Attali, I.: Compiling TYPOL with attribute grammars. In: Proc. PLILP 1988, *LNCS*, vol. 348, pp. 252–272. Springer (1989)
2. Attali, I., Caromel, D., Ehmety, S.O.: A natural semantics for Eiffel dynamic binding. ACM Trans. Program. Lang. Syst. **18**(6), 711–729 (1996)
3. Attali, I., Chazarain, J.: Functional evaluation of strongly non circular Typol specifications. In: Proc. WAGA, *LNCS*, vol. 461, pp. 157–176. Springer (1990)
4. Attali, I., Chazarain, J., Gilette, S.: Incremental evaluation of natural semantics specification. In: Proc. PLILP, *LNCS*, vol. 631, pp. 87–99. Springer (1992)
5. Attali, I., Courbis, C., Degenne, P., Fau, A., Parigot, D., Pasquier, C.: SmartTools: A generator of interactive environments tools. In: Proc. CC, *LNCS*, vol. 2027, pp. 355–360. Springer (2001)
6. Bertot, Y., Castéran, P.: Interactive Theorem Proving and Program Development. Coq'Art: The Calculus of Inductive Constructions. Texts in Theoretical Computer Science. An EATCS Series. Springer (2004)
7. Despeyroux, T.: TYPOL: A formalism to implement natural semantics. Tech. Rep. 94, INRIA (1988)
8. Felleisen, M., Hieb, R.: The revised report on the syntactic theories of sequential control and state. Theor. Comput. Sci. **103**(2), 235–271 (1992)
9. Mosses, P.D.: Modular structural operational semantics. J. Log. Algebr. Program. **60-61**, 195–228 (2004)
10. Nielson, F., Nielson, H.R.: Type and effect systems. In: Correct System Design, Recent Insight and Advances, *LNCS*, vol. 1710, pp. 114–136. Springer (1999)
11. Nielson, H.R., Nielson, F.: Semantics with Applications: An Appetizer. Undergraduate Topics in Computer Science. Springer (2007)
12. Nipkow, T., Paulson, L.C., Wenzel, M.: Isabelle/HOL: A Proof Assistant for Higher-Order Logic, *LNCS*, vol. 2283. Springer (2002)
13. Norell, U.: Dependently typed programming in Agda. In: AFP 2008, Revised Lectures, *LNCS*, vol. 5832, pp. 230–266. Springer (2009)
14. Pettersson, M.: Compiling Natural Semantics, *LNCS*, vol. 1549. Springer (1999)
15. Pfenning, F., Schürmann, C.: System description: Twelf – A meta-logical framework for deductive systems. In: Proc. CADE-16, *LNCS*, vol. 1632, pp. 202–206. Springer (1999)

Chapter 9
A Primer on Type Systems

BENJAMIN C. PIERCE.[1]

Abstract Types are semantic properties of program phrases. For instance, the type of an expression may model what type of value the expression would be evaluated to eventually, for example, the type of natural numbers or of Boolean values in an expression language. Types may be assigned to program phrases statically by means of a *type system* – this is a formal system consisting of inference rules, very much like a semantics definition. Assigned types ("properties") must predict runtime behavior in a sound manner, i.e., the properties should never be violated by the actual runtime behavior. This is also referred to as *type safety* (or *soundness*). The rules making up a type system are easily implemented as *type checkers*, for example, in Haskell, as we will demonstrate. In this chapter, we provide a (very) basic introduction to type systems.

---

[1] I bet that if you were to ask a programming language researcher for recommendations for textbooks on "programming language theory" with good coverage of "type systems", most lists would start with Benjamin C. Pierce's "Types and Programming Languages" [2]. Modest insiders just call it the "TAPL" book. This book and, even more so, the more specialized book "Advanced ..." [3] capture an incredibly thorough and comprehensive discussion of the broad topic of (mostly static) types, taking advantage of Pierce's distinguished academic career in the programming language field.

Artwork Credits for Chapter Opening: This work by Wojciech Kwasnik is licensed under CC BY-SA 4.0. This artwork quotes the artwork *DMT*, acrylic, 2006 by Matt Sheehy with the artist's permission. This work also quotes https://en.wikipedia.org/wiki/File:The_Mulberry_Tree_by_Vincent_van_Gogh.jpg, subject to the attribution "Vincent Van Gogh: The Mulberry Tree (1889) [Public domain], via Wikipedia." This work artistically morphes an image, https://www.cis.upenn.edu/~bcpierce/bio.html, showing the person honored, subject to the attribution "Permission granted by Benjamin C. Pierce for use in this book."

© Springer International Publishing AG, part of Springer Nature 2018
R. Lämmel, *Software Languages*,
https://doi.org/10.1007/978-3-319-90800-7_9

9.1 Types

A type system is a set of rules that assigns types to programs and parts thereof. Types are descriptions of properties that are meant to be abstractions over the runtime behavior of programs. For instance, the type of an expression may model what type of value the expression would be evaluated to at runtime, such that there are different types for numbers, truth values, and other things.

The type system of the simple expression language BTL distinguishes two types:

- nattype: the property of an expression that it evaluates to an element of *nat*, i.e., a natural number;
- booltype: the property of an expression that it evaluates to an element of *bool*, i.e., a Boolean value.

Types may be assigned to expressions, variables, functions, procedures, and so on. Not every syntactic category gives rise to a notion of type by itself. For instance, the statements in an imperative language may not have types themselves, but a type system would still apply to statements in that the well-typed use of variables and operators needs to be checked. Also, the type of a statement in a programming language with exceptions may model what sort of exceptions may be thrown by the statement.

9.2 Typing Judgments

A type system is meant to distinguish well-typed programs, i.e., programs with good properties, from ill-typed programs, i.e., programs that are incorrect or unreasonable in some sense. To this end, one leverages relations over program phrases (statements, expressions, etc.), types, and possibly other data structures such as collections of variable-type pairs. We refer to claims of such relationships as judgments, in fact as typing judgments, to distinguish them from judgments in operational semantics. For instance:

- *typeOf*(*e*, *T*): The expression *e* is of type *T*. This judgment may be suitable, for example, for the type system of an expression language like BTL.
- *typeOf*(*m*, *e*, *T*): The expression *e* is of type *T* in the context *m*, where the context may correspond to, for example, a collection of variable-type pairs. This judgment may be suitable, for example, for the type system of an imperative language like BIPL.
- *wellTyped*(*m*, *s*): The statement *s* is well-typed in the context *m*. This judgment may be suitable, for example, for the type system of an imperative language like BIPL.

In the literature, as a matter of convention, relation symbols are often not alphabetical, nor are they applied in prefix fashion. Instead, some infix or mixfix notation is used. For instance:

- $e : T$ instead of $typeOf(e, T)$.
- $m \vdash e : T$ instead of $typeOf(m, e, T)$.
- $m \vdash s$ instead of $wellTyped(m, s)$.

9.3 Typing Rules

We use inference rules to describe type systems, just as in operational semantics. The rule labels start with $t-\ldots$ ("t" for typing) to distinguish them from the rules for operational semantics. Each typing rule states the conditions (premises) under which program phrases according to a given syntactic pattern are well-typed. In the case of expressions, the typing rules also state the actual type of a given expression.

We are ready to complete the type system for BTL.

Specification 9.1 (Typing rules for BTL expressions)

$$\text{true} : \text{booltype} \qquad\qquad [\text{t}-\text{true}]$$

$$\text{false} : \text{booltype} \qquad\qquad [\text{t}-\text{false}]$$

$$\text{zero} : \text{nattype} \qquad\qquad [\text{t}-\text{zero}]$$

$$\frac{e : \text{nattype}}{\text{succ}(e) : \text{nattype}} \qquad\qquad [\text{t}-\text{succ}]$$

$$\frac{e : \text{nattype}}{\text{pred}(e) : \text{nattype}} \qquad\qquad [\text{t}-\text{pred}]$$

$$\frac{e : \text{nattype}}{\text{iszero}(e) : \text{booltype}} \qquad\qquad [\text{t}-\text{iszero}]$$

$$\frac{e_0 : \text{booltype} \quad e_1 : T \quad e_2 : T}{\text{if}(e_0, e_1, e_2) : T} \qquad\qquad [\text{t}-\text{if}]$$

We read out the rules in the specification above for clarity:

- [t−true], [t−false]: The constants true and false are of type booltype.
- [t−zero]: The constant zero is of type nattype.

- [t−succ], [t−pred]: A term of the form succ(e) or pred(e) is of type nattype, provided e is of type nattype.
- [t−iszero]: A term of the form iszero(e) is of type booltype, provided e is of type nattype.
- [t−if]: A term of the form if(e_0, e_1, e_2) is of type T (either nattype or booltype), provided e_0 is of type booltype and both e_1 and e_2 are of type T.

The big-step style of operational semantics and type systems are very similar. In the case of semantics, the rules state how the constituents of a program phrase (e.g., an expression) are to be evaluated or executed to complete evaluation or execution of the phrase as a whole. In the case of typing, the rules state what conditions have to be satisfied by the constituents for the phrase to be well-typed as a whole.

9.4 Typing Derivations

To attest a certain type for an expression or, more generally, well-typedness for a given phrase, we need to build a derivation tree, in the same way as we used derivation trees for the evaluation or execution of phrases in the context of big-step operational semantics. We use the term "typing derivation" for clarity. Let us prove the following judgment:

$$\text{pred}(\text{if}(\text{iszero}(\text{zero}), \text{succ}(\text{zero}), \text{zero})) : \text{nattype}$$

The typing derivation is shown in Fig. 9.1. Each node in the tree is an instance of a conclusion of an inference rule. The subtrees of a node are instances of the premises of the same rule. The leaf nodes of the tree are instances of axioms. By "instance" we mean that metavariables in the rules are consistently replaced by phrases or data structures, or patterns thereof.

When a given typing judgment cannot be proven, then we speak of a type error. For instance, the following judgment cannot be proven:

$$\text{succ}(\text{true}) : \text{nattype}$$

The type error is that succ must not be applied to a Boolean value.

9.5 Type Safety

A type system can be thought of as rejecting programs that may "go wrong". Such rejection happens ahead of running the program and hence the term "static typing" is used. Any semantics should need to cover only well-typed programs. That is, a semantics does not need to define a possibly nonintuitive semantics for programs that

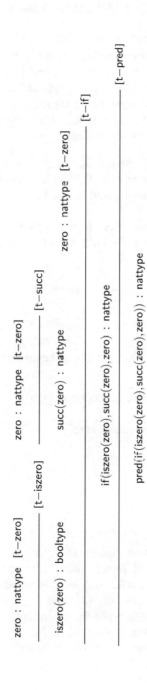

Fig. 9.1 A typing derivation for BTL.

we wish to rule out anyway. Derivation according to a small-step operational semantics would be allowed to get "stuck" for ill-typed programs, as discussed earlier (Section 8.2.2).

Accordingly, a type system must be understood relative to a given semantics since we think of the type system as making predictions about the runtime behavior of program phrases. Thus, a combination of semantics and type system must be consistent in a certain way, giving rise to the notion of type safety or soundness.

We explain type safety in terms of the situation for the expression language BTL. Without loss of generality, we relate a type system to a small-step rather than a big-step operational semantics. Type safety consists of two aspects:

Preservation   For all expressions e, if there exists a type T such that $e : T$ and an expression e' such that $e \rightarrow e'$, then $e' : T$. That is, if the one-step relation returns a new expression, then the new expression has the same type as the initial expression.

Progress   For all expressions e, if there exists a type T such that $e : T$, then either $e \in value$ or there exists an expression e' such that $e \rightarrow e'$. As a corollary, stuck expressions are not well-typed.

Illustration 9.1 (Preservation for BTL)
For instance, consider the following elements of a complete derivation sequence for evaluating a BTL expression; the elements are all of type nattype, *as one can easily verify with the help of the typing rules. Thus, the type* nattype *is indeed preserved:*

$$\mathsf{pred}(\mathsf{if}(\mathsf{iszero}(\mathsf{zero}), \mathsf{succ}(\mathsf{zero}), \mathsf{zero}))$$

$$\Rightarrow \mathsf{pred}(\mathsf{if}(\mathsf{true}, \mathsf{succ}(\mathsf{zero}), \mathsf{zero}))$$

$$\Rightarrow \mathsf{pred}(\mathsf{succ}(\mathsf{zero}))$$

$$\Rightarrow \mathsf{zero}$$

A proof of type safety would thus show that all well-typed expressions preserve their type in derivation sequences and that the semantics never gets "stuck" for well-typed expressions. The definition of type safety may need some adjustment for more complex languages, but the general idea remains the same.

Because of how syntax-driven both semantics and typing rules are, the proofs of these properties are relatively straightforward – at least for simple languages. An essential technique is induction on typing derivations. We refer interested readers to TAPL [2].

Exercise 9.1 (Type safety for functional programs)   [Basic level]
The above formulation is specific to the simple situation of the expression language BTL without context in judgments. Define type safety for the functional programming language BFPL.

Exercise 9.2 (Type safety for big-step style)   [Intermediate level]
The above formulation assumes a small-step semantics. Can you reformulate type safety so that it applies to the setting of big-step operational semantics?

9.6 Type Checking

We have already discussed type checking in an informal manner in Section 5.3.1. Let us now discuss how to implement the inference rules of a type system directly (systematically) for the purpose of type checking. Such an implementation can commence in a manner similar to that for operational semantics (Section 8.1.5). While "executable" operational semantics serve the purpose of interpretation, "executable" type systems do so for *type checking*. That is, a *type checker* is used to verify that the rules of the type system are obeyed by a given program, i.e., the program is well-typed.

Here is how we expect to use a type checker for BTL expressions:

Interactive Haskell session:

```
▶ typeOf (Succ Zero)
Just NatType
- - - - - - - - - - - - - - - - - - - - - - - - - - - - - - - - - - - - - - - - -
▶ typeOf (Succ TRUE)
Nothing
```

We are ready to present the code for the type checker.

Illustration 9.2 (Type checking of expressions)

Haskell module Language.BTL.TypeCheckerWithGuards

```
-- Types of expressions
data Type = NatType | BoolType

-- Well-typedness of expressions
wellTyped :: Expr → Bool
wellTyped e | Just _ ← typeOf e = True
wellTyped e | otherwise = False
```

```
-- Types of expressions
typeOf :: Expr → Maybe Type
typeOf TRUE = Just BoolType
typeOf FALSE = Just BoolType
typeOf Zero = Just NatType
typeOf (Succ e) | Just NatType ← typeOf e = Just NatType
typeOf (Pred e) | Just NatType ← typeOf e = Just NatType
typeOf (IsZero e) | Just NatType ← typeOf e = Just BoolType
typeOf (If e0 e1 e2) |
   Just BoolType ← typeOf e0,
   Just t1 ← typeOf e1,
   Just t2 ← typeOf e2,
   t1 == t2 = Just t1
typeOf _ = Nothing
```

The implementation shown above is based on systematic mapping of typing rules to functional program equations implementing a type checker. That is, the inference rules of the type system are mapped to Haskell equations in a one-to-one manner; this ideal was set out for operational semantics earlier (Section 8.1.5.3).

With reference to the earlier recipe for implementing inference rules (Recipe 8.1) and the "I/O" aspect in particular, the underlying inference rules allow us to implement the type checker in such a manner that it returns the type of an expression as a result, i.e., the type must not be stated upfront.

9.7 More Examples of Type Systems

We define the type systems of a few more "fabricated" languages here.

9.7.1 Well-Typedness of Simple Imperative Programs

Let us define the type system for the imperative programming language BIPL. There are two expression types T: inttype and booltype. As BIPL does not assume explicit variable declarations, we need to somehow "infer" the types of variables. We decide here that the type of a variable is undefined prior to the first assignment, which defines the type for subsequent statements.

The typing judgments for expressions and statements carry a context for the types of variables. (In compilation, we would speak of symbol tables instead of contexts.) We also require auxiliary judgments to describe valid operand and result types for unary and binary operators. Thus:

- $\vdash s$: The program, which is a sequence s of statements, is well-typed.
- $m \vdash s : m'$: The statement s in the context m is of type m'. Both m and m' are collections of variable-type pairs. The first collection, m, models types of

variables prior to statement execution. The second collection, m', models types of variables after execution.

- $m \vdash e : T$: The expression e is of type T in the context m for the collection of variable-type pairs.
- $unary(uo, T) : T'$: The unary operator uo requires the argument type T and the result type T'.
- $binary(bo, T_1, T_2) : T'$: The binary operator bo requires the argument types T_1 and T_2 and the result type T'.

We are ready to complete the type system for BIPL by listing the actual typing rules.

Specification 9.2 (Typing rules for simple imperative programs)

Well-typedness of programs

$$\frac{\emptyset \vdash s : m}{\vdash s} \qquad \text{[t−program]}$$

Types of statements

$$\frac{m \vdash e : T \quad x \notin m}{m \vdash \mathsf{assign}(x, e) : m[x \mapsto T]} \qquad \text{[t−assign1]}$$

$$\frac{m \vdash e : T \quad \langle x, T \rangle \in m}{m \vdash \mathsf{assign}(x, e) : m} \qquad \text{[t−assign2]}$$

$$\frac{m_0 \vdash s_1 : m_1 \quad m_1 \vdash s_2 : m_2}{m_0 \vdash \mathsf{seq}(s_1, s_2) : m_2} \qquad \text{[t−seq]}$$

$$\frac{m_1 \vdash e : \mathsf{booltype} \quad m_1 \vdash s_1 : m_2 \quad m_1 \vdash s_2 : m_2}{m_1 \vdash \mathsf{if}(e, s_1, s_2) : m_2} \qquad \text{[t−if]}$$

$$\frac{m \vdash e : \mathsf{booltype} \quad m \vdash s : m}{m \vdash \mathsf{while}(e, s) : m} \qquad \text{[t−while]}$$

Types of expressions

$$m \vdash \mathsf{intconst}(i) \;:\; \mathsf{inttype}$$ [t−intconst]

$$\frac{m(x) \mapsto T}{m \vdash \mathsf{var}(x) \;:\; T}$$ [t−var]

$$\frac{m \vdash e \;:\; T \quad \mathit{unary}(uo,T) \;:\; T'}{m \vdash \mathsf{unary}(uo,e) \;:\; T'}$$ [t−unary]

$$\frac{m \vdash e_1 \;:\; T_1 \quad m \vdash e_2 \;:\; T_2 \quad \mathit{binary}(bo,T_1,T_2) \;:\; T'}{m \vdash \mathsf{binary}(bo,e_1,e_2) \;:\; T'}$$ [t−binary]

Signatures of operators

$\mathit{unary}(\mathsf{negate},\mathsf{inttype}) \;:\; \mathsf{inttype}$ [t−negate]

$\mathit{unary}(\mathsf{not},\mathsf{booltype}) \;:\; \mathsf{booltype}$ [t−not]

$\mathit{binary}(\mathsf{or},\mathsf{booltype},\mathsf{booltype}) \;:\; \mathsf{booltype}$ [t−or]

$\mathit{binary}(\mathsf{and},\mathsf{booltype},\mathsf{booltype}) \;:\; \mathsf{booltype}$ [t−and]

$\mathit{binary}(\mathsf{lt},\mathsf{inttype},\mathsf{inttype}) \;:\; \mathsf{booltype}$ [t−lt]

$\mathit{binary}(\mathsf{le},\mathsf{inttype},\mathsf{inttype}) \;:\; \mathsf{booltype}$ [t−le]

$\mathit{binary}(\mathsf{eq},\mathsf{inttype},\mathsf{inttype}) \;:\; \mathsf{booltype}$ [t−eq]

$\mathit{binary}(\mathsf{geq},\mathsf{inttype},\mathsf{inttype}) \;:\; \mathsf{booltype}$ [t−geq]

$\mathit{binary}(\mathsf{gt},\mathsf{inttype},\mathsf{inttype}) \;:\; \mathsf{booltype}$ [t−gt]

$\mathit{binary}(\mathsf{add},\mathsf{inttype},\mathsf{inttype}) \;:\; \mathsf{inttype}$ [t−add]

$\mathit{binary}(\mathsf{sub},\mathsf{inttype},\mathsf{inttype}) \;:\; \mathsf{inttype}$ [t−sub]

$\mathit{binary}(\mathsf{mul},\mathsf{inttype},\mathsf{inttype}) \;:\; \mathsf{inttype}$ [t−mul]

The inference rules leverage some special notation:

- $x \notin m$: This form of premise, as exercised in rule [t−assign1], should be read to mean that there is no type T' such that $\langle x, T' \rangle \in m$.
- $m[x \mapsto T]$: This form of premise, as exercised in rule [t−assign1], denotes the variable-type pairs m updated in the position x to be associated with type T while being identical to m in all other positions.
- $m(x) \mapsto T$: This form of premise, as exercised in rule [t−var], applies a map m for variable-type pairs in the sense of function application. The premise fails if the given variable identifier x is not mapped to any type T.

Thus, a program, i.e., in fact, a statement s, is well-typed if there exists some collection m of variable-type pairs such that s, when considered as a statement, is of "type" m starting from the empty collection $\emptyset$.

The typing rules for statements track variable types during execution for the reasons discussed above. That is, variable types are inferred from assignments. The first typing rule for assignments applies when variable x has no type assigned yet. This rule assigns the type of the right-hand side expression to the left-hand side variable. The second typing rule for assignments applies when the left-hand side variable is readily assigned to the right-hand side expression's type; the variable-type pairs are preserved in this case. This also means that a variable cannot change its type.

The typing rule for a statement sequence $\text{seq}(s_1, s_2)$ infers context m_1 from s_1 starting from context m_0 and then it infers context m_2 from s_2 starting from context m_1. The typing rule for if-statements assumes that then- and else-branches agree on the resulting variable-type pairs. The typing rule for while-statements is restrictive in the interest of simplifying the discussion of soundness. That is, no additional variables can have a type assigned within the body of a while-loop.

The typing rules for expressions assign suitable types to the constant forms; the type of a variable is looked up from the context and the operand and result types of unary and binary operators are checked against suitable operator signatures.

Here is how we expect to use the type checker on the sample program for Euclidean division; we supply enough type context for the arguments x and y and type checking determines that the program variables q and r are of type IntType:

Interactive Haskell session:

▶ okStmt euclideanDiv (fromList [("x", IntType), ("y", IntType)])
Just (fromList [("q", IntType), ("r", IntType), ("x", IntType), ("y", IntType)])

We are ready to present the code for the type checker.

Illustration 9.3 (Type checking of imperative programs)

Haskell module Language.BIPL.TypeChecker

```
-- Types of expressions
data Type = IntType | BoolType

-- Variable-type pairs (maps)
type VarTypes = Map String Type

-- Well-typedness of statements
okStmt :: Stmt → VarTypes → Maybe VarTypes
okStmt Skip ctx = Just ctx
okStmt (Assign x e) ctx =
  case typeOfExpr e ctx of
    Nothing → Nothing
    (Just ty) → case lookup x ctx of
      Nothing → Just (insert x ty ctx)
      (Just ty') → if ty==ty' then Just ctx else Nothing
okStmt (Seq s1 s2) ctx =
  case okStmt s1 ctx of
    (Just ctx') → okStmt s2 ctx'
    Nothing → Nothing
okStmt (If e s1 s2) ctx =
  case typeOfExpr e ctx of
    (Just BoolType) →
      case (okStmt s1 ctx, okStmt s2 ctx) of
        (Just ctx1, Just ctx2) →
          if ctx1==ctx2 then Just ctx1 else Nothing
        _ → Nothing
    _ → Nothing
okStmt (While e s) ctx =
  case typeOfExpr e ctx of
    (Just BoolType) →
      case okStmt s ctx of
        (Just ctx') →
          if ctx==ctx' then Just ctx else Nothing
        _ → Nothing
    _ → Nothing

-- Types of expressions
typeOfExpr :: Expr → VarTypes → Maybe Type
typeOfExpr (IntConst i) _ = Just IntType
typeOfExpr (Var x) ctx = lookup x ctx
typeOfExpr (Unary o e) ctx =
  case (o, typeOfExpr e ctx) of
    (Negate, Just IntType) → Just IntType
    (Not, Just BoolType) → Just BoolType
    _ → Nothing
typeOfExpr (Binary o e1 e2) ctx = ...
```

With reference to the earlier recipe for implementing inference rules (Recipe 8.1) and the "I/O" aspect in particular, the variable-type pairs serve both as the argument and the result of the function okStmt for checking well-typedness of statements.

Exercise 9.3 (Local variables in while-loops)   [Basic level]
Suggest a less restrictive typing rule for while-loops such that local variables can be used within loops.

Exercise 9.4 (Variable declarations)   [Basic level]
Revise BIPL to feature explicit variable declarations preceding the statement part so that the types of all variables are declared for the statement part of a program. You may assume the following abstract syntax:

```
// Programs
type program = vardecl∗ × stmt ;
// Variable declarations
type vardecl = string × expr ;
// Statements
symbol skip : → stmt ;
symbol assign : string × expr → stmt ;
symbol seq : stmt × stmt → stmt ;
symbol if : expr × stmt × stmt → stmt ;
symbol while : expr × stmt → stmt ;
// Expressions
...
```

As evident from the syntax, it is assumed here that a variable declaration includes initialization; the initializing expression defines the type of the variable.

Specify the semantics and type system for the revised language. A variable may only be used in the statement part if it has been declared. As before, a variable cannot change its type. It should be clear that the revised typing judgment for statements is no longer expected to assign "types" to variables. We show the original judgment and the intended one for the revision next to each other for clarity:

- $m \vdash s : m'$: *type assignment in the original type system;*
- $m \vdash s$: *well-typedness in the revised type system.*

Exercise 9.5 (Gotos)   [Intermediate level]
Define a type system for BIPL with gotos and without while-loops. (While-loops can be encoded in such a language by means of if-statements and gotos.) The type system must model consistent declaration and referencing of labels. That is, each label can only be placed once in a program. Further, each label referred to in a goto statement must be declared.

9.7.2 Well-Typedness of Simple Functional Programs

Let us define the type system for the functional programming language BFPL.

Specification 9.3 (The type system of simple functional programs)

Metavariables:

- *expression types T:* inttype *and* booltype.

Judgments:

- $\vdash \langle fs, e \rangle$: *the program, which consists of a list fs of functions and a main expression e, is well-typed;*
- $fs \vdash f$: *the function f is well-typed while assuming the list fs of functions as context (to be able to type-check function applications in the body of f);*
- $fs, m \vdash e : T$: *the expression e is of type T in the context fs for the applicable functions and m for argument-type pairs;*
- *auxiliary judgments for signatures of unary and binary operators, as introduced for BIPL.*

Well-typedness of programs

$$\frac{fs = \langle f_1, \ldots, f_n \rangle \quad fs \vdash f_1 \quad \cdots \quad fs \vdash f_n \quad fs, \emptyset \vdash e : T}{\vdash \langle fs, e \rangle} \quad [\text{t}-\text{program}]$$

Well-typedness of functions

$$\frac{fs, [x_1 \mapsto T_1, \ldots, x_n \mapsto T_n] \vdash e : T_0}{fs \vdash \langle x, \langle \langle T_1, \ldots, T_n \rangle, T_0 \rangle, \langle \langle x_1, \ldots, x_n \rangle, e \rangle \rangle} \quad [\text{t}-\text{function}]$$

Types of expressions

$$fs, m \vdash \text{intconst}(i) : \text{inttype} \qquad\qquad\qquad\qquad [\text{t}-\text{intconst}]$$

$$fs, m \vdash \text{boolconst}(b) : \text{booltype} \qquad\qquad\qquad [\text{t}-\text{boolconst}]$$

$$\frac{\langle x, T \rangle \in m}{fs, m \vdash \text{arg}(x) : T} \qquad\qquad\qquad\qquad [\text{t}-\text{arg}]$$

$$\frac{fs,m \vdash e_0 : \text{booltype} \quad fs,m \vdash e_1 : T \quad fs,m \vdash e_2 : T}{fs,m \vdash \text{if}(e_0,e_1,e_2) : T} \quad \text{[t−if]}$$

$$\frac{fs,m \vdash e : T \quad \underline{unary}(uo,T) : T'}{fs,m \vdash \text{unary}(uo,e) : T'} \quad \text{[t−unary]}$$

$$\frac{fs,m \vdash e_1 : T_1 \quad fs,m \vdash e_2 : T_2 \quad \underline{binary}(bo,T_1,T_2) : T'}{fs,m \vdash \text{binary}(bo,e_1,e_2) : T'} \quad \text{[t−binary]}$$

$$\frac{\begin{array}{c} fs,m \vdash e_1 : T_1 \quad \cdots \quad fs,m \vdash e_n : T_n \\ \langle x, \langle \langle T_1,\ldots,T_n \rangle, T_0 \rangle, \langle \langle x_1,\ldots,x_n \rangle, e \rangle \rangle \in fs \end{array}}{fs,m \vdash \text{apply}(x, \langle e_1,\ldots,e_n \rangle) : T_0} \quad \text{[t−apply]}$$

Thus, a program is well-typed if all its defined functions are well-typed and the main expression is of some type T for the empty collection of variable-type pairs. A function is well-typed if its body is of the type T_0 prescribed by its signature while assuming an appropriate context for the function's arguments, as prescribed by the signature as well.

Let us implement a type checker. We aim at making good use of the metalanguage to arrive at concise and idiomatic Haskell code.

Illustration 9.4 (Type checking of functional programs)

Haskell module Language.BFPL.TypeChecker

```
−− Argument−type pairs
type Context = [(String, SimpleType)]

−− Well−typedness of programs
okProgram :: Program → Bool
okProgram (fs, e) = okFunctions && okMain
   where
     okFunctions = and (map (okFunction fs) fs)
     okMain = maybe False (const True) (typeOfExpr fs [] e)

−− Well−typedness of a function
okFunction :: [Function] → Function → Bool
okFunction fs (_, ((ts, res), (ns, body))) = okLength && maybe False (==res) okBody
   where
     okLength = length ns == length ts
     okBody = typeOfExpr fs m body
     m = zip ns ts
```

```
—— Types of expressions
typeOfExpr :: [Function] → Context → Expr → Maybe SimpleType
typeOfExpr _ _ (IntConst _) = Just IntType
typeOfExpr _ _ (BoolConst _) = Just BoolType
typeOfExpr fs m (Arg x) = lookup x m
typeOfExpr fs m (If e0 e1 e2)
   = do
        t0 ← typeOfExpr fs m e0
        t1 ← typeOfExpr fs m e1
        t2 ← typeOfExpr fs m e2
        if t0 == BoolType && t1 == t2 then Just t1 else Nothing
typeOfExpr fs m (Unary o e)
   = do
        t ← typeOfExpr fs m e
        case (o, t) of
           (Negate, IntType) → Just IntType
           (Not, BoolType) → Just BoolType
           _ → Nothing
typeOfExpr fs m (Binary o e1 e2)
   = do
        ...
typeOfExpr fs m (Apply fn es)
   = do
        ((ts, r), _) ← lookup fn fs
        ts' ← mapM (typeOfExpr fs m) es
        if ts == ts' then Just r else Nothing
```

That is, we make good use of list-processing functions in the Haskell code (see the uses of map and mapM, for example) to process lists of functions, argument names, values, etc. Also, we use monad notation (see do ⋯) for the Maybe monad to compose the typing derivations for expressions.

Exercise 9.6 (Type system versus implementation)   [Basic level]
Identify specific idiomatic differences between the original type system of BFPL and the type checker given above. That is, how does the type checker deviate from a mechanical translation of the original inference rules into Haskell?

Exercise 9.7 (Local binding groups)   [Intermediate level]
Define the syntax, the semantics, and the type system for an extended BFPL language with local binding groups based on Haskell's familiar "where" syntax. Consider the following example:

```
—— The factorial function
factorial :: Int −> Int
factorial x =
    if (==) x 0
       then 1
       else (*) x (factorial y)
    where
```

```
y :: Int
y = (−) x 1
```

−− Apply the factorial function
main = print $ factorial 5 *−− Prints 120*

That is, y *is declared locally to* factorial *and it can therefore refer to* x, *which is bound by* factorial.

9.7.3 Well-Formedness of Finite State Machines

Not every software language explicitly involves distinct types of expressions of other syntactic categories. Still, the correct use of the language may be subject to constraints that can be formalized and implemented in ways that are similar to type systems and type checking. In this context, we remind the reader of the earlier discussion of context conditions (Section 3.3).

Exercise 9.8 (Well-formedness of FSMs)   [Intermediate level]
As discussed earlier (Section 5.3.2), FSMs need to satisfy several constraints. Devise inference rules for checking that (i) there is exactly one initial state; (ii) all state declarations have distinct names; (iii) all state ids for targets of transition are resolvable to a state declaration with the same id; and (iv) the transitions of each state are concerned with distinct events.

Summary and Outline

We have given a basic introduction to type systems – these are formal systems for assigning properties to programs and program phrases statically such that these properties correctly and usefully predict the runtime behavior of programs. We have leveraged inference rules for the definition of type systems, just as in the case of operational semantics. Further, we have demonstrated how type systems are implemented as type checkers for rejecting programs that may "go wrong". We have only considered very simple languages. We have not considered type inference (except for tracking variable types in simple imperative programs in Section 9.7.1). A type inference algorithm is supposed to infer types of variables, functions, or other abstractions that lack explicit type declarations – typically with the involvement of polymorphism. To this end, an algorithmic constraint system on non-ground type expressions is leveraged.

In the next chapter, we will discuss the lambda calculus and thereby touch upon some less basic aspects of type systems: scoping rules, polymorphism, structural and nominal typing, and subtyping. Afterwards, we will study denotational semantics as an alternative approach to defining semantics.

In-depth coverage of type systems can be found in the "TAPL" textbook [2]. We also refer to Cardelli and Wegner's seminal text on type systems [1] for an introduction to type systems.

References

1. Cardelli, L., Wegner, P.: On understanding types, data abstraction, and polymorphism. ACM Comput. Surv. **17**(4), 471–522 (1985)
2. Pierce, B.: Types and Programming Languages. MIT Press (2002)
3. Pierce, B.: Advanced Topics in Types and Programming Languages. MIT Press (2004)

Chapter 10
An Excursion into the Lambda Calculus

HENK BARENDREGT.[1]

Abstract The lambda calculus is an idealized programming language which captures the core of functional programming and serves as a notion of computability. The lambda calculus is also a good foundation for studying programming language concepts generally by means of adding dedicated extensions to the basic calculus. Our excursion into the lambda calculus is meant here to let us briefly visit a number of language concepts and aspects of semantics and typing that are of general interest in language design, definition, and implementation. This includes the notions of substitution, fixed-point computation, encoding, and type variance.

---

[1] The lambda calculus (or, in fact, the lambda calculi or the lambda cube [1]) is a beautiful pillar (a formal tool) of theoretical computer science, logic, and programming language theory [2, 3]. It has taken much more than its initial introduction by Alonzo Church to remain relevant to today's research and to have become a standard tool in programming language design and type theory. Henk Barendregt deserves much credit in this regard.

Artwork Credits for Chapter Opening: This work by Wojciech Kwasnik is licensed under CC BY-SA 4.0. This artwork quotes the artwork *DMT*, acrylic, 2006 by Matt Sheehy with the artist's permission. This work also quotes https://commons.wikimedia.org/wiki/File:Van_Gogh_-_Starry_Night_-_Google_Art_Project.jpg, subject to the attribution "Vincent Van Gogh: The Starry Night (1889) [Public domain], via Wikimedia Commons." This work artistically morphes an image, https://en.wikipedia.org/wiki/Henk_Barendregt, showing the person honored, subject to the attribution "By Jan Benda - Own work, CC BY-SA 3.0, https://commons.wikimedia.org/w/index.php?curid=19135230."

© Springer International Publishing AG, part of Springer Nature 2018
R. Lämmel, *Software Languages*,
https://doi.org/10.1007/978-3-319-90800-7_10

10.1 The Untyped Lambda Calculus

We will describe several progressions of the lambda calculus: the pure untyped calculus as a starting point, an extension which adds predefined values and operations (comparable to BTL or BFPL expressions, as discussed earlier), a fixed-point combinator (comparable to recursive functions in BFPL, as discussed earlier), a simply typed calculus, a calculus with support for polymorphism (as present in many languages including Haskell), an extension for records (comparable to, for example, structs in C) and variants (or sums), subtyping for records and variants, and an extension for nominal typing (comparable to algebraic data types in Haskell). We begin with the untyped lambda calculus; this is arguably the simplest calculus in the lambda cube [1].

10.1.1 Syntax

The syntax of the (untyped) lambda calculus is extremely simple. There are three constructs (*lambda*, *var*, and *apply*). Let us look at examples.

The following lambda expression denotes the identity function:

$$lambda(x, var(x))$$

That is, the identity function is represented as a lambda abstraction, i.e., an anonymous function. The first occurrence of x binds the function's argument. The second occurrence of x is in the body of the function, i.e., $var(x)$, thereby referring to the argument. Thus, x is "bound" and x is "returned" – which is why this is the identity function.

The following lambda expression denotes function composition:

$$lambda(f, lambda(g, lambda(x, apply(var(f), apply(var(g), var(x))))))$$

This expression binds three arguments, f, g, and x, by means of a nested lambda abstraction. In the final body, g is applied to x and f is applied on top – which is why this is function composition.

Thus, the constructs of the lambda calculus are these: *variable* (reference), *lambda abstraction*, and *function application*. In the literature, it is common to use a concrete syntax for lambda expressions such as the following:

- x instead of $var(x)$;
- $e_1\ e_2$ instead of $apply(e_1, e_2)$;
- $\lambda x.\ e$ instead of $lambda(x, e)$.

This notation goes with the convention that application associates to the left, for example, $e_1\ e_2\ e_3 = (e_1\ e_2)\ e_3$. We may also abbreviate nested lambda abstractions, for example, $\lambda x_1 x_2.\ e = \lambda x_1.\ (\lambda x_2.\ e)$.

In this concrete syntax, we represent the earlier examples as follows:

> // Identity function
> $\lambda x. x$
> // Function composition
> $\lambda f\, g\, x.\, f\, (g\, x)$

Lambda abstractions are viewed as "values" (normal forms) in the sense of reduction, as we will see below. We use metavariables as follows:

- lambda expressions e;
- variable identifiers x;
- values (lambda abstractions) v.

The lambda calculus is indeed the core of functional programming and, thus, functional programming languages may express lambda expressions. For instance, the identity function and function composition are expressed in Haskell as follows:

Interactive Haskell session:

```
▶ let id = λ x → x
▶ let (.) = λ f g x → f (g x)
▶ id 42
42
▶ (not . not) True
True
```

The concrete syntax of Haskell is slightly different from the proposed notation, but all constructs – lambda abstraction, variable reference, and function application – show up in the session's code. We have leveraged some additional language constructs, let and primitive values, for the purpose of a more accessible and meaningful illustration.

10.1.2 Semantics

Let us discuss the semantics of the untyped lambda calculus – in fact, one specific option such that function arguments are normalized before the function is applied. This option is also referred to as call-by-value as opposed to call-by-need, which would essentially imply that function arguments are evaluated only when they are actually "needed" by the function. The following rules commit to the small-step style of operational semantics.

Specification 10.1 (Call-by-value semantics of untyped lambda calculus)

Reduction of lambda expressions

$$\frac{e_1 \to e_1'}{e_1 \, e_2 \to e_1' \, e_2} \qquad\qquad \text{[app1]}$$

$$\frac{e_2 \to e_2'}{v_1 \, e_2 \to v_1 \, e_2'} \qquad\qquad \text{[app2]}$$

$$(\lambda x. \, e) \, v \to [v/x]e \qquad\qquad \text{[beta]}$$

Values

$$\lambda x. \, e \in value \qquad\qquad \text{[v$-$lambda]}$$

Rule [app1] performs a step on the function position of an application. Rule [app2] assumes a value for the function position and performs a step on the argument position of an application. Rule [beta] leverages a special notation, $[v/x]e$, which denotes the substitution of x by v in e. We will discuss substitution in more detail below. Overall, rule [beta] models what is called *beta reduction* – a function application with a lambda abstraction $\lambda x. \, e$ on the function position and a value v on the argument position performs a step by substituting x by v in e. Rule [v$-$lambda] describes the value form, i.e., the intended normal form.

10.1.3 Substitution

As simple as this semantics may seem, there is some hidden complexity in how exactly substitution (beta reduction) works. Substitution is not specific to the lambda calculus. Substitution is also needed for the binding constructs of other languages. That is, we need to fully understand substitution.

Before we define substitution, we need to discuss the auxiliary notion of free variables, as the distinction between free and bound variables is an important detail constraining substitution. The following recursive function maps a lambda expression to the set of free variables.

Specification 10.2 (Free variables of a lambda expression)

$$FREE(x) \quad = \{x\}$$
$$FREE(e_1 \, e_2) = FREE(e_1) \cup FREE(e_2)$$
$$FREE(\lambda x. \, e) = FREE(e) \setminus \{x\}$$

Thus, all variables occurring in an expression are free unless they are bound in a lambda expression, in which case the variable is bound in the scope of the lambda expression. An expression without free variables is called a *closed expression*; otherwise, it is called an *open expression*. When normalizing a lambda expression, we usually assume that we start from a closed expression. Substitution is defined below.

Specification 10.3 (Substitution for the lambda calculus)
Given expressions e, e′, and a variable x, substitution of x by e within e′ is denoted by [e/x]e′ and defined by case discrimination over e′ as follows:

$$[e/x]x \quad = e$$
$$[e/x]y \quad = y \; if \, x \neq y$$
$$[e/x]e_1 \, e_2 = ([e/x]e_1) \, ([e/x]e_2)$$
$$[e/x]\lambda x. \, e′ = \lambda x. \, e′$$
$$[e/x]\lambda y. \, e′ = \lambda y. \, [e/x]e′ \; if \, x \neq y \; and \; y \notin FREE(e)$$

The first two cases are base cases such that substitution is applied to a variable, which is either the variable x to be replaced or a different variable y. The case for function applications simply pushes substitution into subexpressions. The first case for lambda abstractions cancels substitution, as the variable x in question is re-bound. That is, the substitution does not continue into the body of the lambda abstraction. The second case for lambda abstractions, i.e., the last case, pushes substitution into the body of the lambda abstraction with a bound variable y different from the variable x to be replaced.

Importantly, the last case carries an extra condition which states that y must not be free in the expression e that is meant to replace x. Without this condition, we would allow the free variable y in e to be "captured" by the lambda abstraction. In order to make substitution a total operation, we assume that we apply what is called *alpha conversion* whenever the extra condition is not met. That is, the locally bound y is renamed to another variable so that the last rule can be applied.

In fact, variable identifiers in the lambda calculus can be consistently renamed without changing the semantics of lambda expressions. Expressions that can be converted into each other by alpha conversion are called *alpha-equivalent*. For instance, $\lambda a. \, a$ and $\lambda b. \, b$, both denoting the identity function, are alpha-equivalent. Such consistent renaming is also valid for some binding constructs of many other programming languages.

Exercise 10.1 (Alpha equivalence)   [Basic level]
Implement alpha equivalence in a declarative program. That is, given two expressions, return true if they can be alpha-converted into each other; otherwise, return false.

Exercise 10.2 (Substitution as a total operation)   [Intermediate level]
Implement substitution as a total operation in a declarative program. In order to achieve totality, you will need to implement the last case in Specification 10.3 such that alpha conversion is applied if necessary. A robust scheme is needed to identify a "fresh" variable identifier to be used for alpha conversion.

10.1.4 Predefined Values and Operations

We extend the untyped lambda calculus here to incorporate the expression language BTL, which essentially provides predefined values and operations for natural numbers and Boolean values. The result is also referred to as an applied lambda calculus. This extension is supposed to provide us with a more practically useful calculus. Table 10.1 summarize the abstract and concrete syntax of the calculus.

Table 10.1 Syntax of the applied lambda calculus

Abstract syntax	Concrete syntax
$\mathsf{var}(x)$	x
$\mathsf{lambda}(x,e)$	$\lambda x.\ e$
$\mathsf{apply}(e_1,e_2)$	$e_1\ e_2$
true	true
false	false
zero	zero
$\mathsf{succ}(e)$	succ e
$\mathsf{pred}(e)$	pred e
$\mathsf{iszero}(e)$	iszero e
$\mathsf{if}(e_1,e_2,e_3)$	if e_1 then e_2 else e_3

The small-step operational semantics of the applied lambda calculus is also just the trivial combination of the semantics of the contributing languages. Arguably, this style of composing the untyped lambda calculus and BTL leads to some redundancy because the rules for the constructs succ, pred, iszero, and if involve some elements of function application, which is already present in the untyped lambda calculus.

Exercise 10.3 (Predefined values and operations)   [Intermediate level]
Suggest a more compact applied lambda calculus which addresses the aforementioned redundancy issue.

10.1.5 Fixed-Point Computation

We seem to have arrived at a simple functional programming language. If only we had expressiveness for recursive functions, then we could define, for example, the factorial function on top of addition and multiplication:

add $= \lambda n\ m.$ if iszero n then m else succ $(add$ (pred $n)\ m)$
mul $= \lambda n\ m.$ if iszero n then zero else $add\ m$ $(mul$ (pred $n)\ m)$
$factorial = \lambda n.$ if iszero n then succ zero else $mul\ n$ $(factorial$ (pred $n))$

However, recursive definitions like this are not expressible in the lambda calculus developed thus far; there is no recursive binding construct. As a canny remedy, let us add expressiveness for fixed-point computation. That is, we assume the existence of a fixed-point combinator; it is easily characterized by the following fixed-point property:

$$fix\ f = f(fix\ f)$$

That is, the fixed point of a function f equals the application of the function to the fixed point of the function. While this property essentially defines the meaning of the term "fixed point", it is also directly useful in computing the fixed point, once we have plugged the property into the semantics. We can reformulate the earlier recursive function definitions to make use of fix instead:

add $= $ fix $(\lambda f\ n\ m.$ if iszero n then m else succ $(f$ (pred $n)\ m))$
mul $= $ fix $(\lambda f\ n\ m.$ if iszero n then zero else $add\ m$ $(f$ (pred $n)\ m))$
$factorial = $ fix $(\lambda f\ n.$ if iszero n then succ zero else $mul\ n$ $(f$ (pred $n)))$

Thus, we take a fixed point of a lambda expression with an extra argument f, which corresponds to the assumed fixed point. In this manner, we tie a recursive knot. Let us extend the syntax and semantics of the lambda calculus to include a dedicated expression form fix e. To this end, we essentially turn the earlier fixed-point property into a reduction rule, as defined below.

Specification 10.4 (Small-step operational semantics of *fix*)

Reduction of lambda expressions

$$\frac{e \to e'}{\text{fix } e \to \text{fix } e'} \qquad\qquad \text{[fix1]}$$

$$\text{fix } \lambda x.\ e \to [\text{fix } \lambda x.\ e/x]e \qquad\qquad \text{[fix2]}$$

Rule [fix1] brings the argument of fix into normal form. Rule [fix2] assumes that the argument of fix is a lambda abstraction $\lambda x.\ e$, and it returns e after substituting x by the original fixed-point expression.

10.1.6 Interpretation

Let us implement an interpreter for the untyped lambda calculus in Haskell. To this end, we introduce a language ULL (*U*ntyped *L*ambda *L*anguage). ULL combines the untyped lambda calculus with BTL's expression forms and the *fix* construct. For instance, the "recursive" *add* function can represented in ULL as follows.

Illustration 10.1 (A function for addition)

Haskell module Language.ULL.Sample

```
add = Fix (Lambda "f" (Lambda "n" (Lambda "m"
         (If (IsZero (Var "n"))
            (Var "m")
            (Succ (Apply (Apply (Var "f") (Pred (Var "n"))) (Var "m")))))))
```

Let us implement a data type for representing ULL expressions in Haskell.

Illustration 10.2 (Representation of ULL expressions)

Haskell module Language.ULL.Syntax

```
data Expr
    -- The untyped lambda calculus
  = Var String | Lambda String Expr | Apply Expr Expr
    -- BTL (Basic TAPL Language)
  | TRUE | FALSE | Zero | Succ Expr | Pred Expr | IsZero Expr | If Expr Expr Expr
    -- Fixed-point combinator
  | Fix Expr
```

Interpretation for ULL is implemented by encoding the various small-step operational semantics rules in Haskell; the BTL-related rules are elided below for brevity.

Illustration 10.3 (Implementation of the single-step relation for ULL)

Haskell module Language.ULL.SmallStep

```
step :: Expr → Maybe Expr
step (Apply e1 e2) | not (isValue e1) =
   step e1 >>=λ e1' → Just (Apply e1' e2)
step (Apply e1 e2) | isValue e1 && not (isValue e2) =
   step e2 >>=λ e2' → Just (Apply e1 e2')
step (Apply (Lambda x e1) e2) | isValue e2 =
   substitute e2 x e1
step (Fix e) | not (isValue e), Just e' ← step e = Just (Fix e')
step e@(Fix (Lambda x e')) = substitute e x e'
...
step _ = Nothing
```

Substitution, as needed for beta reduction and fixed-point computations, is implemented as follows.

Illustration 10.4 (Implementation of substitution for ULL expressions)

Haskell module Language.ULL.Substitution

```
substitute :: Expr → String → Expr → Maybe Expr
substitute e x (Var y) | x == y = Just e
substitute e x (Var y) | x /= y = Just (Var y)
substitute e x (Apply e1 e2) = do
  e1' ← substitute e x e1
  e2' ← substitute e x e2
  Just (Apply e1' e2')
substitute e x (Lambda y e') | x == y =
  Just (Lambda y e')
substitute e x (Lambda y e') | x /= y && not (elem y (free e)) = do
  e" ← substitute e x e'
  Just (Lambda y e")
substitute e x (Fix e') = substitute e x e' >>=Just . Fix
...
substitute _ _ _ = Nothing

free :: Expr → [String]
free (Var x) = [x]
free (Apply e1 e2) = free e1 `union` free e2
free (Lambda x e) = [ y | y ← free e, y /= x]
...
```

In order to arrive at a complete interpreter, we also need an operation *steps* for taking the reflexive and transitive closure of the single-step operation *step* in Illustration 10.3. We omit the implementation here because *steps* is defined in just the same way as for the much simper language BTL (Section 8.2.4).

Here is how we can use the interpreter if we assume convenience conversions fromInt and toInt from Haskell's Int type to ULL's (BTL's) natural numbers and vice versa:

Interactive Haskell session:

```
► let (Just r) = steps (Apply (Apply add (fromInt 20)) (fromInt 22))
► toInt r
42
```

That is, we apply the recursive function *add* to 20 and 22 after converting these Haskell Ints into ULL expressions; the result is 42 after converting the ULL expression into a Haskell Int. The convenience conversions allow us to use Haskell's numbers rather than the verbose constructors Zero and Succ. The trivial implementations of the conversions are shown below.

Illustration 10.5 (Conversions between expressions and numbers)

Haskell module Language.ULL.Value

```
...
-- Convert Haskell Int to expression such that isNat is True
fromInt :: Int → Expr
fromInt i | i >= 0 = if i == 0 then Zero else Succ (fromInt (i−1))

-- Convert expression such that isNat is True to Haskell Int
toInt :: Expr → Int
toInt Zero = 0
toInt (Succ e) = toInt e + 1
```

10.1.7 Turing Completeness

As an aside, let us point out that the lambda calculus, without predefined values and operations, is expressive enough to encode such values and operations. Also, the basic untyped lambda calculus is expressive enough to encode a fixed-point combinator. Thus, the basic untyped lambda calculus is Turing-complete, i.e., all computable functions can be encoded in the calculus. Such an encoding is not straightforward, but it may provide insight, which is why we illustrate it here briefly. In particular, we can apply the so-called *Church encoding* for values and operations on Boolean values and natural numbers, as shown in Table 10.2.

That is, Boolean values are essentially encoded as lambda expressions that pick out one of two arguments, thereby immediately enabling an "if-then-else". Natural numbers are encoded in Peano style such that any natural number takes two arguments z and s, the first one corresponding to zero and the second one corresponding to the successor function; the natural number n applies s n times to z.

Table 10.2 Encoding of Boolean values and natural numbers

Value/Operation	Encoding
true	$\lambda t.\, \lambda f.\, t$
false	$\lambda t.\, \lambda f.\, f$
if	$\lambda b.\, \lambda v.\, \lambda w.\, b\, v\, w$
0	$\lambda s.\, \lambda z.\, z$
1	$\lambda s.\, \lambda z.\, s\, z$
2	$\lambda s.\, \lambda z.\, s\, (s\, z)$
3	$\lambda s.\, \lambda z.\, s\, (s\, (s\, z))$
...	...
succ	$\lambda n.\, \lambda s.\, \lambda z.\, s\, (n\, s\, z)$

The encoding of fixed-point computations relies on a lambda expression that "behaves" like the earlier *fix* construct. In fact, there are several different options for *fix* and which of these actually work well depends on the exact choice of the semantics. Here is a fixed-point combinator that can be used together with the call-by-value semantics at hand:

$$fix = \lambda f.(\lambda x.f\,(\lambda v.((x\,x)\,v)))\,(\lambda x.f\,(\lambda v.((x\,x)\,v)))$$

Understanding this combinator properly or deriving it rationally requires some deep insights that go beyond our level of sophistication here, but it may help to observe that the combinator involves some sort of infinite copying behavior, thereby essentially implying that *fix* f is mapped to $f\,(f\,\cdots)$.

10.2 The Simply Typed Lambda Calculus

Let us transition from untyped to typed lambda calculi.

10.2.1 Syntax

We need to revise the syntax of the lambda calculus to incorporate types of variables in lambda abstractions:

- x: variables (as before);
- $\lambda x : T.\, e$: lambda abstractions; x is declared to be of type T;
- $e_1\, e_2$: applications (as before).

We assume that the BTL forms of expressions are added again, so that we are considering an applied calculus. There are types nattype and booltype as in BTL. We also need syntax for a function types:

$$T1 \to T2$$

That is, $T1$ is the argument type and $T2$ is the result type.

10.2.2 Semantics

The semantics of the simply typed lambda calculus is the same as that of the untyped lambda calculus, except that the rule for beta reduction needs to be revised; the type annotation is simply ignored:

$$(\lambda x : T. e)\, v \to [v/x]e \qquad\qquad \text{[beta]}$$

10.2.3 Type System

In the following typing rules, we use labels which start with $t-\ldots$ ("t" for typing) to distinguish them from the rules for operational semantics.

Specification 10.5 (Type system for the simply typed lambda calculus)

$$\frac{x : T \in \Gamma}{\Gamma \vdash x : T} \qquad\qquad \text{[t$-$var]}$$

$$\frac{\Gamma \vdash e_1 : T_1 \to T_2 \quad \Gamma \vdash e_2 : T_1}{\Gamma \vdash e_1\, e_2 : T_2} \qquad\qquad \text{[t$-$apply]}$$

$$\frac{\Gamma, x : T_1 \vdash e : T_2}{\Gamma \vdash \lambda x : T_1.\, e : T_1 \to T_2} \qquad\qquad \text{[t$-$abstr]}$$

In rule [t−var], we assume that the type context Γ provides the type of the variable x. In rule [t−apply], we assume that the function position e_1 in a function application is of a function type and the argument position e_2 is of the corresponding argument type. In rule [t−abstr], when checking the type of the body e, we assume that the context Γ is locally adapted (see "$\Gamma, x : T_1$") to assume that the variable x

from the lambda abstraction is of type T_1; the type of a lambda abstraction is, of course, a function type. The typing rules for BTL's expression forms (Section 9.3) can be trivially adopted; they just need to pass on the typing context Γ.

Exercise 10.4 (Typing rule for fix) [Basic level]
Devise the typing rule for the fixed-point construct. Informally, the type of e in fix *e must be a function type where the argument type equals the result type.*

10.2.4 Type Checking

Let us implement a type checker for the lambda calculus. To this end, we introduce a language TLL (*T*yped *L*ambda *L*anguage). TLL's syntax is exactly the same as ULL's – except for lambda abstractions:

```
-- ULL: Untyped Lambda Language
data Expr = ... | Lambda String Expr | ...
```

```
-- TLL: Typed Lambda Language
data Expr = ... | Lambda String Type Expr | ...
data Type = BoolType | NatType | FunType Type Type
```

For instance, the "recursive" *add* function is encoded as follows.

Illustration 10.6 (A function for addition)

Haskell module Language.TLL.Sample

```
add = Fix (Lambda "f" (FunType NatType (FunType NatType NatType))
            (Lambda "n" NatType
            (Lambda "m" NatType
             (If (IsZero (Var "n"))
               (Var "m")
               (Succ (Apply (Apply (Var "f") (Pred (Var "n"))) (Var "m")))))))
```

We are ready to implement the typing rules as a type checker. The following Haskell code is based on a systematic encoding of the typing rules for the simply typed lambda calculus with predefined values and operations and the *fix* construct; the BTL-related rules are elided again for brevity.

Illustration 10.7 (Type checking of lambda expressions)

Haskell module Language.TLL.Typing

```
-- Context for type checking
type Context = Map String Type

-- Type checking expressions
typeOf :: Context → Expr → Maybe Type
typeOf ctx (Var x) = lookup x ctx
typeOf ctx (Apply e1 e2) = do
  t1 ← typeOf ctx e1
  t2 ← typeOf ctx e2
  case (t1, t2) of
     ((FunType ta tr), ta') | ta == ta' → Just tr
     _ → Nothing
typeOf ctx (Lambda x t e) = do
  let ctx' = insert x t ctx
  t' ← typeOf ctx' e
  Just (FunType t t')
typeOf ctx (Fix e) |
     Just t@(FunType ta tr) ← typeOf ctx e,
     ta == tr =
  Just ta
...
typeOf _ _ = Nothing
```

We can type-check expressions as follows:

Interactive Haskell session:

▶ typeOf empty add
Just (FunType NatType (FunType NatType NatType))

That is, *add* is a function that takes two arguments of the *NatType* and it returns a result of the *NatType*.

10.2.5 Type Erasure

In the simply typed lambda calculus, types do not play any role at runtime. We only declare types as part of the lambda abstractions so that we can check them. In principle, we could also leave out declarations and aim at inference such that we show instead whether types can be assigned to the variables of lambda abstractions. After type checking, we may "erase" the declared types so that we map the syntax of the simply typed calculus to the untyped lambda calculus and fall back to its semantics. Such type erasure is specified below; the rule labels start with $e-\ldots$ ("e" for erasure).

Specification 10.6 (Type erasure for the simply typed lambda calculus)

$$x \rightsquigarrow x \qquad\qquad\qquad\qquad \text{[e−var]}$$

$$\frac{e_1 \rightsquigarrow e_1' \quad e_2 \rightsquigarrow e_2'}{e_1\ e_2 \rightsquigarrow e_1'\ e_2'} \qquad\qquad \text{[e−apply]}$$

$$\frac{e \rightsquigarrow e'}{\lambda x : T.\ e \rightsquigarrow \lambda x.\ e'} \qquad\qquad \text{[e−abstr]}$$

The implementation of type erasure is a straightforward mapping from ULL to TLL as follows.

Illustration 10.8 (Type erasure for TLL)

Haskell module Language.TLL.Erasure

```
import Language.TLL.Syntax as TLL
import Language.ULL.Syntax as ULL
erase :: TLL.Expr → ULL.Expr
erase (TLL.Var x) = (ULL.Var x)
erase (TLL.Lambda x _ e) = (ULL.Lambda x (erase e))
erase (TLL.Apply e1 e2) = (ULL.Apply (erase e1) (erase e2))
erase (TLL.TRUE) = (ULL.TRUE)
...
```

As a result, no interpreter is needed atop the TLL syntax; the earlier interpreter atop the ULL syntax (Section 10.1.6) suffices.

10.3 System *F*

Here, we look briefly at System *F* [12]; this is a lambda calculus which provides a model of *polymorphism*. The general idea underlying the notion of polymorphism is to facilitate declaration of abstractions that can be used for different types. There exist several forms of polymorphism; see, for example, Cardelli and Wegner's seminal text on type systems [5]. System *F* is concerned here with *universal or parametric polymorphism* – this is when abstractions are properly parameterized in types. In System *F*, we have *polymorphic functions* such that arguments and results may be of "arbitrary" types. We also say that System *F* is a polymorphic lambda calculus.

10.3.1 Syntax

Compared with the simply typed lambda calculus, there are the following additional syntactic forms:

- There are these additional forms of expressions:

  - *Type abstractions* $\Lambda X.\, e$: An uppercase lambda expression e is explicitly parameterized by a type variable X.
  - *Type applications* $e[T]$: A type T is passed explicitly as an argument to an uppercase lambda expression e. Type application can be compared to function application.

- There are these additional forms of types:

  - *Polymorphic types* $\forall X.\, T$: The type variable X is explicitly and universally quantified in type T. We use an uppercase lambda ("Λ") to hint at the similarity to normal lambda abstractions, which abstract over values rather than types.
  - *Type variables* X: A type variable can be referred to in constructing type expressions. Type variables should be bound in type expressions, just as regular variable identifiers should be bound in lambda expressions.

  Here are two sample expressions in System F:

- $id = \Lambda X.\, \lambda x : X.\, x$
- $twice = \Lambda X.\, \lambda f : X \rightarrow X.\, \lambda x : X.\, f\ (f\ x)$

The first expression denotes the polymorphic identity function; the second expression denotes a function combinator for applying a function twice. For comparison, in the untyped lambda calculus, the same expressions read as follows:

- $id = \lambda x.\, x$
- $twice = \lambda f\ x.\, f\ (f\ x)$

Table 10.3 shows some attempts of assigning types to expressions that involve the functions *id* and *twice*.

In the row with the "type error", we try to apply the polymorphic function *id* to a Boolean value immediately. This is not correct, because there is a big lambda in front of the small lambda; a type application must precede the function application.

System F and variations thereof are used in the implementation of typed functional programming languages. The actual surface syntax for universal polymorphism may be different in actual functional programming languages. Let us exercise Haskell's situation; we declare and use the functions *id* and *twice* as follows:

Table 10.3 Well- and ill-typedness.

Expression	Type
id	$\forall X. X \to X$
id[booltype]	booltype $\to$ booltype
id[booltype] true	booltype
id true	– type error –
twice	$\forall X. (X \to X) \to X \to X$
twice[nattype]	(nattype $\to$ nattype) $\to$ nattype $\to$ nattype
twice[nattype] λx : nattype. succ x	nattype $\to$ nattype

Interactive Haskell session:

```
▶ let id = λ x → x
▶ let twice = λ f → λ x → f (f x)
▶ :t id
id :: t → t
▶ :t twice
twice :: (t → t) → t → t
▶ id True
True
▶ twice (λ x → x + 1) 40
42
```

That is, in Haskell, type abstractions and type applications are implicit. Also, lambda abstractions do not need to declare types of bound variables. Types use type variables, but without a quantifier; see the type variable t in the types of *id* and *twice*. Thus, universal quantification is implicit.

10.3.2 Semantics

The following rules commit to the small-step style of operational semantics; we also prefer call-by-value just as in the case of the untyped lambda calculus (Section 10.1.2).

Specification 10.7 (Call-by-value semantics of System *F*)

Reduction of lambda expressions

$$\frac{e_1 \to e_1'}{e_1\, e_2 \to e_1'\, e_2} \qquad\qquad \text{[app1]}$$

$$\frac{e_2 \to e_2'}{v_1\ e_2 \to v_1\ e_2'} \qquad\qquad [\text{app2}]$$

$$(\lambda x : T.\ e)\ v \to [v/x]e \qquad\qquad [\text{beta}]$$

$$\frac{e \to e'}{e[T] \to e'[T]} \qquad\qquad [\text{typeapp1}]$$

$$(\Lambda X.\ e)[T] \to [T/X]e \qquad\qquad [\text{typeapp2}]$$

Values

$$\lambda x : T.\ e \in value \qquad\qquad [\text{v--lambda}]$$

$$\Lambda X.\ e \in value \qquad\qquad [\text{v--Lambda}]$$

That is, lambda and type abstractions provide the value forms of the semantics (rules [v−lambda] and [v−Lambda]). The rules for function application, including beta reduction, carry over from the simply typed or the untyped lambda calculus. The rules for type application bring the expression into value form and then use substitution, just as in the case of function application, to replace the type variable of the type abstraction by the argument type.

10.3.3 Type System

The type system of the simply typed lambda calculus is extended as follows.

Specification 10.8 (Type system for System F)

$$\frac{x : T \in \Gamma}{\Gamma \vdash x : T} \qquad\qquad [\text{t--var}]$$

$$\frac{\Gamma, x : T_1 \vdash e : T_2}{\Gamma \vdash \lambda x : T_1.\ e : T_1 \to T_2} \qquad\qquad [\text{t--abstr}]$$

$$\frac{\Gamma \vdash e_1 : T_1 \to T_2 \quad \Gamma \vdash e_2 : T_1}{\Gamma \vdash e_1\ e_2 : T_2} \qquad\qquad [\text{t--apply}]$$

$$\frac{\Gamma, X \vdash e : T}{\Gamma \vdash \Lambda X.\, e : \forall X.\, T} \qquad \text{[t−typeabstr]}$$

$$\frac{\Gamma \vdash e : \forall X.\, T}{\Gamma \vdash e[T_1] : [T_1/X]T} \qquad \text{[t−typeapply]}$$

The rules for variables, lambda abstraction, and function application carry over from the simply typed lambda calculus. The rules for type abstraction and type application are similar to those for lambda abstraction and function application. The type of a type abstraction $\Lambda X.\, e$ is the polymorphic type of e with universal quantification over the type variable X. Just as in the case of lambda abstraction, X is added to the context so that we keep track of big lambdas. The typing rule for type application $e[T_1]$ states that e must be of a polymorphic type $\forall X.\, T$ and the result type is T with X substituted by T_1.

As a testament to the expressiveness of System *F*'s type system consider the problem of self-application, i.e., applying a lambda expression to itself. This may seem to be an obscure problem, but is a good "benchmark" for expressiveness. In the untyped lambda calculus, self-application can be represented trivially:

$$\lambda x.\, x\, x$$

In the simply typed lambda calculus, we are looking for an expression of this form:

$$\lambda x :?.\, x\, x$$

Alas, there is no type that we can assign to x, because we face unresolvable constraints: the type would need to be a function type as well as the argument type of the same function type. Self application can be represented in System *F*, though:

- term: $\lambda x : \forall X.\, X \to X.\, x[\forall X.\, X \to X]\, x$;
- type: $(\forall X.\, X \to X) \to (\forall X.\, X \to X)$.

The reader is invited to figure out an explanation for this encoding.

10.3.4 *Type Erasure*

In System *F*, just as in the simply typed lambda calculus, types are not essential at runtime. We can "erase" type abstractions and applications, as well as the types within lambda abstractions, so that we map the syntax of System *F* to the untyped lambda calculus, as described below.

Specification 10.9 (Type erasure for System F)

$$x \rightsquigarrow x \qquad\qquad\qquad \text{[e−var]}$$

$$\frac{e_1 \rightsquigarrow e'_1 \quad e_2 \rightsquigarrow e'_2}{e_1 \, e_2 \rightsquigarrow e'_1 \, e'_2} \qquad\qquad \text{[e−apply]}$$

$$\frac{e \rightsquigarrow e'}{e[T] \rightsquigarrow e'} \qquad\qquad \text{[erasure−typeapply]}$$

$$\frac{e \rightsquigarrow e'}{\lambda x : T.\, e \rightsquigarrow \lambda x.\, e'} \qquad\qquad \text{[erasure−abstr]}$$

$$\frac{e \rightsquigarrow e'}{\Lambda X.\, e \rightsquigarrow e'} \qquad\qquad \text{[erasure−typeabstr]}$$

Since we can erase all types like this without changing the semantics of expressions, we also say that System F has a type-erasure semantics. If the types are essential in defining the intended semantics of a language, then we speak of a type-passing semantics. For instance, an object-oriented language with some sort of dynamic dispatch may involve some type passing or type tagging so that method dispatch at runtime can be informed by type information available at runtime.

Exercise 10.5 (Implementation of System F)   [Intermediate level]
Implement System F in a declarative program. The type checker assumes that type annotations, type abstractions, and type applications are present. In the syntax, type annotations are optional, thereby simplifying the implementation of type erasure. The interpreter assumes that type annotations, type abstractions, and type applications are gone. You may add predefined values and operations and a fixed-point combinator so that you can test the implementation more easily.

Far more details of System F can be found elsewhere [9, 11].

10.4 Type-System Extensions

Programming languages involve many other language and type-system concepts. For instance, one may want to define types recursively so that recursive data structures can be represented in this manner. One may also want to existentially – as opposed to universally – quantify type variables, thereby being able to "hide" a type, for example, in the context of abstract data type implementation. One may also want to support ad hoc polymorphism or overloading so that some functionality can be implemented for different types. We refer again to [9] for a detailed development in this regard. We refer also to [10] for more advanced type-system concepts. In the rest of this chapter, we discuss simple extensions for records and variants, including aspects of type equivalence, subtyping, recursion, and the distinction between structural and nominal types.

10.4.1 Records and Variants

Here we discuss two forms of type construction which are found, in one form or another, in various programming languages. That is, we introduce *record types* (i.e., products with labeled components) and *variant types* (i.e., sums with labeled operands). Record types go with expression forms of record construction and projection to components. Variant types go with expression forms of variant construction and case discrimination. Such expressiveness corresponds to, for example, algebraic data types in functional programming languages (e.g., Haskell, SML, or Scala). Record types alone are similar to structs in C or records (indeed!) in Pascal.

Let us introduce the expressiveness by means of an example.

Illustration 10.9 (Record and variant types)
Consider the following variant type with record types for the operands:

$rectangle : \{width : \mathsf{floattype}, height : \mathsf{floattype}\} \mid circle : \{radius : \mathsf{floattype}\}$

We take for granted a type floattype *for floating-point numbers. The variant type models two different kinds of "shapes" (record types, in turn) with width and height as components of the rectangle and radius as the one and only component of the circle. The following function computes the circumference of a shape:*

$\lambda s : rectangle : \{width : \mathsf{floattype}, height : \mathsf{floattype}\} \mid circle : \{radius : \mathsf{floattype}\}.$
case s of
  $rectangle : \lambda r : \{width : \mathsf{floattype}, height : \mathsf{floattype}\}. 2 * (r.width + r.height)$
  $\mid circle \quad : \lambda c : \{radius : \mathsf{floattype}\}. 2 * pi * c.radius$

For the sake of readability, we assume here that we are using a lambda calculus (a functional programming language) with suitable literals and infix operators.

Here is an informal description of the syntax and the intended semantics for records and variants:

- Forms of types:

  - Record type $\{l_1 : T_1, \ldots, l_n : T_n\}$: A value of a record type is a n-tuple with components of types $T_1, \ldots, T_n$ and with the components labeled by $l_1, \ldots, l_n$.
  - Variant type $l_1 : T_1 \mid \ldots \mid l_n : T_n$: A value of a variant type is of type T_i for $1 \leq i \leq n$ labeled by l_i.

- Forms of expressions:

  - Record construction $\{l_1 : e_1, \ldots, l_n : e_n\}$: A record is constructed from labeled component values of the expressions $e_1, \ldots, e_n$.
  - Variant construction $l : e$: A variant is constructed by labeling the value of e with l.
  - Component projection for records $e.l$: The component with label l is selected from the record value of e.
  - Case discrimination for variants case e of $l_1 : e_1 \mid \ldots \mid l_n : e_n$: Assuming that e is of a variant type, a case discrimination is performed on the value of e with one case per variant (i.e., per label). When a case i applies, i.e., e evaluates to a value labeled by l_i, then the corresponding function e_i is applied to the value.

Exercise 10.6 (Records and variants in Haskell)   [Basic level]
Implement the type for shapes as well as the function for circumference, as shown in Illustration 10.9, in Haskell. Exercise these options: (i) use ans algebraic data type with regular constructors for shapes; (ii) use Haskell's records; (iii) use the type constructor Either.

The semantics of records and the corresponding typing rules are spelled out below. The "dual" development for variants is left as an exercise for the reader.

Specification 10.10 (Small-step operational semantics of records)

Reduction of expressions

$$\frac{e_{i+1} \to e'_{i+1}}{\{l_1{:}v_1, \ldots, l_i{:}v_i, l_{i+1}{:}e_{i+1}, \ldots, l_n{:}e_n\} \to \{l_1{:}v_1, \ldots, l_i{:}v_i, l_{i+1}{:}e'_{i+1}, \ldots, l_n{:}e_n\}}$$ [record]

$$\frac{e \to e'}{e.l \to e'.l} \qquad \text{[project1]}$$

$$\{l_1 : v_1, \ldots, l_i : v_i, \ldots, l_n : v_n\}.l_i \to v_i \qquad \text{[project2]}$$

Values

$$\{l_1 : v_1, \ldots, l_n : v_n\} \in value \qquad \text{[v-record]}$$

Rule [v−record] states that a record is a value form of expression, provided the labeled components are values. Rule [record] states that a record expression can perform a step when there is still a component that can perform a step. (For what it matters, we pick the leftmost non-value component.) Rules [project1] and [project2] deal with projection. The first rule brings the record into value form. The second rule selects the relevant component.

Exercise 10.7 (Semantics of variants) [Intermediate level]
Define the small-step operational semantics of variants.

Specification 10.11 (Typing for records)

$$\frac{\Gamma \vdash e_1 : T_1 \quad \cdots \quad \Gamma \vdash e_n : T_n}{\Gamma \vdash \{l_1 : e_1, \ldots, l_n : e_n\} : \{l_1 : T_1, \ldots, l_n : T_n\}} \qquad \text{[t-record]}$$

$$\frac{\Gamma \vdash e : \{l_1 : T_1, \ldots, l_i : T_i, \ldots, l_n : T_n\}}{\Gamma \vdash e.l_i : T_i} \qquad \text{[t-project]}$$

Rule [t−record] states that a record expression is of a record type, with the labels from the expression and the component types determined for the labeled components. Rule [t−project] states that $e.l_i$ is of a component type for l_i according to the record type of e.

Exercise 10.8 (Typing for variants) [Intermediate level]
Define the typing rules for variants.

10.4.2 Structural Type Equivalence

The type system with record and variant types, as it stands, is unnecessarily restrictive. The order of operands in types and expressions should not matter. For instance, the following two record types should be equivalent:

- $\{x : \mathsf{floattype}, y : \mathsf{floattype}\}$
- $\{y : \mathsf{floattype}, x : \mathsf{floattype}\}$

This is easily fixed by defining an appropriate type equivalence "$\equiv$" on types so that record types are equivalent if they differ only in terms of order of components, as illustrated in the following table.

Table 10.4 Illustration of type equivalence

1st type	2nd type	"$\equiv$"
floattype	floattype	✓
floattype	booltype	
floattype $\rightarrow$ booltype	floattype $\rightarrow$ booltype	✓
floattype $\rightarrow$ booltype	booltype $\rightarrow$ floattype	
$\{x : \mathsf{floattype}, y : \mathsf{floattype}\}$	$\{y : \mathsf{floattype}, x : \mathsf{floattype}\}$	✓
$\{x : \mathsf{floattype}, y : \mathsf{floattype}\}$	$\{x : \mathsf{booltype}, y : \mathsf{floattype}\}$	
$\{x : \mathsf{floattype}, y : \mathsf{floattype}\} \rightarrow \mathsf{booltype}$	$\{y : \mathsf{floattype}, x : \mathsf{floattype}\} \rightarrow \mathsf{booltype}$	✓
$\{x : \mathsf{floattype}, y : \mathsf{floattype}\} \rightarrow \mathsf{booltype}$	$\{y : \mathsf{floattype}, x : \mathsf{floattype}\} \rightarrow \mathsf{floattype}$	

Exercise 10.9 (Structural type equivalence)   [Basic level]
Specify the equivalence relation "$\equiv$" on types, as illustrated above.

When type equivalence is based on structure, as is the case here, then we speak of structural typing. Type equivalence can also be based on names of types, as we will discuss in a second.

We assume that whenever we are comparing type expressions for equality, then equivalence is meant as opposed to plain syntactical equality. We can plug "$\equiv$" into the type system by the following rule:

$$\frac{\Gamma \vdash e : T' \quad T \equiv T'}{\Gamma \vdash e : T} \qquad \text{[t$-$equiv]}$$

10.4.3 Structural Subtyping

Let us now move from type equivalence to subtyping. It is easy to see that a function which expects – in terms of its type annotation – a record of a specific record type can also be applied soundly to a value of a record type which features additional components or a variant type which features fewer operands. We face a form of polymorphism – in fact, structural subtyping, thereby also providing an instance of the well-known substitution principle [8]. This is illustrated below.

Illustration 10.10 (Structural subtyping)
The function for circumference as of Illustration 10.9 could also be applied to an expression of the following type, which is thus a subtype of the earlier type:

$$rectangle : \{width : \mathsf{floattype}, height : \mathsf{floattype}, filled : \mathsf{booltype}\}$$

This type differs from the original type in that the revised variant for rectangles carries an additional record component "filled" which is obviously not used by projection in the function for circumference. Also, the variant for circles is missing in the revised type; it will thus not be encountered by case discrimination in the function for circumference.

Exercise 10.10 (Structural subtyping)   [Basic level]
Give two types that are not subtypes of the argument type of the function for circumference in Illustration 10.9. One of the types should omit a record component. The other type should include an additional variant.

We assume a subtyping relation "$\subseteq$" to be plugged into the type system by means of adjusting the typing rule for function application. We first recall the subtyping-unaware typing rule in Specification 10.5.

$$\frac{\Gamma \vdash e_1 : T_1 \to T_2 \quad \Gamma \vdash e_2 : T_1}{\Gamma \vdash e_1\, e_2 : T_2} \qquad \text{[t−apply]}$$

The relationship between the argument type of the function and the actual argument type has to be relaxed by a subtyping relation "$\subseteq$"; the labels for the subtyping-related rules start with $s-\dots$ ("s" for subtyping).

Specification 10.12 (Subtyping-aware function application)

$$\frac{\Gamma \vdash e_1 : T_1 \to T_2 \quad \Gamma \vdash e_2 : T_1' \quad T_1' \subseteq T_1}{\Gamma \vdash e_1\, e_2 : T_2} \qquad \text{[s−apply]}$$

We are ready to define the subtyping relation "$\subseteq$". The following rules specify, for example, that a subtype may contain additional components and shared components may be related by subtyping.

Specification 10.13 (Structural subtyping for records)

$$\frac{T \equiv T'}{T \subseteq T'} \qquad\qquad\qquad\qquad\qquad \text{[s−reflexive]}$$

$$\frac{T_1 \subseteq T_2 \quad T_2 \subseteq T_3}{T_1 \subseteq T_3} \qquad\qquad\qquad\qquad \text{[s−transitive]}$$

$$\{l_1{:}T_1,\ldots,l_{n-1}{:}T_{n-1},l_n{:}T_n\} \subseteq \{l_1{:}T_1,\ldots,l_{n-1}{:}T_{n-1}\} \qquad \text{[s−record1]}$$

$$\frac{T_i \subseteq T_i'}{\{l_1{:}T_1,\ldots,l_i{:}T_i,\ldots,l_n{:}T_n\} \subseteq \{l_1{:}T_1,\ldots,l_i{:}T_i',\ldots,l_n{:}T_n\}} \qquad \text{[s−record2]}$$

$$\frac{T_1' \subseteq T_1 \quad T_2 \subseteq T_2'}{T_1 \to T_2 \subseteq T_1' \to T_2'} \qquad\qquad\qquad\qquad \text{[s−funsubtype]}$$

The rules cover only record types; the development for variants is left as an exercise for the reader. We explain the typing rules for "$\subseteq$" one by one as follows:

- [s−reflexive]: The rule models reflexivity of subtyping (under equivalence).
- [s−transitive]: The rule models transitivity of subtyping.
- [s−record1]: A record type with an additional component is a subtype of the record type without that additional component.
- [s−record2]: A record type with type T_i for component l_i is a subtype of a record type that differs only in terms of type T_i' for component l_i, provided it holds that $T_i \subseteq T_i'$.
- [s−funtype]: Function types are in a subtyping relationship such that the domains of the function types are in the reverse direction of subtyping relationship and the ranges are in the same direction of subtyping relationship.

Let us take a closer look at the complex case of function types ([s−funtype]). Because ranges are ordered by subtyping in the same direction as the function types, this is referred to as *covariance*. In the reverse direction, as with the domains, this is referred to as *contravariance*. If we were to rule out any such variance for function types, then this would be referred to as *invariance*. The choice made by rule [s−funtype] is safe in the sense of soundness (Section 9.5).

Exercise 10.11 (Covariance versus contravariance)   [Intermediate level]
Assume a modified rule [s−funtype] *such that covariance is assumed for both the domain and the range of the function type. For this modified system, devise a well-typed expression that gets stuck.*

Exercise 10.12 (Structural subtyping for variants)   [Intermediate level]
Devise subtyping rules for variants. You may try to adapt the rules [s−record1] *and* [s−record2] *to fit variants.*

The subtyping rules as given above are problematic in that they are not really syntax-driven. Owing to the rules [s−reflexive] and [s−transitive], one can construct typing derivations indefinitely. In this sense, the rules are not immediately algorithmic. We need transitivity because of the rules [s−record1] and [s−record2], which only consider pointwise differences. The rule [t−equiv] is also at play; it is needed for type equivalence modulo reordering of operands. It is not too hard, though, to replace all the rules by a single rule which combines the aspects at hand. This is left as an exercise for the reader.

Exercise 10.13 (Algorithmic subtyping)   [Intermediate level]
Devise a reformulation of "⊆" so that the rules are algorithmic, i.e., given two types, there is at most one (finite) typing derivation for a judgment.

10.4.4 Nominal Typing

When type equivalence and subtyping are based on names of types, then we speak of nominal typing. The basic assumption is thus that types are named, subject to an abstraction form for type definition. Types with different names are not equivalent, even if the underlying structural types are.

As a by-product, the proposed form of nominal typing makes it easy to define types recursively, even though, in principle, this could also be achieved without names, i.e., with a fixed-point construction, just as in the case of functions (Section 10.1.5). We will discuss type definitions briefly here, without though considering nominal subtyping, which is of particular interest in the context of OO programming [6, 7]. We assume here that type definitions are add on top of records and variants.

Let us introduce the expressiveness by means of an example.

Illustration 10.11 (Type definitions)
Let us model lists of shapes such that a list either is empty (see the variant labeled nil) or consists of an element as the head and a remaining list as the tail (see the variant labeled cons):

$$\text{newtype } ShapeList = nil : \{\} \mid cons : \{head : Shape, tail : ShapeList\}$$
$$\text{type } Shape \qquad\quad = rectangle : Rectangle \mid circle : Circle$$
$$\text{type } Rectangle \quad\;\; = \{width : \mathsf{floattype}, height : \mathsf{floattype}\}$$
$$\text{type } Circle \qquad\quad = \{radius : \mathsf{floattype}\}$$

We explain the notation as follows. We use N as a metavariable that ranges over names of types. In type expressions, we may refer to named types using, of course, the name. For the sake of matching more realistically how nominal typing shows up in actual programming languages, we actually assume two forms of type definition.

- Type alias declared by type $N = T$: This form only declares an alias N for the structural type T. Referring to N is like copying T literally. No nominal typing is involved.
- New type declared by newtype $N = T$: This form declares a new nominal type N, with T as the underlying structural type. Referring to N is thus not equivalent to T.

We assume that all aliases have been eliminated (i.e., inlined) before even considering typing or semantics. That is, all references to aliases are simply replaced by the underlying structural types. This also implies that aliases must not be defined recursively.

At the expression level, there are these forms:

- $\mathsf{in}_N(e)$: The value of e is injected into the nominal type N provided e is of the underlying structural type of N.
- $\mathsf{out}_N(e)$: The expression e must be of the nominal type N; its value is converted to the underlying structural type of N.

We are ready to define the semantics of nominal types.

Specification 10.14 (Small-step operational semantics of nominal types)

Reduction of expressions

$$\frac{e \to e'}{\mathsf{in}_N(e) \to \mathsf{in}_N(e')} \qquad\qquad\qquad \text{[in]}$$

$$\frac{e \to e'}{\text{out}_N(e) \to \text{out}_N(e')} \qquad\qquad\qquad \text{[out1]}$$

$$\text{out}_N(\text{in}_N(v)) \to v \qquad\qquad\qquad\qquad \text{[out2]}$$

Values

$$\text{in}_N(v) \in value \qquad\qquad\qquad\qquad\qquad \text{[v–in]}$$

By making $\text{in}_N(v)$ a value form, we hint at the basic implementation/representation option of using type names as tags within the actual semantics. This can be compared to carrying type information at runtime, as in object-oriented programming languages with virtual method tables and type inspection [6, 7].

The typing judgment is now of the form $\Gamma, \Delta \vdash e : T$, with Δ corresponding to the type definitions. The following rules only cover the new expressiveness, while we assume that all previous typing rules remain unchanged, except for adding the extra context Δ.

Specification 10.15 (Typing for nominal types)

$$\frac{\text{newtype } N = T \in \Delta \quad \Gamma, \Delta \vdash e : T}{\Gamma, \Delta \vdash \text{in}_N(e) : N} \qquad\qquad \text{[t–in]}$$

$$\frac{\text{newtype } N = T \in \Delta \quad \Gamma, \Delta \vdash e : N}{\Gamma, \Delta \vdash \text{out}_N(e) : T} \qquad\qquad \text{[t–out]}$$

Exercise 10.14 (Nominal subtyping for records) [Intermediate level]
Extend the syntax, semantics, and type system so that nominal type definitions permit nominal subtyping. To this end, assume that nominal record types can explicitly extend an existing nominal record type.

Exercise 10.15 (Classes and "self") [Advanced level]
Formalize some aspects of OO programming as follows. Represent classes as functions (so-called "generators") that are parameterized in "self" and that return a record that models methods as function-typed components that may also refer to "self"; class inheritance corresponds to record update for overriding or to extension for additional members and object construction corresponds to taking the fixed point of generators. See [4] for some background.

Summary and Outline

The lambda calculus is strongly tied to programming language *theory*, but the topic is still important in software language (engineering) *practice*. First, the general notion of a calculus – as an idealized programming language or a core programming language – is a utility that every software language engineer needs to be aware of. In particular, mastery of the calculus notion may help language designers, for example, in the context of identifying the core expressiveness of a domain-specific language. There exist various calculi other than the lambda calculus, for example, in the domains of concurrent programming and mobile computing. Second, the lambda calculus and the extensions in this chapter allowed us to study some important (recurring) language concepts in a compact manner: substitution, call-by-value semantics, recursion, Turing completeness, polymorphism, structural versus nominal typing, and subtyping.

In the following chapter, we will complement the operational approach to defining semantics, which was also exercised throughout the present chapter, with the denotational approach. In the last (technical) chapter, we will discuss a few nontrivial metaprogramming techniques – some of which are also informed by programming language theory.

References

1. Barendregt, H.: Introduction to generalized type systems. J. Funct. Program. **1**(2), 125–154 (1991)
2. Barendregt, H.: The impact of the lambda calculus in logic and computer science. Bulletin of Symbolic Logic **3**(2), 181–215 (1997)
3. Barendregt, H.P., Dekkers, W., Statman, R.: Lambda Calculus with Types. Perspectives in logic. Cambridge University Press (2013)
4. Bracha, G., Lindstrom, G.: Modularity meets inheritance. In: Proc. ICCL, pp. 282–290. IEEE (1992)
5. Cardelli, L., Wegner, P.: On understanding types, data abstraction, and polymorphism. ACM Comput. Surv. **17**(4), 471–522 (1985)
6. Glew, N.: Type dispatch for named hierarchical types. In: Proc. ICFP, pp. 172–182. ACM (1999)
7. Igarashi, A., Pierce, B.C., Wadler, P.: Featherweight Java: a minimal core calculus for Java and GJ. ACM Trans. Program. Lang. Syst. **23**(3), 396–450 (2001)
8. Liskov, B.: Keynote address – Data abstraction and hierarchy. In: Addendum to the Proc. OOPSLA, pp. 17–34. ACM (1987)
9. Pierce, B.: Types and Programming Languages. MIT Press (2002)
10. Pierce, B.: Advanced Topics in Types and Programming Languages. MIT Press (2004)
11. Rémy, D.: Functional programming and type systems: Metatheory of System F (2017). Course notes. Available at `http://cristal.inria.fr/~remy/mpri/`.
12. Reynolds, J.C.: Towards a theory of type structure. In: Proc. Programming Symposium, Proceedings Colloque sur la Programmation, Paris, *LNCS*, vol. 19, pp. 408–423. Springer (1974)

Chapter 11
An Ode to Compositionality

CHRISTOPHER STRACHEY.[1]

Abstract In this chapter, we complement the earlier development of operational semantics with another approach to defining semantics, namely the higher-order functional approach of denotational semantics. We focus here on compositionality, which is a structuring principle for interpreters, analyses, and yet other functionality for languages. We discuss two styles of denotational semantics: the simpler "direct" style and the more versatile "continuation" style capable of dealing with, for example, nonbasic control flow constructs. Denotational semantics can be implemented easily as interpreters, for example, in Haskell, as we will demonstrate.

---

[1] Twenty-five years after his death, two papers by Christoper Strachey appeared [13, 14]: one on his lectures on programming language semantics and another (coauthored with Christopher P. Wadsworth) on continuations. Domain theory would probably not exist without Strachey [11]. My supervisor's generation would have known the work of Strachey (and Scott) through Joseph E. Stoy's textbook [12] and Peter D. Mosses' thesis [5]. I would fall in love with denotational style also, thanks to its applications to parallel and logic programming [6, 2]. Every software language engineer, in fact, every software engineer, should understand and leverage "compositionality" [1].

Artwork Credits for Chapter Opening: This work by Wojciech Kwasnik is licensed under CC BY-SA 4.0. This artwork quotes the artwork *DMT*, acrylic, 2006 by Matt Sheehy with the artist's permission. This work also quotes https://commons.wikimedia.org/wiki/File:Vincent_van_Gogh_-_Vaas_met_tuingladiolen_en_Chinese_asters_-_Google_Art_Project.jpg, subject to the attribution "Vincent Van Gogh: Vaas met tuingladiolen en Chinese asters (1886) [Public domain], via Wikimedia Commons." This work artistically morphes an image, http://www.cs.man.ac.uk/CCS/res/res43.htm, showing the person honored, subject to the attribution "Permission granted by Camphill Village Trust for use in this book."

© Springer International Publishing AG, part of Springer Nature 2018   319
R. Lämmel, *Software Languages*,
https://doi.org/10.1007/978-3-319-90800-7_11

11.1 Compositionality

Denotational semantics [12, 3, 15] is not too popular in today's language definition culture, but the notion of compositionality is. Therefore, we will skip over the mathematical details of denotational semantics here and simply focus on the notion of compositionality. That is, we speak of a compositional semantics when it is defined as a mapping from syntax to semantics with cases for each syntactic pattern such that the meaning of a compound construct is obtained directly and only from the meanings of its constituent phrases ("subterms").

Consider the following two inference rules of a big-step operational semantics for statement sequences and while-loops in an imperative programming language, as discussed earlier (Section 8.1.6.1):

$$\frac{m_0 \vdash s_1 \leadsto m_1 \quad m_1 \vdash s_2 \leadsto m_2}{m_0 \vdash \mathsf{seq}(s_1, s_2) \leadsto m_2} \qquad \text{[SEQ]}$$

$$\frac{m \vdash \mathsf{if}(e, \mathsf{seq}(s, \mathsf{while}(e, s)), \mathsf{skip}) \leadsto m'}{m \vdash \mathsf{while}(e, s) \leadsto m'} \qquad \text{[WHILE]}$$

Rule [SEQ] agrees with the principle of compositionality, while rule [WHILE] does not. That is, the rule [SEQ] for statement sequences applies the judgment for statement execution simply to the two constituents s_1 and s_2 of the sequence $\mathsf{seq}(s_1, s_2)$. By contrast, the rule [WHILE] for while-loops carries a premise with *a newly composed syntactic pattern*. Thus, the meaning of a while-loop $\mathsf{while}(e, s)$ is *not* simply composed from the meanings of its immediate constituents e and s.

Simply speaking, compositionality is good in the same sense as primitive recursion is better understood and better controllable than general recursion. Compositionality simplifies reasoning about the semantics without relying on stepwise computation. Compositionality also helps in separating syntax and semantics in a language definition. Compositionality is not always straightforward to achieve for all language constructs, as we will demonstrate below with a fixed-point semantics of while-loops. To this end, we leverage a different approach to semantics definition: denotational semantics. Within the framework of operational semantics, it appears to be hard to define a compositional semantics of while-loops.

11.2 Direct Style

We develop the basic approach to denotational semantics on the basis of so-called "direct style," which suffices for many programming language constructs; this includes structured programming (sequence, iteration, selection) in imperative programming languages.

11.2.1 Semantic Domains

Denotational semantics assumes that each syntactic category is associated with a semantic domain. We have also used this term earlier in the context of ad hoc interpreters (Section 5.1.1) and operational semantics (Section 8.1.5.1). The difference is that the typical semantic domain of a denotational semantics is a domain of *functions*. Elements of domains directly represent meanings of program phrases; there is no reference to stepwise computation. In the case of the imperative programming language BIPL, we need these domains to be associated with the syntactic categories of statements and expressions:

$$storeT = store \rightarrowtail store \ // \text{Type of store transformation}$$
$$storeO = store \rightarrow value \ // \text{Type of store observation}$$

In these type definitions, we assume the same definitions for *store* and *value* as in the earlier operational semantics (Section 8.1.6.1). That is, *value* denotes the domain of integer and Boolean values, whereas *store* denotes the domain of collections of variable name-value pairs. We can read these definitions as follows. The meaning of a statement is a store transformer, i.e., a function on stores, thereby describing the effect of a given statement on a given store. The meaning of an expression is a store observer, i.e., a function that takes a store and returns a value, where the store may need to be consulted owing to the variable expression form. We assume here that expressions do not modify the store. We deal with partial functions, as denoted by "$\rightarrowtail$" above. The partiality is due to the possibility of nontermination, ill-typed expressions, and undefined variables.

11.2.2 Semantic Functions

Denotational semantics leverages function definitions as opposed to inference rules. The functions assign meanings (compositionally) to the different syntactic categories. In the case of BIPL's imperative programs, we need these functions:

$$\mathscr{S} : stmt \rightarrow storeT \ // \text{Semantics of statements}$$
$$\mathscr{E} : expr \rightarrow storeO \ // \text{Semantics of expressions}$$

That is, the function for statements, $\mathscr{S}$, maps statements to store transformers. The function for expressions, $\mathscr{E}$, maps expressions to store observers.

Compositionality is implied by the following style for defining the semantic functions; in fact, we use a somewhat extreme style for clarity:

$$\begin{aligned}
\mathscr{S}\,[\text{skip}] &= \underline{skip} \\
\mathscr{S}\,[\text{assign}(x,e)] &= \underline{assign}\ x\ (\mathscr{E}\,[e]) \\
\mathscr{S}\,[\text{seq}(s_1,s_2)] &= \underline{seq}\ (\mathscr{S}\,[s_1])\ (\mathscr{S}\,[s_2]) \\
\mathscr{S}\,[\text{if}(e,s_1,s_2)] &= \underline{if}\ (\mathscr{E}\,[e])\ (\mathscr{S}\,[s_1])\ (\mathscr{S}\,[s_2]) \\
\mathscr{S}\,[\text{while}(e,s)] &= \underline{while}\ (\mathscr{E}\,[e])\ (\mathscr{S}\,[s])
\end{aligned}$$

$$\begin{aligned}
\mathscr{E}\,[\text{intconst}(i)] &= \underline{intconst}\ i \\
\mathscr{E}\,[\text{var}(x)] &= \underline{var}\ x \\
\mathscr{E}\,[\text{unary}(o,e)] &= \underline{unary}\ o\ (\mathscr{E}\,[e]) \\
\mathscr{E}\,[\text{binary}(o,e_1,e_2)] &= \underline{binary}\ o\ (\mathscr{E}\,[e_1])\ (\mathscr{E}\,[e_2])
\end{aligned}$$

That is:

- Applications of the semantic functions $\mathscr{S}$ and $\mathscr{E}$ to syntactical patterns or components thereof are surrounded by the so-called Oxford brackets $[\cdots]$. One can trivially check that, in the right-hand sides of equations, the functions are really just applied to components that have been matched on the left-hand sides.
- The intermediate meanings determined for the components are composed by function combinators $\underline{skip}$, $\underline{assign}$, etc. The combinator names are the underlined names of the constructs.
- Some primitive constituents are not mapped. That is, variable names (see the equations for the phrases assign(x,e) and var(x)) and operator symbols (see the equations for the phrases unary(o,e) and binary(o,e_1,e_2)) are directly passed to the corresponding combinators, but no other syntax is passed on or constructed otherwise.
- We apply "curried" notation for the combinators, i.e., function arguments are lined up by juxtaposition as opposed to enclosing them in parentheses, for example, $f\,x\,y$ as opposed to $f(x,y)$.

11.2.3 Semantic Combinators

It remains to define the combinators $\underline{skip}$, $\underline{assign}$, etc. Let us capture their types first, as they are implied by the use of the combinators in the compositional scheme:

$$\begin{aligned}
\underline{skip} &: storeT \\
\underline{assign} &: string \to storeO \to storeT \\
\underline{seq} &: storeT \to storeT \to storeT \\
\underline{if} &: storeO \to storeT \to storeT \to storeT \\
\underline{while} &: storeO \to storeT \to storeT
\end{aligned}$$

$$\begin{aligned}
\underline{intconst} &: int \to storeO \\
\underline{var} &: string \to storeO \\
\underline{unary} &: uo \to storeO \to storeO \\
\underline{binary} &: bo \to storeO \to storeO \to storeO
\end{aligned}$$

Let us define the combinators in a semiformal, intuitive functional notation here. A rigorous development of formal notation for denotational semantics [12, 3, 15] is beyond the scope of this book.

// The identity function for type *store*
$$\underline{skip}\ m\ =\ m$$

// Pointwise store update
$$\underline{assign}\ x\ f\ m\ =\ m[x \mapsto (f\ m)] \text{ if } f\ m \text{ is defined}$$

// Function composition for type *storeT*
$$\underline{seq}\ f\ g\ m\ =\ g\ (f\ m)$$

// Select either branch for Boolean value
$$\underline{if}\ f\ g\ h\ m\ =\ \begin{cases} g\ m \text{ if } f\ m = \text{true} \\ h\ m \text{ if } f\ m = \text{false} \\ undefined \text{ otherwise} \end{cases}$$

We have left out the definition of $\underline{while}$ because it requires some extra effort, as discussed below. For brevity, we have omitted the definition of the combinators needed for $\mathscr{E}$ because the earlier operational semantics of expressions (Section 8.1.6.1) is essentially compositional.

Exercise 11.1 (Denotational semantics of expressions)   [Basic level]
Define the combinators needed for $\mathscr{E}$.

11.2.4 Fixed-Point Semantics

The compositional semantics of while-loops involves a fixed-point construction, as we will clarify now. That is, we aim at a definition of $\underline{while}\ f\ g$ with f as the meaning of the condition and g as the meaning of the loop's body. Let us assume, just for the moment, that we already know the meaning of the while-loop; let us refer to it as t. If so, then it is easy to see that the following equivalence should hold:

$$t \equiv \underline{if}\ f\ (\underline{seq}\ g\ t)\ \underline{skip}$$

That is, by the choice of $\underline{if}$, we test the loop's condition; if the condition evaluates to false, we use the state transformer $\underline{skip}$; otherwise, we sequentially compose the meaning g of the loop's body and the assumed meaning t of the loop itself. Thus, we explicitly construct the meaning of a while-loop, the body of which is executed zero or one times, and we resort to t for repetitions past the first one. It is crucial to understand that we do not use any syntax in this equivalence. Instead, we simply compose meanings.

Alas, we do not yet know t. Let us capture the right-hand side expression of the equivalence as h and parameterize it in t:

$$h\,t \;=\; \underline{if}\; f\; (\underline{seq}\; g\; t)\; \underline{skip}$$

Now consider the following progression of applications of h:

$$h\;undefined$$
$$h\;(h\;undefined)$$
$$h\;(h\;(h\;undefined))$$
$$\vdots$$

Here, *undefined* denotes the completely undefined store transformation, which, given any store m returns a store which maps all variable names to the undefined value. Note that the elements in this progression correspond to approximations to the meaning t of the while-loop that agree with t in terms of the resulting store for the cases of 0, 1, ... required repetitions of the body. Thus, if we can express an unbounded number of applications of h to *undefined*, then we have indeed defined t. This is essentially achieved by taking the fixed point of h. Thus:

$$t \;\equiv\; fix\,h$$

One way to think of *fix* is as being defined "computationally" according to the fixed-point property, as discussed earlier in the context of the lambda calculus (Section 10.1.5). Thus:

$$fix\,k \;=\; k\;(fix\,k)$$

That is, we assume that the fixed point of k is computed by applying k to the computation of the fixed point. Another way to think of *fix* is as being defined as the least upper bound of the elements in the infinite progression described above. The least upper bound is defined here essentially in terms of being more "defined", i.e., returning a less undefined or possibly fully defined store transformer.

To conclude, we define the meaning of a while-loop in terms of the $\underline{while}$ combinator as a fixed point as follows:

$$\underline{while}\; f\; g = fix\,h$$
$$\text{where}$$
$$h\,t = \underline{if}\; f\; (\underline{seq}\; g\; t)\; \underline{skip}$$

Our discussion of fixed points has been very superficial here, and we point to the literature on denotational semantics [12, 3, 15] and on domain theory specifically [11]. In particular, semantic domains and combinators over them must satisfy a number of fundamental properties for such a fixed-point semantics to be well defined in that the fixed point is uniquely defined. To this end, the domains are more than just sets; they are equipped with a partial order to deal with undefinedness and approximation. Also, the combinators need to be monotone and continuous in a specific sense to facilitate fixed-point computation by taking least upper bounds with respect to the said partial orders.

Exercise 11.2 (Existence and uniqueness of fixed points)   [Basic level]
This exercise hints at the challenge of making sure that fixed points exist and are uniquely defined. Define functions a, b, and c on natural numbers such that a has no fixed point, b has exactly one fixed point, and c has an infinite number of fixed points. Use the fixed-point property to check whether a given natural number is indeed a fixed point of a given function. That is, x_0 is a fixed point of f if $f\, x_0 = x_0$.

Regardless of the informality of the development, it is "computationally effective," as a discussion of denotational interpreters shows below.

Exercise 11.3 (Expression-oriented imperative language)   [Intermediate level]
Define the denotational semantics of an imperative language such that the syntactic category for expressions incorporates all statement forms. There were similar assignments for big- and small-step operational semantics in Chapter 8 (Exercises 8.4 and 8.9).

11.2.5 Direct-Style Interpreters

Arguably, semantic domains, functions, and combinators are easily encoded as interpreters in functional programming. Such an implementation benefits from the fact that denotational semantics is clearly a functional approach to defining semantics. That is, domains are types of functions; semantic functions are functions anyway. Semantic combinators are (higher-order) function combinators. The actual details of a systematic and well-defined encoding are nontrivial [8, 9, 10], as there may be some mismatch between the mathematical view of a metanotation for semantics and the actual semantics of the functional metalanguage, but we skip over such details here. We encode denotational semantics in Haskell.

Here is how we expect to use the interpreter for executing the sample program for Euclidean division; we apply values for the variables x and y and execution computes the variables q and r as the quotient and remainder of dividing x by y:

Interactive Haskell session:

```
▶ execute euclideanDiv (fromList [("x", Left 14), ("y", Left 4)])
fromList [("q", Left 3), ("r", Left 2), ("x", Left 14), ("y", Left 4)]
```

Let us start the implementation of an interpreter with a Haskell encoding of the semantic domains as shown below.

Illustration 11.1 (Semantic domains for imperative programs)

Haskell module <u>Language.BIPL.DS.Domains</u>

—— Results of expression evaluation
type Value = Either Int Bool
—— Stores as maps from variable ids to values
type Store = Map String Value
—— Store transformers (semantics of statements)
type StoreT = Store → Store
—— Store observers (semantics of expressions)
type StoreO = Store → Value

The definitions are straightforward. The definition of Store exhibits an element of choice. We could also model stores more directly as functions of type String → Value, but we opt for Haskell's library type Map to model stores as maps (say, dictionaries) from variable names to values because the underlying representation is more convenient to use for testing and debugging, as dictionaries are "observable" as a whole whereas genuine functions can only be "queried" at specific points.

Let us continue the implementation of an interpreter with a Haskell encoding of the compositional mapping over statements as shown below.

Illustration 11.2 (Compositional mapping)

Haskell module <u>Language.BIPL.DS.Interpreter</u>

```
execute :: Stmt → StoreT
execute Skip = skip'
execute (Assign x e) = assign' x (evaluate e)
execute (Seq s1 s2) = seq' (execute s1) (execute s2)
execute (If e s1 s2) = if' (evaluate e) (execute s1) (execute s2)
execute (While e s) = while' (evaluate e) (execute s)

evaluate :: Expr → StoreO
evaluate (IntConst i) = intconst' i
evaluate (Var x) = var' x
evaluate (Unary o e) = unary' o (evaluate e)
evaluate (Binary o e1 e2) = binary' o (evaluate e1) (evaluate e2)
```

That is, the semantic functions $\mathscr{S}$ and $\mathscr{E}$ are called execute and evaluate for clarity, and the underlined combinators of the semiformal development are modeled as primed functions in Haskell; see, for example, skip' instead of *skip*. (By priming, we also avoid clashes. For instance, if is readily taken in Haskell.) There is one equation per language construct. On the left-hand side of an equation, the construct is matched to provide access to the constituents of the construct. On the right-hand side of an equation, the meanings of the constituents are determined by recursive occurrences of the interpreter functions and they are combined by the corresponding semantic combinator.

We complete the implementation of an interpreter with a Haskell implementation of the semantic combinators definitions as shown below.

Illustration 11.3 (Combinators of semantic meanings)

Haskell module Language.BIPL.DS.Combinators

```
skip' :: StoreT
skip' = id
assign' :: String → StoreO → StoreT
assign' x f m = insert x (f m) m
seq' :: StoreT → StoreT → StoreT
seq' = flip (.)
if' :: StoreO → StoreT → StoreT → StoreT
if' f g h m = let Right v = f m in if v then g m else h m
while' :: StoreO → StoreT → StoreT
while' f g = fix h where h t = if' f (seq' g t) skip'
intconst' :: Int → StoreO
intconst' i _ = Left i
var' :: String → StoreO
var' x m = m!x
unary' :: UOp → StoreO → StoreO
unary' Negate f m = let Left i = f m in Left (negate i)
unary' Not f m = let Right b = f m in Right (not b)
binary' :: BOp → StoreO → StoreO → StoreO
...
```

In the code shown above, we make reasonable use of functional programming idioms in Haskell. In the definition of while', we use a polymorphic fixed-point combinator that is readily defined in the Haskell library like this:

```
fix :: (a → a) → a
fix f = f (fix f)
```

Exercise 11.4 (Interpretation without throwing)   [Basic level]
The interpreter may "throw" for different reasons, for example, in the case of applying Boolean negation (Not) to an integer constant. Identify all such reasons and revise the interpreter so that statement execution and expression evaluation do not simply throw, but Nothing of Haskell's Maybe type is returned instead.

The present section can be summarized by means of a recipe.

Recipe 11.1 (Compositional interpretation).

Abstract syntax   Implement abstract syntax, as discussed previously
    (Recipe 4.1).

Semantic domains   *Implement the semantic domains; these are often function types. For instance, the semantic domain for expressions in a language
with variables maps variable identifiers to values.*

Semantic combinators   *There is one combinator per language construct
with as many arguments as there are constituent phrases ("subterms"), with
the argument types equaling the semantic domains for the constituents and
the result type equaling the semantic domain for the construct's category.*

Compositional mapping   *Implement functions from the syntactic to the semantic domains. There is one function per syntactic category. There is one
equation per construct. In each equation, apply the semantic functions to
constituents and combine the results with the combinator for the construct.*

11.3 Continuation Style

We now turn from the direct to the more advanced continuation style of denotational
semantics. The main idea, when one is applying the style to imperative programs,
is to parameterize meanings in the "rest" of the program so that each meaning can
freely choose to deviate from the default continuation, whenever it may be necessary for control-flow constructs such as throws of exceptions or gotos. In functional
programming, there also exists a related style, the *continuation-passing style* (CPS),
which helps with adding error handling to programs and with structuring functional
programs, for example, in the context of implementing web applications [4].

11.3.1 Continuations

In direct style, as assumed so far, control flow is quite limited. To see this, let us
recall that the semantic combinator for sequential composition was defined as follows:

$$\underline{seq} \; : \; storeT \to storeT \to storeT$$
$$\underline{seq} \; f \; g \; m \; = \; g \; (f \; m)$$

Thus, f applies the given store m and passes on the resulting store to g. Now suppose
that f corresponds to a phrase with a goto or a throw of an exception in which case
g should be ignored. Within the bounds of the semantic domains at hand, there is no
reasonable definition for $\underline{seq}$ such that g could be ignored if necessary.

In continuation style, we use more advanced semantic domains; we do not use
"store transformers" but we rather use "store transformer transformers" defined as
follow:

$$storeTT = storeT \twoheadrightarrow storeT$$

The idea is that any meaning is parameterized by a store transformer corresponding to what should "normally" be executed next. We refer to such parameters as continuations. The type and definition of the semantic combinator *seq* are revised as follows:

$$seq \ : \ storeTT \rightarrow storeTT \rightarrow storeTT$$
$$seq \ f \ g \ c \ = \ f \ (g \ c)$$

That is, the sequential composition is parameterized by a continuation c for whatever follows the statement sequence. The order of functionally composing the arguments of *seq* is reversed compared with direct style. This makes sense because we are not composing store transformers; instead, we pass store transformers as arguments.

11.3.2 Continuation-Style Interpreters

We will work out any more details of continuation style in a semiformal notation here. Instead, we will explain details directly by means of interpreters. For now, we just convert the earlier interpreter into continuation style – without yet leveraging the added expressiveness. In the next section, we add gotos to leverage continuation style proper.

We implement the new semantic domain as follows.

Illustration 11.4 (Store transformer transformers)

Haskell module Language.BIPL.CS.Domains

```
type StoreTT = StoreT → StoreT
```

The compositional mapping does not change significantly, as shown below:

Illustration 11.5 (Compositional mapping with continuations)

Haskell module Language.BIPL.CS.Interpreter

```
execute :: Stmt → StoreT
execute s = execute' s id
  where
    execute' :: Stmt → StoreTT
    execute' Skip = skip'
    execute' (Assign x e) = assign' x (evaluate e)
    execute' (Seq s1 s2) = seq' (execute' s1) (execute' s2)
    execute' (If e s1 s2) = if' (evaluate e) (execute' s1) (execute' s2)
    execute' (While e s) = while' (evaluate e) (execute' s)
```

In the code shown above, the top-level function execute maps statements to store transformers and uses the locally defined function execute' to map statements to store transformer transformers starting from the "empty" continuation id.

The semantic combinators have to be changed as follows.

Illustration 11.6 (Combinators of semantic meanings)

Haskell module <u>*Language.BIPL.CS.Combinators*</u>

```
skip' :: StoreTT
skip' = id
assign' :: String → StoreO → StoreTT
assign' x f c sto = c (insert x (f sto) sto)
seq' :: StoreTT → StoreTT → StoreTT
seq' = (.)
if' :: StoreO → StoreTT → StoreTT → StoreTT
if' f g h c = DS.if' f (g c) (h c)
while' :: StoreO → StoreTT → StoreTT
while' f g = fix h where h t = if' f (seq' g t) skip'
```

The combinators differ from direct style as follows:

- skip': The identity function is applied here to store transformers as opposed to stores. The definition models that the current continuation is simply applied.
- assign': The store is transformed, just as in the case of direct style, and then passed to the continuation received.
- seq': The definition models that (the meaning of) the second statement, once applied to the given continuation, acts as a continuation of (the meaning of) the first statement.
- if' : The meaning of an if-statement is the same as in direct style, except that we need to pass the continuation to both branches. We reuse the combinator *DS.if'* of direct style.
- while': The meaning of a while-loop is defined similarly to direct style, except that there is an extra argument for the continuation (suppressed by currying).

11.3.3 Semantics of Gotos

As a simple exercise in leveraging continuation style, we consider an imperative language without while-loops, but with general gotos instead. To this end, we use the following syntax.

Illustration 11.7 (Syntax of imperative statements with gotos)

Haskell module Language.BIPL.Goto.Syntax

```
data Stmt
  = Skip
  | Assign String Expr
  | Seq Stmt Stmt
  | If Expr Stmt Stmt
  | Label String
  | Goto String
```

A sample program follows.

Illustration 11.8 (Euclidean division with goto instead of while)

Haskell module Language.BIPL.Goto.Sample

```
euclideanDiv :: Stmt
euclideanDiv =

    -- Sample operands for Euclidean division
  Seq (Assign "x" (IntConst 14))
  (Seq (Assign "y" (IntConst 4))

    -- Compute quotient q=3 and remainder r=2
  (Seq (Assign "q" (IntConst 0))
  (Seq (Assign "r" (Var "x"))
  (Seq (Label "a")
      (If (Binary Geq (Var "r") (Var "y"))
        (Seq (Assign "r" (Binary Sub (Var "r") (Var "y")))
        (Seq (Assign "q" (Binary Add (Var "q") (IntConst 1)))
            (Goto "a")))
        Skip)))))
```

The denotational semantics of imperative programs with gotos relies on an extra argument for the "goto table" in which to look up the meaning of a label upon encountering a goto. Thus, the semantic domain for meanings of statements evolves as follows.

Illustration 11.9 (Goto tables)

Haskell module Language.BIPL.Goto.Domains

```
type Gotos = [(String, StoreT)] -- Goto tables
type StoreTT' = (StoreT, Gotos) → (StoreT, Gotos) -- Transformation with gotos
```

The compositional mapping is adapted to deal with goto tables, as shown below.

Illustration 11.10 (Compositional mapping with gotos)

Haskell module Language.BIPL.Goto.Interpreter

```
execute :: Stmt → StoreT
execute s = let (c, g) = execute' s (id, g) in c
  where
    execute' :: Stmt → StoreTT'
    execute' Skip = skip'
    execute' (Assign x e) = assign' x (evaluate e)
    execute' (Seq s1 s2) = seq' (execute' s1) (execute' s2)
    execute' (If e s1 s2) = if' (evaluate e) (execute' s1) (execute' s2)
    execute' (Label l) = label' l
    execute' (Goto l) = goto' l
```

The top-level function execute maps statements to store transformers and uses the locally defined function execute' which takes goto tables into account. In fact, as is evident from the definition of StoreTT', the goto table is both received as an argument and returned as part of the result. This may be surprising at first, but in fact the mapping needs to add to the goto table (see the combinator label' in the following illustration) and to read from the goto table (see the combinator goto' in the following illustration).

Illustration 11.11 (Combinators of semantic meanings with gotos)

Haskell module Language.BIPL.Goto.Combinators

```
skip' :: StoreTT'
skip' (c, t) = (c, [])
assign' :: String → StoreO → StoreTT'
assign' x f (c, t) = (λ m → c (insert x (f m) m), [])
seq' :: StoreTT' → StoreTT' → StoreTT'
seq' f g (c, t) = let (c', t') = g (c, t) in let (c", t") = f (c', t) in (c", t'++t")
if' :: StoreO → StoreTT' → StoreTT' → StoreTT'
if' f g h (c, t) = let ((c1, t1), (c2, t2)) = (g (c, t), h (c, t)) in (DS.if' f c1 c2, t1++t2)
label' :: String → StoreTT'
label' l (c, t) = (c, [(l, c)])
goto' :: String → StoreTT'
goto' l (c, t) = (fromJust (lookup l t), [])
```

The combinators are explained one by one as follows:

- skip': The given continuation is simply preserved. The received goto table is not consulted. The returned goto table is empty ([]).
- assign': The store is transformed and then passed to the received continuation. The received goto table is not consulted. The returned goto table is empty ([]).

- seq': The two meanings are essentially composed by function composition, except that the given goto table is passed to both operands and the individually returned goto tables are combined (i.e., appended with (++)) to serve as the resulting goto table for the statement sequence.
- if' : The given goto table is passed to both the then- and the else-branch. The goto tables for the then- and else-branches are combined as the resulting goto table. Other than that, we reuse the semantic combinator of direct style.
- label': The current continuation is captured and associated with the label at hand to form a goto table.
- goto': The current continuation is ignored; in fact, it is replaced by the continuation associated with the given label according to the given goto table.

Exercise 11.5 (Exceptions)   [Intermediate level]
Add the following two statement forms:

- *Throwing an exception* throw(x): *A string x. An exception terminates the regular (sequential) control-flow and propagates through the compound statement until it is handled by a* trycatch *statement (see below) or to the top, where it terminates the program irregularly.*
- *Catching an exception* trycatch(s,x,s'): *While the statement s is being executed, any exception x is caught and s' would be executed. If no exception occurs within s, then the statement behaves just like s. If an exception other than x occurs within s, then the exception is propagated as described above.*

These statement forms should be added by extending the Haskell-based interpreter while leveraging continuation style. This form of exception is developed in some detail in [7].

Exercise 11.6 (Fixed points with gotos)   [Intermediate level]
A recursive let is used in Illustration 11.11, to tie the recursive knot needed for passing the goto table returned by the mapping back into the same mapping. Thus, the semantics is arguably not (obviously) compositional. Revise the semantics so that the recursive let is replaced by some explicit fixed-point construction.

Summary and Outline

We have described the denotational (functional) approach to defining semantics. In its full beauty, denotational semantics is a mathematically elegant approach. We focused here, though, on the key principle of the approach: compositionality, i.e., defining meanings of compound constructs solely in terms of recursively determined meanings of constituent phrases, thereby achieving a full separation of syntax and semantics. We have also touched upon continuation style, which is a sophisticated pattern for structuring semantics definitions (and declarative programs).

In the remaining (technical) chapter, we will discuss a few nontrivial metaprogramming techniques – some of which are also informed by programming language theory. In one case, we will also discuss how denotational semantics can be used to specify program analyses by replacing the semantic algebra for composing meanings by another interpretation geared towards computing program properties that may be useful, for example, for program optimization.

References

1. Blikle, A.: Denotational engineering. Sci. Comput. Program. **12**(3), 207–253 (1989)
2. Brogi, A., Lamma, E., Mello, P.: Compositional model-theoretic semantics for logic programs. New Generation Comput. **11**(1), 1–21 (1992)
3. Gunter, C.: Semantics of Programming Languages: Structures and Techniques. MIT Press (1992)
4. Krishnamurthi, S., Hopkins, P.W., McCarthy, J.A., Graunke, P.T., Pettyjohn, G., Felleisen, M.: Implementation and use of the PLT scheme web server. Higher Order Symbol. Comput. **20**(4), 431–460 (2007)
5. Mosses, P.D.: Mathematical semantics and compiler generation. Ph.D. thesis, University of Oxford, UK (1975)
6. Nielson, F., Nielson, H.R.: Code generation from two-level denotational meta-languages. In: Proc. Programs as Data Objects 1985, *LNCS*, vol. 217, pp. 192–205. Springer (1986)
7. Nielson, H.R., Nielson, F.: Semantics with Applications: An Appetizer. Undergraduate Topics in Computer Science. Springer (2007)
8. Reynolds, J.C.: Definitional interpreters for higher-order programming languages. In: Proc. ACM Annual Conference – Volume 2, ACM '72, pp. 717–740. ACM (1972)
9. Reynolds, J.C.: Definitional interpreters for higher-order programming languages. Higher Order Symbol. Comput. **11**(4), 363–397 (1998)
10. Reynolds, J.C.: Definitional interpreters revisited. Higher Order Symbol. Comput. **11**(4), 355–361 (1998)
11. Stoltenberg-Hansen, V., Lindström, I., Griffor, E.R.: Mathematical Theory of Domains. Cambridge University Press (1994)
12. Stoy, J.E.: Denotational Semantics: The Scott-Strachey Approach to Programming Language Semantics. MIT Press (1977)
13. Strachey, C.: Fundamental concepts in programming languages. Higher Order Symbol. Comput. **13**(1/2), 11–49 (2000)
14. Strachey, C., Wadsworth, C.P.: Continuations: A mathematical semantics for handling full jumps. Higher Order Symbol. Comput. **13**(1/2), 135–152 (2000)
15. Tennent, R.D.: Denotational semantics. In: Handbook of logic in computer science, vol. 3, pp. 169—322. Oxford University Press (1994)

Chapter 12
A Suite of Metaprogramming Techniques

OLEG KISELYOV.[1]

Abstract Metaprogramming may be done with just a few programming techniques: an object-program representation (to capture the syntactical structure of object programs), pattern matching or accessors (to take apart object programs or to select suitable parts thereof), pattern building or constructors (to construct or compose object programs), and a computational model for tree walking (e.g., visitors in OO programming or possibly just recursion). In this chapter, we describe some metaprogramming techniques on the basis of which many metaprograms can be written in a more disciplined style. That is, we describe term rewriting, attribute grammars, multi-stage programming, partial evaluation, and abstract interpretation.

---

[1] Mastery of semantics-based techniques, type-system acrobatics, over-the-head functional programming – these labels pretty reliably map to Oleg Kiselyov without too much risk of hash-code collision. The photo shows him while he was talking about "typed final (tagless-final) style" [7, 34] (http://okmij.org/ftp/tagless-final/) – an advanced topic of metaprogramming not included in this book. One may wonder what a textbook would look like if Oleg was ever to write down a good part of his operational knowledge.

Artwork Credits for Chapter Opening: This work by Wojciech Kwasnik is licensed under CC BY-SA 4.0. This artwork quotes the artwork *DMT*, acrylic, 2006 by Matt Sheehy with the artist's permission. This work also quotes https://en.wikipedia.org/wiki/File:Roses_-_Vincent_van_Gogh.JPG, subject to the attribution "Vincent van Gogh: Roses (1890) [Public domain], via Wikipedia." This work artistically morphes an image, http://www.cs.ox.ac.uk/projects/gip/school/kiselyov.JPG, showing the person honored, subject to the attribution "Permission granted by Oleg Kiselyov for use in this book."

© Springer International Publishing AG, part of Springer Nature 2018
R. Lämmel, *Software Languages*,
https://doi.org/10.1007/978-3-319-90800-7_12

12.1 Term Rewriting

Term rewriting can be viewed as a computational paradigm for describing transformations as a collection of *rewrite rules* which match on object-program patterns and build new patterns from the matched parts in some way. Some implicit or explicit normalization strategy takes care of applying the rules, in some sense, exhaustively. A collection of rewrite rules together with a strategy for their application may be referred to as a *rewrite system*.

In theoretical computer science, rewrite systems are formal entities in themselves (just like grammars) and have been studied very well [16, 39, 17]. In practice, we are interested in metaprogramming systems with support for rewriting such as ASF+SDF [82], TXL [9, 10], Stratego [6], and Rascal [37, 36], and possibly in declarative programming languages that support some form of rewriting. We will exercise term rewriting in Haskell.

12.1.1 Rewrite Rules

As a running example, we will deal with optimization of expression forms; this example was introduced in a pragmatic metaprogramming manner in Section 5.4.1. Our objective here is to show that term rewriting provides a rigorous technique for describing such optimizations. Term rewriting boils down to the declaration and application of rewrite rules such as the following one:

$$(X * Y) + (X * Z) \leadsto X * (Y + Z)$$

This rule captures distributivity for multiplication and addition, as present in many languages. In the rest of this section, we exercise EL (*Expression Language*), which is the language of expression forms that are common to the fabricated imperative and functional programming languages BIPL and BFPL in this book.

As a precursor to setting up a rewrite system, let us collect together several algebraic laws that we assume to hold for expressions. We use uppercase letters $X, Y, Z,$ ... as metavariables for arbitrary expressions so that we can talk about patterns of expressions:

$$
\begin{array}{lll}
X + 0 & = X & \text{-- Unit of addition} \\
X * 1 & = X & \text{-- Unit of multiplication} \\
X * 0 & = 0 & \text{-- Zero of multiplication} \\
X + Y & = Y + X & \text{-- Commutativity of addition} \\
X * Y & = Y * X & \text{-- Commutativity of multiplication} \\
(X + Y) + Z & = X + (Y + Z) & \text{-- Associativity of addition} \\
(X * Y) * Z & = X * (Y * Z) & \text{-- Associativity of multiplication} \\
(X * Y) + (X * Z) & = X * (Y + Z) & \text{-- Distributivity}
\end{array}
$$

We should think of applying these laws – from either left to right or from right to left – to appropriate subterms of a given term such as an EL expression or "bigger" program phrases such as a statement (in BIPL) or a function definition (in BFPL). In sample expressions, we use lowercase letters a, b, c, ... as program variables.

Here is a rewriting step applying the second equation:

$$a + \underline{b * 1} + c = a + \underline{b} + c$$

We have applied the equation from left to right. We have underlined the subexpressions which are instances of the left- and right-hand sides of the equation. We may also use the term "redex" to refer to subterms to which a rewrite rule (or an equation) is applied or applicable.

Exercise 12.1 (Additional rules for expressions) [Basic level]
Identify some additional algebraic laws for EL – specifically also some rules that involve operators that are not exercised by the laws stated above.

When equations are readily directed so that the direction of application is specified, then we speak of rules rather than equations. That is, we use an arrow "⤳" to separate left- and right-hand side, and rules are thus to be applied from left to right. For instance, the first law may reasonably be directed from left to right, as this direction would be useful in applying the rule for the purpose of *simplification*. In fact, the first three equations can be understood as simplification rules, when directed from left to right; in fact, we perform a transition from equations to rules:

$$X + 0 \leadsto X \text{ -- Unit of addition}$$
$$X * 1 \leadsto X \text{ -- Unit of multiplication}$$
$$X * 0 \leadsto 0 \text{ -- Zero of multiplication}$$

That is, a rewrite rule consists of a left- and a right-hand side; these are both patterns of object programs. The assumed semantics of applying a rewrite rule is that the left-hand side is matched with a given term, with the metavariables bound to subterms if matching succeeds; the result is constructed from the bound metavariables according to the right-hand side.

Exercise 12.2 (Semantics of term rewriting) [Intermediate level]
Specify the semantics of applying rewrite rules.

For now, let us use abstract syntax for expressions, as this makes it easy to implement rewrite systems in programming languages. In abstract syntax, the earlier simplification rules look as follows:

$$binary(add, X, intconst(0)) \leadsto X \qquad \text{-- Unit of addition}$$
$$binary(mul, X, intconst(1)) \leadsto X \qquad \text{-- Unit of multiplication}$$
$$binary(mul, X, intconst(0)) \leadsto intconst(0) \text{ -- Zero of multiplication}$$

The abstract syntax is defined as follows.

Illustration 12.1 (Abstract syntax of expressions)

ESL resource <u>languages/EL/as.esl</u>

```
// Expressions
symbol intconst : integer → expr ;
symbol boolconst : boolean → expr ;
symbol var : string → expr ;
symbol unary : uop × expr → expr ;
symbol binary : bop × expr × expr → expr ;

// Unary operators
symbol negate : → uop ;
symbol not : → uop ;

// Binary operators
symbol add : → bop ;
symbol sub : → bop ;
symbol mul : → bop ;
symbol lt : → bop ;
symbol le : → bop ;
symbol eq : → bop ;
symbol geq : → bop ;
symbol gt : → bop ;
symbol and : → bop ;
symbol or : → bop ;
```

12.1.2 Encoding Rewrite Rules

We may encode rewrite rules easily in Haskell, or in any other functional programming language for that matter. That is, rewrite rules become function equations. Functions are used for grouping rewrite rules. We need to be careful to define these functions in such a manner that function application will not throw an exception when the underlying rules are not applicable to a given term. Instead, failure should be communicated gracefully and, thus, we use the Maybe monad. In Section 5.4.1, we already encoded simplification rules in this manner, as we recall here:

```
simplify :: Expr → Maybe Expr
simplify (Binary Add x (IntConst 0)) = Just x
simplify (Binary Mul x (IntConst 1)) = Just x
simplify (Binary Mul x (IntConst 0)) = Just (IntConst 0)
simplify _ = Nothing
```

We may apply the Haskell-based rewrite rules as follows.

Interactive Haskell session:

▶ simplify (Binary Add (Var *"a"*) (IntConst 0))
Just (Var *"a"*)
- -
▶ simplify (IntConst 42)
Nothing
- -
▶ simplify (Binary Add (Var *"a"*) (Binary Add (Var *"b"*) (IntConst 0)))
Nothing
- -
▶ simplify (Binary Add (IntConst 0) (Var *"a"*))
Nothing

The first application succeeds because the simplification rule for the unit of addition is applicable. The second application fails because no simplification rule applies to the expression at hand. Failure of application is modeled by returning *Nothing*. (In an alternative model, the input term could be returned as is if no rule is applicable.) The third application also fails despite the presence of a subexpression to which the simplification rule for the unit of addition would be applicable, but note that we apply simplify directly. We do not in any way descend into the argument to find redexes. Ultimately, we need "normalization", as we will discuss in a second. The fourth application also fails because the simplification rule for the unit of addition only checks for the unit on the right. We may need to combine simplification with the rules for commutativity somehow.

In Haskell, we may also write more versatile rewrite rules taking advantage of functional programming expressiveness. In the following examples, we use guards, extra parameters, and function composition in the "rewrite rules".

Illustration 12.2 (Additional rules illustrating the use of Haskell in rewriting)

Haskell module Language.EL.MoreRules

```
-- Cancel double negation on Ints
doubleNegate (Unary Negate (Unary Negate e)) = Just e
doubleNegate (Unary Negate (IntConst i)) | i <= 0 = Just (IntConst (−i))
doubleNegate _ = Nothing

-- Swap variable names
swap x y (Var z) | z == x = Just (Var y)
swap x y (Var z) | z == y = Just (Var x)
swap _ _ _ = Nothing

-- Compose simplification with optional commute
simplify' x = simplify x `mplus` commute x >>=simplify
```

That is, the doubleNegate function removes two patterns of double negation; the first pattern models double application of the negation operator, and the second pattern models application of the negation operator to a negative number. The swap function is parameterized by two variable names, x and y, and it replaces each occurrence of x by y and vice versa. The simplify' function builds a choice from the plain simplify function such that in the case of failure of simplify, the commutativity rules are applied prior to trying simplify again. Here we assume that we also have "directed" laws for commutativity; the actual direction does not matter in this case, obviously.

Illustration 12.3 (Commutativity for expressions)

Haskell module Language.EL.Rules.Commute

```
commute :: Expr → Maybe Expr
commute (Binary Add x y) = Just $ Binary Add y x
commute (Binary Mul x y) = Just $ Binary Mul y x
commute _ = Nothing
```

We may apply the commutativity-aware definition as follows:

Interactive Haskell session:

▶ simplify' (Binary Add (IntConst 0) (Var "a"))
Just (Var "a")

That is, this application succeeds and returns a simplified term, whereas the application of the original simplify function failed.

12.1.3 Normalization

Rewrite rules only model "steps" of rewriting. We need a normalization strategy atop so that rewrite rules are applied systematically (i.e., repeatedly and exhaustively in some sense). If we had a suitable function normalize, then we might be able to apply the simplify function in the following manner:

Interactive Haskell session:

▶ normalize simplify (Binary Add (Var "a") (Binary Add (Var "b") (IntConst 0)))
Binary Add (Var "a") (Var "b")

Thus, "$a + (b+0)$" is simplified to "$a + b$" when expressed in concrete syntax; we underline again the redex for clarity. However, there seem to be many possible behaviors for normalization, for example: (i) to apply rewrite rules in top-down or bottom-up manner; (ii) to aim at a single or an exhaustive application of the given rules; (iii) to succeed or fail in the case of no applicable rewrite rules; or (iv) to apply rewrite rules only to terms of suitable types or descend into terms to find subterms of suitable types.

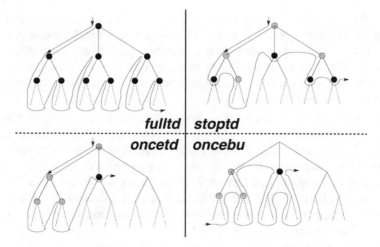

Fig. 12.1 Illustration of different traversal schemes. (Source: [50].) The illustration conveys which nodes are encountered during the traversal and whether the given strategy fails (see the gray nodes) or succeeds (see the black nodes).

Some rewriting approaches tend to favor one "built-in" normalization strategy so that rewrite rules are applied, in some sense, exhaustively [85]. One popular strategy is "innermost" which essentially attempts rules repeatedly in a bottom-up manner until no rule applications are feasible anymore. Other rewriting approaches permit programmers to define normalization strategies. This is the case for the style of (so-called) *strategic programming*, as discussed below. Without such flexibility, programmers end up controlling normalization by more complex rewrite rules.

12.1.4 Strategic Programming

Strategic programming is a discipline which enables the programmer to define and use strategies [86, 87, 50, 51, 52, 85, 6, 49] for applying (collections of) rewrite rules. A suite of reusable normalization strategies is provided to the programmer to choose from, and problem-specific strategies can be defined when necessary.

The notion of strategies is language-independent; it has been realized in several programming languages, for example, in Haskell [51, 52], Java [87], and Prolog [44], and it is available in different metaprogramming systems in one form or another, without necessarily being referred to as strategies; the notion was pioneered in Stratego/XT [86, 6].

Figure 12.1 illustrates a number of "strategic" traversal schemes. All of these schemes are applied to an argument strategy which may be a collection of rewrite rules or a more complex strategy. Let us explain these schemes informally and hint at applications:

fulltd   The argument strategy is applied to all nodes in a top-down, depth-first manner; application needs to succeed for all nodes, otherwise the entire traversal fails. This scheme is used when a transformation should be applied "everywhere". The function *doubleNegate* in Illustration 12.2 could be applied in this manner; the scheme is suitable for finding and eliminating arbitrarily nested occurrences of double negation.

stoptd   This scheme also models top-down, depth-first traversal, but traversal does not visit subtrees for nodes at which application succeeded. This scheme is used when either the existence of redexes below successful nodes can be ruled out to exist or rewrites may create redexes that must not be considered in the interests of termination, for example, when one is inlining recursive abstractions. The function swap in Illustration 12.2 could be applied in this manner. A *fulltd* traversal is not necessary, as redexes for renaming cannot occur inside variables identifier (i.e., strings or lists of characters).

oncebu   The argument strategy is applied to all nodes in a bottom-up manner; traversal stops upon the first successful application. Focusing on one redex at a time is a testament to the overall assumption that a single traversal may be insufficient to find and eliminate all redexes, as rewrites may enable new rewrites. Thus, in general, a repeated application of given rewrite rules may be needed for the sake of completeness. We mentioned *innermost* before as a common normalization strategy; it can be defined by means of repeating *oncebu* until no more redexes are found in this manner.

oncetd   This is just like **oncebu**, but traversal commences in a top-down manner.

Exercise 12.3 (Nonterminating traversal)   [Intermediate level]
Describe a simple, concrete scenario for which a traversal based on **fulltd** *may fail to terminate.*

As an exercise in metaprogramming expressiveness, we would like to give precise definitions of these schemes. In fact, we would like to define the schemes as abstractions in Haskell, thereby revealing the expressiveness that may be needed when a strategic programmer wants to define yet other traversals or schemes for them. We need two special primitives for what we refer to as layer-by-layer traversal; see Fig. 12.2 for an illustration. Let us describe the traversal modeled by these primitives when applied to an argument strategy:

all   The argument strategy is applied to all immediate subterms of a given term; in fact, all applications have to succeed, otherwise the *all* strategy fails. Thus, a (successful) *all* strategy essentially rewrites the immediate subterms (the "children") of a term.

one   The argument strategy is applied to all immediate subterms (from left to right) until one application succeeds. If all applications fail, then the *one* strategy fails too. Thus, a (successful) *one* strategy essentially rewrites one immediate subterm (a "child") of a term.

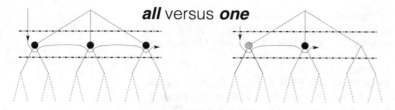

all versus *one*

Fig. 12.2 Layer-by-layer traversal. (Source: [50].)

The following code sketch illustrates how *all* could be defined for expressions:

```
all s (IntConst i) = IntConst <$> s i
all s (BoolConst b) = BoolConst <$> s b
all s (Var v) = Var <$> s v
all s (Unary o e1) = Unary <$> s o <*> s e1
all s (Binary o e1 e2) = Binary <$> s o <*> s e1 <*> s e2
```

That is, the argument s (which is essentially a polymorphic function) is applied to all immediate subterms by combining the applications in the applicative functor style. (We could also use a monadic bind instead.) There is one case for every constructor.

In reality, *all* and *one* are generically defined or definable for all (at least most) Haskell types. For instance, in Haskell's "scrap your boilerplate" (SYB) approach to generic functional programming [45, 46, 47], suitable type-class instances are automatically derived. That is, the code shown would essentially be derived by a tool (such as a compiler).

We are ready to define the earlier traversal schemes as a Haskell library of function combinators. We also provide a few more basic combinators.

Illustration 12.4 (A small strategic programming library)

Haskell module Data.Generics.Strategies

```
— Strategic traversal schemes
fulltd s = s `sequ` all (fulltd s)
fullbu s = all (fullbu s) `sequ` s
stoptd s = s `choice` all (stoptd s)
oncetd s = s `choice` one (oncetd s)
oncebu s = one (oncebu s) `choice` s
innermost s = repeat (oncebu s)

— Basic strategy combinators
s1 `sequ` s2 = λ x → s1 x >>=s2 — monadic function composition
s1 `choice` s2 = λ x → s1 x `mplus` s2 x — monadic choice
all s = ... — magically apply s to all immediate subterms
one s = ... — magically find first immediate subterm for which s succeeds

— Helper strategy combinators
```

```
try s = s `choice` return  -- recover from failure
vary s v = s `choice` (v `sequ` s)  -- preprocess term, if necessary
repeat s = try (s `sequ` repeat s)  -- repeat strategy until failure

-- Strategy builders
orFail f = const mzero `extM` f  -- fail for all other types
orSucceed f = return `extM` f'  -- id for all other types
  where f' x = f x `mplus` return x  -- id in case of failure
```

Thus, the traversal schemes are essentially defined as recursive functions in terms of sequential composition (sequ), left-biased choice, and the traversal primitives all and one. There are also function definitions for "strategy builders" which are needed to turn type-specific rewrite rules into generic functions. This transition is essential for one to be able to process terms of arbitrary types with subterms of different types – not all terms are of types of interest.

Let us illustrate the library in action:

Interactive Haskell session:

```
-- The expression "a + b * 0" with simplification potential
▶ let e1 = Binary Add (Var "a") (Binary Mul (Var "b") (IntConst 0))
-- The expression "((a * b) * c) * d" associated to the left
▶ let e2 = Binary Mul (Binary Mul (Binary Mul (Var "a") (Var "b")) (Var "c")) (Var "d")
-- The expression "0 + a" requiring commutativity for simplification
▶ let e3 = Binary Add (IntConst 0) (Var "a")
- - - - - - - - - - - - - - - - - - - - - - - - - - - - - - - - - - - - - -
-- Incomplete simplification with fulltd
▶ fulltd (orSucceed simplify) e1
Binary Add (Var "a") (IntConst 0)
- - - - - - - - - - - - - - - - - - - - - - - - - - - - - - - - - - - - - -
-- Complete simplification with fullbu
▶ fullbu (orSucceed simplify) e1
Var "a"
- - - - - - - - - - - - - - - - - - - - - - - - - - - - - - - - - - - - - -
-- Incomplete association to the right with fullbu
▶ fullbu (orSucceed associate) e2
Binary Mul (Var "a") (Binary Mul (Binary Mul (Var "b") (Var "c")) (Var "d"))
- - - - - - - - - - - - - - - - - - - - - - - - - - - - - - - - - - - - - -
-- Complete association to the right with innermost
▶ innermost (orFail associate) e2
Binary Mul (Var "a") (Binary Mul (Var "b") (Binary Mul (Var "c") (Var "d")))
- - - - - - - - - - - - - - - - - - - - - - - - - - - - - - - - - - - - - -
-- Apply simplification module commutativity
▶ vary (orFail simplify) (orFail commute) e3
Var "a"
```

Exercise 12.4 (Applicability of innermost)   [Basic level]
Consider again the swap *function of Illustration 12.2. Why would a traversal based on* innermost *not produce the correct result with all occurrences of the two variables consistently swapped?*

The present section is summarized by means of a recipe.

Recipe 12.1 (Design of a strategic program).

Test cases   *Set up test cases for the strategic program, just like for any transformational program (Recipe 5.2). A positive test case consists of an input term and the expected output term. A negative test case consists of an input term and the expectation that the strategy fails.*

Rules   *Implement the basic units of functionality, i.e., (rewrite) rules which match and build patterns of interest and possibly perform other computations along with matching and building.*

Groups   *Group rules into logical units, for example, groups for simplification, normalization, desugaring, and other things. The groups may be specific to the problem at hand. For instance, there may be several groups of optimization rules, subject to separate phases.*

Strategy   *Reuse (i.e., select) or define (i.e., compose) strategy combinators so that they can be applied to the appropriate groups of rules. The combinators may be concerned with traversal or other forms of "control" (e.g., order, alternatives, fixed-point computation).*

Testing   *Test the composed strategy in terms of the test cases.*

12.1.5 Rewriting-Related concerns

12.1.5.1 Other Traversal Idioms

We mention in passing that we have limited ourselves here to *type-preserving* strategies. (We refer to "type" here in terms of the syntactic category of object programs being manipulated.) If we wanted to use rewriting or strategic programming to extract data using so-called *type-unifying* strategies or to perform any other kind of non-type-preserving operations, then we would need additional machinery, but we will not discuss this here. Traversal schemes may also need to maintain additional arguments in the sense of environments and states, so that information is passed down and updated along with traversal. There are also alternative models for combining traversal and rewriting. For instance, traversals may also be set up as walks subject to performing actions that descend into the children, proceed along the siblings, and return to the root [4].

12.1.5.2 Concrete Object Syntax

Rewriting on top of "large" syntaxes may, arguably, benefit from the use of concrete object syntax, as discussed earlier (Section 7.5), because a programmer may recognize object language patterns more easily. Several metaprogramming systems do indeed support concrete object syntax for this reason.

12.1.5.3 Graph Rewriting and Model Transformation

There is the related discipline of graph grammars and transformation [66, 23] – thus, rewriting may instead operate on graphs rather than terms (or trees). In model transformation [14, 56], one may operate on models ("graphs") that are instances of a metamodel with part-of, reference, and inheritance relationships. There exist dedicated model-transformation languages, for example, ATL [31]. These approaches also aim to eliminate boilerplate code for controlling the overall transformation process, including traversal. For instance, ATL provides a refining mode [80] so that transformation rules can be limited to the model elements that need to be replaced.

12.1.5.4 Origin Tracking

In term rewriting (or model transformation), traceability may be desirable in the sense that the "origin" of any given (sub-) term (or model element) can be traced back to some original term (or model element). This idea is captured in a fundamental manner by the notion of origin tracking [18, 88, 65]. For instance, if a semantic analysis was applied to an abstract or intermediate representation in a language implementation, then origin tracking helps in systematically relating back the results of the analysis (e.g., errors or warnings) to the original program. Origin tracking relies on deep support in a metaprogramming or model-transformation system.

12.1.5.5 Layout Preservation

When transforming object programs (by means of rewriting or otherwise), it may be desirable to retain the original layout (white space, line breaks, and even comments) in the programs to the extent possible. For instance, when one is performing a re-engineering transformation on legacy code, the code should be retained as much as possible so that programmers will still recognize their code. Such layout preservation [28, 41, 29] calls for a suitable object-program representation (CST or AST) which incorporates layout. Less obviously, a term-rewriting approach may need to manipulate object-program patterns in a special way so as to retain layout where possible, subject also to possibly incorporating an incremental formatter that applies to fragments without inherited layout or with invalidated layout.

12.2 Attribute Grammars

Attribute grammars (AGs) [40, 3, 60, 25] can be viewed as a computational paradigm for describing translations or analyses by means of adding attributes to nodes in a CST or AST. An AG combines a context-free grammar with computational rules. Each computational rule relates attributes of nonterminal symbols within the scope of a specific context-free rule. The order of computation (attribute evaluation) is not explicitly described, but it can be inferred from the attribute dependencies expressed by the computational rules. In Section 7.3.2, we discussed a limited form of an AG, i.e., grammars enhanced by semantic actions for AST construction to serve as input for a parser generator.

AGs are supported explicitly by some metaprogramming systems with dedicated AG languages, for example, Eli [32], JastAdd [25], Silver [83], or (Aspect) Lisa [60] and these systems support several AG extensions (see, e.g., [33, 48, 42]). The AG style of metaprogramming and computation can also be leveraged if a sufficiently powerful (declarative) metalanguage is used. In particular, AGs can be "encoded" in functional programming [75, 71], as we will show below. Furthermore, a limited form of an AG is also supported by mainstream parser generators such as ANTLR, which we discussed earlier. In this section, we introduce the notion of AGs as a means of approaching analysis and translation problems.

12.2.1 The Basic Attribute Grammar Formalism

We begin with a trivial problem to explain the basics of AGs. In Fig. 12.3, we show an attributed CST for a binary number in the sense of the ("fabricated") Binary Number Language (BNL). Decimal values for the relevant subtrees are shown next to the nodes. That is, the nodes for the individual bits carry attributes for values that take into account the position of each bit. The nodes for bit sequences carry attributes for values that arise as sums of values for subtrees. For instance, the decimal value for the bit sequence 101 is $5 = 4 + 0 + 1$. This trivial (illustrative) example is due to Knuth [40].

We may need additional (auxiliary) attributes to compute the actual decimal values. In one possible model, we may assign a position $(\ldots, 2, 1, 0, -1, -2, \ldots)$ to each bit and maintain the length of a bit sequence so as to be able to actually compute the value for any bit. Table 12.1 shows all attributes that we want to compute.

As the table clarifies, attributes are assigned to nonterminals. An attribute is classified as either inherited or synthesized. We use the classifiers *inherited* ("I") and

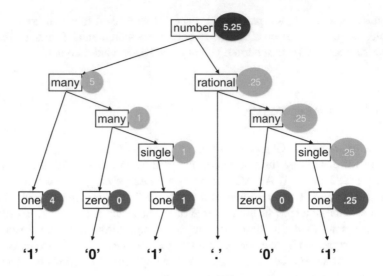

Fig. 12.3 An attributed syntax tree for the binary number 101.01. The attributes attached to the nodes model the decimal value of the subtree at hand.

Table 12.1 Attributes for binary to decimal number conversion

Nonterminal	Attribute	I/S	Type
number	*Val*	S	float
bits	*Val*	S	float
bit	*Val*	S	float
rest	*Val*	S	float
bits	*Pos*	I	integer
bit	*Pos*	I	integer
bits	*Len*	S	natural

synthesized ("S") to express that the attribute is to be passed down or up, respectively, in the tree. This classification has to do with attribute dependencies, as we will see in a second.

An AG associates a collection of computational rules with each context-free rule p. Each computational rule is of the following form:

$$x_0.a_0 = f(x_1.a_1, \ldots, x_m.a_m)$$

where $x_0, \ldots, x_m$ are nonterminals of the context-free rule, $a_0, \ldots, a_m$ are attributes of the nonterminals, and f is any sort of "operation" on the attributes. Conceptually, the computational rules state relationships on attributes. Computationally, these rules, when collected together for all attributes in a CST, can be evaluated to compute all attribute values in some order, subject to respecting the attribute dependencies.

There should be exactly one computational rule for each synthesized attribute of a context-free rule's left-hand side and for each inherited attribute of each nonterminal of a context-free rule's right-hand side. Intuitively, this means that synthesized attributes are indeed computed upwards in the syntax tree, whereas inherited attributes are passed down. Additional constraints are needed to make the AG well defined and, in particular, to avoid cycles [2], but we omit these details here.

We are ready to show all computational rules for number conversion.

Illustration 12.5 (An attribute grammar for number conversion)
Consider the first context-free rule and the associated computational rules:

[number] number : bits rest ;

> $bits.Pos = bits.Len - 1$
> $number.Val = bits.Val + rest.Val$

That is, the inherited attribute Pos of the right-hand symbol bits is equated with the difference between the synthesized attribute Len of the right-hand symbol bits and 1, thereby defining the position of the leading bit in the sequence. The synthesized attribute Val of the left-hand side is equated with the sum of the Val attributes of the right-hand side, thereby combining the value of the integer and the fractional parts of the binary number.

These are the remaining context-free rules and the associated computational rules:

[single] bits : bit ;

> $bit.Pos = bits.Pos$
> $bits.Val = bit.Val$
> $bits.Len = 1$

In the following context-free rule, we assign subscripts 0 and 1 to the different occurrences of bits so that we can refer to the different attributes in the computational rules accordingly:

[many] bits0 : bit bits1 ;

> $bit.Pos = bits0.Pos$
> $bits1.Pos = bits0.Pos - 1$
> $bits0.Val = bit.Val + bits1.Val$
> $bits0.Len = bits1.Len + 1$

[zero] bit : '0' ;

> $bit.Val = 0$

[one] bit : '1' ;

> $bit.Val = 2^{bit.Pos}$

[integer] rest : ;

> *rest.Val* = 0

[rational] rest : '.' bits ;

> *rest.Val* = *bits.Val*
> *bits.Pos* = −1

Figure 12.4 shows the CST for 101.01 with the attributes of the relevant non-terminals. We use superscripts on the attribute names to make them unique across the tree. (The ids model path-based selection of the node. For instance, the id 1.2 states that we select the first subtree of the root and then the second subtree in turn.) In the figure, we also show the attribute dependencies in the tree, as defined by the computational rules; see the dotted arrows. The target of an arrow corresponds to the left-hand side of a computational rule.

It is worth noticing how the attribute dependencies point downwards and upwards in the tree. Consider, for example, Len^1, which is computed upwards in the tree and is used in initializing Pos^1, which is then used in computing other positions downwards the tree.

12.2.2 Attribute Evaluation

Given a CST and an AG, the process of computing all attributes for the CST is referred to as attribute evaluation. There are various methods of attribute evaluation [2]; one overall option is to perform static code generation for a tree walk so that the computations can be performed for any given CST without any run-time analysis. We will not discuss the corresponding technicalities here. Conceptually, we may view attribute evaluation as a simple mathematical problem in the sense of solving a system of equations.

Consider again Fig. 12.4 which encodes all the context-free rules involved and assigns unique names to all the attributes involved. For each context-free rule applied, we instantiate its computational rules for the unique attribute names taken from the CST. For instance, the root of the CST shown, with its two children, corresponds to an application of the rule [number]. Accordingly, we instantiate the computational rules as follows:

$$Pos^1 = Len^1 - 1$$
$$Val = Val^1 + Val^2$$

The left child (id 1) with its two children (ids 1.1 and 1.2) corresponds to an application of the rule [many]. Accordingly, we instantiate the computational rules as follows:

$$Pos^{1.1} = Pos^1$$
$$Pos^{1.2} = Pos^1 - 1$$
$$Val^1 = Val^{1.1} + Val^{1.2}$$
$$Len^1 = Len^{1.2} + 1$$

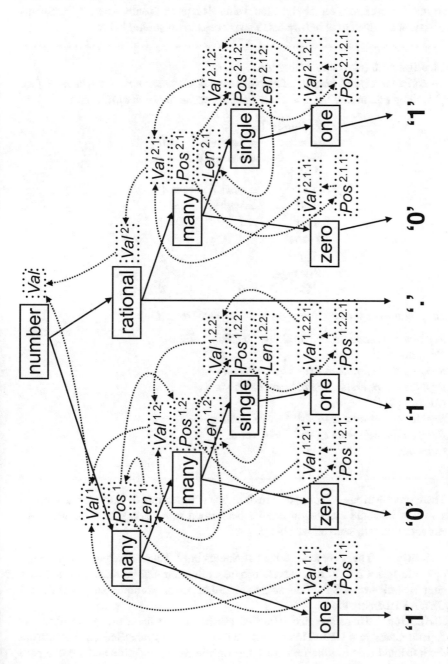

Fig. 12.4 Attributes to be evaluated for a CST of a binary number.

Once we have collected all these equations for all the applications of context-free rules together in a CST, we can simply start replacing references to attributes by values. The process starts with replacement for attributes with computational rules by constant expressions on the right-hand side. The process ends when replacements have assigned values to all attributes. The process is illustrated below.

Illustration 12.6 (Attribute evaluation)
Let us consider a much simplified example: the binary number 1 for which we face the following equations; we also show the final value for each attribute:

$$
\begin{aligned}
&// \,[\text{number}] \\
&\quad Pos^1 &&= Len^1 - 1 &&= 0 \\
&\quad Val &&= Val^1 + Val^2 &&= 1 \\
&// \,[\text{single}] \\
&\quad Pos^{1.1} &&= Pos^1 &&= 0 \\
&\quad Val^1 &&= Val^{1.1} &&= 1 \\
&\quad Len^1 &&= 1 &&= 1 \\
&// \,[\text{one}] \\
&\quad Val^{1.1} &&= 2^{Pos^{1.1}} &&= 1 \\
&// \,[\text{integer}] \\
&\quad Val^2 &&= 0 &&= 0
\end{aligned}
$$

The solution of the equation system commences as follows:

- *Replace references to Val^2 and Len^1 by their values.*
- *Compute Pos^1.*
- *Replace the reference to Pos^1 by its value.*
- *Replace the reference to $Pos^{1.1}$ by its value.*
- *Compute $Val^{1.1}$.*
- *Replace the reference to $Val^{1.1}$ by its value.*
- *Replace the reference to Val^1 by its value.*
- *Compute Val.*

There exist various AG classes which impose constraints on attribute dependencies so that attribute evaluation can be performed more easily or efficiently. We briefly mention two such classes here:

S-attribution   There are synthesized attributes only. Thus, all dependencies point upwards in a CST. In this case, attribute evaluation can be accomplished as a simple walk over CSTs. This scheme facilitates, for example, simple forms of CST/AST construction.

L-attribution   There are also inherited attributes, but there are no right-to-left dependencies in a CST. This means that we can pass inherited attributes from the left-hand side to inherited attributes on the right-hand side and we can pass synthesized attributes of any nonterminal on the right-hand side to inherited attributes on the right-hand side if they are further to the right. In this case, attribute evaluation can be also be accomplished by a simple walk, which can be carried out during parsing if the CST is built from left to right.

Let us consider an S-attributed variation on the running example.

Illustration 12.7 (An S-attributed variation on number conversion)
Compared to Illustration 12.5, we do not use not any attributes for positions in the following variation. These are the computational rules:

[number] number : bits rest ;

> $number.Val = bits.Val + rest.Val$

[single] bits : bit ;

> $bits.Val = bit.Val$
> $bits.Len = 1$

[many] bits0 : bit bits1 ;

> $bits0.Val = bit.Val * 2^{bits1.Len} + bits1.Val$
> $bits0.Len = bits1.Len + 1$

[zero] bit : '0' ;

> $bit.Val = 0$

[one] bit : '1' ;

> $bit.Val = 1$

[integer] rest : ;

> $rest.Val = 0$

[rational] rest : '.' bits ;

> $rest.Val = bits.Val / 2^{bit.Len}$

It should be clear by now that the computational rules in an AG are necessarily tied to the underlying CST structure. That is, given two context-free grammars that generate the same language (i.e., set of strings), the two grammars may require different computational rules to achieve the same ultimate result. We use the term "result" here in the sense of a dedicated synthesized attribute of the start symbol such as the decimal value of a binary number in the running example. The dependence between context-free and computational rules is illustrated below.

Illustration 12.8 (A left-recursive variation on Illustration 12.7)
The rule [many] *for bit sequences was defined in right-recursive style in Illustration 12.7. If we use left-recursive style instead, then the associated computational rules are adapted as follows:*

[many] bits0 : bits1 bit ;

$bits0.Val = 2 * bits1.Val + bit.Val$
$bits0.Len = bits1.Len + 1$

12.2.3 Attribute Grammars as Functional Programs

Attribute grammars provide a declarative computational paradigm that is actually very similar to (some form of) functional programming. That is, we may encode AGs as disciplined functional programs [75, 71]. One encoding scheme may be summarized as follows:

- Without loss of generality, we operate on the abstract as opposed to the concrete syntax. That is, we interpret computational rules on top of algebraic constructors as opposed to context-free rules.
- We associate each syntactic category (sort) with a function with one equation per alternative (constructor) to model the associated computational rules. That is, a function's patterns match on the syntactic structure. The inherited attributes of the category become function arguments, whereas the synthesized attributes become function results. Overall, we switch from the use of attribute names to the use of positions in argument lists and result tuples.
- Types of attribute values and operations on these types – as they are used in the computational rules – are also modeled in the functional program.

This encoding is illustrated for the AG for binary-to-decimal number conversion; see Illustrations 12.9 and 12.10 below.

Illustration 12.9 (Representation of binary numbers)

Haskell module Language.BNL.Syntax

```
data Number = Number Bits Rest
data Bits = Single Bit | Many Bit Bits
data Bit = Zero | One
data Rest = Integer | Rational Bits
```

Illustration 12.10 (Binary-to-decimal number conversion)

Haskell module Language.BNL.Conversion

```
number :: Number → Float
number (Number bs r) = val0
  where
    (len1, val1) = bits bs pos1
    pos1 = len1 − 1
    val2 = rest r
```

```
val0 = val1 + val2

bits :: Bits → Int → (Int, Float)
bits (Single b) pos = (1, bit b pos)
bits (Many b bs) pos0 = (len0, val0)
  where
    val1 = bit b pos0
    (len1, val2) = bits bs pos1
    pos1 = pos0 − 1
    len0 = len1 + 1
    val0 = val1 + val2

bit :: Bit → Int → Float
bit Zero _pos = 0
bit One pos = 2^^pos

rest :: Rest → Float
rest Integer = 0
rest (Rational bs) = val
  where
    (_len, val) = bits bs pos
    pos = −1
```

Because of the generality of attribute grammars, the result of encoding may be such that function arguments depend on results. This is indeed the case for the example at hand; consider the function corresponding to the rule [number], which we repeat for clarity:

```
number (Number bs r) = val0
  where
    (len1, val1) = bits bs pos1
    pos1 = len1 − 1
    val2 = rest r
    val0 = val1 + val2
```

The result of applying the function bits includes the length len1 of the bit sequence, which is then used in setting up pos1, i.e., the position of the leading bit in the sequence, to be passed as an argument to the same function application. This functional program is sound only for lazy (as opposed to eager) language semantics. Thus, AGs can be said to be declarative because no particular order of computation is expressed directly; instead, an order must be determined which respects attribute dependencies. Lazy evaluation happens to determine a suitable order.

Exercise 12.5 (An AG for translation)   [Intermediate level]
The running example (binary-to-decimal number conversion) can be seen as a trivial form of translation. Let us consider a more significant form of translation: imperative statements are to be mapped to bytecode (Section 5.2), just as in a real compiler. Devise an AG for this purpose.

12.2.4 Attribute Grammars with Conditions

AGs are routinely used to impose "context conditions" on syntactical structure, as discussed as a general concern earlier (Section 3.3). That is, we may use AGs effectively to represent the typing and name-binding rules of a software language. If we want to model conditions, then, in principle, we can simply use computational rules on Boolean-typed attributes. Alternatively, we may assume a more convenient AG notation with explicit support for conditions in addition to regular computational rules. Attribute evaluation is supposed to "fail" if any condition does not hold.

We now discuss conditions for a somewhat more complex example of an AG specification. Specifically, we consider an imperative language with a nested block structure: EIPL (*E*xtended *I*mperative *P*rogramming *L*anguage), which is an extension of BIPL. Each block (scope) may declare variables and (parameterless) procedures. The use of variables and procedures entails some nontrivial conditions to be understood relative to an *environment* maintaining scopes. Consider the following sample.

Illustration 12.11 (An imperative program with block structure)

EIPL resource languages/EIPL/sample.eipl

```
 1  begin
 2    var x = 0;
 3    proc p { x = x + x; }
 4    proc q { call p; }
 5    begin
 6      var x = 5;
 7      proc p { x = x + 1; }
 8      {
 9        call q;
10        write x;
11      }
12    end
13  end
```

In particular, the sample program declares a variable x and a procedure p in two different scopes. Thus, it is important to understand what the different references to x and p actually resolve to. We assume lexical (static) scope here. The call to q (line 9) in the inner block makes q call p (line 4) in the outer block, whose reference to x (line 3) resolves to the x in the outer block (line 2). (If we assume dynamic scope instead, then x (line 3) resolves to the x in the inner block (line 6), as the call chain departed from there.)

We can model such conditions in an AG. In the following example, we mark conditions with the keyword "require".

Illustration 12.12 (An attribute grammar for checking block structure)
Within the conditions and computational rules, we use the following function and condition symbols on attributes of an assumed type Env *for environments:*

empty   *This is the representation of the empty environment, i.e., an empty collection of scopes from which to start the semantic analysis.*
enterScope   *This function modifies an environment to enter a new (nested) scope.*
noClash   *This condition checks that a name is not yet bound in the current scope of the given environment.*
addVar   *This function adds a variable with a name and a type to the current scope of the given environment.*
addProc   *This function adds a procedure with a name to the current scope of the given environment.*
isVar   *This condition checks that a name can be resolved to a variable in the current scope or an enclosing scope of the given environment.*
getType   *The type of the variable is returned. The type is only defined if isVar holds.*
isProc   *This condition checks that a name can be resolved to a procedure in the current scope or an enclosing scope of the given environment.*

program : scope ;

   $scope.EnvIn = empty$

scope : *'begin'* decls stmt *'end'* ;

   $decls.EnvIn = enterScope(scope.EnvIn)$
   $stmt.EnvIn = decls.EnvOut$

decls0 : decl decls1 ;

   $decl.EnvIn = decls0.EnvIn$
   $decls1.EnvIn = decl.EnvOut$
   $decls0.EnvOut = decls1.EnvOut$

decls : ;

   $decls0.EnvOut = decls0.EnvIn$

[var] decl : *'var'* name *'='* expr *';'* ;

   require $noClash(decl.EnvIn, name.id)$
   $decl.EnvOut = addVar(decl.EnvIn, name.Id, expr.Type)$
   $expr.EnvIn = decl.EnvIn$

[proc] decl : *'proc'* name stmt ;

   require $noClash(decl.EnvIn, name.id)$
   $decl.EnvOut = addProc(decl.EnvIn, name.Id)$
   $stmt.EnvIn = decl.EnvIn$

[skip] stmt : *';'* ;

[assign] stmt : name '=' expr ';' ;

>   **require** *isVar(stmt.EnvIn, name.Id)*
>   **require** *getType(stmt.EnvIn, name.Id) = expr.Type*
>   *expr.EnvIn = stmt.EnvIn*

[call] stmt : *'call'* name ';' ;

>   **require** *isProc(stmt.EnvIn, name.Id)*

[scope] stmt : scope ;

>   *scope.EnvIn = stmt.EnvIn*

// Remaining statement forms omitted for brevity
...

[intconst] expr : integer ;

>   *expr.Type = intType*

[var] expr : name ;

>   **require** *isVar(expr.EnvIn, name.Id)*
>   *expr.Type = getType(expr.EnvIn, name.Id)*

// Remaining expression forms omitted for brevity
...

Exercise 12.6 (Recursive procedures)   [Basic level]
Does the given AG permit (model) recursive procedures? Discuss how to change the AG so that recursive procedures are expressed or not expressed.

Exercise 12.7 (Functional encoding for block structure)   [Basic level]
Exercise the functional program encoding (Section 12.2.3) for the given AG. (See the repository for additional positive and negative test cases.) You may use Boolean-typed attributes for the conditions or, instead, operate in the Maybe monad.

Exercise 12.8 (An interpreter for EIPL)   [Intermediate level]
Implement an interpreter that includes block structure.

12.2.5 Semantic Actions with Attributes

In Section 7.3.2, we discussed semantic actions as a means of injecting statements of the target language for parser generation into a grammar. Specifically, we used semantic actions for AST construction during parsing. A parser description with semantic actions can be considered a limited form of an AG because computational actions are associated with context-free grammar productions.

In fact, parser generators may also support proper synthesized and inherited attributes. In particular, S-attribution is supported by the "typical" parser generator. This is demonstrated for ANTLR below. That is, we transcribe the S-attributed grammar variation on binary-to-decimal number conversion (Illustration 12.7) quite directly to ANTLR notation.

Illustration 12.13 (Binary-to-decimal number conversion)

ANTLR resource languages/BNL/ANTLR/BnlBnfConversion.g4

```
grammar BnlBnfConversion;
@header {package org.softlang.bnl;}

number returns [float val]
    : bits rest WS? EOF { $val = $bits.val + $rest.val; }
    ;
bits returns [float val, int len]
    : bit { $val = $bit.val; $len = 1; }
    | bits1=bits bit { $val = 2*$bits1.val + $bit.val; $len = $bits1.len + 1; }
    ;
bit returns [int val]
    : '0' { $val = 0; }
    | '1' { $val = 1; }
    ;
rest returns [float val]
    : { $val = 0; }
    | '.' bits { $val = $bits.val / (float)Math.pow(2, $bits.len); }
    ;
WS : [ \t\n\r]+ ;
```

While ANTLR does not support AGs in their full generality, ANTLR's support goes beyond S-attribution. That is, L-attribution (i.e., a limited form of inherited attributes on top of S-attribution) is also supported. We demonstrate L-attribution with a parser for FSML below. We use a synthesized attribute for the constructed AST. We use inherited attributes to pass appropriate "context" for AST construction.

Illustration 12.14 (A parser for finite state machines)

ANTLR resource languages/FSML/Java/FsmlToObjects2.g4

```
grammar FsmlToObjects2;
@header {package org.softlang.fsml;}

fsm returns [Fsm result] :
    { $result = new Fsm(); }
    state[$result]+
    EOF
```

```
    ;
state[Fsm result] :
  { boolean initial = false; }
  ('initial' { initial = true; })?
  'state' stateid
  { String source = $stateid.text; }
  { $result.getStates().add(new State(source, initial)); }
  '{' transition[$result, source]* '}'
    ;
transition[Fsm result, String source] :
  event
  { String action = null; }
  ('/' action { action = $action.text; })?
  { String target = source; }
  ('−>' stateid { target = $stateid.text; })?
  { $result.getTransitions().add(new Transition(source, $event.text, action, target)); }
  ';'
    ;
...// Lexical syntax as before
```

That is, we pass the FSM to the nonterminals *state* and *transition* as context so that states and transitions can be added to the appropriate collections in the scope of the corresponding productions. We also pass the state id of a state declaration to each of its transitions so that it can be used as the target state id when an explicit target is omitted.

The parser is invoked like this:

```
Fsm fsm = parser.fsm().result;
```

Thus, the FSM is retrieved as the result of invoking the method *fsm*, i.e., we access the synthesized attribute result of the nonterminal *fsm*.

Let us return to the more significant AG for checking imperative programs with block structure (Section 12.2.4) and implement the AG with ANTLR. The following ANTLR code takes advantage of the imperative nature of the host language such that the environment is implemented as a global attribute rather than passing the object reference for the environment with attributes and copy rules.

Illustration 12.15 (Checking block structure)

ANTLR resource languages/EIPL/ANTLR/EiplChecker.g4

```
1  grammar EiplChecker;
2  @header {package org.softlang.eipl;}
3  @members {
4  public boolean ok = true;
5  public Env env = new Env();
6  }
7
8  program : scope EOF ;
9  scope : { env.enterScope(); } 'begin' decl* stmt 'end' { env.exitScope(); } ;
```

```
10   decl :
11          'var' NAME '=' expr ';'
12          { ok &= env.noClash($NAME.text); env.addVar($NAME.text, $expr.type); }
13       |
14          'proc' NAME stmt
15          { ok &= env.noClash($NAME.text); env.addProc($NAME.text); }
16       ;
17   stmt :
18          ';'
19       |
20          NAME '=' expr ';'
21          { ok &= env.isVar($NAME.text) && env.getType($NAME.text) == $expr.type; }
22       |
23          'call' NAME ';'
24          { ok &= env.isProc($NAME.text); }
25       |
26          scope
27       |
28          // Remaining statement forms omitted for brevity
29          . . .
30       ;
31   expr returns [Env.Type type] :
32          INTEGER
33          { $type = Env.Type.IntType; }
34       |
35          NAME
36          { ok &= env.isVar($NAME.text); $type = env.getType($NAME.text); }
37       |
38          expr1=expr '+' expr2=expr
39          {
40            ok &= $expr1.type == Env.Type.IntType
41               && $expr2.type == Env.Type.IntType;
42            $type = Env.Type.IntType;
43          }
44       |
45          // Remaining expression forms omitted for brevity
46          . . .
```

In line 9, we use a new symbol, exitScope, to exit the scope by means of a side effect. In the original formulation of the AG, there is no counterpart because the basic formalism is free of side effects. In various semantic actions, for example, in lines 12 and 15, we adapt a global attribute ok, as declared in line 4, to communicate condition failures, if any.

The use of global attributes may be acceptable if the technology-defined order of executing semantic actions and thus the order of side effects on the global attributes are easily understood to be correct. We mention in passing here that there exist AG extensions that aim at avoiding laborious computational "copy rules" in a more declarative manner [24, 33, 5].

We need a concrete realization of environments, as accessed within the conditions and computational rules. That is, we assume a corresponding type *Env*, as implemented below. We assume here again that ANTLR is used together with Java.

Illustration 12.16 (The environment for checking block structure)

Java source code <u>org/softlang/eipl/Env.java</u>

```
import java.util.Stack;
import java.util.HashMap;

public class Env {
  public enum Type { NoType, IntType, BoolType }
  private abstract class Entry { String id; }
  private class VarEntry extends Entry { Type ty; }
  private class ProcEntry extends Entry { }
  private Stack<HashMap<String, Entry>> stack = new Stack<>();
  public void enterScope() { stack.push(new HashMap<>()); }
  public void exitScope() { stack.pop(); }
  public boolean noClash(String id) { return !stack.peek().containsKey(id.intern()); }
  public void addVar(String id, Type ty) {
    VarEntry entry = new VarEntry();
    entry.ty = ty;
    stack.peek().put(id.intern(), entry);
  }
  public void addProc(String id) { stack.peek().put(id.intern(), new ProcEntry()); }
  public boolean isVar(String id) { return chase(id.intern()) instanceof VarEntry; }
  public boolean isProc(String id) { return chase(id.intern()) instanceof ProcEntry; }
  public Type getType(String id) {
    Entry entry = (VarEntry) chase(id.intern());
    return entry instanceof VarEntry ? ((VarEntry) entry).ty : Type.NoType;
  }
  private Entry chase(String id) {
    Entry entry = null;
    for (HashMap<String, Entry> map : stack)
      if (map.containsKey(id)) {
        entry = map.get(id);
        break;
      }
    return entry;
  }
}
```

In particular, lexical scopes are maintained as a stack of hash-maps – one hash-map per scope. Variables and procedures are searched for in the environment by a stack traversal, i.e., starting at the top of the stack, which is the current scope.

The present section is summarized by means of a recipe.

Recipe 12.2 (Design of an attribute grammar).

Syntax   *Define the underlying syntax, typically, by means of a context-free grammar. (Tree grammars may be used instead of context-free grammars, for example, in the form of algebraic data types in a functional program* *encoding.) In this manner, we can already separate valid inputs from invalid inputs, subject to implementing the grammar as a syntax checker (Recipe 2.5).*

Test cases   *Set up test case for the AG. In particular, a positive test case consists of a valid input and the expected output which is to be modeled eventually as a dedicated attribute of the start symbol.*

Attributes   *Associate the grammar symbols with attributes (their names and types), thereby expressing what sort of information should be available at what sort of node in the parse tree. Mark the attributes as either synthesized or inherited, in accordance with attribute dependencies.*

Computations and conditions   *Define computational rules for each context-free grammar rule, all synthesized attributes of the left-hand side nonterminal and all inherited attributes of the right-hand side nonterminals. If necessary, impose additional conditions on the attributes. (At this point, one may need to commit to a particular AG system or to an encoding of the AG, for example, as a functional program.)*

Testing   *Test attribute evaluation in terms of the test cases. This may also entail parsing.*

12.3 Multi-Stage Programming

Multi-stage programming is a style of metaprogramming that is particularly useful for program generation, i.e., for writing programs that generate programs or parts thereof at compile time or runtime. A "stage" is essentially a point in time at which programs or parts thereof are compiled, generated, or evaluated, i.e., compile time versus runtime versus different stages at runtime [78, 76, 77]. We focus here on compile-time metaprogramming as a form of multi-stage programming, which means that parts of the program are executed at compile time to compute and compile additional parts of the program (again at compile time).

The motivation for multi-stage programming is often performance in the presence of using more or less advanced abstraction mechanisms. In a simple case, program generation may help to inline function applications for arguments that are known at compile time, as we will demonstrate below. In a more advanced case, program generation may help with providing domain-specific concepts in a performant and possibly type-safe manner.

Multi-stage programming is clearly a form of metaprogramming, as a multi-stage program is essentially a program generator with the metalanguage and the object language being the same language. (In reality, the language of generated code may be restricted compared with the full metalanguage.) Multi-stage programming language extensions do not just strive for syntactically correct generated code, but name-binding and typing rules may also be guaranteed (more or less) statically.

12.3.1 Inlining as an Optimization Scenario

In the sequel, we briefly demonstrate multi-stage programming in terms of Haskell's Template Haskell extension [69] for compile-time metaprogramming. We discuss a very simple scenario – essentially, programmatic inlining of recursive function applications. Template Haskell has seen many uses, especially also in the context of optimizations for DSLs [67].

Consider the recursive function definition as follows.

Illustration 12.17 (A power function)

Haskell module Power

```
power :: Int → Int → Int
power n x =
  if n==0
    then 1
    else x * power (n−1) x
```

Now assume that within some part of our program, we need the exponent 3 time and again. We may even define a dedicated application of the power function and use it as illustrated below:

Interactive Haskell session:

```
▶ let power3 = power 3
▶ power3 3
27
- - - - - - - - - - - - - - - - - - - - - - - - - - - - - - - - - - - - - - - - - - - - -
▶ power3 4
64
```

Alas, the overhead of applying the recursively defined power function is incurred, even for applications of power3 unless we imagine a Haskell compiler that somehow decides to inline recursive function applications in some way. Multi-stage programming allows us to express explicitly that nonrecursive code is to be generated on the basis of the known exponent.

12.3.2 Quasi-Quotation and Splicing

In Template Haskell, we may define a variation on the power function which is recursive at compile time, and generates nonrecursive code for a fixed first argument, as shown below.

Illustration 12.18 (A staged power function)

Haskell module UntypedPower

```
power :: Int → Q Exp → Q Exp
power n x =
  if n==0
    then [| 1 |]
    else [| $x * $(power (n−1) x) |]

mk_power :: Int → Q Exp
mk_power n = [| λ x → $(power n [| x |]) |]
```

Notice that the structure of the code is very similar to the original power function. There is an additional function, mk_power, that we will explain in a second. The following elements of multi-stage programming are at play:

- We use quasi-quote brackets [| ⋯ |] (or Oxford brackets) to quote Haskell code, thereby expressing that the corresponding expression evaluates to code. For instance, for the base case of power we simply return the code 1.
- Within the brackets, we use splicing $(⋯) to insert code that is computed when the quasi-quoted code is constructed. For instance, for the recursive case of the power function, we insert the code returned by the recursive application of the code-generating function.
- We use the quotation monad Q in places where we compute code. This monad takes care of fresh-name generation, reification (program inspection), and error reporting.
- The type Exp stands for "Haskell expressions". By using the quasi-quote brackets, we enter a scope in which Haskell expressions are constructed (in fact, "computed") as results.

The additional function mk_power serves the purpose of applying power to an actual exponent. A lambda abstraction is constructed to receive the missing argument x; the body of the function splices in the code generated for a given exponent n. Here is a demonstration where we apply the generated function and inspect the generated code for clarity:

Interactive Haskell session:

```
▶ let power3 = $(mk_power 3)
▶ power3 3
27
- - - - - - - - - - - - - - - - - - - - - - - - - - - - - - - - - - - - - - - -
▶ power3 4
64
- - - - - - - - - - - - - - - - - - - - - - - - - - - - - - - - - - - - - - - -
▶ runQ (mk_power 3) >>=putStrLn . pprint
λ x_0 → x_0 * (x_0 * (x_0 * 1))
```

At the last prompt, we use the "run" function of Template Haskell's quotation monad (i.e., runQ) to actually perform code generation in the Haskell session, and we pretty print the code, as shown. The generated code clearly conveys that the recursive definition of the power function was unfolded three times, ending in the base case.

Exercise 12.9 (Fine-tuning the code generator)   [Intermediate level]
The generated code clearly involves an unnecessary multiplication with "1" at the right end of the multiplication. It is reasonable to expect that the compiler may take care of this by implementing a unit law for multiplication. However, whether or not a particular compiler optimization is available and applicable is generally a complicated matter. So we might prefer to make the code generator avoid the unnecessary multiplication in the first place. Adjust the generator accordingly so that it returns this code instead:

λ x_0 → x_0 * (x_0 * x_0)

12.3.3 More Typeful Staging

Arguably, the staged code discussed above lacks some important type information that might be valuable for a user of the code generator and helpful in type checking. Most notably, the revised power function takes an argument of type Exp and its result is of type Exp too. Thus, we neither document nor enforce the condition that the power function operates on Ints. Template Haskell also provides a more typeful model such that we can track the expected type of Haskell expressions, as demonstrated below.

Illustration 12.19 (A more typefully staged power function)

Haskell module TypedPower

```
1  power :: Int → Q (TExp Int) → Q (TExp Int)
2  power n x =
3    if n==0
4      then [|| 1 ||]
5      else [|| $$x * $$(power (n−1) x) ||]
6
7  mk_power :: Int → Q (TExp (Int → Int))
8  mk_power n = [|| λ x → $$(power n [|| x ||]) ||]
```

That is, we use the type constructor TExp (lines 1 and 7) instead of Exp, thereby capturing the expected type of expression. The power function is more clearly typed now in that it takes an Int and code that evaluates to an Int; the function returns code that evaluates to an Int (i.e., the actual expression for computing the power). We use "typed" quasi-quote brackets $[|| \cdots ||]$ (e.g., in line 4) and "typed" splices $\$\$(\cdots)$ (e.g., in line 5). Other than that, the program generator remains unchanged, and it can be also used in the same manner as before. Incorrect uses would be caught by the type system at the time of checking the quasi-quotes in the staged abstractions, i.e., even before applying the staged abstractions.

In staging, as much as in using macro systems, one needs to be careful about unintended name capture so that names from the generated code do not interfere in an unintended manner with other names in scope, thereby giving rise to a notion of *hygiene* [1].

Staging does not need to involve systematic quasi-quotation and splicing, as demonstrated by the "Scala-Virtualized" approach [64]. In this approach, overloading is used in a systematic manner so that the transition between regular code and quoted code ("representations") is expressed by type annotations. This idea, which relies on some Scala language mechanisms, was fully developed in the body of work on *LMS* (Lightweight Modular Staging) with applications of staging for the benefit in performance across different domains [63, 74, 30, 38], for example, database queries or parsing.

This concludes our brief discussion of multi-stage programming. There exist different language designs that support multi-stage programming. In a simple case, macro systems may be used for program generation. In the case of the language C++, its template system caters for a form of multi-stage programming, i.e., template metaprogramming [84, 70, 59]. We have exercised Template Haskell [69], thereby taking advantage of dedicated language support multi-stage programming, including means of quotation and splicing. MetaML [79], MetaOCaml [54, 35], and Helvetia [62] also provide such support. There exists scholarly work comparing or surveying approaches in a broader context [15, 61, 19, 72].

Exercise 12.10 (A recipe for multi-stage programming)   [Intermediate level]
Describe a recipe for the design of a multi-stage program (Recipe 12.3). Aim at adopting the style for recipes used elsewhere in this book. In particular, you may consult Recipe 12.4 for inspiration, as it is concerned with the problem of partial evaluation, which is closely related to multi-stage programming. In the view of the breadth of the field of multi-stage programming, as indicated by the discussion of related work above, you are advised to focus your recipe on the kind of optimization that we demonstrated above.

Recipe 12.3 (Design of a multi-stage program).   *See Exercise 12.10.*

12.4 Partial Evaluation

Partial evaluation[2] is a style of metaprogramming where a program is systematically
"refined" on the basis of partially known program input so that a partially evaluated
(specialized) program is computed; the primary objective is optimization [27, 22].
Partial evaluation is based essentially on one simple idea: evaluate (execute) a program to the extent possible for incomplete input. The result of partial evaluation is
a specialized program, also referred to as a *residual program.*

Partial evaluation has applications in, for example, modeling [81], model-driven
development [68], domain-specific language engineering [26], generic programming [53], and optimization of system software [55]. The technique of partial evaluation is particularly useful and well understood when the program is an interpreter
and the partially known program input is the program to be interpreted. In this case,
one gets essentially a compiler.

We introduce partial evaluation (or program specialization) by means of writing
a simple partial evaluator for a simple, pure, first-order, functional programming
language. In particular, we will show that the partial evaluator can be derived as
a variation on a compositionally defined interpreter. The style of partial evaluator
developed here is called an *online* partial evaluator because it makes decisions about
specialization as it goes, based on whatever variables are in the environment at a
given point during evaluation [27]. (An *offline* partial evaluator performs a static
analysis of the program to decide which variables will be considered known versus
unknown.)

12.4.1 The Notion of a Residual Program

We pick up essentially the same example that we studied in the context of multi-
stage programming, i.e., the application of the power function with a known exponent. However, this time around, we separate the metalanguage and the object
language: Haskell versus a "fabricated" functional language (BFPL). That is, we
use an object program as follows.

---

[2] Acknowledgment and copyright notice: This section is derived from a tutorial paper, jointly
written with William R. Cook [8], who has kindly agreed to the material being reused in this book.
The tutorial was published by EPTCS, subject to the rule that copyright is retained by the authors.

Illustration 12.20 (A power function and an application thereof)

BFPL resource languages/BFPL/samples/power.bfpl

```
power :: Int -> Int -> Int
power n x =
  if (==) n 0
    then 1
    else (*) x (power ((-) n 1) x)

main = print $ power 3 2 -- Prints 8
```

Now let us suppose that only the value of the exponent is given, while the base remains a variable. A partial evaluator should return the following code:

```
(*) x ((*) x ((*) x 1))
```

In infix notation:

```
x * x * x * 1
```

That is, partial evaluation should specialize the program such that the recursive function is essentially inlined as many times as needed for the different exponents encountered recursively. In contrast to multi-stage programming, we do not want to "instrument" the power function in any way (by quasi-quotation and such); instead, inlining should be triggered by setting the corresponding function argument to unknown.

We use Haskell as the meta-language for implementing the partial evaluator. We take advantage of the fact that we have already implemented an interpreter for the object language (BFPL) in Haskell in Section 5.1.3. The power function is easily represented as a Haskell term as shown below.

Illustration 12.21 (The power function in abstract syntax)

Haskell module Language.BFPL.Samples.Power

```
power :: Function
power = (
  "power",
  (([IntType, IntType], IntType),
   (["n", "x"],
     If (Binary Eq (Arg "n") (IntConst 0))
       (IntConst 1)
       (Binary Mul
          (Arg "x")
          (Apply "power" [Binary Sub (Arg "n") (IntConst 1), Arg "x"]))))))
```

This is the signature of a regular interpreter function (Illustration 5.8):

eval :: Program → Value

A "total evaluator" can handle applications of the power function only if the arguments denote values; evaluation fails if missing arguments are dereferenced:

Interactive Haskell session:

▶ eval ([power], (Apply *"power"* [IntConst 3, IntConst 2]))
Left 8
- -
▶ eval ([power], (Apply *"power"* [IntConst 3, Arg *"x"*]))
*** Exception: ...

A partial evaluator is similar to an interpreter, but it returns residual code instead of values. For now, we assume a simple scheme of partial evaluation such that a residual expression is returned:

peval :: Program → Expr

A partial evaluator agrees with a total evaluator, i.e., a regular interpreter, when values for all arguments are provided. However, when an argument is a variable without binding in the environment, some operations cannot be applied, and they need to be transported into the residual code:

Interactive Haskell session:

▶ peval ([power], (Apply *"power"* [IntConst 3, IntConst 2]))
IntConst 8
- -
▶ peval ([power], (Apply *"power"* [IntConst 3, Arg *"x"*]))
Binary Mul (Arg *"x"*) (Binary Mul (Arg *"x"*) (Binary Mul (Arg *"x"*) (IntConst 1)))

12.4.2 Interpretation with Inlining

Let us implement the envisaged partial evaluator by enhancing a regular interpreter with inlining. In principle, the approach presented here works for any interpreter following the scheme of, more or less closely, big-step operational or denotational semantics.

Illustration 12.22 (An interpreter with inlining of function applications)

Haskell resource languages/BFPL/Haskell/Language/BFPL/Inliner.hs

```
1   type Env = Map String Expr
2
3   peval :: Program → Expr
4   peval (fs, e) = f e empty
```

```
5     where
6       f :: Expr → Env → Expr
7       f e@(IntConst _) _ = e
8       f e@(BoolConst _) _ = e
9       f e@(Arg x) env =
10        case Data.Map.lookup x env of
11            (Just e') → e'
12            Nothing → e
13      f (If e0 e1 e2) env =
14        let
15          r0 = f e0 env
16          r1 = f e1 env
17          r2 = f e2 env
18        in
19          case toValue r0 of
20            (Just (Right bv)) → if bv then r1 else r2
21            Nothing → If r0 r1 r2
22      f (Unary o e) env =
23        let r = f e env
24        in case toValue r of
25            (Just v) → fromValue (uop o v)
26            _ → Unary o r
27      f (Binary o e1 e2) env = ...
28      f (Apply fn es) env = f body env'
29        where
30          Just (_, (ns, body)) = Prelude.lookup fn fs
31          rs = map (flip f env) es
32          env' = fromList (zip ns rs)
33
34    −− Attempt extraction of value from expression
35    toValue :: Expr → Maybe Value
36    toValue (IntConst iv) = Just (Left iv)
37    toValue (BoolConst bv) = Just (Right bv)
38    toValue _ = Nothing
39
40    −− Represent value as expression
41    fromValue :: Value → Expr
42    fromValue (Left iv) = IntConst iv
43    fromValue (Right bv) = BoolConst bv
```

The inlining partial evaluator deviates from the regular interpreter as follows:

- The partial evaluator maps expressions to residual expressions, whereas the regular interpreter maps expressions to values. Values are trivially embedded into expressions through the constant forms of expressions, subject to the conversions fromValue and toValue (lines 34–43).
- The partial evaluator uses an environment (line 1) which maps argument names to expressions, whereas the regular interpreter's environment maps argument names to values. This is necessary when function arguments cannot be evaluated completely and, thus, residual code needs to be passed to the applied function.

- The cases of the partial evaluator for the different expression forms (lines 7–32) are systematically derived from the cases of the regular interpreter (Illustration 5.8) by performing regular evaluation when subexpressions are values and returning residual code otherwise. The cases are explained one by one as follows:

  IntConst/BoolConst   A constant is partially evaluated to itself, just like in the regular interpreter.

  Arg   An argument is partially evaluated to a value according to the variable's binding in the environment, just like in the regular interpreter, if there is a binding. Otherwise, the variable is partially evaluated to itself; the regular interpreter fails in this case.

  If   An if-statement can be eliminated such that one of the two branches is chosen for recursive (partial) evaluation, just like in the regular interpreter, if the condition is (partially) evaluated to a Boolean value. Partial evaluation fails for an integer value, just like regular interpretation. If the condition is not partially evaluated to a value, an if-statement is reconstructed from the partially evaluated branches.

  Unary/Binary   The corresponding operation is applied to the (partially) evaluated arguments, just like in the regular interpreter, if these are all values. Otherwise, a unary/binary expression is reconstructed from the partially evaluated arguments.

  Apply   Partial evaluation involves argument (partial) evaluation, environment construction, and (partial) evaluation of the body in the new environment, just like in the regular interpreter – except that expressions for the partially evaluated arguments are passed in the environment in the case of the partial evaluator, as opposed to values in the case of the regular interpreter.

The treatment of if-statements and function applications is naive. In particular, partial evaluation of a function application may diverge, as illustrated by the following example:

Interactive Haskell session:

```
-- Result shown in concrete BFPL/Haskell syntax for clarity
▶ peval ([power], (Apply "power" [Arg "n", IntConst 2]))
if ((==) n 0)
  then 1
  else (*) 2 (if ((==) ((−) n 1) 0)
              then 1
              else (*) 2 (if ((==) ((−) ((−) n 1) 1) 0 ...))
```

The position with '...' proxies for infinite inlining. That is, in this example, the function power is applied to a specific base, 2, but the exponent remains a variable, n. Inlining diverges because the recursive case of power is expanded indefinitely.

Nevertheless, inlining is useful in a relatively well-defined situation. Before we generalize from inlining to full-fledged program specialization, let us discuss some variations on inlining by means of exercises.

Exercise 12.11 (Inlining with pairs)   [Intermediate level]
Extend the functional language to support pairs. The following expression forms
should be supported:

```
data Expr = ...
  | Pair Expr Expr -- Construction of a pair
  | Fst Expr -- 1st projection
  | Snd Expr -- 2nd projection
```

Another form of type is needed as well:

```
data Type = ... | PairType Type Type
```

For instance, a swap function for pairs of ints is defined as follows:

```
-- Haskell counterpart for comparison
-- swap :: (Int, Int) -> (Int, Int)
-- swap x = (snd x, fst x)
swap :: Function
swap =
  ( "swap",
    ( ([PairType IntType IntType], PairType IntType IntType),
      ("x", Pair (Snd (Arg "x")) (Fst (Arg "x")))
    )
  )
```

Extend the regular interpreter to support pairs. To this end, you also need to
extend the type of values. Assume the following variant, which favors a dedicated
algebraic data type over the use of Either:

```
data Value = IntValue Int | BoolValue Bool | PairValue Value Value
```

The extended interpreter must support this application:

Interactive Haskell session:

► evaluate ([swap], (Apply *"swap"* [Pair (IntConst 2) (IntConst 3)]))
PairValue (IntValue 3) (IntValue 2)

Extend the inliner to cover pairs so that it supports this application:

Interactive Haskell session:

► peval ([swap], (Apply *"swap"* [Pair (Arg *"x"*) (Arg *"y"*)]))
Pair (Arg *"y"*) (Arg *"x"*)

Exercise 12.12 (Loop unrolling in imperative programs)   [Advanced level]
Let us consider partial evaluation in the context of an imperative language. This exercise is concerned with an optimization which is somewhat similar to function inlining. The optimization is to unroll loops in an imperative language. Consider the following imperative program for exponentiation, with base x, *exponent* n, *and result* r:

BIPL resource languages/BIPL/samples/exp-loop.bipl

```
{
  r = 1;
  while (n >= 1) {
    r = r * x;
    n = n - 1;
  }
}
```

Now suppose the exponent is known: n = 3. *In the absence of a known base* x, *a partial evaluator may still unroll the loop three times, since the loop condition depends only on* n. *This unrolling may result in code like this:*

BIPL resource languages/BIPL/samples/exp-unrolled.bipl

```
{
  r = 1;
  r = r * x;
  n = n - 1;
  r = r * x;
  n = n - 1;
  r = r * x;
  n = n - 1;
}
```

A data-flow analysis may determine that the result r *does not depend on* n *and, thus, all assignments to* n *may be removed. Such slicing may result in code like this:*

BIPL resource languages/BIPL/samples/exp-sliced.bipl

```
{
  r = 1;
  r = r * x;
  r = r * x;
  r = r * x;
}
```

Implement a partial evaluator for the unrolling part of this optimization.

12.4.3 Interpreter with Memoization

The proper treatment of recursive functions requires us to synthesize *residual programs* instead of just residual expressions. Also, we need to memoize specialization in a certain way, as we will discuss in a second. We need a partial evaluator of the following type:

peval :: Program → Program

The idea here is that the incoming function definitions and the main expression are specialized such that the resulting main expression refers to specialized function definitions. A given function definition may be specialized several times depending on the statically known argument values encountered. For instance, exponentiation with the exponent 3 would be specialized as follows; the result is shown in Haskell's concrete syntax for the sake of readability:

```
power'a x = x * power'b x
power'b x = x * power'c x
power'c x = x * power'd x
power'd x = 1
```

The names of the specialized functions are fabricated from the original name by some qualification scheme to account for disambiguation. Thus, specialized function definitions have been inferred for all the inductively encountered values 3, 2, 1, and 0 for the exponent. Subject to an inlining optimization, we obtain the familiar expression for x to the power 3. The inlining needed here is trivial, in that we would only inline nonrecursive functions. The "heavy lifting" is due to specialization.

Here is a demonstration of the implemented specializer; it returns the same specialized program, in abstract syntax.

Interactive Haskell session:
```
▶ peval ([power], (Apply "power" [IntConst 3, Arg "x"]))
([
    ("power'a", (([IntType], IntType), (["x"],
      Binary Mul (Arg "x") (Apply "power'b" [Arg "x"])))),
    ("power'b", (([IntType], IntType), (["x"],
      Binary Mul (Arg "x") (Apply "power'c" [Arg "x"])))),
    ("power'c", (([IntType], IntType), (["x"],
      Binary Mul (Arg "x") (Apply "power'd" [Arg "x"])))),
    ("power'd", (([IntType], IntType), (["x"],
      IntConst 1)))
  ],
  Apply "power'a" [Arg "x"]
)
```

Exercise 12.13 (Inlining nonrecursive functions)   [Intermediate level]
Implement an analysis (in Haskell) to determine for a given functional (BFPL) pro-
gram the set of names of nonrecursive functions. For instance, all of the above func-
tions power'a, ..., power'd *should be found to be nonrecursive. Hint: This analysis*
can be described like this:

- *Start from the empty set of nonrecursive functions.*
- *Repeat the following step as long as new nonrecursive functions are still found:*

    - *Include a function in the set if it only applies functions that are already known*
      to be nonrecursive. (Thus, initially, a function is included if it does not apply
      any function – power'd in our example.)

Complement the analysis for nonrecursive functions to obtain the simple inlining
optimization discussed above.

Let us illustrate how program specialization should handle the diverging example that we faced earlier. Program specialization should carefully track argument
lists for which specialization is under way or has been completed. This solves the
termination problem:

Interactive Haskell session:

```
▶ peval ([power], (Apply "power" [Arg "n", IntConst 2]))
( [
    ("power'a", (([IntType], IntType), (["n"],
        If (Binary Eq (Arg "n")
            (IntConst 0))
            (IntConst 1) (Binary Mul
                            (IntConst 2)
                            (Apply "power'a" [Binary Sub (Arg "n") (IntConst 1)]))))))
  ],
  Apply "power'a" [Arg "n"]
)
```

Thus, the original definition of power has been specialized such that the argument position for the statically known base is eliminated. Note that the specialized
function is recursive.

The program specializer is derived from the inliner and thus from the regular
interpreter by making adaptations as described below. Overall, inlining is tamed so
that termination is guaranteed. During inlining (in fact, specialization), specialized
functions are aggregated in a data structure:

```
peval :: Program → Program
peval (fs, e) = swap (runState (f e empty) [])
    where
        f :: Expr → Env → State [Function] Expr
        ...
```

The state monad is applied to the result type to aggregate specialized functions along the way. The environment is of the same type as in the regular interpreter:

```
type Env = Map String Value
```

That is, the environment binds variables to values as opposed to expressions, as in the case of the naive inliner. Thus, the environment only serves to represent statically known arguments. Statically unknown arguments are preserved within the definitions of the specialized functions.

The cases for all constructs but function application can be taken from the inliner – except that we need to convert to monadic style, which is a simple, systematic program transformation in itself [43, 20], routinely performed by functional programmers. Thus, recursive calls to the specializer are not used directly in reconstructing terms, but their results are sequenced in the state monad. For instance:

```
f (Binary o e1 e2) env = do
  r1 ← f e1 env
  r2 ← f e2 env
  case (toValue r1, toValue r2) of
    (Just v1, Just v2) → return (fromValue (bop o v1 v2))
    _ → return (Binary o r1 r2)
```

It remains to define the case for partial evaluation of function applications; this case is significantly more complex than in the regular interpreter or the inliner. The case is presented below.

Illustration 12.23 (Specializing function applications)

Haskell resource languages/BFPL/Haskell/Language/BFPL/Specializer.hs

```
1   f (Apply fn es) env = do
2     -- Look up function
3     let Just ((ts, t), (ns, body)) = Prelude.lookup fn fs
4     -- Partially evaluate arguments
5     rs ← mapM (flip f env) es
6     -- Determine static and dynamic arguments
7     let trs = zip ts rs
8     let ntrs = zip ns trs
9     let sas = [ (n, fromJust (toValue r)) | (n, (_, r)) ← ntrs, isJust (toValue r) ]
10    let das = [ (n, (t, r)) | (n, (t, r)) ← ntrs, isNothing (toValue r) ]
11    -- Specialize body
12    let body' = f body (fromList sas)
13    -- Inlining as a special case
14    if null das then body'
15    -- Specialization
16    else do
17      -- Fabricate function name
18      let fn' = fn ++ show sas
19      -- Memoize new residual function, if necessary
20      fs' ← get
21      when (isNothing (Prelude.lookup fn' fs')) (do
```

```
22        -- Create placeholder for memoization
23        put (fs' ++ [(fn', undefined)])
24        -- Partially evaluate function body
25        body" ← body'
26        -- Define residual
27        let r = ((map (fst . snd) das, t), (map fst das, body"))
28        -- Replace placeholder by actual definition
29        modify (update (const r) fn'))
30        -- Apply the specialized function
31        return (Apply fn' (map (snd . snd) das))
```

Here the following steps are performed:

1. The applied function is looked up (lines 2–3) and the arguments are evaluated (lines 4–5), just like in the regular interpreter. As a reminder, the list of function declarations is an association list mapping function names to lists of argument types ts, the result type t, argument names ns, and the body.
2. The partially evaluated arguments are partitioned into static arguments sas and dynamic arguments das (lines 6–10). Static arguments are values; dynamic arguments exercise other expression forms.
3. The body of the specialized function is obtained by partially evaluating the original body in the variable environment of the static variables (lines 11–12). In fact, we use a let-binding; the actual specialization needs to be demanded in a monadic computation (lines 14 and 25).
4. If there are no dynamic arguments, we switch to the behavior of the interpreter by (partially) evaluating the body of the applied function (lines 13–14).
5. The "identity" (name) of the specialized function is derived by concatenating the name of the applied function and the string representation of the actual values of the static arguments (lines 17–18); see Exercise 12.14 for a discussion of naming.
6. We need to remember (memoize) function specializations so that a function is not specialized again for the same static arguments, thereby guarding against infinite inlining (lines 19–29).
7. In order to deal with recursion, it is important that the specialized function has already been added to the state before its body is obtained so that it is considered known during specialization. To this end, an undefined function, except for the name, is initially registered as a placeholder (lines 22–23), to be updated later (lines 28–29).
8. The argument list of the specialized function (the "residual") includes only variables for the dynamic positions (lines 26–27). The specialized function is ultimately applied to the dynamic arguments; the expression for that application serves as the result of partial evaluation (lines 30–31).

Exercise 12.14 (Readable function names)   [Intermediate level]
In the illustration of the specializer, we used readable names for the specialized functions, power'a, . . . , power'd, *in the specialized program. The actual implementation applies a rather crude approach to memoization:*

let fn' = fn ++ show sas

That is, it uses the string representation of the list of static arguments as part of the fabricated function name. For instance, power'a *would be rendered as* "power[(\"n\", Left 3)]". *Revise the specializer so that readable (short) function names, as assumed in the illustration, are indeed fabricated.*

As a hint at a more interesting partial evaluation scenario, consider the following problem related to the language of finite state machines (FSML), as discussed in detail in Chapter 2. We would like to apply partial evaluation in the context of model-driven development such that partial evaluation of a model interpreter for a statically known model (an FSM) provides us with a code generator. That is, a program specializer, when applied to the model interpreter with a static FSM and a dynamic event sequence, creates essentially a compiled version of the model [21]. The tutorial notes [8] describe the development of a sufficiently powerful specializer for an FSML-like interpreter.

The present section is summarized by means of a recipe.

Recipe 12.4 (Design of a partial evaluator).

Interpreter   Pick a regular interpreter (Recipe 5.1) from which to start.

Test cases   Set up test cases for the partial evaluator. A positive test case consists of a program (to be partially or totally evaluated), the input of the program, the partitioning thereof in terms of what parts are known versus unknown to the partial evaluator, the output of the program, and the partially evaluated program.

Code domains   Extend the domains used by the regular interpreter, specifically those for results, to be able to represent code.

Code generation   Complement the regular interpreter by extra cases that cover unknown input ("dynamic variables"). That is, when subexpressions cannot be evaluated to apply the regular interpreter's operations (e.g., if-then-else or addition), the corresponding expression is reconstructed from the recursively specialized subexpressions. Memoization is needed to avoid infinite code generation.

Testing   Validate each test case as follows: the regular interpreter computes the expected output from the given program and the input; the partial evaluator computes the partially evaluated program from the given program and the part of the input known to the partial evaluator; and the regular interpreter computes the expected output from the partially evaluated program and the remaining input.

12.5 Abstract Interpretation

Abstract interpretation is a semantics-based technique for *program analysis*. The expectation is that any such analysis will soundly predict the runtime behavior at some level of abstraction. We will describe two analyses by abstract interpretation: a form of type checking (Chapter 9), and "sign detection" for program variables to be used in program optimization. We will use denotational semantics or denotational style interpreters (Chapter 11) as a starting point for abstract interpreters, because the underlying compositional scheme of mapping syntax to semantics makes it easy to replace systematically the semantic domains of a standard semantics and the corresponding combinators by versions that serve the purpose of a specific program analysis.

12.5.1 Sign Detection as an Optimization Scenario

We would like to optimize imperative programs on the basis of knowing just the signs but not the precise values of some program variables. Here we assume that signs may be determined by a static analysis for "sign detection". The following program is amenable to such an optimization.

Illustration 12.24 (A program with an optimization opportunity)

BIPL resource *languages/BIPL/samples/abs.bipl*

```
{
    ...
    y = x * x + 42;
    if (y < 0)
        y = −y;
    ...
}
```

The basic laws of arithmetic suggest that the variable y in this program must be positive by the time it is tested by the condition of the if-statement. Thus, the condition must evaluate to false, which implies that the then-branch will never be executed. On the basis of such a static analysis, i.e., without knowing the exact input x, the program could be optimized. In this example, we consider the signs *Pos*, *Neg*, and *Zero* of variables in the program as properties of interest for abstract interpretation. Compare this with the standard semantics, where we care about actual numbers stored in variables. We can calculate on signs pretty much like on numbers, as illustrated by the following function tables for the arithmetic and comparison operators on signs:

*	Neg	Zero	Pos	?
Neg	Pos	Zero	Neg	?
Zero	Zero	Zero	Zero	Zero
Pos	Neg	Zero	Pos	?
?	?	Zero	?	?

+	Neg	Zero	Pos	?
Neg	Neg	Neg	?	?
Zero	Neg	Zero	Pos	?
Pos	?	Pos	Pos	?
?	?	?	?	?

<	Neg	Zero	Pos	?
Neg	?	True	True	?
Zero	False	False	True	?
Pos	False	False	?	?
?	?	?	?	?

In these tables, we use "?" to denote that the sign or truth value of an operand or result has not been assigned. For the program in Illustration 12.24, we can assign sign *Pos* to y because, for all possible signs of x, the result of x∗x has sign *Pos* or *Zero* and thus the addition of 42 implies sign *Pos* for x∗x+42. Hence, the condition must evaluate to False and the code in the then-branch is dead.

Abstract interpretation has found many application areas; see, for example, [13] for an application to refactoring and [12] for an application to grammar analysis and parsing. This section relies completely on representing abstract interpretation in Haskell, as opposed to using any semiformal notation for semantics or analysis. The development will be cursory and pragmatic overall. A thorough development can be found elsewhere [58, 57]. Also, Cousot & Cousot's line of seminal work on the subject may be consulted; see [11] for their first paper on the subject.

12.5.2 Semantic Algebras

An abstract interpreter can be seen as a variation on a regular interpreter where semantic domains and combinators are defined differently. In order to be able to explore such a variation in an effective manner, we revise a denotational interpreter so that it is parameterized in the semantic domains and combinators. This is done here for an imperative programming language (BIPL) and its direct-style denotational semantics.

That is, we aim at factoring out the algebra (an abstract data type) of meanings; we use the term "semantic algebra". We begin by identifying the corresponding signature as shown below.

Illustration 12.25 (Signature of semantic algebras)

Haskell module Language.BIPL.Algebra.Signature

```
-- Aliases to shorten function signatures
type Trafo sto = sto → sto -- Store transformation
type Obs sto val = sto → val -- Store observation
-- The signature of algebras for interpretation
data Alg sto val = Alg {
  skip' :: Trafo sto,
  assign' :: String → Obs sto val → Trafo sto,
  seq' :: Trafo sto → Trafo sto → Trafo sto,
  if' :: Obs sto val → Trafo sto → Trafo sto → Trafo sto,
  while' :: Obs sto val → Trafo sto → Trafo sto,
  intconst' :: Int → Obs sto val,
```

```
  var' :: String → Obs sto val,
  unary' :: UOp → Obs sto val → Obs sto val,
  binary' :: BOp → Obs sto val → Obs sto val → Obs sto val
}
```

That is, the signature is defined as a record type Alg. The record type carries one member for each language construct. There are type parameters sto and val for stores and values. These type parameters enable different type definitions for concrete and abstract interpreters and, in fact, for different abstract interpreters implementing different program analyses.

Given an actual algebra of the signature, an interpreter (an analysis) can be defined by simply recursing into program phrases and combining the intermediate meanings according to the operations of the algebra, as shown below.

Illustration 12.26 (The compositional scheme)

Haskell module Language.BIPL.Algebra.Scheme

```
interpret :: Alg sto val → Stmt → sto → sto
interpret a = execute
  where
    —— Compositional interpretation of statements
    execute Skip = skip' a
    execute (Assign x e) = assign' a x (evaluate e)
    execute (Seq s1 s2) = seq' a (execute s1) (execute s2)
    execute (If e s1 s2) = if' a (evaluate e) (execute s1) (execute s2)
    execute (While e s) = while' a (evaluate e) (execute s)
    —— Compositional interpretation of expressions
    evaluate (IntConst i) = intconst' a i
    evaluate (Var n) = var' a n
    evaluate (Unary o e) = unary' a o (evaluate e)
    evaluate (Binary o e1 e2) = binary' a o (evaluate e1) (evaluate e2)
```

The interpreter is equivalent to the earlier direct-style denotational interpreter (Illustration 11.2), except that the semantic combinators are not functions in scope, but instead are looked up as record components from the argument algebra a. Thus, interpretation is completely parametric at this stage.

12.5.3 Concrete Domains

The "standard semantics" can now be simply represented as a specific algebra – a record; we also speak of "concrete domains". The record components, as shown below, directly correspond to the top-level functions modeling semantic combinators, as defined in the underlying denotational interpreter (Illustration 11.3).

Illustration 12.27 (An algebra for interpretation)

Haskell module Language.BIPL.Algebra.StandardInterpreter

```
1   type Value = Either Int Bool
2   type Store = Map String Value
3   algebra :: Alg Store Value
4   algebra = a where a = Alg {
5     skip' = id,
6     assign' = λ n f m → insert n (f m) m,
7     seq' = flip (.),
8     if' = λ f g h m → let (Right b) = f m in if b then g m else h m,
9     while' = λ f g → fix (λ x → if' a f (seq' a g x) (skip' a)),
10    intconst' = λ i → const (Left i),
11    var' = λ n m → m!n,
12    unary' = λ o f m →
13      case (o, f m) of
14        (Negate, Left i) → Left (negate i)
15        (Not, Right b) → Right (not b),
16    binary' = λ o f g m → ...
17  }
```

Thus, the algebra commits to the sum of Int and Bool for values (line 1), and to maps from strings to values for stores (line 2), and it designates the usual operations for combining meanings. For instance, if-statements are eventually handled by a dispatch on a condition's two possible values, True and False (line 8).

12.5.4 Abstract Domains

An abstract interpretation devises abstract domains to analyze programs statically, as opposed to a description of the precise semantics in terms of its so-called concrete domains. For instance, an abstract interpretation for type checking would use abstract domains as follows:

```
data Type = IntType | BoolType  −− Instead of values
type VarTypes = Map String Type  −− Instead of stores
```

That is, abstract interpretation should compute variable-to-type maps as opposed to proper stores, i.e., variable-to-value maps. The idea is then that the semantic combinators on abstract domains are defined similarly to those for the concrete domains. In algebraic terms, we use (chain-) complete partial orders (CCPO or CPO). An abstract interpretation for sign detection would use abstract domains as follows:

```
data Sign = Zero | Pos | Neg | BottomSign | TopSign
data CpoBool = ProperBool Bool | BottomBool | TopBool
type Property = Either Sign CpoBool
type VarProperties = Map String Property
```

The key type is Sign, with constructors Zero, Pos, Neg for different signs of numbers. The type abstracts from the Int type used in the standard interpreter. The type Sign features additional constructors BottomSign and TopSign as least and greatest elements, which are needed for technical reasons. BottomSign ($\perp$) proxies for the analysis not having identified the sign yet. TopSign ($\top$) proxies for the analysis having failed to identify the sign. The type CpoBool adds least and greatest elements to Haskell's Bool. The type Property is a sum over Sign and CpoBool, and it thus abstracts from Value as a sum over Int and Bool in the standard interpreter. The type VarProperties abstracts from Store in the concrete interpreter, i.e., it maps variables to abstract values ("properties") rather than concrete values.

Let us take a closer look at the abstract domain for signs. We provide an implementation as follows.

Illustration 12.28 (Signs of numbers)

Haskell module Data.CPO.Sign

```
1   data Sign = Zero | Pos | Neg | BottomSign | TopSign
2
3   instance Num Sign
4     where
5       fromInteger n
6         | n > 0 = Pos
7         | n < 0 = Neg
8         | otherwise = Zero
9
10      TopSign + _ = TopSign
11      _ + TopSign = TopSign
12      BottomSign + _ = BottomSign
13      _ + BottomSign = BottomSign
14      Zero + Zero = Zero
15      Zero + Pos = Pos
16      ...
17
18   instance CPO Sign where
19      pord x y | x == y = True
20      pord BottomSign _ = True
21      pord _ TopSign = True
22      pord _ _ = False
23      lub x y | x == y = x
24      lub BottomSign x = x
25      lub x BottomSign = x
26      lub _ _ = TopSign
27
28   instance Bottom Sign where
29      bottom = BottomSign
```

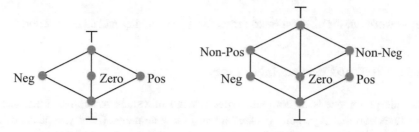

Fig. 12.5 Two options for an abstract domain of signs.

The excerpts given here illustrate the following aspects of signs:

- Signs are "abstract" numbers; Haskell's library type class Num is instantiated for type Sign (lines 3–16), paralleling the standard instance for type Int. The type-class member fromInteger (lines 5–8) is the explicit manifestation of abstraction: integers are mapped to signs. Further, we hint at the addition operation on signs (lines 10–15). Several other operations on signs have been omitted for brevity.
- Signs form a partial order, and there are least and greatest elements; see the instances of dedicated type classes CPO and Bottom (lines 18–29). In Fig. 12.5, we show two options for a partial order on signs with different degrees of precision; the algebraic data type shown earlier corresponds to the less precise option on the left. We use Hasse diagrams for illustration. The idea is that the least element ⊥ is the initial element for any sort of approximative, fixed point-based analysis (see below for details), whereas the greatest element ⊤ is the indicator of failure of analysis. We show two options for the abstract domain of signs in the figure because we want to indicate that one can make a trade-off in abstract interpretation or program analysis more generally, in terms of precision of results versus time and space complexity required.

For an abstract interpretation to be sound with regard to a given standard semantics and to enable effective computation of uniquely defined fixed points, various properties have to be satisfied by the abstract domains [57, 73], which we mention here only in passing. In general, abstract domains need to define chain-complete partial orders (ccpos). Further, there also needs to be a mapping from concrete to abstract domains (see fromInteger above) such that partial orders are preserved and homomorphisms are defined, i.e., mapping concrete values to abstract values and then combining abstract values with the abstract semantic combinators equals combining concrete values and mapping the result.

Exercise 12.15 (More discriminative signs)   [Basic level]
Implement the more precise option shown in Fig. 12.5.

12.5.5 Examples of Abstract Interpreters

Let us work out the abstract interpreters for type checking and sign detection.

12.5.5.1 A Type-Checking Interpreter

The interpreter needs to compute types instead of values for expressions, and it computes variable-type pairs (in fact, a map) for statements. Clearly, type checking can fail, which happens when the given program or some phrase of it does not type-check. As discussed earlier (Chapter 9), we do not want the type checker to "throw" in the Haskell sense. Instead, we expect to observe failure of type checking on the basis of wrapping the result types of the type checker in the Maybe monad.

Here is how we expect to use the type checker:

Interactive Haskell session:

▶ interpret TypeChecker.algebra euclideanDiv (fromList [("x", IntType), ("y", IntType)])
Just (fromList [("q", IntType), ("r", IntType), ("x", IntType), ("y", IntType)])

That is, we type-check the sample program for Euclidean division We supply enough type context for the arguments x and y. Type checking infers that the program variables q and r are of type IntType.

The simple signature introduced above (Illustration 12.25) does not give us control to add Maybe to the result types in semantic domains. We need a more general, monadic signature as follows:

Illustration 12.29 (Monadic semantic algebras)

Haskell module <u>Language.BIPL.MonadicAlgebra.Signature</u>

```
—— Aliases to shorten function signatures
type Trafo m sto = sto → m sto —— Store transformation
type Obs m sto val = sto → m val —— Store observation
—— The signature of algebras for interpretation
data Alg m sto val = Alg {
  skip' :: Trafo m sto,
  assign' :: String → Obs m sto val → Trafo m sto,
  seq' :: Trafo m sto → Trafo m sto → Trafo m sto,
  ...
}
```

That is, the type synonyms Trafo and Obs at the top (lines 1–2) for transformers and observers wrap the result in a type constructor m. The compositional scheme for monadic algebras is the same as for non-monadic ones (Illustration 12.26). We define an algebra for type checking as follows.

Illustration 12.30 (An algebra for type checking)

Haskell module Language.BIPL.MonadicAlgebra.TypeChecker

```
1   data Type = IntType | BoolType
2   type VarTypes = Map String Type
3   algebra :: Alg Maybe VarTypes Type
4   algebra = Alg {
5     skip' = Just,
6     assign' = λ x f m → f m >>=λ t →
7       case lookup x m of
8         (Just t') → guard (t==t') >> Just m
9         Nothing → Just (insert x t m),
10    seq' = flip (<=<),
11    if' = λ f g h m → do
12      t ← f m
13      guard (t==BoolType)
14      m1 ← g m
15      m2 ← h m
16      guard (m1==m2)
17      Just m1,
18    while' = λ f g m → do
19      t ← f m
20      guard (t==BoolType)
21      m' ← g m
22      guard (m==m')
23      Just m,
24    intconst' = const (const (Just IntType)),
25    var' = λ x m → lookup x m,
26    unary' = λ o f m → f m >>=λ t →
27      case (o, t) of
28        (Negate, IntType) → Just IntType
29        (Not, BoolType) → Just BoolType
30        _ → Nothing,
31    binary' = λ o f g m → ...
32  }
```

We discuss the first few record components as follows:

skip′   The transformer returns the given variable-type map as is (line 5).

assign′   The right-hand side expression is type-checked and its type, if any, is bound to t (line 6). The variable-type map m is consulted to see whether or not the left-hand side variable x has an associated type (line 7). If there is a type, it must be equal to t (line 8); otherwise, the map is adapted (line 9).

seq′   Flipped monadic function composition composes type checking for the two statements (line 10).

if′   The condition is type-checked and its type, if any, is bound to t (line 12); the guard checks that t equals BoolType (line 13). The then- and else-branches are type-checked for the same input map m and the result maps, if any, are bound to m1 and m2 (lines 14–15). The two maps are checked to be equal; this is one sound option for if-statements (Section 9.7.1) (line 16), and either of them (in fact, m1) is finally returned (line 17).

Exercise 12.16 (Fixed-point semantics of while-loops)   [Basic level]
Why does the semantic combinator while' *for type checking not involve a fixed-point computation, whereas it does in the case of standard semantics?*

Exercise 12.17 (Algebras with monadic binding)   [Intermediate level]
Would it make sense to factor out monadic binding, as exercised extensively in the algebra above, into the compositional scheme?

12.5.5.2 A Sign-Detection Interpreter

Let us set up a test case for sign detection first. We pick a program that involves a while-loop so that we are bound to also discuss the intricacies of fixed-point semantics. In fact, we offer two variations on a program computing the factorial of an argument x in the hope that sign detection works equally well for these variations; see below.

Illustration 12.31 (A program for the factorial (V1))

BIPL resource <u>languages/BIPL/samples/factorialV1.bipl</u>

```
// Assume x to be positive
y = 1;
i = 1;
while (i <= x) {
  y = y * i;
  i = i + 1;
}
```

Illustration 12.32 (A program for the factorial (V2))

BIPL resource <u>languages/BIPL/samples/factorialV2.bipl</u>

```
// Assume x to be positive
y = 1;
while (x >= 2) {
  y = y * x;
  x = x - 1;
}
```

We want sign detection to infer that the variable y is positive after execution of the program. As we will see, the minor idiomatic differences between the two variants will cause a challenge for the program analysis. That is, an initial, more straightforward version of the analysis will fail to predict the sign of y in the second variant. A refined, more complex version will succeed, though.

Here is how we expect the program analysis for sign detection to work:

Interactive Haskell session:

► interpret analysis facv1 (fromList [("*x*", Left Pos)])
fromList [("*i*", Left Pos), ("*x*", Left Pos), ("*y*", Left Pos)]

That is, applying the analysis to the first variant of the factorial code (facv1) and setting up x with sign Pos as a precondition, we find that y has sign Pos after program execution; the signs for the other program variables also make sense.

We define an algebra for sign detection as follows.

Illustration 12.33 (An algebra for sign detection)

Haskell module Language.BIPL.Analysis.BasicAnalysis

```
 1  type Property = Either Sign CpoBool
 2  type VarProperties = Map String Property
 3  algebra :: Alg VarProperties Property
 4  algebra = a where a = Alg {
 5    skip' = id,
 6    assign' = λ n f m → insert n (f m) m,
 7    seq' = flip (.),
 8    if' = λ f g h m →
 9      let Right b = f m in
10        case b of
11          (ProperBool True) → g m
12          (ProperBool False) → h m
13          BottomBool → bottom
14          TopBool → g m `lub` h m,
15    while' = λ f g → fix' (λ x → if' a f (x . g) id) (const bottom),
16    intconst' = λ i → const (Left (fromInteger (toInteger i))),
17    var' = λ n m → m!n,
18    unary' = λ o f m →
19      case (o, f m) of
20        (Negate, Left s) → Left (negate s)
21        (Not, Right b) → Right (cpoNot b),
22    binary' = λ o f g m → ...
23  }
```

We discuss the semantic combinators one by one as follows:

skip', assign', seq' These cases (lines 5–7) are handled in the same manner as in the standard semantics. That is, it does not matter if we operate on concrete or abstract stores when it comes to the empty statement, assignment, and sequential composition.

if′   There is a case discrimination with respect to the truth value computed for the condition of the if-statement (lines 8–14); the first two cases correspond to those also present in the standard semantics (True and False, lines 11–12). The third case (line 13) applies when the truth value is not (yet) defined, in which case the resulting variable-property map is also undefined, i.e., bottom. The fourth case (line 14) applies when the truth value is "over-defined", i.e., the analysis cannot derive any precise value, in which case the least upper bound of the variable-property maps for the then- and else-branches are computed. This is discussed in more detail below.

while′   A fixed point is computed in a manner similar to the standard semantics (line 15), except that a different fixed-point combinator fix′ is assumed here, which aims at finding a fixed point computationally and effectively by starting from an initial approximation bottom. This is discussed in more detail below.

intconst′   The constant is mapped to a sign by plain abstraction (line 16), i.e., the Int is first mapped to an Integer so that the fromInteger member of the type class Num, as discussed above (Illustration 12.28), can be applied.

var′   This case (line 17) is handled in the same manner as in the standard semantics.

unary′ and binary′   Just as in the standard semantics, operations are applied to the arguments, except that we operate on the abstract domains here: Sign and CpoBool.

One crucial aspect is the treatment of if-statements in the case where the truth value for the condition cannot be precisely determined. In this case, the analysis approximates the resulting property-type map by simply assuming that either of the two branches may be executed and, thus, the least upper bound (LUB) of the two branches is taken. Here we rely on LUBs on maps to be defined in a pointwise manner as follows.

Illustration 12.34 (Partial order on maps with pointwise LUB)

Haskell module Data.CPO.Map

```
instance (Ord k, CPO v) => CPO (Map k v) where
  pord x y = and (map (f y) (toList x))
    where f y (k,v) = pord v (y!k)
  lub x y = foldr f y (toList x)
    where f (k,v) m = Data.Map.insert k (lub v (y!k)) m
instance (Ord k, CPO v) => Bottom (Map k v) where
  bottom = empty
```

If the two branches of an if-statement disagree in the sign of a variable (Pos versus Neg versus Zero), then the combined value is Top. This causes a precision challenge, to be discussed in a second.

Another crucial aspect is the treatment of while-loops in terms of the required fixed-point computation. We a dedicated fixed-point combinator as follows.

Illustration 12.35 (Fixed-point computation with iterands)

Haskell module Language.BIPL.Analysis.Fix

```
fix' :: Eq a => ((a → a) → a → a) → (a → a) → a → a
fix' h i x = limit (iterate h i)
   where limit (b1:b2:bs) = if b1 x == b2 x then b1 x else limit (b2:bs)
```

This combinator is polymorphic, but let us explain it in terms of the abstract domains at hand. The type variable a proxies for abstract stores (i.e., type VarProperties). Thus, the combinator, in this instance, returns an abstract store transformer. It is parameterized in the "transformer transformer" h, from which we can take a fixed point, an initial transformer i to start off the iteration, and an abstract store x. With iterate, the combinator builds an infinite list by applying h to i 0, 1, 2, ... number of times. With the local helper limit, the combinator finds the position in the list such that the applications of two consecutive elements b1 and b2 to x are the same; b1 is thus the fixed point, i.e., the store transformer for the while-loop.

We are now ready to apply the program analysis:

Interactive Haskell session:

```
▶ interpret BasicAnalysis.algebra facv1 (fromList [("x", Left Pos)])
fromList [("i", Left Pos), ("x", Left Pos), ("y", Left Pos)]
- - - - - - - - - - - - - - - - - - - - - - - - - - - - - - - - - - - - - - - - -
▶ interpret BasicAnalysis.analysis facv2 (fromList [("x", Left Pos)])
fromList [("x", Left TopSign), ("y", Left TopSign)]
```

Our analysis finds the expected sign for the first variant (Illustration 12.31); it fails for the second variant (Illustration 12.32), as it reports TopSign for y. Generally, program analysis (whether based on abstract interpretation or not) may be challenged by such precision issues. In this particular case, the origin of the problem lies in the handling of if-statements. The abstract store transformer for an if-statement will assign TopSign all too easily to variables whenever the condition evaluates to TopBool which may happen easily. Consider the second variant again; variable x is decremented in the loop body and, by the rules for signs, the sign of x is going to be TopSign. Thus, the truth value of the loop's condition is going to be TopBool.

Let us hint at a possible improvement. Given the abstract input store m for the if-statement, we do not simply compute the abstract output stores for the two branches from the given map m and combine them, but instead determine a smaller abstract store to serve as the input for each branch. For the then-branch, we determine the largest store such that the condition evaluates to True, and likewise for the else-branch. We revise the algebra accordingly as follows.

Illustration 12.36 (A refined algebra for sign detection)

Haskell module <u>Language.BIPL.Analysis.RefinedAnalysis</u>

```
 1  algebra :: Alg VarProperties Property
 2  algebra = a where a = Alg {
 3     ...
 4     if' = λ f g h m →
 5       let Right b = f m in
 6         case b of
 7           (ProperBool True) → g m
 8           (ProperBool False) → h m
 9           BottomBool → bottoms m
10           TopBool → g (feasible True f m) `lub` h (feasible False f m)
11             where feasible b f m = lublist (bottoms m) [ m' |
12                     m' ← maps (keys m),
13                     m' `pord` m,
14                     Right (ProperBool b) `pord` f m' ],
15     ...
16  }
```

The refinement concerns the TopBool case for if' (lines 10–14). That is, g and h are not directly applied to m, as before. Instead, a variable-property map is computed for each branch by the function feasible. This function generates all maps m' such that they assign properties to the same variables as in m (line 12), they are less defined than or equally defined as m (line 13), and they permit the evaluation of the condition f for the given Boolean value *b* (line 14).

We apply the refined program analysis as follows:

Interactive Haskell session:

▶ interpret RefinedAnalysis.algebra facv1 (fromList [(*"x"*, Left Pos)])
fromList [(*"i"*, Left Pos), (*"x"*, Left Pos), (*"y"*, Left Pos)]

- -

▶ interpret RefinedAnalysis.algebra facv2 (insert *"x"* (Left Pos) empty)
fromList [(*"x"*, Left TopSign), (*"y"*, Left Pos)]

Thus, we infer sign Pos for y for both variants of the program now. Nevertheless, there is room for improvement, as illustrated by the following exercises.

Exercise 12.18 (More precise domains)   [Intermediate level]
As the analysis stands, when applied to the second variant of the factorial program, it maps x to Top. *Refine the analysis so that it can make a more precise prediction. This exercise may require an adaptation of the abstract domains for signs.*

Exercise 12.19 (Precise squaring) [Intermediate level]
The present section started with an example in which the sign of an input variable x *was not fixed (Illustration 12.24) and, thus,* BottomSign *should be assigned to* x*. The analysis, as it stands, would be too imprecise to serve for this example. For instance, consider squaring* x*. Per the rules we would assign* BottomSign*∗*BottomSign = BottomSign *to* x*∗*x*, even though we "know" that the result of squaring a number* x *has sign* Zero *or* Pos *no matter what the sign of* x*. Refine the analysis accordingly.*

The present section is summarized by means of a recipe.

Recipe 12.5 (Design of an abstract interpreter).

Interpreter   *Pick a compositional interpreter (Recipe 11.1) from which to start.*

Abstract domains   *Define the abstract domains as abstraction from the concrete domains in the underlying interpreter so that the properties of interest (e.g., signs) are modeled. Abstract domains include bottom (⊥ = "undefined") and top (⊤ = "overdefined") as abstract values, subject to a partial order for undefinedness.*

Test cases   *Set up test cases for the abstract interpreter. A test case consists of an input term and the expected result of the analysis, thereby exercising the abstract domains. A positive test case does not exercise top for the result. Explore the precision the analysis by also incorporating negative test cases, as variations on positive test cases, for which the analysis returns top.*

Parameterization   *Factor the compositional interpreter to become parametric in the semantic domains and semantic combinators, thereby enabling the use of the abstract domains for the analysis at hand.*

Testing   *Test the abstract interpreter in terms of the test cases.*

Summary and Outline

We have presented term rewriting and attribute grammars as computational paradigms for developing certain kinds of metaprograms in a more disciplined way. Term rewriting fits well with rule-based transformational problems, for example, refactoring and optimization. Attribute grammars fit well with tree-annotation problems and, specifically, with translations and analyses. We have also presented (compile-time) multi-stage programming and partial evaluation as powerful program optimization techniques and abstract interpretation as a semantics-based method for analysis. Multi-stage programming serves the purpose of program generation by allowing one to derive optimized code based on appropriately "quasi-quoted code and splices". Partial evaluation serves the purpose of program specialization by allowing one to derive optimized code based on an appropriately refined interpreter, which, in the case we considered, combines function inlining and memoization for arguments. Abstract interpretation may serve, for example, the purpose of optimization.

This ends the technical development presented in this book. We will now wrap up the book in the Postface.

References

1. Adams, M.: Towards the essence of hygiene. In: Proc. POPL, pp. 457–469. ACM (2015)
2. Alblas, H.: Attribute evaluation methods. In: Proc. SAGA, *LNCS*, vol. 545, pp. 48–113. Springer (1991)
3. Alblas, H., Melichar, B. (eds.): Attribute Grammars, Applications and Systems, International Summer School SAGA, 1991, Proceedings, *LNCS*, vol. 545. Springer (1991)
4. Bagge, A.H., Lämmel, R.: Walk your tree any way you want. In: Proc. ICMT, *LNCS*, vol. 7909, pp. 33–49. Springer (2013)
5. Boyland, J.T.: Remote attribute grammars. J. ACM **52**(4), 627–687 (2005)
6. Bravenboer, M., Kalleberg, K.T., Vermaas, R., Visser, E.: Stratego/XT 0.17. A language and toolset for program transformation. Sci. Comput. Program. **72**(1-2), 52–70 (2008)
7. Carette, J., Kiselyov, O., Shan, C.: Finally tagless, partially evaluated: Tagless staged interpreters for simpler typed languages. J. Funct. Program. **19**(5), 509–543 (2009)
8. Cook, W.R., Lämmel, R.: Tutorial on online partial evaluation. In: Proc. DSL, *EPTCS*, vol. 66, pp. 168–180 (2011)
9. Cordy, J.R.: The TXL source transformation language. Sci. Comput. Program. **61**(3), 190–210 (2006)
10. Cordy, J.R.: Excerpts from the TXL cookbook. In: GTTSE 2009, Revised Papers, *LNCS*, vol. 6491, pp. 27–91. Springer (2011)
11. Cousot, P., Cousot, R.: Abstract interpretation: A unified lattice model for static analysis of programs by construction or approximation of fixpoints. In: Proc. POPL, pp. 238–252. ACM (1977)
12. Cousot, P., Cousot, R.: Grammar semantics, analysis and parsing by abstract interpretation. Theor. Comput. Sci. **412**(44), 6135–6192 (2011)
13. Cousot, P., Cousot, R., Logozzo, F., Barnett, M.: An abstract interpretation framework for refactoring with application to extract methods with contracts. In: Proc. OOPSLA, pp. 213–232. ACM (2012)
14. Czarnecki, K., Helsen, S.: Feature-based survey of model transformation approaches. IBM Syst. J. **45**(3), 621–646 (2006)
15. Czarnecki, K., O'Donnell, J.T., Striegnitz, J., Taha, W.: DSL implementation in MetaOCaml, Template Haskell, and C++. In: Domain-Specific Program Generation, International Seminar, Dagstuhl Castle, Germany, March 23-28, 2003, Revised Papers, *LNCS*, vol. 3016, pp. 51–72. Springer (2004)
16. Dershowitz, N.: A taste of rewrite systems. In: Functional Programming, Concurrency, Simulation and Automated Reasoning: International Lecture Series 1991-1992, McMaster University, Hamilton, Ontario, Canada, *LNCS*, vol. 693, pp. 199–228. Springer (1993)
17. Dershowitz, N., Jouannaud, J.P.: Rewrite systems. In: Handbook of Theoretical Computer Science B: Formal Methods and Semantics, pp. 243–320. North-Holland (1990)
18. van Deursen, A., Klint, P., Tip, F.: Origin tracking. J. Symb. Comput. **15**(5/6), 523–545 (1993)

19. Erdweg, S.: Extensible languages for flexible and principled domain abstraction. Ph.D. thesis, Philipps-Universität Marburg (2013)
20. Erwig, M., Ren, D.: Monadification of functional programs. Sci. Comput. Program. **52**, 101–129 (2004)
21. Futamura, Y.: Partial evaluation of computation process — an approach to a compiler-compiler. Higher Order Symbol. Comput. **12**, 381–391 (1999)
22. Hatcliff, J.: Foundations of partial evaluation and program specialization (1999). Available at http://people.cis.ksu.edu/~hatcliff/FPEPS/
23. Heckel, R.: Graph transformation in a nutshell. ENTCS **148**(1), 187–198 (2006)
24. Hedin, G.: An overview of door attribute grammars. In: Proc. CC, *LNCS*, vol. 786, pp. 31–51. Springer (1994)
25. Hedin, G.: An introductory tutorial on JastAdd attribute grammars. In: GTTSE 2009, Revised Papers, *LNCS*, vol. 6491, pp. 166–200. Springer (2011)
26. Hudak, P.: Modular domain specific languages and tools. In: Proc. ICSR, pp. 134–142. IEEE (1998)
27. Jones, N.D., Gomard, C.K., Sestoft, P.: Partial evaluation and automatic program generation. Prentice-Hall, Inc. (1993)
28. de Jonge, M.: Pretty-printing for software reengineering. In: Proc. ICSM 2002, pp. 550–559. IEEE (2002)
29. de Jonge, M., Visser, E.: An algorithm for layout preservation in refactoring transformations. In: Proc. SLE 2011, *LNCS*, vol. 6940, pp. 40–59. Springer (2012)
30. Jonnalagedda, M., Coppey, T., Stucki, S., Rompf, T., Odersky, M.: Staged parser combinators for efficient data processing. In: Proc. OOPSLA, pp. 637–653. ACM (2014)
31. Jouault, F., Allilaire, F., Bézivin, J., Kurtev, I.: ATL: A model transformation tool. Sci. Comput. Program. **72**(1-2), 31–39 (2008)
32. Kastens, U., Pfahler, P., Jung, M.T.: The Eli system. In: Proc. CC, *LNCS*, vol. 1383, pp. 294–297. Springer (1998)
33. Kastens, U., Waite, W.M.: Modularity and reusability in attribute grammars. Acta Inf. **31**(7), 601–627 (1994)
34. Kiselyov, O.: Typed tagless final interpreters. In: Generic and Indexed Programming – International Spring School, SSGIP 2010, Revised Lectures, *LNCS*, vol. 7470, pp. 130–174. Springer (2012)
35. Kiselyov, O.: The design and implementation of BER MetaOCaml – System description. In: Proc. FLOPS, *LNCS*, vol. 8475, pp. 86–102. Springer (2014)
36. Klint, P., van der Storm, T., Vinju, J.J.: RASCAL: A domain specific language for source code analysis and manipulation. In: Proc. SCAM, pp. 168–177. IEEE (2009)
37. Klint, P., van der Storm, T., Vinju, J.J.: EASY meta-programming with Rascal. In: GTTSE 2009, Revised Papers, *LNCS*, vol. 6491, pp. 222–289. Springer (2011)
38. Klonatos, Y., Koch, C., Rompf, T., Chafi, H.: Building efficient query engines in a high-level language. PVLDB **7**(10), 853–864 (2014)
39. Klop, J.W.: Term rewriting systems. In: Handbook of Logic in Computer Science, pp. 1–117. Oxford University Press (1992)
40. Knuth, D.E.: Semantics of context-free languages. Mathematical Systems Theory **2**(2), 127–145 (1968)
41. Kort, J., Lämmel, R.: Parse-tree annotations meet re-engineering concerns. In: Proc. SCAM, pp. 161–168. IEEE (2003)
42. Lämmel, R.: Declarative aspect-oriented programming. In: Proc. PEPM, pp. 131–146. University of Aarhus (1999)
43. Lämmel, R.: Reuse by program transformation. In: Selected papers SFP 1999, *Trends in Functional Programming*, vol. 1, pp. 144–153. Intellect (2000)
44. Lämmel, R.: Scrap your boilerplate – Prologically! In: Proc. PPDP, pp. 7–12. ACM (2009)
45. Lämmel, R., Jones, S.L.P.: Scrap your boilerplate: a practical design pattern for generic programming. In: Proc. TLDI, pp. 26–37. ACM (2003)
46. Lämmel, R., Jones, S.L.P.: Scrap more boilerplate: reflection, zips, and generalised casts. In: Proc. ICFP, pp. 244–255. ACM (2004)

47. Lämmel, R., Jones, S.L.P.: Scrap your boilerplate with class: extensible generic functions. In: Proc. ICFP, pp. 204–215. ACM (2005)
48. Lämmel, R., Riedewald, G.: Reconstruction of paradigm shifts. In: Proc. WAGA, pp. 37–56 (1999). INRIA Technical Report
49. Lämmel, R., Thompson, S.J., Kaiser, M.: Programming errors in traversal programs over structured data. Sci. Comput. Program. **78**(10), 1770–1808 (2013)
50. Lämmel, R., Visser, E., Visser, J.: The essence of strategic programming (2002). 18 p.; Unpublished draft; Available at http://citeseerx.ist.psu.edu/viewdoc/download?doi=10.1.1.198.8985&rep=rep1&type=pdf
51. Lämmel, R., Visser, J.: Typed combinators for generic traversal. In: Proc. PADL, *LNCS*, vol. 2257, pp. 137–154. Springer (2002)
52. Lämmel, R., Visser, J.: A Strafunski application letter. In: Proc. PADL, *LNCS*, vol. 2562, pp. 357–375. Springer (2003)
53. Landauer, C., Bellman, K.L.: Generic programming, partial evaluation, and a new programming paradigm. In: Proc. HICSS-32. IEEE (1999)
54. Lengauer, C., Taha, W. (eds.): Special issue on the first MetaOCaml Workshop 2004. Sci. Comput. Program. (2006)
55. McNamee, D., Walpole, J., Pu, C., Cowan, C., Krasic, C., Goel, A., Wagle, P., Consel, C., Muller, G., Marlet, R.: Specialization tools and techniques for systematic optimization of system software. ACM Trans. Comput. Syst. **19**(2), 217–251 (2001)
56. Mens, T.: Model Transformation: A Survey of the State of the Art, pp. 1–19. John Wiley & Sons, Inc. (2013)
57. Nielson, F., Nielson, H.R., Hankin, C.: Principles of Program Analysis, corrected 2nd printing edn. Springer (2004)
58. Nielson, H.R., Nielson, F.: Semantics with Applications: An Appetizer. Undergraduate Topics in Computer Science. Springer (2007)
59. Porkoláb, Z., Sinkovics, Á., Siroki, I.: DSL in C++ template metaprogram. In: CEFP 2013, Revised Selected Papers, *LNCS*, vol. 8606, pp. 76–114. Springer (2015)
60. Rebernak, D., Mernik, M., Henriques, P.R., Pereira, M.J.V.: AspectLISA: An aspect-oriented compiler construction system based on attribute grammars. ENTCS **164**(2), 37–53 (2006)
61. Renggli, L.: Dynamic language embedding with homogeneous tool support. Ph.D. thesis, Universität Bern (2010)
62. Renggli, L., Gîrba, T., Nierstrasz, O.: Embedding languages without breaking tools. In: Proc. ECOOP, *LNCS*, vol. 6183, pp. 380–404. Springer (2010)
63. Rompf, T.: The essence of multi-stage evaluation in LMS. In: A List of Successes That Can Change the World – Essays Dedicated to Philip Wadler on the Occasion of His 60th Birthday, *LNCS*, vol. 9600, pp. 318–335. Springer (2016)
64. Rompf, T., Amin, N., Moors, A., Haller, P., Odersky, M.: Scala-Virtualized: linguistic reuse for deep embeddings. Higher Order Symbol. Comput. **25**(1), 165–207 (2012)
65. van Rozen, R., van der Storm, T.: Origin tracking + + text differencing = = textual model differencing. In: Proc. ICMT, *LNCS*, vol. 9152, pp. 18–33. Springer (2015)
66. Rozenberg, G. (ed.): Handbook of Graph Grammars and Computing by Graph Transformation. World Scientific Publishing Company (1997). Volume 1: Foundations
67. Seefried, S., Chakravarty, M.M.T., Keller, G.: Optimising embedded DSLs using Template Haskell. In: Proc. GPCE, *LNCS*, vol. 3286, pp. 186–205. Springer (2004)
68. Shali, A., Cook, W.R.: Hybrid partial evaluation. In: Proc. OOPSLA, pp. 375–390. ACM (2011)
69. Sheard, T., Peyton Jones, S.L.: Template meta-programming for Haskell. SIGPLAN Not. **37**(12), 60–75 (2002)
70. Siek, J.G., Taha, W.: A semantic analysis of C++ templates. In: Proc. ECOOP, *LNCS*, vol. 4067, pp. 304–327. Springer (2006)
71. Sloane, A.M., Kats, L.C.L., Visser, E.: A pure embedding of attribute grammars. Sci. Comput. Program. **78**(10), 1752–1769 (2013)
72. Smaragdakis, Y.: Structured program generation techniques. In: GTTSE 2015, Revised Papers, *LNCS*, vol. 10223, pp. 154–178. Springer (2017)

73. Stoltenberg-Hansen, V., Lindström, I., Griffor, E.R.: Mathematical Theory of Domains. Cambridge University Press (1994)
74. Sujeeth, A.K., Brown, K.J., Lee, H., Rompf, T., Chafi, H., Odersky, M., Olukotun, K.: Delite: A compiler architecture for performance-oriented embedded domain-specific languages. ACM Trans. Embedded Comput. Syst. **13**(4), 1–25 (2014)
75. Swierstra, S.D., Alcocer, P.R.A., Saraiva, J.: Designing and implementing combinator languages. In: Advanced Functional Programming, Third International School, Braga, Portugal, September 12-19, 1998, Revised Lectures, *LNCS*, vol. 1608, pp. 150–206. Springer (1999)
76. Taha, W.: A gentle introduction to multi-stage programming. In: Domain-Specific Program Generation, International Seminar, Dagstuhl Castle, Germany, March 23-28, 2003, Revised Papers, *LNCS*, vol. 3016, pp. 30–50. Springer (2004)
77. Taha, W.: A gentle introduction to multi-stage programming, part II. In: GTTSE 2007, Revised Papers, *LNCS*, vol. 5235, pp. 260–290. Springer (2008)
78. Taha, W., Sheard, T.: Multi-stage programming. In: Proc. ICFP, p. 321. ACM (1997)
79. Taha, W., Sheard, T.: MetaML and multi-stage programming with explicit annotations. Theor. Comput. Sci. **248**(1-2), 211–242 (2000)
80. Tisi, M., Mart/́ınez, S., Jouault, F., Cabot, J.: Refining models with rule-based model transformations. Tech. rep., Inria (2011). Research Report RR-7582. pp.18
81. Ulke, B., Steimann, F., Lämmel, R.: Partial evaluation of OCL expressions. In: Proc. MODELS, pp. 63–73. IEEE (2017)
82. van den Brand, M., Sellink, M.P.A., Verhoef, C.: Generation of components for software renovation factories from context-free grammars. Sci. Comput. Program. **36**(2-3), 209–266 (2000)
83. Van Wyk, E., Bodin, D., Gao, J., Krishnan, L.: Silver: An extensible attribute grammar system. Sci. Comput. Program. **75**(1-2), 39–54 (2010)
84. Veldhuizen, T.: Template metaprograms. C++ Rep. **7**(4), 36—43 (1995)
85. Visser, E.: A survey of strategies in rule-based program transformation systems. J. Symb. Comput. **40**(1), 831–873 (2005)
86. Visser, E., Benaissa, Z., Tolmach, A.: Building program optimizers with rewriting strategies. In: Proc. ICFP, pp. 13–26. ACM Press (1998)
87. Visser, J.: Visitor combination and traversal control. In: Proc. OOPSLA, pp. 270–282. ACM (2001)
88. Williams, K., Wyk, E.V.: Origin tracking in attribute grammars. In: Proc. SLE, *LNCS*, vol. 8706, pp. 282–301. Springer (2014)

Postface

Abstract We wrap up this book by (i) restating the importance of competence software languages in the broader context of computer science and IT; (ii) summarizing the key concepts of software languages as captured in this book; (iii) identifying the omissions in this book, to the extent they are clear to the author; (iv) listing complementary textbooks; and (v) listing relevant academic conferences. In this manner, we also provide pointers to further reading of different kinds.

The importance of Software Language Engineering

Software language engineering (SLE) basically proxies for software engineering with awareness of the languages involved such that software artifacts are treated in a syntax- and semantics-aware manner and particular attention is paid to software language definition and implementation, as well as other phases of the software language lifecycle. A "philosophical" discussion of the term "software languages" and the engineering thereof can be found elsewhere [39].

SLE is becoming a fundamental competence in computer science, best comparable to competences in algorithms, data structures, networking, security, software architecture, design, testing, formal methods, data mining, and artificial intelligence. The importance of SLE competence has increased in recent years and may continue to increase because of general developments in computer science. That is, while the classic language implementation tasks, i.e., the design and implementation of interpreters and compilers for mostly general-purpose programming languages, affect only a few software engineers directly, software engineers and other IT professionals and scientists are increasingly ending up in more diverse contexts with relevance to SLE such as the following:

- Design, implementation, and usage of internal and external DSLs that support problem or technical domains, for example, user interfaces, web services, configuration, testing, data exchange, interoperability, deployment, and distribution.

© Springer International Publishing AG, part of Springer Nature 2018
R. Lämmel, *Software Languages*,
https://doi.org/10.1007/978-3-319-90800-7

- Software reverse engineering and re-engineering in many forms, for example, analysis of projects regarding their dependence on open-source software, integration of systems, and migration of systems constrained by legislation or technology.
- Data extraction in the context of data mining, information retrieval, machine learning, mining software repositories, big data analytics, data science, computational social science, digital forensics, and artificial intelligence, with diverse input artifacts to be parsed and interchange formats to conform to.

Software Languages: Key Concepts

What are the key concepts regarding software languages? In this particular book, we have identified, explained, illustrated, and connected some concepts, as summarized below.

The basic starting point is (object program) *representation* of artifacts that are software language elements so that they are amenable to programmatic processing, i.e., *metaprogramming*. Thus, a *metaprogram* is a program that processes other programs or software artifacts that are elements of software languages. Ordinary programming languages may serve for metaprogramming, but we may also use more specialized *metaprogramming languages* or *systems* with dedicated metaprogramming expressiveness (e.g., for *term rewriting* or *concrete object syntax*) and infrastructure (e.g., for *template processing* or *parser generation*).

The *syntax* of a software language defines the language as a set of strings, trees, or graphs; it also defines the structure of software language elements, thereby facilitating their representation in metaprograms. Different formalisms may be used for syntax definition, for example, *grammars*, *signatures*, or *metamodels*. We may check for *conformance*, i.e., given a string, a tree, or a graph, we may check whether it complies with a given syntax definition. We may also engage in *parsing*, such that we analyze the structure of some input and possibly map language elements from *concrete syntax* to *abstract syntax*. We may further engage in *formatting* such that we render language elements according to some concrete syntax.

The syntax (and semantics) of syntax definitions gives rise to a *metametalevel*. It is important to master representation and syntax across *technological spaces* [76] because one is likely to encounter different spaces in practice.

The *semantics* of a software language defines the meaning of language elements. A software language engineer may not be interested in the formal study of semantics in itself, but may be very well interested in the applications of semantics for the purpose of (metaprograms for) *interpretation* (i.e., actual or *abstract interpretation*), *semantic analysis* (e.g., *well-formedness* or *type checking*), *transformation* (e.g., *optimization* or *refactoring*), and *translation* (e.g., *compilation* or *code generation* in a DSL implementation). We contend that there is simply no reasonable way to author metaprograms without some degree of understanding of the *operational* or *denotational* semantics of the object and metalanguages involved. All these metaprograms are syntax-driven and essentially rule-based in how they interpret, analyze, transform, or translate object programs. In more disciplined cases, these metaprograms may obey the principle of *compositionality* (i.e., some kind of structural recursion).

Omissions in This Book

This book describes the author's particular view of the software language world and it is limited by what can be reasonably fitted into a book, also taking into account a certain target audience and making certain assumptions about the background of readers, as discussed in the Preface. Thus, omissions are to be expected, and we itemize them here. We do this also to support further reading, maybe also in the context of research-oriented course designs. We group these omissions by major software language topics.

Meta-programming In this book, we favor a grammarware- and metaprogramming-based view of software languages; we have complemented this view with occasional excursions into the technological space of *model-driven engineering (metamodeling, model transformation)* [10, 125]. We implemented transformations in the style of rewriting; we did not properly describe or exercise *model transformation languages* [92, 26, 58, 2, 60]. The coverage of metaprogramming is limited in this book. We focused mainly on source-code analysis and manipulation, where source code should again be understood in a broad sense, not limited to programming languages. We managed an excursion to program generation. We did not cover *reflection* or limited (disciplined) concepts derived from reflection [67, 36, 30], *bytecode analysis and manipulation* [27, 21], higher-level programming constructs for modularity with lower-level semantics involving reflection, for example, *context-oriented programming* (COP) [50], *aspect-oriented programming* (AOP) [65, 78, 149, 64, 66], or *morphing* [54].

Domain-specific languages This book provides a backbone regarding representation, syntax, parsing, formatting, basic language concepts, interpretation, and typing for DSLs or software languages generally. Coverage of domains was very sparse; some additional problem domains for DSLs are, for example, telecom services, insurance products, industrial automation, medical device configuration, ERP configuration, and phone UI applications [139]. The book also left out the interesting topic of *domain-specific optimization* [75, 12, 68]. We adopted a basic metaprogramming approach without explicit dependence on or systematic discussion of more advanced features of *metaprogramming languages* and *systems* [52, 151, 152, 93, 118, 19, 35, 32, 29, 143, 124], and also without coverage of DSL development with *language workbenches* [33, 34, 62, 61, 147, 145, 148, 141]. We focused on textual concrete syntax; we did not cover *visual syntax* [88, 96, 73], in particular, we did not cover it in terms of editing. We also omitted coverage of *syntax-directed editing* [11, 119] and *projectional editing* [142, 146, 144]. Overall, we did not cover the lifecycle of DSLs too well; we provided some implementation options, but we were very sparse on design. Some recommended further reading is [52, 151, 152, 93, 118, 19, 35, 32, 29, 143, 124]. There were also specific topics on the *software language lifecycle* that fell off the desk, unfortunately, for example, *test-data generation* [114, 89, 13, 48, 17, 134, 136, 47, 77, 59, 82] and *language-usage analysis* [72, 43, 80, 7, 22, 38, 81].

Compilation   As *compiler construction* is a well-established subject with excellent textbook coverage (see the next section), the present book makes no attempt at covering compiler construction. It so happens that simple aspects of frontends and translation were covered, but the more interesting aspects of the vital use of *intermediate representations* and *high-* and *low-level optimizations* were not. These days, *compiler frameworks*, as a form of language infrastructure possibly including runtime system components, support compiler construction, for example, LLVM [83], which is widely used, or more specialized frameworks [28, 115, 37, 20, 86] that target different architectures or optimization philosophies. Another interesting framework is Graal/Truffle, which combines aspects of cross-compilation and interpreter specialization [153, 31, 120].

Grammars   While we covered tree-based abstract syntax definition by means of algebraic signatures, we did not discuss the related notion of *tree grammars* [23]. While we covered graph-based abstract syntax definition (i.e., metamodeling, including reference relationships), we did not discuss the related field of *graph grammars* [122]. As for string languages, we focused completely focused on context-free grammars, and did not cover other grammar formalisms such as *regular grammars* [53] and *parsing expression grammars* (PEGs) [40]. Regular grammars are useful, for example, for efficient scanning [1] and lexical fact extraction [101, 70]. PEGs provide an alternative formalism for parsing.

Parsing   We did not explore *grammar classes* and we dealt superficially with *parsing algorithms* [1, 45], thereby leaving out a discussion of the space of options with regard to precise recognition, efficiency, restrictions imposed on the grammar author, and guarantees regarding grammar ambiguities. Increasingly, "generalized" parsing approaches are being used: *generalized LR parsing* [140, 117], *generalized LL parsing* [57, 126], LL($*$) [109], and PEGs [40]. We certainly also missed various forms of parsing used in software engineering. For instance, there are specific forms of grammars (or parsing) such as *island* or *tolerant grammars*, aiming at robustness in the in response to the complexity of language syntax, diversity of dialects, or handling parser errors in an interactive context [97, 98, 71, 104].

Semantics and types   We covered the basics of semantics and types, aiming at the pragmatic realization of interpreters and type checkers. While we developed the basics of operational and denotational semantics, we did not cover some of the refinements that improve usability, for example, modular operational semantics [100], action semantics [99], and monad transformers [85]. We also did not cover approaches to semantics that are less directly usable for interpretation – in particular, all forms of axiomatic semantics [51, 138]. We skipped over the foundations of formal semantics and type systems; we refer to the next section for textbooks on programming language theory. We focused on "classical" static typing; we omitted several advanced concepts, for example, effect systems [102], liquid types [121], soft typing, gradual typing [18, 130, 131, 132], dependently typed programming [90, 106, 107, 15], and the scale between *static* and *dynamic typing* [91]. We touched upon *type safety*, but omitted a proper discussion of the more general notion of (mechanized) *metatheory* [113, 4], which might possibly also depend on *theorem provers* or *proof assistants*, for example, Twelf [112, 84], Coq [8], and Isabelle/HOL [105], or *dependently typed* programming languages, for example, Agda [14, 107].

Language concepts We exercised a range of languages for illustration. We did not intend to cover programming paradigms systematically; see the next section for textbook recommendations. Various language concepts were not covered, for example, object-oriented programming (OOP) [55, 16], type dispatch or type case [44, 24, 25], polytypic or generic functional programming [56, 49, 79], and information hiding or data abstraction [95, 133, 150]. We covered some parts of the lambda cube [6]; we did not cover complementary calculi, for example, process calculi or process algebras (CCS, CSP, π-calculus, etc.) [5, 94, 123] for concurrent programming.

Complementary Textbooks

This book can be usefully compared and complemented with textbooks in neighboring areas. In this manner, we may also provide pointers to further reading. We have classified textbooks into the following categories:

Programming language theory Textbooks in this category cover topics such as lambda calculi, formal semantics, formal type systems, metatheory, and program analysis. Examples include Pierce's "Types and Programming Languages" [113], Friedman and Wand's "Essentials of Programming Languages" [42], and Gunter's "Semantics of Programming Languages: Structures and Techniques" [46]. We also refer to Nielson and Nielson's "Semantics with Applications: An Appetizer" [103] as an introductory text and Slonneger and Kurtz' "Formal Syntax and Semantics of Programming Languages" [135] for a less formal, more practical approach to programming language theory.

The present book covers only some basic concepts of formal semantics and type systems, such as interpretation based on big-step and small-step semantics, the scheme of compositional (denotational) semantics, and type checking – without covering language concepts deeply, and without properly covering fundamental aspects such as metatheory (e.g., the soundness property on pairs of semantics and type system). This book goes beyond textbooks on programming language theory by covering the lifecycle, syntax implementation (parsing and formatting), and metaprogramming with applications to, for example, software reverse engineering and re-engineering.

Programming paradigms Textbooks in this category cover various paradigms (such as the imperative, functional, logical, and OO paradigms). The organization may be more or less aligned with an assumed ontology of language concepts. Typically, an interpreter-based approach is used for illustration. Examples include Sebesta's "Concepts of Programming Languages" [128], Sethi's "Programming Languages: Concepts and Constructs" [129] and Scott's "Programming Language Pragmatics" [127]. These books also cover, to some extent, programming language theory and compiler construction.

The present book is not concerned with a systematic discussion of programming paradigms and programming language concepts. Nevertheless, the book exercises (in fact, "defines") languages of different paradigms and discusses various language concepts in a cursory manner. This book goes beyond textbooks on programming paradigms by covering metaprogramming broadly, which is not a central concern in textbooks on paradigms.

Compiler construction   This is the classical subject in computer science that, arguably, comes closest to the subject of software languages. Examples of textbooks on compiler construction and overall programming language implementation include Aho, Lam, Sethi, and Ullman's seminal "Compilers: Principles, Techniques, and Tools" [1], Louden's "Compiler Construction: Principles and Practice" [87], and Appel's product line of textbooks such as Appel and Palsberg's " Modern Compiler Implementation in Java" [3].

The present book briefly discusses compilation (translation), but it otherwise covers compiler construction at best superficially. For instance, lower-level code optimization and code generation are not covered. This book covers language implementation more broadly than textbooks on compiler construction, with regard to both the kinds of software languages and the kinds of language-based software components. Most notably, this book covers metaprogramming scenarios other than compilation, and metaprogramming techniques other than those used in a typical compiler.

Hybrids   There are a number of books that touch upon several of the aforementioned topics in a significant manner. There is Krishnamurthi's "Programming Languages: Application and Interpretation" [74], which combines programming language theory and programming paradigms in a powerful manner. There is Ranta's "Implementing Programming Languages: An Introduction to Compilers and Interpreters" [116] with coverage of programming paradigms and compiler construction. There is also Stuart's "Understanding Computation: From Simple Machines to Impossible Programs" [137], which is exceptionally broad in scope: it covers various fundamental topics in computer science, including parsing and interpretation; it explains all notions covered to the working Ruby programmer in a pragmatic manner.

The present book aims at a deeper discussion of the implementation and lifecycle of software languages in the broader context of software engineering, with the central topic being metaprogramming in the sense of source-code analysis and manipulation.

Domain-specific languages   There are some more or less recent textbooks on DSLs. Fowler's "Domain-Specific Languages" [41] discusses relatively basic or mainstream OO techniques and corresponding patterns for language implementation and embedding specifically. Kleppe's "Software Language Engineering: Creating Domain-Specific Languages Using Metamodels" [69] and Kelly and Tolvanen's "Domain-Specific Modeling: Enabling Full Code Generation" [63] exercise the modeling- and metamodeling-based view of language design and implementation, as opposed to the use of standard programming languages and language implementation technology. Voelter et al.'s "DSL Engineering: Designing, Implementing and Using Domain-Specific Languages" [143] focuses on specific technologies such as MPS, xText, and Stratego/Spoofax. Parr's "Language Implementation Patterns: Techniques for Implementing Domain-Specific Languages" [108] is a practical guide to using the ANTLR technology for language implementation. Bettini's "Implementing Domain-Specific Languages with Xtext and Xtend" [9] focuses on practitioners specifically interested in the Xtext stack.

The present book is not limited to domain-specific languages; it discusses software languages in a broad sense. Programming languages and semantics-based techniques such as partial evaluation and abstract interpretation are also covered to some extent. The book discusses software language engineering without commitment to a specific metaprogramming system.

Software Languages in Academia

Let us now connect the broad area of software languages to some established academic conference series. In this manner, we will also hint at resources for carrying out research on software languages. The conferences listed below are loosely ordered by decreasing coverage of the software language area. Thus, we start off with the conferences on Software Language Engineering and close the list with more specialized conferences focusing on specific aspects of software languages or specific categories such as programming languages. It goes without saying that this selection and its ordered presentation, just as much as the characterization of the individual conferences series, are subjective. We link each conference acronym to its manifestation in the DBLP database.

- SLE^3: **Software Language Engineering**. This conference series covers the full range of software language topics in a balanced manner. The conference series was specifically created to unite the different perspectives on software languages such as those in the communities of grammarware and modelware.
- $SCAM^4$: **Source Code Analysis and Manipulation**. This conference series takes a broad view of source code and covers a wide range of forms and purposes of software analysis and transformation such as parsing, smells, metrics, slicing, and clone detection.

---

[3] SLE: http://dblp.uni-trier.de/db/conf/sle/ (at DBLP)

[4] SCAM: http://dblp.uni-trier.de/db/conf/scam/ (at DBLP)

- *MODELS*[5]: **Model Driven Engineering Languages and Systems**. This conference series covers the field of software languages in terms of modeling, meta-modeling, and model transformation while assuming an increasingly broad interpretation of modeling etc.
- *ECMFA*[6]: **European Conference on Model Driven Architecture - Foundations and Applications**. This conference series is similar to MODELS.
- *MODELSWARD*[7]: **Model-Driven Engineering and Software Development**. This conference series is similar to MODELS.
- *ICMT*[8]: **International Conference on Model Transformation**. This conference series covers the field of software languages in terms of model transformation while assuming an increasingly broad interpretation of model transformation by being inclusive in terms of technological spaces.
- *MSR*[9]: **Mining Software Repositories**. This conference series covers analysis of all kinds of artifacts in the broad sense of software repositories – not just source code, but also commit messages and bug reports. The conference series goes beyond the field of software languages by being also inclusive of methods from the fields of text analysis, natural language processing, information retrieval, machine learning, and data mining.
- *ICPC*[10]: **International Conference on Program Comprehension**. This conference series focuses on methods and tools for program comprehension, which includes a wide range of types of software analysis, visualization, cognitive theories, and other things. Software languages play a key role in terms of the artifacts to be analyzed.
- *SANER*[11]: **Software Analysis, Evolution, and Reengineering** (formerly WCRE (Working Conference on Reverse Engineering) and Conference on Software Maintenance and Reengineering (CSMR)). This conference series covers the broad areas of software reverse engineering, software re-engineering, and – even more broadly – software maintenance, software evolution, and software analysis. Software languages play a key role in terms of the artifacts to be analyzed or transformed.
- *ICSME*[12]: **International Conference on Software Maintenance and Evolution** (formerly ICSM (International Conference on Software Maintenance)). This conference series is similar to SANER.
- *CC*[13]: **Compiler Construction**. This conference series focus on language implementation, specifically compiler construction, which is a classic core component

---

[5] MODELS: http://dblp.uni-trier.de/db/conf/models/ (at DBLP)

[6] ECMFA: http://dblp.uni-trier.de/db/conf/ecmdafa/ (at DBLP)

[7] MODELSWARD: http://dblp.uni-trier.de/db/conf/modelsward/ (at DBLP)

[8] ICMT: http://dblp.uni-trier.de/db/conf/icmt/ (at DBLP)

[9] MSR: http://dblp.uni-trier.de/db/conf/msr/ (at DBLP)

[10] ICPC: http://dblp.uni-trier.de/db/conf/iwpc/ (at DBLP)

[11] SANER: http://dblp.uni-trier.de/db/conf/wcre/ (at DBLP)

[12] ICSME: http://dblp.uni-trier.de/db/conf/icsm/ (at DBLP)

[13] CC: http://dblp.uni-trier.de/db/conf/cc/ (at DBLP)

of the software language field. Language implementation aspects other than those directly relevant to compilation are not systematically covered.

- *PEPM*[14]: **Partial Evaluation and Semantic-Based Program Manipulation**. This conference series is concerned with program manipulation, partial evaluation, and program generation. The focus is on semantics-based methods and programming languages (including domain-specific languages) as opposed to engineering and software languages generally.
- *ICSE*[15]: **International Conference on Software Engineering**. This conference series covers software engineering broadly. A significant percentage of ICSE papers involve language-centric tools and methods, for example, in the sense of refactorings, IDEs, and automated testing. Combinations of software language engineering and empirical software engineering are common – just as in the case of the MSR conferences.
- *ASE*[16]: **Automated Software Engineering**. This conference series is similar to ICSE, except that it entirely focuses on automated aspects of software engineering.
- *PLDI*[17]: **Programming Language Design and Implementation**. This conference series covers all areas of programming language research, including the design, implementation, theory, and efficient use of languages. There is a clear focus on implementation, though, for example, innovative and creative approaches to compile-time and runtime technology and results from implementations.
- *POPL*[18]: **Principles of Programming Languages**. This conference series covers all aspects of programming languages and programming systems. Historically, POPL papers have been theoretical – they develop formal frameworks; more recently, experimental papers and experience reports have been encouraged.
- *ECOOP*[19]: **European Conference on Object-Oriented Programming**. This conference series covers all areas of object technology and related software development technologies with a focus on foundations (semantics, types, semantics-based tools, language implementation).

In addition to the established conferences listed above, let us also point out an emerging conference series, `http://programming-conference.org/`, which is associated with a dedicated journal, `http://programming-conference.org/journal/`. This conference series promises, as it develops further, to be very relevant in terms of software language topics.

It would also be useful to itemize journals in a similar manner, but we leave this as an "advanced exercise" to the reader. One could, for example, set up and execute a suitable methodology to review computer-science journals in terms of their coverage

---

[14] PEPM: `http://dblp.uni-trier.de/db/conf/pepm/` (at DBLP)

[15] ICSE: `http://dblp.uni-trier.de/db/conf/icse/` (at DBLP)

[16] ASE: `http://dblp.uni-trier.de/db/conf/kbse/` (at DBLP)

[17] PLDI: `http://dblp.uni-trier.de/db/conf/pldi/` (at DBLP)

[18] POPL: `http://dblp.uni-trier.de/db/conf/popl/` (at DBLP)

[19] ECOOP: `http://dblp.uni-trier.de/db/conf/ecoop/` (at DBLP)

of the software language area. To this end, one could follow common guidelines for a systematic mapping study [110, 111].

Feedback Appreciated

Readers are strongly encouraged to get in touch with the book's author, who is looking forward to incorporating any feedback received into a future revision of this book and to advertise contributed resources. Please see the book's website[20] for contact information.

References

1. Aho, A., Monica S., Sethi, R., Ullman, J.: Compilers: Principles, Techniques, and Tools. Addison Wesley (2006). 2nd edition
2. Amrani, M., Combemale, B., Lucio, L., Selim, G.M.K., Dingel, J., Traon, Y.L., Vangheluwe, H., Cordy, J.R.: Formal verification techniques for model transformations: A tridimensional classification. J. Object Technol. **14**(3), 1–43 (2015)
3. Appel, A., Palsberg, J.: Modern Compiler Implementation in Java. Cambridge University Press (2002). 2nd edition
4. Aydemir, B.E., Bohannon, A., Fairbairn, M., Foster, J.N., Pierce, B.C., Sewell, P., Vytiniotis, D., Washburn, G., Weirich, S., Zdancewic, S.: Mechanized metatheory for the masses: The PoplMark challenge. In: Proc. TPHOLs, *LNCS*, vol. 3603, pp. 50–65. Springer (2005)
5. Baeten, J.C.M., Weijland, W.P.: Process Algebra. Cambridge University Press (1990)
6. Barendregt, H.: Introduction to generalized type systems. J. Funct. Program. **1**(2), 125–154 (1991)
7. Baxter, G., Frean, M.R., Noble, J., Rickerby, M., Smith, H., Visser, M., Melton, H., Tempero, E.D.: Understanding the shape of Java software. In: Proc. OOPSLA, pp. 397–412. ACM (2006)
8. Bertot, Y., Castéran, P.: Interactive Theorem Proving and Program Development. Coq'Art: The Calculus of Inductive Constructions. Texts in Theoretical Computer Science. An EATCS Series. Springer (2004)
9. Bettini, L.: Implementing Domain-Specific Languages with Xtext and Xtend. Packt Publishing (2013)
10. Bézivin, J.: Model driven engineering: An emerging technical space. In: GTTSE 2005, Revised Papers, *LNCS*, vol. 4143, pp. 36–64. Springer (2006)
11. Borras, P., Clément, D., Despeyroux, T., Incerpi, J., Kahn, G., Lang, B., Pascual, V.: CENTAUR: the system. In: Proc. SDE 1988, pp. 14–24. ACM (1989)
12. van den Bos, J., van der Storm, T.: Domain-specific optimization in digital forensics. In: Proc. ICMT, *LNCS*, vol. 7307, pp. 121–136. Springer (2012)
13. Boujarwah, A., Saleh, K.: Compiler test suite: Evaluation and use in an automated test environment. Inf. Softw. Technol. **36**(10), 607–614 (1994)
14. Bove, A., Dybjer, P., Norell, U.: A brief overview of Agda – A functional language with dependent types. In: Proc. TPHOLs, *LNCS*, vol. 5674, pp. 73–78. Springer (2009)
15. Brady, E.: Idris, a general-purpose dependently typed programming language: Design and implementation. J. Funct. Program. **23**(5), 552–593 (2013)

---

[20] http://www.softlang.org/book

16. Bruce, K.B., Schuett, A., van Gent, R., Fiech, A.: PolyTOIL: A type-safe polymorphic object-oriented language. ACM Trans. Program. Lang. Syst. **25**(2), 225–290 (2003)
17. Burgess, C.J., Saidi, M.: The automatic generation of test cases for optimizing Fortran compilers. Inf. Softw. Technol. **38**(2), 111–119 (1996)
18. Cartwright, R., Fagan, M.: Soft typing. In: Proc. PLDI, pp. 278–292. ACM (1991)
19. Ceh, I., Crepinsek, M., Kosar, T., Mernik, M.: Ontology driven development of domain-specific languages. Comput. Sci. Inf. Syst. **8**(2), 317–342 (2011)
20. Chandramohan, K., O'Boyle, M.F.P.: A compiler framework for automatically mapping data parallel programs to heterogeneous MPSoCs. In: Proc. CASES, pp. 1–10. ACM (2014)
21. Chiba, S.: Load-time structural reflection in Java. In: Proc. ECOOP, *LNCS*, vol. 1850, pp. 313–336. Springer (2000)
22. Collberg, C.S., Myles, G., Stepp, M.: An empirical study of Java bytecode programs. Softw., Pract. Exper. **37**(6), 581–641 (2007)
23. Comon, H., Dauchet, M., Gilleron, R., Löding, C., Jacquemard, F., Lugiez, D., Tison, S., Tommasi, M.: Tree automata techniques and applications. Available at http://www.grappa.univ-lille3.fr/tata (2007)
24. Crary, K., Weirich, S., Morrisett, J.G.: Intensional polymorphism in type-erasure semantics. In: Proc. ICFP, pp. 301–312. ACM (1998)
25. Crary, K., Weirich, S., Morrisett, J.G.: Intensional polymorphism in type-erasure semantics. J. Funct. Program. **12**(6), 567–600 (2002)
26. Czarnecki, K., Helsen, S.: Feature-based survey of model transformation approaches. IBM Syst. J. **45**(3), 621–646 (2006)
27. Dahm, M.: Byte code engineering. In: Java-Informations-Tage, pp. 267–277 (1999)
28. Dai, X., Zhai, A., Hsu, W., Yew, P.: A general compiler framework for speculative optimizations using data speculative code motion. In: Proc. CGO, pp. 280–290. IEEE (2005)
29. Degueule, T.: Composition and interoperability for external domain-specific language engineering. Ph.D. thesis, Université de Rennes 1 (2016)
30. Denker, M.: Sub-method structural and behavioral reflection. Ph.D. thesis, University of Bern (2008)
31. Duboscq, G., Würthinger, T., Mössenböck, H.: Speculation without regret: Reducing deoptimization meta-data in the Graal compiler. In: Proc. PPPJ, pp. 187–193. ACM (2014)
32. Erdweg, S.: Extensible languages for flexible and principled domain abstraction. Ph.D. thesis, Philipps-Universität Marburg (2013)
33. Erdweg, S., van der Storm, T., Völter, M., Boersma, M., Bosman, R., Cook, W.R., Gerritsen, A., Hulshout, A., Kelly, S., Loh, A., Konat, G.D.P., Molina, P.J., Palatnik, M., Pohjonen, R., Schindler, E., Schindler, K., Solmi, R., Vergu, V.A., Visser, E., van der Vlist, K., Wachsmuth, G., van der Woning, J.: The state of the art in language workbenches – conclusions from the language workbench challenge. In: Proc. SLE, *LNCS*, vol. 8225, pp. 197–217. Springer (2013)
34. Erdweg, S., van der Storm, T., Völter, M., Tratt, L., Bosman, R., Cook, W.R., Gerritsen, A., Hulshout, A., Kelly, S., Loh, A., Konat, G.D.P., Molina, P.J., Palatnik, M., Pohjonen, R., Schindler, E., Schindler, K., Solmi, R., Vergu, V.A., Visser, E., van der Vlist, K., Wachsmuth, G., van der Woning, J.: Evaluating and comparing language workbenches: Existing results and benchmarks for the future. Comput. Lang. Syst. Struct. **44**, 24–47 (2015)
35. Erwig, M., Walkingshaw, E.: Semantics first! – rethinking the language design process. In: Proc. SLE 2011, *LNCS*, vol. 6940, pp. 243–262. Springer (2012)
36. Fähndrich, M., Carbin, M., Larus, J.R.: Reflective program generation with patterns. In: Proc. GPCE, pp. 275–284. ACM (2006)
37. Falk, H., Lokuciejewski, P.: A compiler framework for the reduction of worst-case execution times. Real-Time Systems **46**(2), 251–300 (2010)
38. Favre, J., Gasevic, D., Lämmel, R., Pek, E.: Empirical language analysis in software linguistics. In: Proc. SLE 2010, *LNCS*, vol. 6563, pp. 316–326. Springer (2011)
39. Favre, J.M., Gasevic, D., Lämmel, R., Winter, A.: Guest editors' introduction to the special section on software language engineering. IEEE Trans. Softw. Eng. **35**(6), 737–741 (2009)

40. Ford, B.: Parsing expression grammars: A recognition-based syntactic foundation. In: Proc. POPL, pp. 111–122. ACM (2004)
41. Fowler, M.: Domain-Specific Languages. Addison-Wesley (2010)
42. Friedman, D., Wand, M.: Essentials of Programming Languages. MIT Press (2008). 3rd edition
43. Gil, J., Maman, I.: Micro patterns in Java code. In: Proc. OOPSLA, pp. 97–116. ACM (2005)
44. Glew, N.: Type dispatch for named hierarchical types. In: Proc. ICFP, pp. 172–182. ACM (1999)
45. Grune, D., Jacobs, C.: Parsing Techniques: A Practical Guide. Monographs in Computer Science. Springer (2007). 2nd edition
46. Gunter, C.: Semantics of Programming Languages: Structures and Techniques. MIT Press (1992)
47. Harm, J., Lämmel, R.: Two-dimensional approximation coverage. Informatica (Slovenia) 24(3) (2000)
48. Harm, J., Lämmel, R., Riedewald, G.: The Language Development Laboratory — LDL. In: Proc. NWPT, pp. 77–86 (1997). Research Report 248. University of Oslo
49. Hinze, R.: A new approach to generic functional programming. In: Proc. POPL, pp. 119–132. ACM (2000)
50. Hirschfeld, R., Costanza, P., Nierstrasz, O.: Context-oriented programming. J. Object Technol. 7(3), 125–151 (2008)
51. Hoare, C.: An axiomatic basis for computer programming (reprint). Commun. ACM 26(1), 53–56 (1983)
52. Hoare, C.A.R.: Hints on programming language design. Tech. rep., Stanford University (1973)
53. Hopcroft, J., Motwani, R., Ullman, J.: Introduction to Automata Theory, Languages, and Computation. Pearson (2013). 3rd edition
54. Huang, S.S., Smaragdakis, Y.: Morphing: Structurally shaping a class by reflecting on others. ACM Trans. Program. Lang. Syst. 33(2), 6 (2011)
55. Igarashi, A., Pierce, B.C., Wadler, P.: Featherweight Java: a minimal core calculus for Java and GJ. ACM Trans. Program. Lang. Syst. 23(3), 396–450 (2001)
56. Jansson, P., Jeuring, J.: Polyp – A polytypic programming language. In: Proc. POPL, pp. 470–482. ACM (1997)
57. Johnstone, A., Scott, E.: Modelling GLL parser implementations. In: Proc. SLE 2010, LNCS, vol. 6563, pp. 42–61. Springer (2011)
58. Jouault, F., Allilaire, F., Bézivin, J., Kurtev, I.: ATL: A model transformation tool. Sci. Comput. Program. 72(1-2), 31–39 (2008)
59. Kalinov, A., Kossatchev, A., Petrenko, A., Posypkin, M., Shishkov, V.: Coverage-driven automated compiler test suite generation. ENTCS 82(3) (2003)
60. Kappel, G., Langer, P., Retschitzegger, W., Schwinger, W., Wimmer, M.: Model transformation by-example: A survey of the first wave. In: Conceptual Modelling and Its Theoretical Foundations – Essays Dedicated to Bernhard Thalheim on the Occasion of His 60th Birthday, LNCS, vol. 7260, pp. 197–215. Springer (2012)
61. Kats, L.C.L., Visser, E.: The Spoofax language workbench. In: Companion SPLASH/OOPSLA, pp. 237–238. ACM (2010)
62. Kats, L.C.L., Visser, E.: The Spoofax language workbench: rules for declarative specification of languages and IDEs. In: Proc. OOPSLA, pp. 444–463. ACM (2010)
63. Kelly, S., Tolvanen, J.: Domain-Specific Modeling. IEEE & Wiley (2008)
64. Kiczales, G.: Aspect-oriented programming. In: Proc. ICSE, p. 730. ACM (2005)
65. Kiczales, G., Lamping, J., Mendhekar, A., Maeda, C., Lopes, C.V., Loingtier, J., Irwin, J.: Aspect-oriented programming. In: Proc. ECOOP, LNCS, vol. 1241, pp. 220–242. Springer (1997)
66. Kiczales, G., Mezini, M.: Aspect-oriented programming and modular reasoning. In: Proc. ICSE, pp. 49–58. ACM (2005)
67. Kiczales, G., des Rivieres, J., Bobrow, D.G.: The Art of the Metaobject Protocol. MIT Press (1991)

68. Kim, Y., Kiemb, M., Park, C., Jung, J., Choi, K.: Resource sharing and pipelining in coarse-grained reconfigurable architecture for domain-specific optimization. In: Proc. DATE, pp. 12–17. IEEE (2005)
69. Kleppe, A.: Software Language Engineering: Creating Domain-Specific Languages Using Metamodels. Addison-Wesley (2008)
70. Klusener, A.S., Lämmel, R., Verhoef, C.: Architectural modifications to deployed software. Sci. Comput. Program. 54(2-3), 143–211 (2005)
71. Klusener, S., Lämmel, R.: Deriving tolerant grammars from a base-line grammar. In: Proc. ICSM, pp. 179–188. IEEE (2003)
72. Knuth, D.E.: An empirical study of FORTRAN programs. Softw., Pract. Exper. 1(2), 105–133 (1971)
73. Kolovos, D.S., Rose, L.M., bin Abid, S., Paige, R.F., Polack, F.A.C., Botterweck, G.: Taming EMF and GMF using model transformation. In: Proc. MODELS, LNCS, vol. 6394, pp. 211–225. Springer (2010)
74. Krishnamurthi, S.: Programming Languages: Application and Interpretation. Brown University (2007). https://cs.brown.edu/~sk/Publications/Books/ProgLangs/
75. Kronawitter, S., Stengel, H., Hager, G., Lengauer, C.: Domain-specific optimization of two Jacobi smoother kernels and their evaluation in the ECM performance model. Parallel Processing Letters 24(3) (2014)
76. Kurtev, I., Bézivin, J., Akşit, M.: Technological spaces: An initial appraisal. In: Proc. CoopIS, DOA 2002, Industrial track (2002)
77. Lämmel, R.: Grammar testing. In: Proc. FASE, LNCS, vol. 2029, pp. 201–216. Springer (2001)
78. Lämmel, R.: A semantical approach to method-call interception. In: Proc. AOSD, pp. 41–55. ACM (2002)
79. Lämmel, R., Jones, S.L.P.: Scrap your boilerplate: a practical design pattern for generic programming. In: Proc. TLDI, pp. 26–37. ACM (2003)
80. Lämmel, R., Kitsis, S., Remy, D.: Analysis of XML schema usage. In: Proc. XML (2005)
81. Lämmel, R., Pek, E.: Understanding privacy policies – A study in empirical analysis of language usage. Empir. Softw. Eng. 18(2), 310–374 (2013)
82. Lämmel, R., Schulte, W.: Controllable combinatorial coverage in grammar-based testing. In: Proc. TestCom, LNCS, vol. 3964, pp. 19–38. Springer (2006)
83. Lattner, C., Adve, V.S.: LLVM: A compilation framework for lifelong program analysis & transformation. In: Proc. CGO, pp. 75–88. IEEE (2004)
84. Lee, D.K., Crary, K., Harper, R.: Towards a mechanized metatheory of standard ML. In: Proc. POPL, pp. 173–184. ACM (2007)
85. Liang, S., Hudak, P., Jones, M.P.: Monad transformers and modular interpreters. In: Proc. POPL, pp. 333–343. ACM (1995)
86. Liang, Y., Xie, X., Sun, G., Chen, D.: An efficient compiler framework for cache bypassing on GPUs. IEEE Trans. CAD Integr. Circ. Syst. 34(10), 1677–1690 (2015)
87. Louden, K.: Compiler Construction: Principles and Practice. Cengage Learning (1997)
88. Marriott, K., Meyer, B. (eds.): Visual Language Theory. Springer (1998)
89. Maurer, P.: Generating test data with enhanced context-free grammars. IEEE Softw. 7(4), 50–56 (1990)
90. McBride, C.: Epigram: Practical programming with dependent types. In: Proc. AFP, LNCS, vol. 3622, pp. 130–170. Springer (2004)
91. Meijer, E., Drayton, P.: Static typing where possible, dynamic typing when needed: The end of the cold war between programming languages (2005). Available at http://citeseerx.ist.psu.edu/viewdoc/summary?doi=10.1.1.69.5966
92. Mens, T.: Model Transformation: A Survey of the State of the Art, pp. 1–19. John Wiley & Sons, Inc. (2013)
93. Mernik, M., Heering, J., Sloane, A.M.: When and how to develop domain-specific languages. ACM Comput. Surv. 37(4), 316–344 (2005)

94. Milner, R.: Communicating and Mobile Systems: The π-calculus. Cambridge University Press (1999)
95. Mitchell, J.C., Plotkin, G.D.: Abstract types have existential type. ACM Trans. Program. Lang. Syst. **10**(3), 470–502 (1988)
96. Moody, D.L.: The physics of notations: Toward a scientific basis for constructing visual notations in software engineering. IEEE Trans. Softw. Eng. **35**(6), 756–779 (2009)
97. Moonen, L.: Generating robust parsers using island grammars. In: Proc. WCRE, pp. 13–22. IEEE (2001)
98. Moonen, L.: Lightweight impact analysis using island grammars. In: Proc. IWPC, pp. 219–228. IEEE (2002)
99. Mosses, P.D.: Theory and practice of action semantics. In: Proc. MFCS, *LNCS*, vol. 1113, pp. 37–61. Springer (1996)
100. Mosses, P.D.: Modular structural operational semantics. J. Log. Algebr. Program. **60-61**, 195–228 (2004)
101. Murphy, G.C., Notkin, D.: Lightweight lexical source model extraction. ACM Trans. Softw. Eng. Methodol. **5**(3), 262–292 (1996)
102. Nielson, F., Nielson, H.R.: Type and effect systems. In: Correct System Design, Recent Insight and Advances, *LNCS*, vol. 1710, pp. 114–136. Springer (1999)
103. Nielson, H.R., Nielson, F.: Semantics with Applications: An Appetizer. Undergraduate Topics in Computer Science. Springer (2007)
104. Nilsson-Nyman, E., Ekman, T., Hedin, G.: Practical scope recovery using bridge parsing. In: Proc. SLE 2008, *LNCS*, vol. 5452, pp. 95–113. Springer (2009)
105. Nipkow, T., Paulson, L.C., Wenzel, M.: Isabelle/HOL: A Proof Assistant for Higher-Order Logic, *LNCS*, vol. 2283. Springer (2002)
106. Norell, U.: Towards a practical programming language based on dependent type theory. Ph.D. thesis, Department of Computer Science and Engineering, Chalmers University of Technology (2007)
107. Norell, U.: Dependently typed programming in Agda. In: AFP 2008, Revised Lectures, *LNCS*, vol. 5832, pp. 230–266. Springer (2009)
108. Parr, T.: Language Implementation Patterns: Techniques for Implementing Domain-Specific Languages. Pragmatic Bookshelf (2010)
109. Parr, T., Fisher, K.: LL(*): The foundation of the ANTLR parser generator. In: Proc. PLDI, pp. 425–436. ACM (2011)
110. Petersen, K., Feldt, R., Mujtaba, S., Mattsson, M.: Systematic mapping studies in software engineering. In: Proc. EASE, Workshops in Computing. BCS (2008)
111. Petersen, K., Vakkalanka, S., Kuzniarz, L.: Guidelines for conducting systematic mapping studies in software engineering: An update. Inf. Softw. Technol. **64**, 1–18 (2015)
112. Pfenning, F., Schürmann, C.: System description: Twelf – A meta-logical framework for deductive systems. In: Proc. CADE-16, *LNCS*, vol. 1632, pp. 202–206. Springer (1999)
113. Pierce, B.: Types and Programming Languages. MIT Press (2002)
114. Purdom, P.: A sentence generator for testing parsers. BIT **12**(3), 366–375 (1972)
115. Raghavan, P., Lambrechts, A., Absar, J., Jayapala, M., Catthoor, F., Verkest, D.: Coffee: COmpiler Framework for Energy-aware Exploration. In: Proc. HiPEAC, *LNCS*, vol. 4917, pp. 193–208. Springer (2008)
116. Ranta, A.: Implementing Programming Languages: An Introduction to Compilers and Interpreters. College Publications (2012)
117. Rekers, J.: Parser generation for interactive environments. Ph.D. thesis, University of Amsterdam (1992)
118. Renggli, L.: Dynamic language embedding with homogeneous tool support. Ph.D. thesis, Universität Bern (2010)
119. Reps, T.W., Teitelbaum, T.: The Synthesizer Generator – A System for Constructing Language-Based Editors. Texts and Monographs in Computer Science. Springer (1989)
120. Rigger, M., Grimmer, M., Wimmer, C., Würthinger, T., Mössenböck, H.: Bringing low-level languages to the JVM: Efficient execution of LLVM IR on Truffle. In: Proc. VMILSPLASH, pp. 6–15. ACM (2016)

121. Rondon, P.M., Kawaguchi, M., Jhala, R.: Liquid types. In: Proc. PLDI, pp. 159–169. ACM (2008)
122. Rozenberg, G. (ed.): Handbook of Graph Grammars and Computing by Graph Transformation. World Scientific Publishing Company (1997). Volume 1: Foundations
123. Sangiorgi, D., Walker, D.: The π-calculus: A Theory of Mobile Processes. Cambridge University Press (2001)
124. Schauss, S., Lämmel, R., Härtel, J., Heinz, M., Klein, K., Härtel, L., Berger, T.: A chrestomathy of DSL implementations. In: Proc. SLE. ACM (2017). 12 pages
125. Schmidt, D.C.: Guest editor's introduction: Model-driven engineering. IEEE Computer **39**(2), 25–31 (2006)
126. Scott, E., Johnstone, A.: Structuring the GLL parsing algorithm for performance. Sci. Comput. Program. **125**, 1–22 (2016)
127. Scott, M.: Programming Language Pragmatics. Morgan Kaufmann (1996). 3rd edition
128. Sebesta, R.W.: Concepts of Programming Languages. Addison-Wesley (2012). 10th edition
129. Sethi, R.: Programming Languages: Concepts and Constructs. Addison Wesley (1996). 2nd edition
130. Siek, J.G., Taha, W.: Gradual typing for functional languages. In: Proc. Workshop on Scheme and Functional Programming, pp. 81–92. University of Chicago (2006)
131. Siek, J.G., Taha, W.: Gradual typing for objects. In: Proc. ECOOP, *LNCS*, vol. 4609, pp. 2–27. Springer (2007)
132. Siek, J.G., Vitousek, M.M., Cimini, M., Boyland, J.T.: Refined criteria for gradual typing. In: Proc. SNAPL, *LIPIcs*, vol. 32, pp. 274–293. Schloss Dagstuhl – Leibniz-Zentrum für Informatik (2015)
133. Simonet, V.: An extension of HM(X) with bounded existential and universal data-types. In: Proc. ICFP, pp. 39–50. ACM (2003)
134. Sirer, E.G., Bershad, B.N.: Using production grammars in software testing. In: Proc. DSL, pp. 1–13. USENIX (1999)
135. Slonneger, K., Kurtz, B.: Formal Syntax and Semantics of Programming Languages. Addison Wesley (1995)
136. Slutz, D.: Massive stochastic testing for SQL. Tech. Rep. MSR-TR-98-21, Microsoft Research (1998). A shorter form of the paper appeared in the Proc. VLDB 1998
137. Stuart, T.: Understanding Computation: From Simple Machines to Impossible Programs. O'Reilly (2013)
138. Tennent, R.: Specifying Software. Cambridge University Press (2002)
139. Tolvanen, J., Kelly, S.: Defining domain-specific modeling languages to automate product derivation: Collected experiences. In: Proc. SPLC, *LNCS*, vol. 3714, pp. 198–209. Springer (2005)
140. Tomita, M.: An efficient context-free parsing algorithm for natural languages. In: Proc. IJCAI, pp. 756–764. Morgan Kaufmann (1985)
141. Visser, E., Wachsmuth, G., Tolmach, A.P., Neron, P., Vergu, V.A., Passalaqua, A., Konat, G.: A language designer's workbench: A one-stop-shop for implementation and verification of language designs. In: Proc. SPLASH, Onward!, pp. 95–111. ACM (2014)
142. Voelter, M.: Embedded software development with projectional language workbenches. In: Proc. MODELS, *LNCS*, vol. 6395, pp. 32–46. Springer (2010)
143. Voelter, M., Benz, S., Dietrich, C., Engelmann, B., Helander, M., Kats, L.C.L., Visser, E., Wachsmuth, G.: DSL Engineering – Designing, Implementing and Using Domain-Specific Languages. dslbook.org (2013)
144. Voelter, M., Lisson, S.: Supporting diverse notations in MPS' projectional editor. In: Proc. GEMOC@Models 2014, *CEUR Workshop Proceedings*, vol. 1236, pp. 7–16. CEUR-WS.org (2014)
145. Voelter, M., Ratiu, D., Kolb, B., Schätz, B.: mbeddr: instantiating a language workbench in the embedded software domain. Autom. Softw. Eng. **20**(3), 339–390 (2013)
146. Völter, M., Siegmund, J., Berger, T., Kolb, B.: Towards user-friendly projectional editors. In: Proc. SLE, *LNCS*, vol. 8706, pp. 41–61. Springer (2014)

147. Völter, M., Visser, E.: Language extension and composition with language workbenches. In: Companion SPLASH/OOPSLA, pp. 301–304. ACM (2010)
148. Wachsmuth, G., Konat, G.D.P., Visser, E.: Language design with the Spoofax language workbench. IEEE Softw. **31**(5), 35–43 (2014)
149. Wand, M., Kiczales, G., Dutchyn, C.: A semantics for advice and dynamic join points in aspect-oriented programming. ACM Trans. Program. Lang. Syst. **26**(5), 890–910 (2004)
150. Wehr, S., Lämmel, R., Thiemann, P.: JavaGI: Generalized interfaces for Java. In: Proc. ECOOP, *LNCS*, vol. 4609, pp. 347–372. Springer (2007)
151. Wile, D.S.: Lessons learned from real DSL experiments. In: Proc. HICSS-36, p. 325. IEEE (2003)
152. Wile, D.S.: Lessons learned from real DSL experiments. Sci. Comput. Program. **51**(3), 265–290 (2004)
153. Würthinger, T.: Graal and Truffle: Modularity and separation of concerns as cornerstones for building a multipurpose runtime. In: Proc. Modularity, pp. 3–4. ACM (2014)

Index

© Springer International Publishing AG, part of Springer Nature 2018   415
R. Lämmel, *Software Languages*,
https://doi.org/10.1007/978-3-319-90800-7

Printed in the United States
By Bookmasters